Emanuel Swedenborg

Swedenborg Studies/No. 9
Monographs of the Swedenborg Foundation

Emanuel Swedenborg

THE DEVELOPMENT OF HIS THOUGHT

MARTIN LAMM

TRANSLATED BY TOMAS SPIERS AND ANDERS HALLENGREN

Swedenborg Foundation Publishers
West Chester, Pennsylvania

First published in Swedish as *Swedenborg: En Studie Över Hans Utveckling Till Mystiker Och Andeskådare* (Stockholm: Hugo Gebers Förlag, 1915) ©1915 Martin Lamm
Second Swedish edition, 1987, by Hammarström & Åberg Bokförlag, with a foreword by Olle Hjern and afterword by Inge Jonsson

The foreword by Paul Valéry appeared in the first translation of *Swedenborg* (Paris: Libraire Stock, Delamain & Boutelleau, 1936) and is reproduced by permission of the estate of Paul Valéry and Éditions Stock.

Swedenborg Studies is a scholarly series published by the Swedenborg Foundation. The primary purpose of the series is to make materials available for understanding the life and thought of Emanuel Swedenborg (1688–1772) and the impact his thought has had on others. The Foundation undertakes to publish original studies and English translations of such studies and to republish primary sources that are otherwise difficult to access. Proposals should be sent to: Senior Editor, Swedenborg Studies, Swedenborg Foundation, 320 North Church Street, West Chester, Pennsylvania 19380.

Library of Congress Cataloging-in-Publication Data

Lamm, Martin, 1880–1950
[Swedenborg. English]
Emanuel Swedenborg: the development of his thought / Martin Lamm ; translated by Tomas Spiers and Anders Hallengren.
p. cm. – (Swedenborg studies ; no. 9)
Includes bibliographical references and index.
ISBN 0-87785-193-X (hc) — ISBN 0-87775-194-8 (pbk)
I. Swedenborg, Emanuel, 1688–1772. I. Title. II. Series.

BX8748 .L3613 2000
289'.4'092–dc21 00–059537

Edited by Richard Smoley
Designed by Sans Serif, Inc., Saline, Michigan
Set in Granjon by Sans Serif, Inc.
Printed in the United States of America.

Contents

THOUGHTS AFTER READING MARTIN LAMM'S *SWEDENBORG*

by Paul Valéry

The noble name of Swedenborg sounds strange to us. It awakens all the depths of confused thoughts surrounding the fantastic image of a singular personage, less defined by history than created by literature. I confess that until recently all I knew of him was the remains of readings of many years ago.

Seraphitus-Seraphita, by Balzac and a chapter of Gérard de Nerval had previously been my only sources, and into these I had not dipped for some thirty years.

This fading recollection, nevertheless, retained a charm for me. The simple syllabic resonance of the magic name, when I chanced to hear it, evoked memories of incredible associations, of the fascinations of a chimerical science, of the marvel of the considerable influence emanating from reveries; in a word, I loved to picture the uncertain figure of the seer in the frame of the century in which I would choose to have lived.

I think to myself that his epoch was one of the most brilliant and whole that humanity can know. Therein we find the scintillating finale of one world and the strenuous birth pangs of another, the most refined art, all the forces and graces of the spirit. There was magic and differential calculus, the most cynical of the cynics, and the most bizarre among the dreamers. A surplus of intelligence was not lacking, balanced—at times within the same minds—by an astounding credulity. All the themes of limitless intellectual curiosity that the Renaissance had recaptured from the ancients or drawn from its own euphoria reappear in the eighteenth century more alive, sharper, and more precise.

Europe, then, accepts the coexistence of mutually contradictory systems. That is the characteristic of a "modern" type of civilization. Rome and Alexandria had already known such an accumulation of contradictory theses, publicly manifested and debated. In these ancient capitals, the diversity of cults and philosophies were in ferment: no one could ignore, in those environments of fiery intellectualism, the fact that every speculative question had more than one answer. The end product of such relationships and exchanges, often visible in a specific individual, incarnates the disorder and richness of an era.

In the eighteenth century, while the d'Alemberts, the Clairauts, the Eulers were building a rigorously antiseptic, mechanical world on the foundation of entirely novel resources of mathematical analysis; while others researched biology, visualizing diverse philosophies of living nature and striving to trace the origins of what they believed about matter; while the great Linnaeus undertook the immense task of classifying all living organisms, others elaborated diverse metaphysics—still in the footsteps of the ancients—or extrapolated from Gassendi, Descartes, Spinoza, Leibniz, or Malebranche. In the theological camp, Jansenists, Quietists, and many of other hues disputed among themselves the possession of truth and the empire of souls. Thus, there was no dearth of vigorous spirits.

But if freedom of inquiry—having become almost legitimate everywhere—if the progress of the exact sciences, their stunning success, and the discovery of the entire shape of the world had created a kind of encyclopedic appetite—an attitude that rejected nothing—this same thirst for knowledge and power did not disdain the exploration of the intellectual penumbra even into those suspect shadows in which, from the most remote antiquity, the imagination of a larger number of individuals locates the wellspring of power and knowledge and the source of secrets of supernatural importance.

So curiosity and hope coexist in more than one spirit in an

astonishing combination. Men like Leibniz or Boyle may appear to us to be too rich in concerns that are too disparate; and the association, in Newton, of the interpretation of the Apocalypse (by way of hypotheses on the astronomy of the Argonauts) with the formulation of the mathematics of fluxion and the theory of universal attraction disconcerts us. But their century abounds in research in all disciplines; and the necessary passion, the cultivation of observation and experiment, does not deliver them from the temptations offered by doctrines and practices mysteriously transmitted.

(I observe in passing that the most prudent and the most positive science of those who dedicate themselves to it with the ardor that leads to discovery demands a certain thirst for marvels. The prodigious, the unexpected, deriving from rigorous deduction or a faultless experimental procedure, endows the mind with one of the deepest joys anyone can know.)

We find, therefore, in the eighteenth century, the generalization, almost the vulgarization, of both normal and degenerate varieties, which kindle the desire to know more than one can know. Adepts multiply, initiates abound, charlatans swarm. The social and political role of the occult becomes immense.

Credulity and skepticism have never been as closely associated and as impartially distributed among the human race as they then were. The symbolism that decodes the universe like a hieroglyphic text; the hermeneutics that attributes to the Scriptures an interpretation more profound than the sense of the letter; the theosophy that awaits and receives communication from an immediate light; and—still more daring, more disturbing, and ambitious in their operating procedures—magic, alchemy, divination by stars, by dreams, by evocation—all coexist in more than one spirit along with the most limpid culture and the discipline of the exact sciences.

Such is the mental environment, the intellectual theater, that the name Swedenborg recalls to me. These three syllables were for me only a kind of musical resonance, an incantatory formula, evoking a fantastic image of the secret spiritual life of the epoch of Louis XV. I never thought that I would go further and consider with an entirely new and personal interest a personage who for a long time only appeared to me as among the shadows of a society voluptuously curious about the arcane.

But the book I have just read turns my thoughts to an entirely different Swedenborg. The vague and Hoffmanesque idea that my ignorance formed of this man is transformed into that of a figure no less enigmatic, but precise—powerfully interesting, whose intellectual history enlivens a quantity of problems of first importance in the domain of the psychology of consciousness.

I have read the work of Martin Lamm with an increasing eagerness. There I saw take form, in chapter after chapter, the extraordinary romance of a "second life." I say "romance" because, during my reading, I naively felt that intense eagerness for the sequel, that thirst for the future by which we are ordinarily carried away in the productions aimed at making us anticipate the delights of *adventure*.

Of course, the adventure in question is not one of those whose recital intoxicates and captivates the immense majority of readers: it unfolds in the most private domains of the inmost life and on the unmarked frontiers where the forces, the ambitions, the lights within us manifest themselves, opposing one another as they oppose, on the other hand, the ordinary phenomena of the "external world." But in my personal opinion, it is not tales of voyages to the periphery of reality, recitals of marvels, epic or dramatic narrations that lead to the study of the inexhaustible creator and universal transformer that we call *Spirit*.

The Swedenborg to whom Martin Lamm's book introduces me is a being who has known, experienced, and traversed all the states or phases of the most intense and most complete physical life, since he appears to have scoured the intellectual spectrum even to certain extremes that might be called abnormal if this term—a purely negative one to my mind—did not introduce too summary or too simple a judgment. The analysis of his successive works, masterfully handled by the author, presents the development of a prestigious *case* that anyone, according to the nature of his own mind, can meditate upon and interpret in his own way; be he a historian, a psychiatrist, a mystic—even a poet—he can study, comment upon, admire, or classify at will.

Whatever treatment the attentive reader might give to his perusal of the volume, he will necessarily be amazed by its fullness and clarity. He will give respectful consideration to the sum of knowledge, the quality of the work, and the intellectual vigor that an examination and exposition of the whole of the enormous work of Swedenborg requires. This labor is, I imagine, one that is neither constantly pleasant nor easy, although we find, in places, bits of great poetic beauty, delicious visions appearing to transcendental infancy. But it contributes an incomparable document of interest that I would never have even suspected without the effort to which Lamm has gone to reduce to essentials an immense amount of material and to guide us among the Swedenborgian infernos and paradises. In his preface, he modestly reduces his role to the study of the origins of the theosophy of Swedenborg, a task in which he became engaged in the course of his researches regarding "the mystical-sentimental current in Swedish eighteenth-century literature which opens the way for Romanticism and later merges with it." But he will be found, I think, to have delineated a unique personage in the great drama of the human spirit.

That is not all. A book, to my eyes, has value according to the number and the novelty of the problems it creates, stimulates, or reanimates in my mind. Works that demand or postulate the passivity of the reader are not to my taste. I expect my readings to generate such comments, reflections, such sudden arrests that suspend consideration, illuminate perspectives, and suddenly reawaken our profound curiosity, the particular interests of our personal researches, and the direct feeling of our fully alive involvement.

So, in a few words, I am going to try to give an idea of some of the emerging questions that Martin Lamm's book calls forth in me.

Swedenborg appears to me to have been the exemplar and the subject of one of the most remarkable and complete internal transformations. This was accomplished in several stages over the course of sixty years. This transformation of a psychic life, observed and recorded in the chronological sequence of his writings, is that of a man of vast culture, who could at the outset be regarded as a savant and philosopher of the type characteristic of his time, but who changes imperceptibly into a mystic around his fortieth year.* The first modification, adequately fostered by his early education, comes from the mysticism of his father and the environment of his earlier impressions. Nevertheless, how does one pass from a mechanistic view of the world and from habits ingrained by the practice of precise observations of natural science to meditations of theological origin, to the focusing of thought upon questions derived from Scripture and tradition? How does this displacement of values come about?

Even so, it is not that ordinary attention is transferred from one object to another or that a certain custom of theoretical thought is substituted for another. We find a little later that a rarer and more profound alteration becomes pronounced: from the theoretical and speculative phase, busied with reasonings about the dogma of the Fall or about the nature of angels, Swedenborg advances to another state in which *it is not the ideas themselves that are in question*, but *consciousness itself.* The theoretical phase is succeeded by one in which interior happenings occur that do not possess the purely transitory and plausible character of ordinary thought, but which introduce into the consciousness an *awareness of forces and presences* that are apart from the self, that stand before him, not as responses or arguments or ordinary intuitions, but as phenomena. So we see dissertation and dialectic replaced by *reporting* and description; that is to say, the conditions and means of intellectual research—doubt, formulation of the plurality of possibilities, choice, demonstration, etc.—are dispossessed by a perception that carries immediate and invincible certitude. This kind of certitude is not comparable to that expressed by the term "evidence": evidence, after all, is a reaction of our mind in which *we recognize ourselves*, while mystic certitude stems from the impression of an existence independent of self, which objects and tangible bodies commonly give us; that impress themselves upon us *as long as they are alien to us.* That is why this introduction of forces and presences just

**Editor's Note.* Swedenborg is usually thought to have had his first mystical experience in his mid-fifties.

spoken of can well be regarded as the formation of a second "reality," or a second order, and the possession of such a double pluralism defines the state of the mystic.

But with Swedenborg, theoretical activity does not entirely vanish in the face of direct perception. It resumes its role of construction and justification. It is natural for a mind so strongly endowed and cultivated to establish between his two realities relations that are as systematic as possible, and he constitutes a type of method to which a quasi-scientific framework can be attributed. That is what Swedenborg has done with his famous theory of correspondences, in which he combined several metaphysical, Kabbalistic, or magical traditions, with their initial rationalism, on the one hand, and the discoveries which the awakening of his new faculty offers him on the other.

This theory enables him to construct a tabulation, a dictionary, in which, to each object of ordinary world experience or each word of common language, a being or object in the "spiritual" world responds. Physical laws themselves are to be translated in "spiritual" terms.

Here is another question posed by the reading of Martin Lamm's book. What is to be understood by the word *spiritual*? I might easily have passed this over and allowed myself to believe that I understood it. I have heard the term a thousand times. I have used it times without number. But here I find in it a scope and importance that demand a pause.

I said to myself: ordinary philosophical vocabulary allows me the vice of necessarily appropriating the appearance of a technical language, although truly precise definitions are no less necessarily lacking—for there are only precise *instrumental* definitions (that is, they are reduced to actions, like displaying an object or performing an operation). It is impossible to guarantee that a unique, uniform, and constant sense can be attributed to words like *reason*, *universe*, *cause*, *matter*, or *idea*. It most often turns out that every effort to predicate the significance of such terms ends by introducing, under the same name, a new object of thought *that is opposed to the prior one to the extent that it is new.*

But the mystical vocabulary is much more elusive still. Here the value attributed to the elements of discourse is not merely a personal one, but one arising from exceptional moments or states of the subject. It is not only that it lacks independence from the subject who thinks and speaks, but it even depends upon his state. Besides, among mystics, the sense perceptions themselves receive values no less singular than those attached to words. A fortuitous sound or (as occurred with Jacob Boehme) a reflection from a tin plate is not limited to what it is and the association of ideas that can be derived from them: they assume the force of a happening, and by its *actio praesentiae*, they become "catalysts," provoking a change of state.

So the subject passes into his second life without difficulty—as though the initial phenomenon were a common element, a point of contact or of the welding of two "universes."

That is the way of essential terms among the mystics. They have one meaning according to which they belong in the dictionary of common usage, and another meaning whose resonance only develops in the domain of the "internals" of a specific person. The ambivalence of this double function results in the facility of passage from the normal to the privileged state, *the effortless going and coming between two worlds.* This latter remark seems important to me: it permits us to avoid confusing mysticism with delirium. Delirium blends worlds and values: mysticism of Swedenborg's type discriminates to the point of presenting the table of their correspondences as a problem and a task. Moreover, his activities in the ordinary world, his relations with its beings and objects, are perfectly normal and irreproachably conventional.

In the case under consideration, *spiritual* is a key word, the significance of which is a resonance. It does not bring to mind the object of thought. It responds to the need of expressing that what one says does not have its aim or value in what one sees; furthermore, it indicates that what one thinks has neither its aim nor its value in what can be thought. It is a sign that, in the form of an epithet, suggests that we reduce the objects and occurrences of ordinary life and sensory reality to the condition of simple symbols and that warns us besides of the symbolic nature of our thought itself. The "spiritual" world gives the visible world its true meaning, but is itself only the symbolic expression of an essential, inaccessible world where the distinction between "being" and "awareness" ceases.

The principal fact (for the psychologist) that all this proposes for study is the following: someone experiences and assures himself that his thought might manifest something other than the thought itself. The mystic or spiritual event is *par excellence* the presumed introduction or intervention of quasi-phenomena, of impulsive forces, of judgments, etc., in the group of attributes of a *self*, that the *self* does not recognize as its own, which it can only attribute to an *other*—in the domain where there is normally no *other*, the invisible domain of the *self*.

No doubt what is produced *in us* is often enough a surprise *for us*; and it astonishes us sometimes by a superior quality; sometimes, on the contrary, by a weakness or a deficiency that reveals itself. We find ourselves now more, now less than "ourselves." But we do not, nevertheless, cease to attribute these digressions to some more or less intimate or functional origin, as we do when an unexpected bodily sensation surprises us. A sudden pain transforms our idea of ourselves just as does a flash of exquisite pleasure, but it never occurs to us that these incidents or occurrences are not of our own substance, of which they are only a rarely induced faculty. The mystic, however, feels the externality, or rather the extraneousness, of the source of images, of emotions, of words, of impulses that reach him by an internal route. He is constrained to grant them the force of reality; but as he cannot confuse *this reality* with *the reality of everybody*, his life is a progression between two universes of equal existence, but of very unequal importance.

It is here that the question is posed that I cannot undertake to answer. Can I even enunciate it clearly?

How can we conceive that a man such as Swedenborg—profoundly cultured, accustomed to serious labors of a scientific nature and meditations in which logic and internal concentration are long sustained, accustomed to observe the formation of his thought and to move forward within himself, all the while preserving awareness of the activities of his mind—could have failed to discern the action even of that mind in the production of images, of admonitions, of "verities" that came to him from a secret source? These productions are strange, no doubt; but not so strange that one could not recognize upon reflection the elements borrowed from ordinary life experience. How could he fail to see that our spiritual formations are part of the group of combinations that can be composed in us on the basis of our sensory acquisitions and of our psychic and affective possibilities and freedoms? While Swedenborg the scholar had surely considered the sensory world as the superficial aspect of a psychomechanical world, according to Descartes or Newton, Swedenborg the mystic considered this superficial sensory aspect of naive intuition as the expression of a "spiritual" world. *If, then, this spiritual world is revealed by some supernatural power, this power chose to express in Swedenborg the appearances that were suitable to teach any untutored person.*

I have italicized these words; but I can insist still more strongly upon the idea that they express by means of the following remark: the most extravagant vision of a visionary can always be brought back or traced to a single deformation of observable reality, with preservation of the conditions of consciousness, and this vision can, moreover, be described in terms of ordinary language. But let us think about the structure and form of the universe that the tools of mathematics and instruments of science offer us today. There, on the one hand, results are positive, because they refer to the powers of action; on the other, they penetrate the unintelligible, shake the venerable "categories of understanding," disparage even the notions of law and cause—to the extent that the ancient "reality" of yore becomes a simple statistical effect, although the imagination itself, producer of all "visions" possible, and the "usual language," their means of expression, find themselves paralyzed, incapable of communicating to us what our instruments and calculations oblige us to try to think about.

The Swedenborgian universe, the spiritual world, the home of conjugial love in the sphere of angels and spirits, is, then, "human, all too human," too like our own, while the universes of scientific fabrication (and even those conceived of in the time of Swedenborg) are, on the contrary, more and more "inhuman": we find in them neither marriages nor good conversation nor shining virgins; and they are impotent to serve as symbols of anything at all, being themselves mere symbols, tensors, operators, matrices, and symbols whose concrete significance escapes us.

I have spoken of all this only to insist on the question that I consider essential in this case: *how is a Swedenborg possible?* What must be assumed to consider the coexistence of the qualities of a learned engineer, of an eminent government official, of a man wise in practical matters and learned in every field, with the characteristics of a visionary who has no hesitation in writing out and publishing his visions, in allowing himself to be known as one visited by the inhabitants of another world, taught by them, and living a part of his life in their mysterious company?

Moreover, it is certainly insufficient to speak only of coexistence: it is necessary also to take note of a certain collaboration, the most remarkable and astonishing example of which is given by the doctrine of representations and correspondences.

It is hard for me to believe that this work was not thought out and composed by an author more systematic and master of himself than one inspired and lost in contemplation. The concern for order, the drive and painstaking definition, the well-arranged introduction of new ideas are very apparent and must have demanded a considerable logical labor, which contrasts curiously with the content of dreams. But more extraordinary yet is the part of this system where Swedenborg develops the correspondences of organs and membranes. There he displays remarkably precise and detailed anatomical knowledge, and he expresses himself like a man who has deeply reflected about the problems of physiology, knowledge, and reflections of which he makes use to interrelate all the parts of the organism, the strangest significances, evaluations, or "spiritual" creations. This mixture of understanding, method, and dream, of perfect and sure lucidity and imaginary analogy, is so difficult to accept that one would sometimes be tempted to suspect the good faith of our visionary were it not that the considerable labor applied, the duration and continuity of the effort, along with the evident impersonality of character, did not render incredible the hypothesis of a fraudulent undertaking, of a huge lie in the grand manner.

Swedenborg himself answered anxious questioners about his own faith in his personal illuminations by saying, "*Haec vera sunt quia signum habeo*" (These are truths because I have the sign). The "sign" sufficed to dissipate all internal resistance and to consecrate the intimate union between Swedenborg the rationalist, physicist, practical and social man, with the familiar of spirits and confidant of angels. These sublime and marvelous relations did not in the least embarrass him in his extensive social contacts, and he maintained these as he maintained an honest man's relationships with his contemporaries, just as casually and habitually as anyone who frequents different "social circles" (such as those of business and those of recreation) sustains and interrelates their varying activities.

The nature of this "sign" is not explained to us. His silence may be attributed to fear of seeing this basis of inmost life contested, or perhaps lest the virtue of the sign and its secret should vanish. But also the very difficulty of describing it would have constrained him to keep silence about it. It is common knowledge that whatever fixes our mind on a certainty is indefinable. So I am not going to try to figure it out but will, nevertheless, venture a certain analogy by way of simple suggestion.

I visualize, then, a kind of "force" and consistency that affirms or confirms in us an opinion or a resolution because it conforms entirely to the needs of our sensibility. If we receive from an external source something for which we have an intense desire, it seems to us that this thing that satisfies us so perfectly is as though produced by our own desire. We find that such an idea presented to us delights us as though the desire to be delighted materialized itself; we find that a certain piece of work is so well done for us that it is as though done by us; and we say the same of a person; and this invincible and immediate sentiment is an indubitable "sign": for we cannot doubt that what we want is pleasing to us or that what overwhelms us leaves no room for the slightest hesitation.

By what "sign" does an artist know that at such-and-such an instant he is in his "truth" and perceives the necessity, along with the voluptuousness (the two mingling), of his creative act?

The "sign" of Swedenborg was perhaps only the sensation of energy, of a fullness of happiness and well-being that he always felt when giving himself up to the production and organization of his spiritual world, and the certitude of his creative delights could no doubt suffice to defer his doubts indefinitely and to rein his critical sense.

Yes, the Swedenborg case proposes to us, it seems, certain alleged facts that boil down neither to mystic vision nor to the avowed existence of a particular sign.

This sign metamorphoses from a thought, at first quite scientific and metaphysico-theological, into an intuitive "second reality," and is worked by degrees into a transcendental doctrine. And these degrees are marked by properly hallucinatory "subjective" occurrences, of which the scene in the London inn is entirely characteristic.

Must the account of it by the theosopher himself be accepted as correct? The importance of this question will be seen. The correctness I have in mind is not that which depends upon Swedenborg's good faith. Let us accept that as integral. But the most sincere man in the world, expressing what he has seen, particularly what he has seen in the domain where he alone could have seen it, inevitably alters this condition of singularity *merely by the use of ordinary language,* which adds to the no less inevitable alteration due to the act of direct memory, that results from the fragmentation into words and the laws of combination or form of syntax. In the order of practical communication, these alterations are generally negligible and are rectified, moreover, by common experience: the common sensory environment verifies the accord of our signals. But every *description* of our separate perceptions radically destroys what would be the most precious of these perceptions to know and decipher.

That is why I am very far from trusting the attempted analyses that are so fashionable today, when it seems that a new key of dreams has been forged.

The dream is a hypothesis, because we never know it except as a memory, but this memory is necessarily a structured one. We construct and redesign our dream; we express it, we attribute a sense to it, it becomes tellable: history, scenes, role of personages, and in the scenario of recollections the role of the awakening, the recognition, are indiscernible. It happens that we recount this dream: the hearer translates the recital in turn according to his own system of images: if the study of dreams piques him, he will reason on the basis of what he imagines, which is a transmutation of a transmutation.

The translation of a translation may well conserve something, but *not what cannot be verbalized.* What cannot be spoken is precisely what is important for us to grasp; that which would give us some idea of what *consciousness while asleep* can be; the production and substitution of quasi-phenomena, the perpetual aborning state of a mental life of no return, which is essentially instantaneous. But to speculate about the *recitation* of a dream is to operate on the result of an *activity* of the night before, the hypothetical original having lost the substance of its nature and become an abstract reconstruction—like a statue that no longer presents the intimate causal relation between the form and the living matter of the model. In sum: we reason on the schema of a totally consummated event, and we interpret it; but a schema is the result of sundry *acts,* and these acts are those of the waking state; it must be "awakened" to *express.*

But suppose that we should try, on the other hand, to modify voluntarily our waking perceptions and representations so as to diminish their significative effect, to exhaust their transitive and conventional effect (as happens in the case of a word repeated until it loses its meaning). We then observe some features of a state of which the dream state might be the limit. Moreover, we observe quite clearly, when we feel the mind overcome by sleep, that we waver in some way between two worlds, the stronger of which dissolves gradually into the weaker. Then we see take form the manner of transformation of consciousness that will rule in the dream universe. Admitting (for purely hypothetical purposes) that this universe is distinguished from the preceding one by the development of every impression that affects us, we shall have some idea of what might happen under the influence of sleep when our residual sensorium is excited by organic incidents or by external activities that are insufficient to induce a total change of our state—that is, an awakening.

Analogous characteristics, I think, must be found in "visions." The modes of transformation of appearances there must strongly resemble those of our dreams. There we have what I believe I have verified in some cases by careful study of certain accounts by visionaries selected from the most naive examples. This means, in effect, that the document emanates from a subject as poorly educated, and also as *unimaginative* as possible, in order that the production of images be as free as possible from secondary motives and corrections.

With regard to Swedenborg, the conditions are entirely the opposite, and they are very unfavorable for an examination of the degree of precision in the report he has recorded for us in his writings. Indeed, certain details of the celebrated vision in London seem to me to be of the kind that "are not invented," that is, which seem to me to be impossible to represent a desire, preceded by an intent, to respond to some conscious demand.

I have allowed myself to delve into considerations of which it is only necessary to remember this: that I would never finish were I to pursue all the questions with which Martin Lamm's book deals.

I began without suspecting that I was entering an enchanted forest where every step raised sudden flights of ideas; where avenues of brilliant hypotheses proliferated, of psychological ambushes and echoes; where each glance reveals perspectives bristling with enigmas; where the intellectual visitor is infected with excitement, strays, loses, finds the trail, and loses it again. But this is not at all to waste one's time. I love the hunt for hunting's sake, and there are few hunts more rewarding than the hunt for the mystery of Swedenborg.

Introduction to First Swedish Edition (1915)

This book owes its birth to my studies of the mystical-sentimental current in Swedish eighteenth-century literature which opens the way for Romanticism and later merges with it. When it then became a matter of closer treatment of the doctrine of Swedenborg and its important role in Sweden as well as abroad, I soon became aware of the fact that it was impossible to base it on earlier accounts. It also became evident that Swedenborg's system remains unintelligible without establishing its relation to the philosophical concepts developed in his works on physical and natural sciences, on which it is founded. I was, therefore, compelled to examine more closely the genesis of Swedenborgian theosophy: here I bring the result of these researches, and I hope that, despite its inadequacy, this work can be of some use to future scholars in a field still very much neglected in my country.

It is apparent how my subject is thereby restricted. I have said nothing of the importance of Swedenborg to his contemporaries and to posterity, cherishing the hope of a discussion of it in detail in another context. Of Swedenborg's biography, I have only included what has seemed to me to be necessary to clarify his religious development. I have touched upon his researches in the natural sciences only insofar as they have seemed to me to have exercised influence upon his later thought. I have deliberately neglected those parts of his system that I have judged of little importance and found without relation to the fundamental ideas that govern his development. Diverse comparisons with other theological and philosophical systems suggest themselves. I have noted only those that can demonstrate a serious influence upon his thought or contribute a complementary clarification. One often finds unverified hypotheses put forth according to which Swedenborg appears to rely upon such-or-such an author. In general, it has seemed to me superfluous to discuss them. Indeed, most of the time they appear to rest upon purely external similarities, and can only testify to a general trait of affinity common to all speculation tinged with mysticism.

There is no ratio between the relative lack of international literature regarding Swedenborg and its scholarly value. Inestimable help has been furnished to me by the great collections of biographical sources, the bibliographies, editions of texts, etc., published by the Swedenborgian societies. Those works on Swedenborg whose research I have made use of are cited in the respective places. An overall bibliography has not seemed to me to be necessary: it suffices to refer the reader to the good chronological account of Swedenborg studies published by Hjalmar Holmquist in the *Kyrklig Tidskrft* of 1909.[1]

Swedenborg supplied almost all his works—of his scientific period as well as his theological period—with sequential numeration of paragraphs, so I have confined myself in my translated quotations to referring to the work and number in question.[2] The passages to which I refer should be located without any difficulty. I reproduce the Latin text only when it seems to me particularly interesting to

1. *Editor's Note.* For an updated bibliography of scholarly work published since the first publication of this book, the reader should refer to Anders Hallengren, "Bibliography," in *Gallery of Mirrors: Reflections of Swedenborgian Thought* (West Chester, Penna.: Swedenborg Foundation, 1998), 163–196. For a complete bibliography of Swedenborg's works and that of his commentators, see William Ross Woofenden, *Swedenborg Explorer's Guidebook* (to be published in 2001 by the Swedenborg Foundation).

2. *Editor's Note:* As is customary in Swedenborgian studies, the numbers following titles refer to paragraph or section numbers, which are uniform in all editions, rather than to page numbers. In this edition, the section symbol (§) precedes numbered references to Swedenborg's works. All other numbers in references indicate page numbers from Martin Lamm's original research.

know its exact tenor. Even the frequent summaries of Swedenborg's statements—made necessary by Swedenborg's extremely lengthy style, with its irreproducible inflections of works and convoluted sentence structure—are all accompanied by this kind of reference. Any other method would have caused a multiplication of the size of the present volume.

Finally, I offer my cordial thanks to all those who have helped me with their good advice and bibliographical data, above all Professor Frey Svenson, the Assistant Professors K.B. Westman and A. Phalén, and to Mr. A.H. Stroh, M.A.

MARTIN LAMM
Uppsala, May 1915

Introduction to the Present Edition

by James F. Lawrence

The publication in the English-speaking world of Martin Lamm's seminal work on Swedenborg is much more significant than it might appear upon a casual glance through the volume. Lamm's treatise is significant not only because it represents the most important scholarly study on Swedenborg ever undertaken in his native land and continues to be regarded in European academic circles as the cornerstone of scholarship on Swedenborg, but also because it provides a highly provocative thesis—namely, that Swedenborg's theological system (and in particular the "science of correspondences") was already developed before his supposed illumination and prophetic calling. In fact, Lamm believes that, however interesting it may be for students of the paranormal, Swedenborg's famed mode of revelatory perception—of "things seen and heard"—was completely unnecessary as a means of insight, because all of his core concepts had been developed and were at-hand when he began his theological works.

For the scholarly study of Swedenborg, Lamm's perspective is one that must be engaged and weighed against other views. For the religious devotee of Swedenborg's theological system, this work provides fascinating new possibilities of understanding the development of Swedenborg's thinking, particularly on the one doctrine that would become his chief distinguishing method as a biblical expositor.

Alfred Acton developed the most accepted view for those in the various branches of the New Jerusalem churches in his *An Introduction to the Word Explained: A Study of the Means by which Swedenborg the Scientist Became the Theologian and Revelator* (Bryn Athyn, Penna.: Academy of the New Church, 1927). The main purpose of Acton's work is to show how Swedenborg was prepared by God to become a Christian revelator appropriate for the modern era. Often simply referred to as "Swedenborg's preparation," Swedenborg's scientific period is regarded as creating a general structure of rational thought capable of supporting a reasonable system of religious values, communicated expressly by the Lord, usually through the agency of angels. These ideas and values would become the "heavenly doctrines"—a revelatory body of work that in some ways restored ancient understandings, but in some ways also presented a more sophisticated interpretation than any before grasped by humankind.

Whereas Acton (and Lamm notes others such as Alfred Stroh) believes that scientific theories rendered general supportive structures for the theosophical ideas, Lamm's goal is to demonstrate that the two periods of Swedenborg's studies are so thoroughly continuous that there is really no leap in ideation that renders extrasensory revelatory experience as necessary.

My own reading of Swedenborg's story is that Lamm's thesis does no damage to what most devout believers understand. The fact that something happened causing Swedenborg to cease scientific pursuits and to commit his attention exclusively to biblical and theological discussions for the better part of the remaining three decades of his life is not undercut by the possibility that Swedenborg already understood a cosmology and ontology that would house the "heavenly doctrines." Certainly, before the time of his calling, he had not felt the need to apply his developing philosophy to the Christian faith. However, Lamm's position does not adequately account for the fact that Swedenborg went into his theological phase with much "old church" conceptions of key doctrines, writing several exploratory works he did not publish which demonstrate that he still believed in a personified Devil; in a Godhead of three Persons; in the Creation being out of "nothing." In numerous important respects, Swedenborg's theology underwent substantial new developments after his prophetic calling.

Some devoted Swedenborgians may feel dismay in Lamm's tone. He is clearly not an adherent of Swedenborg's religious system, and he makes it plainly evident that he does not believe Swedenborg's supposed seership has any important role in the actual ideas that flowed from his pen. But Swedenborg often remarked that divine providence uses the minds and works of people in ways that they do not themselves perceive. I feel this way about Martin Lamm. His work has brought a new depth of insight into how thoroughly Swedenborg's scientific effort prepared him to understand how the Bible could contain an inner sense. The aids Lamm brings in filling out the story of Swedenborg's training only deepens my awe of the seer's biography.

On the other hand, Lamm's practical approach to Swedenborg's religious calling has its drawbacks. His treatment of the seer's "religious crisis" and mystical experiences is by far the weakest aspect of Lamm's investigation, and it is here that the scholar wanders out of his expertise. His analysis of Swedenborg's dream journal seems to be amateurish in the year 2000. When Lamm wrote this work, the modern understanding of dreams was in its infancy. Freud's first published writings were only a decade old and had not penetrated the university realm. Carl Jung's work had scarcely begun.

We now stand upon a full century of psychological investigation that has yielded a much advanced understanding of dream activity. What Lamm sees as bizarre and disjointed images and ideas in the dream journal, we now know to be a different kind of symbolic language that occurs within everyone's mind during sleep. Swedenborg's dream journal is remarkable not for its sexual aspects or disturbing images—although, for the mid-eighteenth century, Swedenborg's own attempts at interpretation are astonishing in their perceptiveness, as is his ability to put his interpretations to practical use—but as a window to a soul about to be transformed.

Lamm's attempts to diagnose Swedenborg's mental state in his supposed "alert" spiritual visions also seem beyond his professional ken. Without citing any specific comparisons, Lamm declares his conclusion that Swedenborg follows the form of "the vast majority of mystics"—namely, that his personal sense of mystical experience is in response to an emotional crisis. His terminology of "pseudohallucinations" to describe Swedenborg's spiritual mode of perception seems clinical, and his analysis betrays his prejudice that this mode of perception was neither necessary nor valuable to the outcome of Swedenborg's writings.

Yet, the excitement arising from a clearer understanding of how Swedenborg arrived at his mature "science of correspondences"—surely, his most striking doctrine and the one for which he is so highly regarded in metaphysical circles, even as "correspondences" have been cause for his dismissal in traditional Christian circles—alone makes this work invaluable to Swedenborg students of all persuasions.

As a longtime student myself, I welcome the opportunity to engage what is the most important modern study of Swedenborg in his homeland.

Emanuel Swedenborg

o n e

Early Years

"The name of my son *Emanuel* means *God with us,* in order that he may ever be reminded of the presence of God and the intimate, holy and secret union in which we by faith stand with our propitious and gracious God."

Such is the note—the only one, moreover, that he devotes to his oldest son—that is found in the autobiography of the venerable Jesper Swedberg.[1] It is significant that the name Swedenborg received at baptism is, according to his father's interpretation, meant to symbolize the *unio mystica,* that "secret union" with God in and through faith, which constitutes the lifeblood of all Christian mysticism.

All the biographies of Swedenborg agree in tracing to the paternal home itself the prime origin of his evolution into a mystic. They point to the conformity between the character and philosophy of the father and that of the son with such persistence that one is tempted to react against the exaggerations of this thesis. It is beyond doubt that, in a general way, Jesper Swedberg and his son represent two rather different fundamental types in the gallery of religious personages. Despite these allowances, there remain enough essential traits common to both that it is hard to understand Emanuel Swedenborg without knowing his father.

In his external appearance, Jesper Swedberg was typical of the upright pastors of the seventeenth century. He was a native of the Bergslag mining district, where, according to his own statement, in his youth everybody was dressed "like honest and grave clergymen." It is with "the heart filled with bitterness" that he sees the elegant clergymen ecclesiastics of the new century "deck themselves with blond and powdered perukes, showering a veritable white snowfall over the back and shoulders of their silk mantles."[2] The preserved portraits we have of him show a confident and rustic visage of a man from Dalecarlia; and in his sermons, he does not spare drastic though fatuous invectives against the vanity and impiety of his time.

Nevertheless, this powerful preacher of the old stock, who himself relates how the dragoons of Charles XI, when for the first time they reported for examination on the catechism, cringed before him "as they never trembled in the face of the enemy," hid beneath that stern surface the tender and childlike soul of a dreamer. Early in his life he had come in contact with Arndt and Scriver, German forerunners of Pietism. These two theologians were particularly pleasing to his spirit because they demanded of their followers a true purity of conduct even more than a dogmatic faith, and their works breathed a warmth of feeling that he found lacking in the rigid, formal Protestant orthodoxy of the seventeenth century.

Swedberg also felt a live sympathy for what the Pietists' doctrine contained by way of mysticism, since, as he says of the works of Scriver, "they lead us toward spiritual unity, to the holy and sacred mystic community with Jesus Christ."[3] In the course of time, he also became acquainted with later Pietist authors and felt attracted to them, as well as to the serene devotion of Swedish Pietist circles with whom he found himself in touch, without ever considering himself as standing outside of orthodox Protestantism. The subtleties of dogmatics were entirely alien to his spirit, and Tottie rightly takes note of his fundamental "lack of scientific interest," his indifference with respect to any attempt "to justify to the mind the very essence of faith and to make of it, in the slightest degree, a matter of knowledge."[4] He gave short shrift to any theological speculation with the ancient adage of Tertullian, "*credo quia absurdum,*" and, he said, "I believe because this is impossible for me to understand and, even more so, to do."

This innocent purity of heart, reflected in his diary, is found in his sermons as well. These are both numerous and rather compendious. Jesper Swedberg was, in fact, infected by an ineradicable desire to write and print. He himself attributed this disposition to his baptismal name, which in Hebrew is said to signify "he shall write." He declared that ten wheelbarrows would hardly be enough to transport what he had written or published. "And still," he adds, "there is much unprinted material, yes, almost as much." Let it be added parenthetically that it was from his father that Swedenborg inherited this productivity. This assumed such proportions with him that the psychiatrist Gilbert Ballet appears seriously inclined to find therein a symptom of mental disorder.[5] As to form, the collections of sermons published by Jesper Swedberg are far from qualifying as a literary effort, and the same can be said of his hymns.

But, as Schück points out, as with the homiletic literature of the seventeenth century, they are distinguished by their subjectivism, by the absence of all dogmatic polemic, and by their practical spirit.[6] In Swedberg's religious tracts, one finds no abstract or irksome commentary: everything becomes simple and concrete. He modernizes the parable of the prodigal son with the same naivety and directness as of the school dramas of the Reformation: a fastidious young "lord" has delighted in *lettres d'amour* and harlot songs," instead of taking "in hand the precious book of Sirach."[7] And in his sermons, he willingly abandons the text of the day to illustrate, by living examples drawn from his own experience, the teachings he especially wishes to engrave upon the minds of his hearers. Swedberg particularly loves to expatiate on the miracles or the apparitions of which he himself is the object or the witness. Thus, during Advent, while preaching about the Last Judgment, he points to the appearance in Sweden of a number of precursory signs that indicate that the time is near. He recalls "the terrible great comet" of 1680; he relates that three evenings in succession he has seen "thick pools of blood large as tub bottoms" floating in Lake Barken in Dalecarlia; he reminds the congregation of the recent earthquake in Västergötland; he speaks "of a woman who called herself Sophia" who, during the summers of 1698 and 1699, traveled all through the Bergslag and Västmanland, announcing the approaching ruin of Sweden. But what appears to him, more than any other sign, to indicate the proximity of the Last Judgment, is that "the brute creatures are bringing forth offspring wearing that offensive headdress called 'fontang' which is extremely displeasing to God, the angels and to every pious man." It is thus that, on February

4, 1696, a cow on the island of Gotland had brought forth, giving voice to prolonged bellows, a calf with a "fontang" (protuberance) half an ell long on its head.[8]

For Jesper Swedberg, the earth on which we live is a world of perpetual miracles. The Pauline allegory on the lamentations of the creature is, for him, a truth so literal that he believes he hears the animals everywhere, and even inanimate objects, lament over the sins of mankind.[9] "For even the creature destitute of life or reason possesses a sensibility, an intelligence, and a voice." If a poacher plunders fish from a lake, it is found that the fish disappear; if apples are stolen from a tree, one will notice that it will no longer yield such rich harvests. Even household furnishings deplore the transgressions of man: "It seems to me that, when one hears a sudden creaking of a chest or cupboard, this involves something that has suffered abuse. They become alarmed and bemoan the triumph of a wickedness which offends God and saddens the angels."[10]

But at the same time, nature is the herald of resurrection. When autumn comes, swallows plunge to the bottoms of lakes and remain there lifeless until the return of summer. If, after cutting down flowers and plants and reducing them to powder, this is buried, it will be noticed that they grow up again as beautiful as before. Truly, everything on this earth, even inanimate objects, actually proclaims eternity and testifies to God's kingdom of blessedness:

> Where is job? In the Holy City
> where the angels sing a new song
> and the bells are tolling in the king's palace.
> Oh, if we were only there! Oh, if we were only there![11]

It is around this "Holy City" that Jesper Swedberg's thoughts constantly revolve, and his ardent imagination tries to visualize the life that awaits him there. In the course of his voyage to Hamburg, when parting from the celebrated orientalist Edzardus, he asks him, in what language they will converse when they meet again in the realm of the heavens. His friend remains silent, so Swedberg adds, "I believe it will be in the *tongue of the angels.* Just as angels converse with a Swede in Swedish, and German with a German, or in English with an Englishman and so on. I will then be allowed to speak to Abraham, Isaac, and Jacob, and they will respond in Swedish. . . . For I cannot believe that we are to lose the gift of speech there. To speak is, as we know, a human quality."[12]

This concept of the tongue of angels seems, in the mind of Jesper Swedberg, to have evolved gradually into a sense close to the ideas Swedenborg would form about it. In a Lenten sermon, Swedberg tells his flock that, in the kingdom of heaven, we shall regain "our languages" as well as "all the knowledge that we have laboriously collected here below. . . . And I believe, for example, that when we converse with Abraham, and he with us, we shall speak our Swedish language, which he will understand, and he will reply in Hebrew, which we shall also understand. And when we talk with Saint Peter, we shall talk our Swedish language, and he will answer us in his Greek or Syriac language."[13]

Swedberg is equally convinced that, from the high heavens, the blessed continue to be interested in their kinsmen on earth. For the deceased have not lost their memory, "but this recollection has become purer, more refined, sharper." Therefore, they also have a "holy feeling" when their loved ones on earth repent from their sins.[14] On the witness of "second-sighted persons," Swedberg holds it quite certain that "with God's permission, the shapes of the dead can appear to the living," and only "the atheists and those abandoned by God" are capable of denying "the existence of ghosts."[15] But, above all, he holds that man is in contact with heaven through the mediation of angels. They still move between heaven and earth like the angels on the ladder Jacob saw in his dream. The angels are "servant spirits" sent to watch over men on this low earth. Every human being has one or more such "caring spirits" who looks after him when the Evil One "who roves like a roaring lion" threatens to devour him. We shall see that these obliging spirits were later taken up by Swedenborg in his theosophy, even under the same name. Swedberg sees a manifest proof of this protection by the spirits in the fact that "drunkards and other intemperates frequently conduct themselves as though, if they had ten lives, they could not even preserve one." In spite of this, they are protected from the gravest dangers because their angels are around them.[16]

Moreover Jesper Swedberg knows from experience that he has one of these guardian angels at his side. Already in his student years at Uppsala, he has been visited by one of these angels, who appears to him in his study-chamber and recommends that he read Scriver, Arndt, and other authors.[17] He also has other manifest proofs that the devil, who fears lest he become dangerous to his empire, has tried to destroy him. At the age of seven years, he narrowly escapes from being precipitated by the devil into a millrace; and, shortly before his appointment to the bishopric of Skara, God reveals to him in a dream that Satan will continue to persecute him in Västergötland, and "would cruelly pounce on me with the intention to murder me." Armed with a spear, Satan follows the carriage with bursts of sardonic laughter; finally, upon awakening, Swedberg sees his enemy "clearly" standing in the moonlight. It is only by constant prayer and the singing of hymns that he succeeds in driving away the demon. In reality, from the age of thirteen, Swedberg experiences prophetic dreams and apparitions, often of a marked hallucinatory nature, while fully awake. As he preaches in the pulpit, he hears on many occasions—as do his listeners—choirs of angels singing hymns to the accompaniment of an invisible organ.[18]

Swedberg also evinced the same interest in the apparitions experienced by others as in his own. It appears that, little by little, the episcopal manse of Brunsbo became the center of all the superstition that still flourished in Sweden at that time. It was the rendezvous of the maidservants who were possessed or speaking with tongues; once any miraculous events were heard of in the diocese, the old bishop was called, who, by his prayers, the laying on of hands, or other similar means, exorcized the devil and healed those who had drawn upon themselves the punishment of God by some particularly grave sin. He says himself that even in England, Holland, and elsewhere abroad, his exorcisms were spoken of. It was especially told of him that he had succeeded, one day at Brunsbo, in expelling the devil who appeared to him in the guise of a cavalier through a small hole in a windowpane in the manse.

Jesper Swedberg is often classed as a mystic. This is true only if the term is used in its most general application, that is to say as indicating a certain bent towards superstition together with a visionary inclination. But Swedberg has little in common with the great family of mystics to which his son belonged. His religiosity is entirely unreflective and, despite its warmth, lacks that depth of feeling, that faculty of self-analysis that characterizes true mysticism. It never rises to the bliss of ecstasy any more than it founders in the torments of endless broodings. It is an innocent, old-time Swedish religiosity, healthy to the core, which, impelled by an infantile curiosity, seeks to open the door slightly to the supersensory world.

This quality attaches itself also to the visions of Jesper Swedberg. While the visions of true mystics are generally confused and enigmatic, acquiring deep meaning only through symbolic interpretation, those of Swedberg constitute concrete images, which only confirm his own notions, built on popular tradition, of the life hereafter. Take, for example, the first of the visions, which he says he has seen regarding heaven and hell at thirteen years of age. It is easy to see that it directly reproduces the old religious paintings found in churches and which stimulated his childish imagination. The Savior stands in person before a large basin filled with warm water, washing those he wants to save and introducing them immediately thereafter into the "heavenly hall" to the right where the elected sit, "entirely naked in common felicity and joy in a holy ignorance of evil and a perfect innocence." Swedberg then is led to the left and enters into hell where the condemned give themselves to rude, lascivious dances in a pit exhaling sulfurous vapors. "And, despite their efforts to escape from the pit, I saw them pushed back into the abyss with blows of iron pitchforks amidst frightful wails and atrocious hissings."[19] As we see, this is the traditional representation of hell found on altarpieces since the Middle Ages. It does not seem to me correct when Holmquist likens this conception of heaven and hell, in its smallest details, to the more characteristically, uniquely personal conception of Swedenborg, which are speculatively structured and entirely symbolic.[20]

The theological conceptions of Swedberg are marked by the same straightforward simplicity. We have already had occasion to note the little importance he accords to dogma, placing above all else the concordance of life and doctrine. The "*Theologia verbalis,*" Swedberg writes in his autobiography, "has never appealed to me but the *theologia realis*. '*If you know these things,*' says the Most High Teacher, *'blessed are you if you do them'* (John 13:17). The Savior of us all says, *'Do, do, do,'"* [21] Therefore, he consistently comes to rise up against the abuse by the prevailing orthodoxy of the doctrine of justification by faith alone; of "solifidism," as he himself expresses it. Already, on the occasion of his journey abroad, he is deeply grieved to observe that, impelled by their conviction of the importance for salvation of good works, the French Catholics busy themselves with quantities of acts of charity to which Protestant countries remained quite indifferent. "They, in their erroneous creed, innocently follow the teachings of Christ; we, in our doctrine of *sovereign faith (stortro),* which predominates in our country, practice no good works."[22]

This regrettable state of things appears still more clearly to Swedberg as his new episcopal functions permit him to know better the religious situation of his diocese, and more particularly among his clergy. Everywhere he observes that the teaching of Luther is misunderstood and that good deeds are considered to be superfluous provided one has the true faith. "They all go to church regularly and the holy table is approached on the dates fixed, besides continuing to live in various sinful deeds of the flesh. No need to worry: the 'sovereign faith' will do it."[23] A faith without good deeds, in Swedberg's opinion, is not a living faith at all; it is "a cerebral faith and not a faith of the heart, a shadow without a body, a dead faith and not a living one, indeed, a devilish faith, one I call the 'sovereign faith' in which Christianity takes refuge, and on which God may have mercy."[24]

It was especially the necessity, proclaimed by the Pietists, of a sincere repentance and a pious life that above all made him so sympathetic towards them; and time after time he complains that no one can live piously, insist on keeping the Sabbath, and combat drunkenness without exposing oneself to the charge of Pietism by the clergy: "You are a Pietist, you." He hopes for a new reformer who, preaching the unity of works and faith, will inspire Protestantism, congealed in a loveless orthodoxy, with a new life. "O my God, Thou who awakened Luther and endowed him with the spirit of fearlessness, to introduce anew the Christian doctrine of faith, send us also a Luther who, with the same spirit of fearlessness and the same blessed energy, may reestablish a Christian life!"[25] As we know, it was Emanuel

Swedenborg who came to consider it as his mission in life to become this new Luther.

We may conclude from the preceding that Swedberg did not, by his polemic against sovereign faith, consider himself in opposition to Luther. This is confirmed in his long study of the Protestant conception of faith in his *Casa Pauperum, Gaza Divitum* (House of the Poor, Treasure of the Wealthy; Iskara, 1723). In this work, Swedberg seeks to demonstrate, with the help of ample quotations from Luther, that the latter, when establishing his doctrine of justification by faith, desired to create precisely that living faith proclaimed by Swedberg and his favorite Pietist authors; Luther ought not to be considered in any way as the inspirer of the "sovereign faith" that was dominant at the time. All things considered, Swedberg does not seem to be aware of deviating in the least from Luther's doctrine. There is, then, no reason to see in Swedberg a direct representative of the heterodox doctrine that characterizes Swedenborg and which already appears in his very first work on a theological subject, *De Fide et Bonis Operibus*, published in 1738, and in which Luther's interpretation of the Pauline doctrine on justification by faith alone is specifically denounced as a falsification of the biblical text. But it is clear that, all things considered, the tendencies of Swedberg head in the same direction. It is equally possible that his middle-of-the-road position to some extent depends on his aversion to all dogmatic polemics.

The preceding brief characterization unfortunately permits only a rather incomplete view of the spiritual atmosphere of the home in which Swedenborg was born and reared. A more detailed exposition would have required more extensive extracts from the works and the autobiography of Jesper Swedberg, more than space here allows. So I have to refer the reader interested in this matter to the very complete biography of Swedberg written by [Henry William] Tottie.

The element that had the greatest influence on Emanuel Swedenborg's development was evidently his father's belief in a supersensory world that is capable of manifesting itself to us and directly intervening in our life. At that time, there were of course numerous Swedish homes where one could tell of wonderful dreams and visions and in which spirit apparitions and miraculous happenings were daily occurrences. During Swedenborg's childhood, the ideas of the Enlightenment had not yet made their entry into Sweden, and many of the phenomena for which a scientific explanation was found fifty years later still appeared to be unfathomable mysteries. But in the house of Jesper Swedberg, these miracles and these visions displayed a notably more important role than in most contemporary homes. These were not simply incidents that were discussed in idle moments and promptly forgotten in the course of daily occupations: they were real happenings, leaving their imprint on the life of the whole family. In this family circle, where all the children, except for one daughter who entered the world on Easter Monday, were born on a Sunday, every event, even the most insignificant, was considered to have a particular meaning; and an effort was made to discover the intervention of spirits in everything. The old bishop was surely not the only one to sense the presence of the devil everywhere, wandering through the manse like a "roaring lion" to devour him, or to believe that good angels of God constantly came to his rescue. From Swedberg's autobiography, it appears that the entire family shared his conception of life, according to which fires, accidents, sickness, and poor harvests were regarded as so many chastisements of God, or as so many trials or afflictions. Happy occurrences, on the contrary, constituted recompense. Jesper Swedberg loved to compare his own destiny and that of his family to that of Job and his house. To judge from the comparison that he himself made between the one and the other, it appears that his own existence was more full of blessings than of hard trials.

For the God who was adored in the home of Swedberg was not only the zealous guardian of good morals and the judge threatening the eternal punishments of hell, he was also the tender father above all, only resorting to the punishment of his children when so constrained and obliged, in the end always ready to forgive. In tracing God's protecting hand in everything, the Swedbergs had approached him so closely that he had been changed almost into a friendly household spirit, watching over the larder and the stables, never permitting anything in the house to go wrong as long as one did not disturb him intentionally.

In consequence, domestic worship around Jesper Swedberg's hearth never assumed the aspect of severe observance that was characteristic of most of the Protestant families at that time: it was rather a vesperal repose from the labors of the day. Moreover, this worship had an aesthetic quality that was certainly very rare in those days. Swedberg, like his son Emanuel after him, loved music above all. "For God has endowed beautiful music with incredible force." And in his provident goodness, God had endowed Swedberg's house with an excellent musician. "God has granted me the grace that Doctor Hesselius is a good violoncellist, and he plays beautiful and divine hymns every evening; which permits me to go to my rest with a peaceful and content spirit."[26]

How easy it is to imagine what such an evening in that paternal home must have been! The venerable bishop relates with his customary innocence how God has guided him throughout the phases of his life and how many manifest signs of God's grace and omnipotence he has seen. And the evening closes with the chant, to the accompaniment of Hesselius' violoncello, of one of the hymns, of such noble simplicity and beauty, that Jesper Swedberg has composed or translated; for example the "*Hymnus de Sanctis Angelis*" of Melanchthon, which so well reflects his religious views:

> Glory be to God
> for holy angels' watch
> that he by grace me vouchsafes
> against all evil powers.
> Provided, off they go
> as winds on his command
> to surround and defend
> the pious one who is righteous.
>
> They come to visit me
> as in ancient Israel.
> They bring me out of danger
> like Daniel in days of yore.
> They lead me by the hand
> as Lot out of fire and embers,

as Peter out of straits,
as Paul out of distress.

And when on earth it happens
that a drudging sinner
repents and is reformed,
caring for his soul,
then in the heavenly kingdom
angelic rejoicing is heard:
We have got an equal!
Glory be to God!

It is in this environment, where each felt himself under "the guardianship of holy angels," where faith and intuition transformed reality into a beautiful dream and the dream was taken as a part of reality, where the naive religiosity of the old Swedes was mingled with a sensibility full of warmth that already augured the new age—it is in this environment that Emanuel Swedenborg grew up. We readily understand how strongly such a milieu could have contributed to the development of his natural and hereditary tendency as a dreamer and visionary.

It is our misfortune that we know only about Swedenborg's early days from what he told in his old age. The most complete account that we have of the religious events of his first years is to be found in a letter written to Gabriel Beyer, dated November 14, 1769:

> I want to tell you here how my early childhood was. From my fourth to my tenth year, my thoughts were constantly focused upon God, blessedness, and the *passiones spirituales* of mankind. I repeatedly revealed things that astonished my father and my mother and caused them to consider that angels spoke through me. From my sixth to my twelfth year, my pleasure was to discuss with clergymen regarding faith, that the life thereof is love, that the love that vivifies is love for one's neighbor, and that God has given faith to all men, but that only those have truly received it practice that love; then I knew of no other faith than that God created Nature and sustains it and that He gives men

> understanding and good nature and all that flows therefrom. The learned faith, which is that God the Father imputes His Son's justification to whomsoever and whensoever He wishes, even to those who have done no penance, was then unknown to me; and had I known of it, then as now, it would have gone far above my comprehension.[27]

Obviously, this exposition cannot be accepted without reserve as the faithful expression of Swedenborg's religious state during his childhood. Like most great mystics, he has evidently unconsciously romanticized his recollections in the conviction of having been the elected instrument of God from the beginning. In particular, his statement that he did not know or accept the orthodox doctrine of atonement as a child seems less than credible. It would be difficult to explain why, in such a case, he was loyal to this doctrine preceding his theological period. On the other hand, everything suggests the accuracy of his recollections when he relates that, during his early childhood, he gave himself up to long meditations about "God, blessedness, and the *passiones spirituales* of mankind," that he discussed these things with the clergy, and that his parents regarded him as a religious prodigy.

That Swedenborg had been in mystical states already during his childhood years, foreshadowing his later visionary period, is a fact made clear by a declaration found in his *Spiritual Diary* §3464, pointed out by Tafel.[28] Referring to "internal breathing," by means of which during his theosophical period Swedenborg believed himself able to enter into communication with the angels and spirits, he relates that he acquired the habit of this exercise while saying his morning and evening prayers during his childhood. If the descriptions of this "internal respiration" given later by Swedenborg, consisting of an inhibition of external respiration, and allowing only imperceptible and silent respiratory exchange, are studied more closely, we realize that we here have a phenomenon that is known and described by a number of different mystics. It is a suspension of breathing that often accompanies mystical states of mind, contemplation, or inarticulate "mental" prayer. It brings forth a state of trance during which the subject feels separated from the external world and at the same time is suffused by an interior light. His emotions attain a fervor and his thoughts gain a clarity that he does not experience under normal conditions. This suspension of respiration often constitutes the prelude to visions of a hallucinatory character.[29] The phenomenon appears to have been first produced with Swedenborg in an unconscious manner, but he later learned, he tells us, to induce it by intense mental concentration. In this state, he believed he could suspend his external breathing for a whole hour and during this time could find himself in communion with angels and spirits. As can be seen, this respiratory inhibition constitutes a direct opening of the spiritual visions of Swedenborg, and we shall see later what an important role it has played in the evolution of his philosophy towards mysticism.

The information we possess regarding Swedenborg's childhood, scanty though it be, nevertheless gives us an idea of the difference between his temperament and that of his father. From the first, we find in Swedenborg a speculative interest that was entirely lacking in Jesper Swedberg. Likewise, even in childhood, Swedenborg's religiosity assumes an ecstatic character of which no equivalent can be found in the father.

From the very beginning, one has the impression of a more introverted and complicated nature in Swedenborg, in which nothing remains of the basically healthy confidence of Jesper Swedberg. It is because of this that Swedenborg, unlike his father, cannot walk around in serene unconcern in a fairytale land of wonder enchanted with miracles, rejoicing in each new apparition as a sign of divine power and goodness. His brain knows rest only when it has succeeded in finding an explanation for a phenomenon, in penetrating the causes of such occurrences. All the miracles he witnesses or that are related to him in his father's house do not merely turn his own imagination toward the supernatural; for him, from the beginning, they constitute so many problems demanding solution. In his search for answers, he addresses himself first to the sciences that seem to him the most exact in their methods and results. He demands of mathematics and mechanics the explanation of the creation and subsistence of the universe, then searches anatomy for the definitive solution of the mysteries of the soul. But despite all his classifications and his analogical inferences, he does not reach the goal he seeks. There are always some phenomena that evade all rational explanations; and, unconsciously, step by step, he introduces more mystical elements into his philosophy. Like most mystics, Swedenborg took his definitive turn toward mysticism as a result of a personal crisis. But he was committed to the road leading to it well before this crisis.

In fact, even at the time when he was professing a philosophy so distinctly mechanistic that it attracted a certain amount of attention abroad, we detect in Swedenborg's mind a leaven of mysticism derived from his paternal inheritance. It is a feeling of the existence of a higher world, to which our own world has a relationship. It is in vain that he asserts on many occasions that such a world is beyond our knowledge, which is reduced to the limits of our sensory perceptions. In spite of everything, he is pursued by the desire to learn something of life beyond the grave and of the secret influence of higher powers upon our earthly life. In his dreams and in his visions, the supersensory world meets him in perceptible forms; finally, he believes he has found the key to the spiritual world in the doctrine of correspondences. It is then that he commits himself to the gigantic task of explaining, in terms of natural science, not only the visible universe but also the unknown world on high. Starting with the human anatomy, his *Animal Kingdom* attempts an empirical penetration, not merely of the essence of the soul and its intercourse with the body, but even the state of the soul after physical death. But this work never reaches its appointed goal; while it is in progress, Swedenborg receives a divine apparition commanding him to renounce the natural sciences and confine himself exclusively to work *in spiritualibus*.

Thus it is that the mystical tendencies he has for so long tried to restrain by scientific criticism finally win. His patrimony claims its rights. It is significant that, during that decisive crisis, which we know about from his *Journal of Dreams*, Swedenborg repeatedly sees in the dreams his paternal home on the Great Square in Uppsala and hears the admonitory voice of his father. His reflective spirit will never allow him to attain the happy state of naive faith possessed by Jesper Swedberg, and he often speaks with envy of the poor in spirit "who believe and do not see."

Nevertheless, it appears that something of the childish trust of his father casts its glow on his closing years. Times of temptation and spiritual conflict are now past and, in his home at Hornsgatan, he peacefully awaits the hour when he will enter forever the world of spirits he has visited so often in his visions. Each year he feels his soul become more harmonious and secure. He even tells his visitors that his physical health improves from day to day and that he is growing new teeth to replace those he had lost.

It seemed too that Swedenborg had a certain physical resemblance to his father, of which the portraits that we possess of each of them give no idea. Carl Gustaf Tessin, who once "from pure curiosity to make the acquaintance of a strange personality," paid Swedenborg a visit, found his "countenance perfectly like that of the late Bishop Swedberg; but shorter in stature, with weak eyes, a large mouth, pale complexion, friendly, cheerful, and talkative."[30] In his stuttering speech, Swedenborg talked to Tessin regarding human destiny after death and the various heavens and hells. He told his visitor that "whenever he is alone he is visited by angels and by the deceased." These are the "guardian spirits" of his father, who have never left him and who serve as intermediaries with the spiritual world. Despite all the divergences, Swedenborg's philosophy returns to the same point as the innocent superstition of his father: a sense of never-ceasing union with the transcendental and divine.

Contemporary anecdotes relate that the gate to Swedenborg's yard was never locked and that, during his last sojourn in Paris, he had never once locked his doors. When his servant, being concerned, once warned him how easily he could be burglarized, Swedenborg responded with a smile that the servant no doubt was unaware of the faithful guardian he had at his door. In addition, he felt himself personally to be under the constant "guardianship of the holy angels."

After his father's appointment to the bishopric of Skara, Swedenborg went to live with his brother-in-law, Erik Benzelius, in order to pursue university studies under his supervision. To judge from the correspondence between them, Erik Benzelius appears to have been the relative closest to Swedenborg during the next decades; and it is natural to suppose that this brother-in-law, thirteen years older than he, exercised considerable influence over Swedenborg, who at that time was in the most receptive age. It is certain that it was primarily his brother-in-law to whom he owed the love for science that dominated his adult life.

Erik Benzelius is one of the most magnificent representatives of the second flowering of the humanism that arose in Sweden during the last decades of her political grandeur. While the multiplication of scientific material and the broadening of horizons had already forced a specialization in the field of science in other countries, Sweden, where the Renaissance had only tardily penetrated and taken root, still possessed a phalanx of late-born humanists for whom specialization did not exist and whose interest and zeal embraced every area of contemporary science. With the greater number of them, this desire for universal scientific conquest (which Schück rightly compares to the great-power policy pursued by Sweden) demanded a disastrous dispersion of energy that resulted, in many cases, in an accomplishment that did not match up to their genius. The contemporary field of science had become too vast to be grasped in its totality by a single scholar, however energetic. Moreover, the cultural isolation of Sweden, as well as its limited means, constituted additional obstacles that were difficult to overcome. So it is that, among the great Swedish scholars at the close of the seventeenth century, some, like Rudbeck, established magnificent systems, although fantastic and devoid of any critical spirit, while others became scholarly compilers, as well-known abroad as in their own country, inspirers of various movements but themselves incapable of concentrating upon a homogeneous lifework.

Erik Benzelius belonged in this second category. His own scholarship included ancient manuscripts, comparative philology, Nordic archaeology, and history, both ecclesiastical and literary—in other words, all the humanistic sciences that were pursued at this time. He was also keenly interested in the many new branches of natural science and their practical application. The scientific thrust of the Swedish "Era of Liberty" (1718–1772) owes much to him for the creative impulses that he stimulated, and notably for the foundation of the first Swedish scientific society, the *Collegium curiosorum,* and the two that succeeded it—the *Bokvettsgillet* and *Vetenskapssocieteten*—as well as for the creation of the first Swedish scientific and literary journal.

The active role Benzelius played in the practical organization of scientific studies at the University of Uppsala should not be forgotten. Either directly or through the mediation of friends, or friends of friends, he was in contact with all scholarly Europe, and it was due to his initiative that a goodly number of young students with promising futures found the means to perfect their education abroad. Nevertheless, his personal scholarly production never attained the level worthy of the central position he had enjoyed in Sweden and in the scientific life of his age. His historical researches largely remained in the form of lecture notes, and the two great works that he had projected—editions of Philo Judaeus and Ulfilas—were not published in his lifetime. The first of these two works was anticipated by an English edition, and the second was only published seven years after Benzelius' death, but was already antiquated. By that time, two young authors, Sotberg and Ihre, equipped with a more modern education in philology, had produced a text and translation of Ulfilas.[31]

Despite this, Swedenborg found in his brother-in-law the surest scientific guide and best-qualified supervisor in the scientific circles of the time. From his relations with Benzelius, he also absorbed some of the universal scientific enthusiasm. In fact, we find in Swedenborg's letters to his brother-in-law a reflection of this enthusiasm for every new discovery and problem of the human spirit. In the first letter he writes to Benzelius from London, Swedenborg tells him about his visit to the tomb of the celebrated humanist Isaac Casaubon in Westminster Abbey. He "was seized," he says, "with such great love of this hero of learning" that he kissed the tomb and immediately composed some Latin verses in honor of Casaubon.[32]

Through Benzelius, then, Swedenborg is directly connected to the generation of scholars active towards the end of Sweden's age of grandeur. Actually, the scientific impulses Swedenborg received during his years of study in Rudbeck's Uppsala appear to me to deserve the same attention as those he found later in the England of Newton. Although the methods he learned in London are those of modern empiricism, his whole conception of the goals and possibilities of science come largely from his formative years at Uppsala. Despite all the respect that he feels for experimentation, a respect that he proclaims on many occasions, he often lacks the patience indispensable for every experimenter. From the beginning, he addresses himself to the great hypotheses that seek to explain the universe. If we have correctly understood the indications from the experts in this respect, the greatest discoveries of Swedenborg in the various scientific fields are to be regarded as brilliant and daring combinations of facts, which were only demonstrated by later generations, rather than the slow fruit of exacting research. The sober motto of Newton, *Hypotheses non fingo,* could not be applied to Swedenborg who, on the contrary, had only too great a propensity for hypotheses. It follows that his discoveries belong in an entirely different category than those bearing the stamp of the century of empiricism. They are the offspring of the magnificent, boldly constructive spirit of conquest, which inspired the sciences at Uppsala under the aegis of Rudbeck.

Among all the more or less happy comparisons that have been made between Swedenborg and other great minds—and all, from Plato to Goethe, have been drawn upon—none appears to me so legitimate as that which joins his name with that of Rudbeck. Certainly, Swedenborg, during much of his scientific youth, was a faithful adept of the doctrines of the *Atlantica*: we know, in effect, that in his work on *The Level of Waters* he believes that his theory of the primitive insularity of Sweden contributes "plausible confirmations" to the hypothesis, "naturally and laudably deduced by Rudbeck from the works of numerous learned men," according to which Sweden was at one time "the great island of Atlantis."[33] And when, in another of his works, he demonstrates that, because the earth's orbiting of the sun had formerly been more rapid, a perpetual springtime reigned over the whole globe, he concludes that the "late Rudbeck," who was often accused of being "inspired by a blind patriotism rather than regard for the truth," was perhaps not wrong in supposing that Sweden had in the past enjoyed a climate similar to that of Florence, and that it really was the cradle of humanity.[34]

But what is much more remarkable than these direct references, which simply prove that Swedenborg remained unshakably loyal to the authority of Rudbeck which so far had not yet been recognized in Sweden, is the concordance one finds between the conceptions and the scientific methods of these two thinkers. Thus, Swedenborg grants to tradition the same validity as Rudbeck does.[35] And, like Rudbeck, he attempts no critique of his sources. These are not only the biblical accounts of the earthly paradise, the Flood, the ages of the antediluvians, and so on, which his geological theories are drawn upon to corroborate, but even all the cosmogonic conceptions of mythology and of the poetry of classical antiquity. His cosmological system permits him to confirm the descriptions by Hesiod and his successors; of the "world egg" from which the sun and planets emerged; of Plato's conceptions of a subsolar world and his myth of Atlantis; of the recitations of Ovid on the four ages of the earth. Homer himself, that "sire of all poets," seems to have given voice to a profound truth when he tells us that "Pallas, Venus, and all the other gods of lust have lived on this earth and associated with men." In effect, Swedenborg understands by this that "the earth was formerly like heaven and the age like a celestial amusement."[36]

Swedenborg, then, like Rudbeck, considers all tradition, whether from the Bible or from ancient mythology, to be the allegorical, if not literal, expression of historical truth. Like Rudbeck, he tries to discover in every ancient legend and in all ancient history the same historical events mentioned in the Bible, even though they may at times appear in somewhat different form. As we shall see later, this notion will follow him into his theosophical period during which he creates, by a kind of amalgam of Genesis with the accounts of Hesiod and the four ages of Ovid, a strange fable of the evolution of the human race from its childhood.

Another trait in Swedenborg that is reminiscent of Rudbeck is his incredible power of combination. Without entering into Rudbeck's favorite domain—etymological explanation—he displays the same boldness as the latter in skillfully regrouping facts for his own purposes, especially when it comes to discovering the allegorical implications in the accounts of ancient writers or of the Bible. In this respect, his scientific works already foreshadow his biblical exegesis.

But Swedenborg especially resembles Rudbeck in the scope of the tasks that he sets for himself from the beginning. He rarely occupies himself with problems of detail: they have no interest in themselves. He immediately attacks the deepest problems, such as the origin of our planetary system or the first state of the earth. His optimistic self-confidence yields nothing to Rudbeck, any more than does his patriotism. In both thinkers, a vast universal learning in all the many fields of human knowledge is joined with an indisputable practical sense and great ability for logical demonstration. Both construct gigantic systems upon arguments that are in appearance perfectly coordinated. But neither takes the time to verify adequately the solidity of his premises and, therefore, ends up building castles in the air. The Atlantis of Rudbeck and the spiritual world of Swedenborg do not, perhaps, have much in common in their construction; but both are products of the same scientific imagination, nourished and exalted by an age when every day the spirit of discovery opened new horizons to the human spirit.

two

The Mechanistic View of the World

It is clear from Swedenborg's letters to Erik Benzelius that it was largely under the influence of the latter that he came to dedicate the greater part of his scientific studies to the natural sciences, particularly mathematics and mechanics. Evidently, his intent was to devote his life to applied mechanics, and consultations had been in course already in 1710 to gain him an apprenticeship under Christopher Polhem. This collaboration was nevertheless deferred at the time,[37] since Swedenborg had obtained his father's permission to undertake the trip abroad for which he had so long hoped.

The real goal of this voyage was, quite naturally, England, at that time the center of modern natural science. To this destination, Swedish university youth, once having completed their academic studies, made a pilgrimage in their desire to acquire practical instruction, which the Swedish universities with their obsolete equipment could not yet provide.

It is almost superfluous to emphasize the considerable influence of this sojourn in England on Swedenborg's subsequent development. His own letters to Benzelius are eloquent enough in this respect. Once disembarked, he becomes intoxicated by the passion for research that holds sway in that country. He undertakes the study of everything, mathematics, mechanics, astronomy. He enters into daily relationship with the most illustrious scholars of Europe, discoursing with Flamsteed and Halley, listening to the lectures of Newton. He has, as he writes to Benzelius, such an "immoderate desire" for studies that he even takes domicile with watchmakers or instrument makers, lodging successively with one and the other in the hope of discovering their professional secrets. After a short time, his imaginative mind has formulated a series of hypotheses and theories that he submits to Swedish scholars for evaluation. And following his return from England, he lists, in a letter to Benzelius, no less than fourteen sensational inventions, the description of which he has sent to his father. These, among other things, include a submarine, a steam engine, and an aircraft. It is almost too much of a good thing, suggesting one of the favorite subjects of contemporary satire, the "gadgeteer" whose mind seethes with the most diverse ideas, who has a formula for condensation of air into solid form, who knows how to extract solar rays from cucumbers, etc., a caricature that age sketched of its own inventive mania, of its incurably optimistic faith in the ability of science to perform the impossible.

It is most probable that the religious interests of his earlier youth found themselves largely relegated to the background as a consequence of this enthusiastic devotion to scientific matters. The example that Holmquist cites regarding this state of mind, the passage in a letter to Benzelius in which Swedenborg speaks of the superstition of the Catholic Church historian Vastovius is, despite his prudence, rather characteristic.[38] Even more eloquent in this respect is perhaps the allusion found in a letter addressed to Benzelius (*Opera* I, §217) from the year 1712 where Swedenborg, indignant because his father has left him without money, remarks that "it is difficult to live like the maid in Schone, without either food or drink." The reference is to a maid, Ester Jönadotter of Norre-Åby, who lived without nourishment during six years. This was one of the great miracles that Jesper Swedberg himself had witnessed and that he had related in detail in his sermons "in order that neither we nor our descendants should never forget such a miracle of God."[39] The old bishop would no doubt have taken deeply to his heart the irreverent tone of his son when mentioning the incident.

In general, in the letters from his trip and the years following, Swedenborg appears more like a man of the world. He is completely absorbed by his scientific theories and by the expectation of celebrity and the scientific recognition that cannot fail to accrue to him once they are published. He has a rather high opinion of himself. The best example of this can be found in the proposition he submits to Benzelius to reduce the salaries of the professors in order to provide a position for him at Uppsala. When this is rejected by Benzelius, he suggests suppressing a chair of theology or medicine. He expresses himself in rather disdainful terms regarding Swedish scholars and their Cartesian "prejudices." And it is precisely this scientific ambition that, at the time of his religious crisis, he will consider the greatest and most difficult to eradicate of his sins. His relations with his family seem, at least at times, rather cold. His father appears to entertain some doubts about his scientific future or at least about the possibility of his carving out an assured future for himself in this line; it is only with difficulty that he is induced to provide his son with the means needed for his studies.

This exclusive orientation toward pure science and this newly acquired self-confidence are easily explained by Swedenborg's conviction that he is standing at the springs of modern science. It could be anticipated that this atmosphere would forever stifle all tendency toward mysticism in him. The survival of these tendencies, observable to a certain extent in the philosophical works appearing in the decades after his voyage to England, suggests the question whether, even in the environment of sober empiricism he experienced during his sojourn in England, there were not some factors acting in the opposite direction. We are unable to analyze here in all its facets an age customarily seen too much in the light of the succeeding period, that of the French Enlightenment. We shall only try to deal with certain factors whose role had a certain importance, especially for Swedenborg.

Without any doubt, the time of Newton is above all the golden age of the empirical methods and the experiment. The natural sciences now acquire a cultural hegemony that they have never known. If, prior to this period, theology and philosophy had alternately, by turns, proclaimed themselves to be the science of sciences, it is now the natural sciences that lend the support of their arguments to theological and philosophical verities and that impose their methods on these disciplines. New thought, stimulated by empiricism and by the newly acquired freedom of the press, for certain pioneers, has in an amazingly short time made a clean sweep of all authorities and traditions. It has also created on scientific bases a philosophy that, by its materialistic and atheistic consequences, by its pitiless critique of the Bible, and by its elimination of every supernatural element, anticipates that of the Encyclopedists.

In the fervor to demonstrate the stages that led to the ideas of the French Enlightenment, the Enlightenment's free-wheeling predecessors were later accorded an importance they did not have in their own time. No account was taken of diametrically opposed tendencies that animated most of the guiding spirits of the age—which explains why, at the very hour the ideas of the Enlightenment in the form of the *Encyclopedia* win a definitive victory, all over cultured Europe those forces that were to cause their downfall were already in action and, in fact, proselytizing.

The era of Newton was a time of crisis, and, like all similar periods, it was animated by a contradictory spirit that is difficult to penetrate. When the chains imposed on human thought by orthodoxy and philosophic rationalism were struck off, the free practice of scientific studies was not the only impulse to be awakened. Mysticism also acquired a freedom of action that allowed it influence on public opinion. Not only did it flourish within sects that, in England as everywhere else, now had their heyday, but it took over the new science, seeking in scientific discoveries the justification of its own dreams.

Here we find historical authentication, frequently confirmed, of the fact that the occasions when experimental sciences succeed in opening new horizons for the human spirit are often also the times when superstition and mysticism enlarge their domain and recruit new followers. This is not only the result of the fact that the empirical sciences are in their beginnings related to magic, that historically chemistry is the daughter of alchemy. It is also because scientific experiments generate new results without being able to explain them satisfactorily; thus, they entice impatient minds to supernatural interpretations. The brilliant scientific period of the last fifty years is particularly illustrative in this respect. Almost every unexplained scientific discovery—notably those of interest in the psychophysical field—has given birth to new forms of mysticism; and in many cases, the researchers themselves have inadvertently abandoned the field of the exact sciences in favor of fantastic speculations.

Naturally, the temptation was even stronger at the beginning of the eighteenth century. The new science was born of the philosophy of nature of the preceding century, a philosophy with strong elements of occultism and Kabbalah. Long after it abandoned the methods of past times in order to devote itself exclusively to experimentation, it continued to exhibit a taste for occult speculations. It is thus, for example, that Thomasius, one of the greatest German pioneers of the Enlightenment, was the disciple of Robert Fludd and published books with the clear imprint of occultism. Robert Boyle, one of the founders of modern chemistry and one of the teachers of Swedenborg, was deeply interested in alchemy as well as in all sorts of mystical speculations.

It was the same in Sweden. Urban Hiärne, because of his scientific work, can be considered as one of the great pioneers of the Enlightenment; moreover, he contributed in large measure to a more modern outlook by his agitation against the trials for witchcraft. Yet he was also a lover of alchemy and astrology and published an ardent defense of Paracelsus. Polhem, with whom Swedenborg directly collaborated, was not at all, as we shall see, a stranger to mystical concepts or the interest in occultism. And this scenario repeats itself in all countries.

The great rationalistic system of the seventeenth century had drawn a very clear demarcation between the domains of faith and of science, and step by step people became lulled by the illusion that these two would henceforth not disturb each other. The great discoveries that marked the turn of the century threatened to demolish these hopes. The traditional proofs of religious truths became useless, and the theologians who had hardly had time to reconcile Christianity and Cartesianism suddenly found themselves faced by new scientific facts whose consequences appeared to lead to materialism and atheism.

The theologians were not alone in dreading such a use of the new discoveries. The scientists themselves, who often came from very religious families and whose faith had resisted their own scientific works, considered, not without horror, the dangerous weapons against religion that could be forged out of the material from their research. Naturally, they also feared that the modern science would be discredited by being used as a pretext by freethinkers. Thus, one finds in their own and their followers' writings constant attempts to reconcile the new concepts of nature with biblical text. Each sought to prove that, far from undermining belief in God and the immortality of the soul, the new doctrine furnished new and powerful arguments on behalf of these ideas. It is in England, where this spirit ruled among the majority of scientific personalities, that this form of apologetics found the largest number of propagators. It is for this reason that Robert Boyle founded in London a special institute for public conferences where various orators might demonstrate that the new science, far from being opposed to the cardinal truths of faith, had a necessary connection with them.[40] It was particularly important to prove that the new ideas on the origin of the world responded point by point to the creation story in Genesis. In the earliest cosmological works of Swedenborg are found similar attempts to establish the validity of the Mosaic cosmology from the perspective of natural science. The seven days of creation, the earthly paradise, the Flood, the origin of the rainbow, all the details of the biblical tradition, found entirely satisfactory confirmation in the new naturalistic conception. The burden was "to approve nothing unacceptable to the word of God and to irrefutable reason."

It is in connection with this strange current of the time, in which an anxious eye was kept on the past lest contact with authority and tradition be lost, that we must also see the philosopher who, for his contemporaries as for posterity, most clearly summed up the world of ideas of the empirical sciences and with Newton stood as the intellectual master of the century: John Locke. We have all the more reason to dwell a moment upon this illustrious philosopher in that his *Essay Concerning Human Understanding* played a decisive role in Swedenborg's development and even extended an influence far into his theosophical period.

The view that only credits Locke with empiricism and sensationalism, and sees in his masterwork merely a more cautious version of the same doctrine that was openly professed by the Encyclopedists, has been generally abandoned in our time by the historians of philosophy. It is above all thanks to the very complete study by Hertling,[41] from which I have drawn the major part of the following account, that the amalgam of empirical and rationalistic reasonings that characterize Locke's philosophy have been brought out, and that, for this reason, the true purpose pursued by the author of the *Essay* has appeared to us under a new light. Far from constituting—as contemporaries including Voltaire believed—a lethal blow against all metaphysics, far from seeking to create doubts about the existence of God, the immortality of the soul, and the validity of moral law, the *Essay* was written with the apparent aim of arming religion and morality against the consequences of the naturalistic philosophy that threatened to overthrow them.[42]

In reality, the extensive study of empirical knowledge, which occupies the larger part of the work, leads to the Platonic idea that no true knowledge of the physicosensory world, which is in the process of constant modification, can exist. We can only gain real knowledge by means of general concepts, which exist solely in the domain of ideas.[43]Along with sensation and reflection, which, while collecting and extrapolating the elements of our conception of things, provide us with a relative knowledge of phenomena within and outside ourselves, there exists an intuitive and demonstrative knowledge that permits us to affirm with ample evidence the concordance of two ideas, and teaches us to recognize necessary truths. It follows that true knowledge is not rooted in experience; it is independent of experience and surpasses it. Knowledge assumes the form of necessary and general judgments by which we affirm the objective relations between ideas we have perceived.[44] Not only does the universality of geometric propositions depend on this knowledge, but also all the verities that we necessarily must acknowledge, such as our own existence, the existence of God, of life after death, etc. No doubt these "eternal verities" are not inborn, but every human being possessing ordinary human faculties finds himself obliged to recognize them once he directs his thoughts to the examination of his own ideas.[45]

From an epistemological standpoint, one may realize, as Hertling has pointed out,[46] that to read into Locke's work any attempt to establish, in agreement with Kant, the impossibility of metaphysics is completely unwarranted. On the contrary, Locke acknowledges the highest degree of evidence for the knowledge of the existence of God, and in the *Essay*, one can find numerous forms of metaphysical reasoning. Locke believes that we are able, with the same degree of plausibility as that accepted for the establishment of scientific theories, to accept the existence of angels who surpass us by various degrees of perfection and who lead us, through gradations analogous to those we observe in nature, toward the infinite perfection of the Creator. At many points in his work, he speculates on the nature of these angels and their faculty of assuming corporeal form, a faculty that he is disposed to accept on the authority of the Church Fathers. He maintains that our conceptions of a spiritual substance are at least as clear as those of a material substance and speaks clearly of the existence of a "world of the intellect" that is "certainly more extensive and beautiful than the material world."[47]

In the mind of Locke, therefore, there exists not only a clearly rationalistic conception coexistent with his empiricism, but also a certain element of mysticism that is obviously akin to Neoplatonic philosophy, including his conception of intuition as a sort of spiritual sight, a kind of inner light that imposes itself irresistibly upon our eyes from the moment they focus upon it. One can say as much regarding his idea of two worlds as well as his belief in spirits and their faculty of materialization.

Today there is almost general agreement in seeking the origin of this mystical element in the relationship between Locke and the philosophical school that, at this time in England, was the clearest expression of the opposition to the materialism of Hobbes as well as to the rationalism of Descartes, who despised mysticism. Here we refer to the group of Platonic thinkers known as the Cambridge School, of which Ralph Cudworth and Henry More were the principal representatives. All were theologians and Puritans, and their thinking always retained a trace of these elements. Against the mechanical philosophy of nature, they raised a conception of nature that was heavily impregnated with theology, and they borrowed the principal elements of this view from Neoplatonism and the Christian Platonism of the Church Fathers. But they were also in close touch with the mystical philosophy of the Renaissance and the following centuries, particularly with that of Paracelsus. Most of them were pure mystics by temperament, for whom apparitions and ghosts were an absolute, complete reality, and who were given to magic and to a Kabbalistic exegesis of the Bible. They maintained continuous personal relations with several leaders of modern science, whom they regarded as allies in the struggle against atheists and materialists. They exercised a considerable influence not only on Locke but also on Newton and Boyle.

We shall see further on how much in common the Cambridge theologians have with the system in which the mystic philosophy of Swedenborg appears for the first time in manifest form, a system that is found in the *Economy of the Animal Kingdom* and works of the same period. Up to a certain point, this kinship certainly depends on the fact that both the Cambridge School and Swedenborg have drawn from the same sources—Neoplatonism and the Church Fathers, themselves influenced by Neoplatonism—and on the whole proceed from related currents of thought. Swedenborg no doubt knew of the Cambridge School and was influenced by it. As we shall see further on, his work confirms that he knew, at least at second hand, of the philosophy of Cudworth and More.

Subjected to the alternating influence of contemporary science and a philosophy colored by theology, the *Essay Concerning Human Understanding* became a work that, despite a logical reconciliation of pure form, reflects the irreducible antagonism of contemporary doctrines. Thus in the second book of the *Essay*, one reads that "in [experience] all our knowledge is founded and from that it ultimately derives itself." But the author declares, in book four, that "on . . . intuition . . . depends all certainty and evidence of all our knowledge."[48] Toward the end of his study, Hertling rightly points out that the empirical tendencies of Locke's philosophy are those that were especially active at the time following. But he goes perhaps too far in thinking the rationalistic tendencies of Locke passed by the contemporary world entirely unperceived. Without being comparable to the former, from a historical viewpoint, the rationalistic tendency has certainly been for many minds, by the very fact that it was mingled with the empirical tendencies, the starting point of a philosophy entirely opposed to the sensationalistic doctrine of the Enlightenment that can also be deduced from Locke's *Essay*. In this, it contributed to the mystic and idealistic reaction that did not delay in coming to the surface. It is at least in this sense that the rationalism of Locke has acted on Swedenborg. His philosophy, born of a basically empirical outlook, found precisely in Locke's thesis of intuition the fulcrum of support that permitted him to evolve toward a pronounced mysticism without abandoning his earlier theories.

One of the most characteristic of the Swedish representatives of this schism between the old and new that I have tried to sketch was Christopher Polhem, Swedenborg's leading scientific mentor. By temperament a protagonist of empiricism and applied mechanics, Polhem still remained, in many aspects of his philosophical convictions, an adherent of metaphysics and the traditional philosophy of nature. On his return from England, Swedenborg became associated with him in a scientific relationship as his amanuensis; Swedenborg often helped Polhem to record his scientific ideas. Consequently, it has been very difficult to establish the true parenthood of a few of Swedenborg's early papers, since they are also found among Polhem's own papers and in the latter's handwriting. Under these circumstances, it is hard to define in a more precise manner Polhem's influence over Swedenborg. Bring[49] and Stroh[50] both point out that this influence must have been considerable. It is, then, of great importance to study Polhem's philosophy of nature more closely. Having only in a few cases had the opportunity to study Polhem's unedited and difficult-to-decipher manuscripts, I am obliged to have recourse to extracts furnished by Bring.

Whenever Swedenborg found the occasion during his theosophical period to characterize Polhem, with whom he seems to have broken off in 1719 for personal reasons, he always depicted him as a cunning, out-and-out atheist: Polhem had confirmed himself in the belief that God does not exist, that all is natural and mechanical, and that men and animals are mere inflated mechanisms. He is also portrayed as given to magic. As punishment for the lack of faith manifested in this world he is, in the spiritual world, condemned to the fabrication of mechanical birds, cats, etc.[51] This description of

Polhem's atheism is obviously exaggerated. From excerpts of the correspondence between Polhem and Benzelius that are quoted in Bring, it is quite clear that, in Polhem's opinion, one should not question the text of the Bible. "It is not Christian," he says, "to doubt the words of Moses, dictated by the Holy Spirit, and even less the words of Christ." He was equally convinced "that between the word of Moses and the properties of nature no contradiction exists provided one accepts certain rules dictated by reason, without which man is like an animal without a soul"[52] Nonetheless, he pushes the intervention of reason rather far when he tries, for example, to disengage himself from the story of Creation by maintaining that the Mosaic version is only applicable "to the origin of his people and had taken a very limited region of the world for its entirety."

The cosmological theories of Polhem appear to rest essentially on a Cartesian basis. It may be true, he declares, that parts of Descartes' thesis are subject to revision, but certain others appear to him as "proven." "For," he says, "one observes the rather strange fact that all the properties of nature are founded on mathematical and mechanical principles."[53] This same mechanistic viewpoint is found in the earlier scientific works of Swedenborg. However, Polhem mingles with those physical theories of Descartes, which he retained, a certain number of other conceptions that appear partly to be echoes of older systems of the philosophy of nature, partly derived from newer scientific theories and partly the fruit of his own hardly methodical speculations. Thus, he differs from the Cartesian theory of the elements and states that all particles of matter take the form of spheres. Here he appeals, as he often does, to the testimony of the senses. "All bodies perceptible to the senses, as well as matter itself, attest that the spherical form is the most favorable to motion, as is the property of fluid matter." Consequently, the space between particles of matter should consist of a "pure vacuum," and this void should be "almost as extensive as matter, in the bosom of which one can affirm that the divine is omnipresent." This void is, in effect, the area of "a perpetual motion outside of matter, motion that can only be God himself, who constitutes its essence."[54]

In another passage, Polhem speaks "of the four infinites of time and space, the center and the concept of which is God himself."[55] This conception, which seems to identify God with the infinity of time and space, is found rather often among the naturalists of the time. It is also found among certain mystic naturalists, hostile to the rationalism of Descartes, Leibniz, and Wolff, who appear to them to place God outside the world and thereby render his existence highly doubtful. These philosophers identify God with the absolute "universal" space that surrounds matter and occupies the interstices between the most minute particles of this matter and even, for certain ones among them, the internal space of matter. This, in their mind, is the only way to elude the hypothesis of an infinite matter and at the same time to establish the omnipresence of God. They invoke the words of the Gospel: "Through Him we live and move and have our being." This is notably the point of view of the German philosopher Andreas Rüdiger, who, as we shall see, certainly influenced Swedenborg.[56] It is difficult to decide whether Polhem was also influenced by Rüdiger or whether he has been inspired by a more ancient philosophy. This view of matter does not appear, however, to have been a systematically developed concept for Polhem; for, in another exposition. he tries in effect to reconcile the biblical doctrine of creation from nothing with the hypothesis of a medium "more subtle than air . . . that our gross senses are unable to perceive," and that consequently appears to us to be nothingness. God has made finite matter out of this infinite matter.[57]

This subtle matter, which Polhem at times identifies with God and at times considers as coeternal with God, will also serve him in explaining all spiritual functions. In his "Thoughts on the Existence of Spirits," the manuscript of which is in the Royal Library in Stockholm, he speaks scornfully of the "learned men," who "have taken upon themselves to writing about immaterial things, such as the soul, thoughts, angels, and God Himself." That, in his opinion, is a vain attempt, man being incapable of "conceiving anything beyond matter." But now experience proves that our thoughts "have the same activity as our senses; in other words, that they depend on the nourishment of the body, that they are susceptible to work and fatigue, whence it can be concluded that they must possess a material quality, all motion being a function of matter, however rarified it may be." And granted that "formal matter" acts upon our senses, that the air with its tremulations impinges upon our eardrums and the undulations of the ether upon the eye, why should not a "more refined matter than the ether affect our thought, or the organ of thought in the brain?"

Thus, Polhem envisages a more subtle, shifting matter in which thoughts are motions of a similar kind as sound waves or the "undulations" of light, although much more rapid. Just as sound can pass through a wall and sight through the "hardest diamond," so, he believes, nothing can resist the vibrations of thought. This explains the mutual awareness that two intimate friends—or children and parents or a husband and wife—can create over a distance of several miles. If one of these suffers a trauma, mortal anguish, or great joy, and at the same time concentrates his thought on the absent one, a certain communication of these feelings will often, if not always, be produced. If one of the two perceives in a dream the misfortune or prosperity of the other, it is nothing but "the motion of thought substance between them." In the same vein, Polhem explained the apparitions of ghosts and phantoms.

This concept of wonderfully subtle matter, occupying the entire universe and carrying the thought of one individual to another to any distance, is found among numerous occult authors of the sixteenth and seventeenth centuries, including Cornelius Agrippa von Nettesheim and Paracelsus. It is one of the ideas that led to Mesmer's discovery of animal magnetism. We see, then, how Polhem, through his constant efforts in the natural sciences to apply the laws of mechanics and through his reluctance to "comprehend" anything whatsoever "outside matter, its figure and motion," approaches unconsciously the mystical form of the philosophy of nature. His naive materialism, which identifies divinity with infinite space and spirit with matter, leaves the field open to theosophical conclusions. We have just seen from his hypothesis of "thought substance" that he has now acquired the means of proving scientifically the reality of telepathy and ghosts. His point of departure is exactly the reasoning by which spiritism has tried over the last centuries under various names to explain scientifically spirit appearances.

It has not been possible for me to establish up to what point Polhem advanced his theorizing in this respect. Nonetheless, it appears that the brief account of his philosophy just given suffices to demonstrate that Swedenborg had already discerned in his mentor reasonings associated with theosophical theories, in effect inviting this kind of speculation.

In the earliest works of Swedenborg—even in those of which his authorship is beyond all question—we find repeated echoes of Polhem's outlook. It is thus that Swedenborg earnestly adopts his master's hypothesis of the spherical form of the basic particles of which matter is composed, and he seeks with even more eagerness to establish that all organic life, including our mental activities, is really only a series of motions subject to the same laws as the phenomena perceptible to our senses. Such is the leading idea that inspires two of his first physiological works, "Proofs Showing That Our Vital Essence Consists Mostly of Minute Vibrations; that is to say, 'Tremulations," published in *Daedalus Hyperboreus* in 1718, and a 1719 manuscript on "The Anatomy of Our Most Subtle Nature, Showing That Our Motive and Vital Essence Consists of Tremulations."[58] The mechanical explanation that he gives here of the vital functions of human beings had been set forth previously by the Italian Borelli in his work *De motu animalium*, to which Polhem also had recourse[59] and which had been used by Descartes and Baglivi. Swedenborg refers to these predecessors but believed he had "confirmed and developed" their theory in a more complete manner. "For I consider my proofs as new and my own and the idea itself to be another's" (*Opera*, I, §297).

What is noteworthy is that Swedenborg does not remain content, as his predecessors did, to apply the mechanistic theory of tremulations to the circulation of the blood and the nervous system, but that he extends it, like Polhem, to practically the whole of humanity's spiritual life. He cites the same examples of telepathy and thought transmission as Polhem and believes himself warranted in concluding that the thoughts of the nonreasoning animals are no more than tremulations produced by external sensations. He does not pronounce directly in these works on the nature and activity of human reason, but it is evident that he considers them to be of a similar order.

Swedenborg's marked propensity at this time to follow Polhem's example in effacing every line of demarcation between spirit and matter stands out with even greater clarity in a letter that he wrote to Erik Benzelius in 1719. The latter seems to have suggested that the sun was the abode of the damned. Swedenborg, on the contrary, opined, in *Opera* V, §294, that the sun, the center of our solar system, was the residence of the blessed, for the good reason that

> The subtlest of all atmospheres, and the finest essence wherein is the minutest element, are in the sun, for the nearer to the sun, the finer; and in its center is presumably such fineness that the particles are almost devoid of composition and put off the denomination of matter and also of form, weight, and many other properties possessed by compound particles. And it would also seem likely that in their finest, must be the finest of beings. A god, an angel, a thing which moreover has nothing of matter in its being, must be especially in its own element; like seeks like, and the finer does not naturally seek the grosser; so it could rather be believed (although I readily leave this to my brother's judgment) that God has this seat in the sun, as the Bible says.[60]

It is easy to see where Swedenborg got the idea for this theory. Descartes, as we know, postulated as a first and most subtle element, the most tenuous of elements, solar matter, matter aflame, the finest and most active in the cosmos, which formed the sun and fixed stars and fills the intercorpuscular space between all other elements. In his *Prodromus Principiorum* of 1721, Swedenborg holds that the spaces between particles are occupied by this fiery matter. He proposes that this matter is refined to the point of no longer warranting the name "matter" and that it should be postulated as the abode of God, the angels, and all things whose essence contain nothing of matter.

There is no difficulty in tracing the relationship between Swedenborg's early ideas in natural philosophy and those of Polhem. With the aim of rigorously applying the laws of mechanics, both assume that the spiritual is only a higher exponent of the material, that thought is only a refined form of action. But it is clearly evident that this identification of spirit and matter opens the door to a theosophical conception of the universe. It is only too easy to reverse the argument and consider matter as the ultimate reflection of spirit and motion as a shadow image of thought. Here, as often happens, the naively scientific outlook bridges the gulf to mysticism.

The same tendencies detected in Swedenborg's early scientific works are again found in his cosmogonic system as it was elaborated in the *Principia* in 1734. His main purpose is still to give a complete explication of the origin of the universe through the application of mathematical and mechanical laws and to reduce all organic life to motion. In his cosmology, based on the vortical theory of Descartes, he consequently starts with the mathematical point as the principle underlying all natural particles, arguing that nature is obedient to the same laws as geometry, with nothing nongeometrical existing in nature and vice versa.[61] This indivisible unit devoid of spatial extension is found midway between the infinite, out of which it is created, and the finite world, of which it is the source. "It is comparable to the two-faced Janus, seeing in opposite directions simultaneously, each of his two faces turned toward one of the two universes" (*Prodromus* §31).

The point is created by motion from the infinite. This motion naturally must be pure motion, which is not subject to mechanical laws. Furthermore, the point embraces nothing substantial or susceptible of being put in motion, so its motion becomes an interior state, a tendency (*conatus*) toward motion. Possessing only a single limit and not, therefore, enclosing any space, it cannot be considered as spatial in terms of finite objects. But if one compares it to pure motion, from which it emanates, one is forced to recognize it in a moment of analogy as possessing some spatial aspect (*intellectum spatium*).

The fact that Swedenborg assigns to the "natural" point an intermediate position between the finite and the infinite depends upon the fact that he considers everything that is finite as subject to the laws of mechanics. For him, as for Polhem, the concepts of the finite and matter coincide. The point, having no spatial extension, cannot be considered as finite. Being derived directly from the infinite, it preserves something of the spirit of the infinite.

It is not within the purview of this study to indicate how, starting with the natural point, Swedenborg structured his very complicated cosmology. I can more appropriately pass over this question since we already have rather good summaries of the system put forth in *Principia*, to which I refer the reader.[62] The infinite provides only the first creative impulse by way of the point that proceeded out of it. Thereupon, the points existing everywhere are those that, by their motion, give rise to aggregates that are progressively more and more complex. In the first particle thus created, *primum finitum,* the "first finite" or *primum substantiale*, the first purely spatial particle, we discern two tendencies, produced by the motion of points within the particles: one tending toward equilibrium and the other in the opposite direction. The result of these two tendencies is that the more complex elementary particles enclose, along with passive substances, active substances representing motion.

What characterizes the whole system is that Swedenborg, who accepts the theory of attraction but rejects the Newtonian doctrine of the void and the action at a distance, structures the entire universe down to its most minute particle by analogy with the planetary world. His *prima finita* are already terrestrial globes in miniature, moving spirally and turning around their own axes. Every evolution and every differentiation are entirely a function of motion.

The entire universe, whose birth we are thus shown, is subject to mechanical laws. "*Ipse mundus tam elementaris quam mineralis et vegetalis, pariter anatomico animalis pure mechanicus est*", Prodromus §9). The mechanical forces that determine the movement of planets in their orbits are identical to those that, through the nervous system, fibers, and muscles, set the different parts of the body of human and animal into motion. The heart functions as a pump, the lungs as bellows, and all our sensory perceptions can likewise be explained in mechanical terms. In his *Prodromus Philosophiae Ratiocinantis de Infinitio*, published the same year, Swedenborg extends the laws of mechanics to the soul itself. Every created thing known to us is subject to the laws of geometry and mechanics, so we must necessarily conclude, by way of analogy, that the situation is the same with the soul. Although the imperfection of our investigative resources has not permitted us to discover the soul's mechanism, there is no reason to conclude that we shall never succeed someday (*Prodromus* §197). Swedenborg even goes so far as to call the soul a machine and only emphasizes that it should not be viewed as an inanimate machine, but as a *machina animata* (*Prodromus* §190).

Being finite and subject to the laws of mechanics and geometry, the soul must necessarily possess spatial and material extension, which Swedenborg assumes unhesitatingly. Its seat is in the whole of the body, but is primarily localized in the finest of its tissues, notably in the brain and the spinal chord (*Prodromus* §256ff.). Since the soul constitutes the most subtle substance of the body, we know for sure that it is immortal, for it could never be destroyed by any grosser elements. It escapes decomposition and cannot perish by air or in any other way. At the moment of physical death, it frees itself from the organic tissues and is concentrated into a whole, even if a few scattered parts of it perish (*Scientific and Philosophical Treatises,* 31–32). The functions of the soul consist of movements that are produced in the tissues of the brain and the subtle fluid they contain.

As one can see, Swedenborg here still holds to the conception regarding the soul and its functions that we found earlier in the work on "tremors," a concept whose origin we have been able to trace to Polhem. But this concept is here accompanied by an argument that well proves that Swedenborg, far from wishing to undermine faith in God and the immortality of the soul, tries, on the contrary, to strengthen that faith by his theory. He says that by proclaiming the soul to be spiritual, the philosophers have succeeded neither in explaining its relationship with the body—the Cartesian hypothesis on the intermediate role of the "animal spirits" being in his eyes no more than provisional—nor in understanding its existence in the midst of a finite universe. The philosophers' mysterious descriptions and scholastic distinctions lead many readers to doubt—if not openly, at least in their hearts—the very existence of the soul and to believe that nothing distinguishes us from the animals (*Prodromus* §198ff). Another of Swedenborg's works from the same period says that to postulate the unknowable nature of the soul and to make of it something occult and entirely removed from the senses is the shortest way to atheism and materialism.[63]

This kind of reasoning is in no way as idiosyncratic to Swedenborg as one may be tempted to believe. Time and again philosophers have, in an effort to save themselves from the supposed skeptical consequences of Descartes' and Leibniz's dualism, attributed a spatial extension to the soul and envisaged the existence of reciprocal relationships between soul and body. And it is precisely this same reasoning that we find again with certain writers who have felt the influence of mystical doctrines. Here I shall only cite two with whom Swedenborg is evidently familiar and who have undoubtedly contributed to strengthen his conclusions on the spatiality of the soul.

Henry More, an English contemporary of Descartes, influenced the Newtonian conception of space, as well as that of Locke and even (directly or indirectly) that of Kant, as recent research has strongly emphasized. More assigned to his philosophy the task of "reintroducing God into the world by the same door through which Descartes had attempted to shut him out." In the course of a direct polemic with Descartes, More denies that extension constitutes matter. Space is a reality that exists outside bodies and our own thought. Every real thing consequently displays a certain extension. God is the subject of absolute space. The soul is as spatial and extended as the body. Starting with this theory, More then launches into speculations on the presence of spirits in space and into the four-dimensional character of space—ideas that were later picked up by spiritualism. More was, moreover, a manifest theosophist, and he gave himself up to Kabbalistic interpretations of the Bible that rather closely resemble those of Swedenborg.[64]

Perhaps even closer to Swedenborg, we find a contemporary German philosopher, Andreas Rüdiger, who strongly felt the influence of More as well as that of the English alchemist Robert Fludd. In his chief work, *Physica Divina,* Rüdiger sought to reconcile the mystic doctrines of the two English philosophers with the latest discoveries of science and philosophy. This *Physica Divina,* along with another work by the same author, *Von Wesen der Seele,* published in 1727, and in which Rüdiger expounds his conception of the soul by way of notes on the work of Christian Wolff, formed part of the rather restricted library of Swedenborg.

Rüdiger, having more or less the same conception of space as More, whom he often cites, states that everything finite, and consequently the soul itself, must have extension. He points out that the soul's activity necessarily assumes a substratum for this activity; we may not, then, identify the soul with the natural point. This is exactly the reasoning that we find again in Swedenborg (*Prodromus* §178ff.).

Just as Swedenborg already seems to do (*Prodromus* §204), Rüdiger adheres to the traducianist doctrine, according to which the soul is propagated by the paternal sperm, a doctrine that coexists quite often with that of the materiality of the soul. Rüdiger adduces the same proofs of the immortality of the soul as Swedenborg: due to its subtle character the soul could not be destroyed by the effect of natural causes (*Physica Divina,* 773). The reasons that determined Rüdiger to acknowledge the spatiality of the soul are precisely those that appeared to be decisive for Swedenborg: for the one as for the other, it is impossible to otherwise establish the existence of the soul within nature and, even less, its relationship with the body. It is probable that Swedenborg was acquainted with Rüdiger and that his reading of the German philosopher strengthened in his mind the conception of the soul's materiality that he had already acquired from Polhem, inasmuch as his contemporaries themselves have remarked the similarity of the two doctrines. In a review of the work of Swedenborg, published in 1735 in the *Acta Eruditorum,* it is observed, apropos of the Swedenborgian doctrine of a soul subjected to mechanical and physical law, that the same thesis is already found in Rüdiger, "whom the author appears to have frequently followed."

Thanks to his theory of the spatiality of the soul, Swedenborg comes to set a very definite line of demarcation between the infinite and the created universes. And the principal aim of the *Prodromus* is precisely to give a clear proof of the existence of God and of his relations with the universe. After having expounded in detail the physico-theological proof of God's existence (that is, that the need for a constructor is established by the ingeniousness and perfection of the mechanism), Swedenborg undertakes an ardent polemic, on the one hand against the pantheism that confuses finite nature with its infinite cause, and on the other, against anthropomorphic conceptions of God.

In an extensive argument that is not lacking in interest, Swedenborg seeks to prove that, in their tentative efforts to define the divinity, the various philosophical schools have attributed human qualities to it or have identified it with nature itself. He concludes that no finite attribute can be applied to the infinite (*Prodromus* §100). For him, as for the Neoplatonists, God is indeterminable. And

Swedenborg already appears to foresee the difficulties that this conception cannot fail to raise. The infinite is the cause of the finite. But in the effect nothing of the cause subsists. Divinity cannot be placed in direct relation with a finite and imperfect universe (*Prodromus* §194ff).

Swedenborg attempts to avoid the notion of God's directly creating the universe by supposing that he who is and who was from all eternity the Son of God, has served as a link between cause and effect, between the infinite and the finite. Since this Son is one with the Father, it is not a question of mediated creation, although Swedenborg further maintains that only the *primum creatum*, the natural point, which has nothing of matter and which possesses the supreme perfection, is a direct creation of God. All the rest of the universe derives from this initial point. To the degree that things issue from the infinite in a more mediated fashion, they have become less and less perfect, taking on more and more natural elements and less and less of the divine. The first created *primitivum* alone, then, is of immediate divinity: everything else in the universe is only mediately divine. For nothing can persist and live in the universe that has not its source and cause in the infinite (*Prodromus* §159).

It is plain that we have here the framework of an emanationist system, similar to that that we find again in Swedenborg during his next period of development. In his above cited work *De Mechanismo Animae et Corporis* (*Scientific and Philosophical Treatises* §24), which is considered to be preparatory to the *Prodromus*, Swedenborg has scaled all the steps of the ladder beyond the limits of the sensory universe. For him, matter must exist that is even more simple than the initial matter of nature, and there must be souls still more subtle and active than ours. Swedenborg recalls that theology acknowledges the existence of various categories of angels: angels whose mission is to carry out the judgments of God; guardian angels watching over the human creature and leading him according to God's designs; angels carrying the soul into heaven; and finally, evil angels of grosser nature. And he concludes that such angels or mediating substances must exist with souls like ours but serve at a subtler level as intermediaries for the divine providence. As we see, Swedenborg's imagination already begins to become involved in a world of supersensory beings who will, during the course of his theosophical period, completely occupy his interest.

It is, nevertheless, in the epistemological outline that serves as an introduction to the *Principia* that Swedenborg's imminent evolution towards mysticism stands out most clearly. Here he adopts the traditional division of the soul into an inferior vegetative soul, the *animus,* and the *mens,* which is the reason proper. From the external sense organs, sensations are transmitted through ever more subtle media to the *animus* and thence to the *mens.* In its innermost active element, which we cannot explain with our mathematical laws, these sensations are turned into knowledge. We cannot, then, have access to knowledge except through the senses. But there is more. It is only progressively, in the course of our physical development, that the fine tissues that serve as intermediaries between the senses and the soul can be cultivated and acquire their right function. And it is only by the experience painfully accumulated by our ancestors and transmitted from generation to generation and by using geometry and philosophy as means that we have reached our present stage of knowledge. Just imagine a human creature having grown up without education among wild animals or apes, or even outside any sort of animal culture: what bestiality would not be his? Education alone creates and forms the human being and distinguishes it from the animal (*Prodromus* §§4–5).

This fundamental conception of the origin and conditions of human knowledge, of which Swedenborg here makes himself the interpreter, is nothing more than the empiricism of Locke. How often, in the course of the era of the French Enlightenment, has not the example mentioned above been used to illustrate the narrowness of the gap that separates the primitive human from the animal, and how that human, whose soul at birth is a *tabula rasa*, depends on impressions from the outside world!

For Swedenborg, this state of dependence on experience constitutes a shortcoming in our knowledge. For him, it is exclusively to the Fall of the first man and woman that we owe our inability to acquire knowledge except through our senses; our incapacity to pursue the deductive method without prior induction depends on the fact that our spiritual machinery has fallen into disorder. If this mechanism had continued to function in its original state, we would have the most perfect and precise knowledge without the help of experience.

In his original state of integrity, the first human must have had a perfect contiguity throughout his whole system. Such a person could be compared to the world, in which the rays of the sun, thanks to the contiguity of the elements through which they travel, freely strike the eyes. Likewise, all impressions striking the senses of this first human freely find their way to his most subtle and active mental organs. Such a perfect being would be capable of rapidly acquiring, through the sole mediation of the senses, all the philosophy and experiential knowledge he needed. He likewise would enjoy the most perfect cogitative faculty. Such a human could truly feel himself in the center of the universe and at a glance (*uno quasi intuitu*) could embrace its entire periphery. By his knowledge of causes and the interrelationship of everything, he would also know the past, present, and future (*Prodromus* §23). With respect to God, he would have a pure love devoid of all fear. And since God loves us to the same degree that we love him, we would have been the object of divine love.

How different is the human situation after the Fall! Pleasures and desires have destroyed the slender tissues that transmit the stirrings of the organs of the body to the *animus* and to the *mens*. The *mens* can only imperfectly exercise over the individual the rule of which it has been despoiled. Thick clouds have gathered between the sun and his eyes and, if the sun's rays nevertheless manage to penetrate the overcast, they transmit only a refracted and distorteded image. We can no longer see the sun (*Prodromus* 24–25). And just as our reason is obscured, our love of God is polluted by fleshly desires. We can no longer establish a relationship with God other than through Christ, provided we try to live by his example.

As we see, Swedenborg conceives the knowledge for which humanity was originally created as a kind of irradiation of divine light. Here we find in outline form the Neoplatonic concept of God as a spiritual sun that will become a central principle of Swedenborgian doctrine beginning with the *Economy of the Animal Kingdom*. From this point on, we can glimpse the reasoning that will later serve as the decisive base for Swedenborg's whole theological system: among all created beings, humanity alone is not "in order"; because of the Fall, we have put ourselves beyond the reach of direct diving inflow. In his theological works, Swedenborg maintains that people of the oldest church, "the Adamites," were in direct contact with the divinity and that the organs of their souls functioned in all their original integrity. For this reason, they had a direct conception of good and truth; and they could immediately discover the correspondences, the spiritual and heavenly equivalents, in terrestrial phenomena. Thus, they could intuitively acquire knowledge of things and their ends.

Thus assuming the existence of an intuitive knowledge with Adam before the Fall, Swedenborg involves himself in a reasoning dear to many Christian mystics, for whom Adam was endowed, in his original state of integrity, with intuitive knowledge. It is only after the Fall that all direct relations between God and man were broken. Finding themselves in a stage of mystic intuition, the mystics considered themselves as enjoying the same state as Adam before the Fall. Among many of them, this rationale was developed into a psychological construction. They sought to explain the imperfection of our present knowledge by the circumstance that the Fall broke one of the springs of our spiritual mechanism and that, from then on, the latter has functioned only imperfectly.

To give a concrete example of this conception, I refer to the exposition by the great Belgian physician and natural philosopher T.B. van Helmont, in his treatise on *Intellectus Adamicus*.[65] This example is even more interesting since there is reason to believe that the psychological system later developed by Swedenborg is not without dependence on the theories of the Belgian scholar.

In the state of ignorance of good and evil, Adam's intellect (his *mens*) ruled as its sovereign mistress over his body, and he consequently possessed perfect knowledge of all things. *"Siquidem oblato objecto non antea viso, noverat penitissimas ejus proprietates"* (If some object was brought before him that he had not previously seen, he knew its deepest characteristics; see above). It was only after the Fall that the lower soul (*anima sensitiva*) was created, enveloping the *mens* and making it impossible for the latter to transmit the divine light to the body or to rule over it. In this way, humanity's knowledge became obscured: it found itself dependent on the sensory world, and human love became impure. Death alone restores its primitive clarity to the mind. But even in these stifling temptations of the flesh and resorting to meditation, human beings can immerse themselves entirely in divinity and feel, for brief moments, the divine light illuminating the soul, enjoying intuitive knowledge, the only truth, and becoming one with divinity.

Nothing in the *Principia*, any more than in Swedenborg's other works of the same period, acknowledges the possibility that the fallen human creature can partake in knowledge of this nature. But the fact that Swedenborg believed in the existence of this knowledge in primordial man, along with his mistrust of empirical knowledge, constitutes a psychological foreshadowing of the way by which he will pass on to mysticism.

The anonymous author of the review published in the *Acta Eruditorum* of 1735, while expounding the *Prodromus* in complimentary and courteous terms, leaves it to be clearly understood in places that the theories of the author, in his opinion, lead to materialism. Swedenborg's characterization of the soul, "the most subtle part of our body," cannot fail, the reviewer says, to appear "somewhat gross" (*duriusculum*) to many minds. He considers that the acceptance of this postulate necessarily implies the conclusion that matter is susceptible of thinking, and can, as a composition of substances, be dissolved and destroyed by natural causes. "The partisan followers of the notion of influx find here the magnificent consequences which the principle of a physical union (between body and soul) imposes upon them."[66] And in his *Theologia Naturalis,* Wolff categorically asserts that the acceptance of the spatiality of the soul inevitably leads to materialism.[67] He particularly inveighs against those materialists—"whether they recognize themselves as such or not"—who reach this conclusion from supposing that simple being is nothing but the mathematical point and who therefrom make a complex substance of the soul. This is probably the passage where Swedenborg thought he was referred to, when in his journal he records, under date of July 20, 1736, that he has read the *Theologia Naturalis* of Wolff, "in which there appears somewhat to be a question of my person, without name."[68]

It is easily understood that Swedenborg's rigorous application of the mechanistic principle may have subjected him to the accusation of materialism. He attributed to the soul, not only spatial extension, but—contrary to Rüdiger—a certain elasticity, and he was without doubt sincerely convinced that it was only a more subtle body. His hypothesis, according to which certain parts of the soul could be lost in the universal space at the moment of death, adequately demonstrates how precarious were the proofs of immortality that he adduced for himself. For him, the functions of the soul were still only a transmission of motion. To be sure, he admitted the existence of an active principle, the equivalent of which was not present in animals, but not once is it seen how this activity differs from what he assumes to exist in all the particles of matter. It might well appear that his mechanical cosmology tends to reduce the role of God to that of first cause, the creator of the natural point from which the whole visible universe evolves.

But in reality, although they were as yet not clearly formulated, Swedenborg's tendencies were already oriented in an entirely different direction. Through his mechanistic interpretation of physical and psychic processes, he seeks to demonstrate that all motion and all life have their existence only from the infinite that is origin, cause, and end, and that the body lives and moves only from the soul. The entire universe is directly or mediately divine (*Prodromus* §160ff.). It is thus, in his imagination, that the immense universal mechanism, moving according to mechanical laws, step by step lays the basis for the conception of the grand universal organism, of the greatest human, drawing its life and activity from the infinite. Likewise for the ordinary man, the microcosm, all life, and all consciousness are but an irradiation of divine light. When Swedenborg undertakes to pull down the wall erected between spirit and matter by Cartesianism, he is certainly driven above all by the desire to regard all spiritual phenomena as material in a way explicable according to mechanical law. When his mystical tendencies become progressively more marked and his religious interests carry him beyond his scientific interests, he comes to draw the opposite conclusions from the same monistic point of view. He comes to spiritualize the entire universe and to consider the body as the ultimate reflection of the soul.

three

A Mystical Philosophy of Nature

The years immediately following the publication of the *Principia* are of particular importance in life of Emanuel Swedenborg. It is the period of his first mystical experiences, dreams, and waking visions, which presage all his later spirit encounters. It is the period when his ideas are transformed into a philosophy of nature tinged with theology, which later becomes the foundation of his theosophy.

The main problem for Swedenborg's research at this time was the question of the nature of the soul and its relation to the body. We have seen how this problem had preoccupied him from the beginning of his scientific activities and how he tried to solve it in different ways without achieving any satisfactory result. Now, the question absorbs his mind completely, obliging him to abandon his studies of mechanics to focus his zeal on physiological and psychological research. As is well known, it is in his two great works, *Economy of the Animal Kingdom* and *Animal Kingdom,* that he presents his new and epoch-making ideas in the field of cerebral physiology. This altered orientation of his scientific labors in itself explains, to a certain degree, the change that took place in his outlook.

The world picture he found in contemporary philosophy and in the medical works with which he then became acquainted was for the most part organic. The strictly Cartesian mechanistic view of nature had gradually lost all its support. Newton had already broken with the prevailing concepts when he saw in attraction not only a reciprocal mechanical action between bodies but also a nonmaterial force ruling over matter. Drawing this metaphysical conclusion from the law of gravity, Newton aligned himself, as has been frequently remarked, with the ideas of the Cambridge Platonists. By introducing a "plastic force" into their system and acknowledging the existence of spatial but immaterial spiritual substances as intermediaries between God and matter, the Platonists sought to discard, in favor of teleological and organic concepts, every mechanical explanation of nature, which, in their opinion, could only lead to materialistic and atheistic results. The explanation of distant action of a body given by Newton tended also in the same direction. "*Das mathematische Gesetz wird unter dem Namen der Fernkraft versinnbildlicht und anthromorphisiert*" (The mathematical principle becomes symbolized and anthropomorphized under the name of "gravity").[69]

Leibniz's philosophy aimed at reconciling the Cartesian view of nature with the Aristotelian teleological view, achieving a compromise between the mechanical and organic interpretations of the universe. Leibniz reached this conclusion by considering bodies as representations of an internal, nonmaterial force. While he kept the mechanical interpretation of physical phenomena, his monadology gave the very nature of things an explanation that transformed the universe into a living whole occupied by animated substances. Lasswitz emphasized that this metaphysical interpretation of the universe by Leibniz's successors was directly applied to physical phenomena.[70] And it is thus that his monadology became the starting point for most of the attempts to substitute the hylozoistic doctrine of living molecules for mechanical atomism, a doctrine that we find also among a good number of philosophers and naturalists of the eighteenth century.

As we have seen, Swedenborg was already acquainted with Leibniz and, with respect to certain details, was influenced by him. Nevertheless, the latter does not appear to have been granted full credit in the mind of Swedenborg until, in the course of writing the *Principia,* he found occasion to renew his acquaintance with the Leibnizian doctrine, although in the somewhat diluted form it took in the works of Christian Wolff. To Swedenborg, these works constituted, at the time, the last word in philosophical science, to which he referred even while holding a quite different point of view.

Contemporaneous with Leibniz, and partly under his influence, the same tendency toward an organic conception of the universe appeared in the physical and natural sciences, particularly in medicine, where the main thrust previously had been toward interpretation of physiological phenomena as purely mechanical or chemical processes. The most characteristic expression of this tendency is the theory known as "animism," whose founder, the celebrated doctor Georg Ernst Stahl, was represented by several of his works in Swedenborg's library. In Stahl's system, the soul (*anima*) structures the body for its own purposes, and the organs have life only through it. Maladies are caused by psychic malfunctions, which are in large part healed by altering the psychic regime.[71]

Because of their metaphysical point of departure, Stahl and his school opposed all detailed study of anatomy. But a clearly organic perspective was attained even in this domain through other avenues. With the aid of a microscope, living elements seemed to be perceived everywhere—in the sperm, in the blood, and even in the ovaries. Things apparently devoid of life are themselves filled with living organisms. Leeuwenhoeck discovered a multitude of infusorians in a drop of water. As a result of these discoveries, the concept of inorganic matter, which was the basis of the atomism of the seventeenth century, gave way to diverse and rather obscure theories about organic matter as a kind of whole that is made up of living microscopic entities, whose combinations produce individuals that are more and more differentiated. This molecular theory found its principal protagonist in George Buffon, for whom infusorians were animal molecules; but it had, both before and after Buffon, notable representatives in the field of medicine and in the natural sciences.

In agreement with this discovery stands the old doctrine of spontaneous generation or *generatio aequivoca,* again picked up by most of the molecularists, which has numerous parallels with this theory. Some among them acknowledged that every living being is born of spontaneous generation (*generatio aequivolata*), while others restricted this hypothesis to lower microscopic forms. It is to this reasoning that Swedenborg rallies in *De Mechanismo Animae et Corporis,*

(*Scientific and Philosophical Treatises* §27). Here, invoking a number of fantastic examples, he maintains that every part of an animal can evolve into a new animal. Moreover, even in the course of his theological period, he continues to adhere to the concept of spontaneous generation for the lower animals.

This altered view of nature was validated in all fields. The great Haller, a contemporary of Swedenborg, is not the only one to welcome a new target for his activity in creating what he calls "*belebte Anatomie*." In all circles, among scholars and thinkers as well as among poets, the same trend appears: to see organic life where their precursors discerned only mechanical or chemical transformations. The diatribe of young Thorild against "these mechanical, soulless minds who strive to present nature as inanimate clockwork" is characteristic of efforts throughout the eighteenth century to see something of life in nature, a tendency that well explains many facets of the spiritual life of that century.

With regard to Swedenborg, we should bear in mind that he witnessed the dawn of that development. A large share of the discoveries that furnished a scientific basis for the new organic conception of the world were yet to be made or lay almost unknown. To cite only one example, Haller's doctrine of irritability, which is probably the starting point of the explanation of physiological processes that was laid down by the next generation of scientists, was published almost simultaneously with *Economy of the Animal Kingdom*. It follows that Swedenborg, like his contemporaries, could not develop the organic theory in all its details and that he often resorted to old hypotheses. But he also mixed a certain number of mystical speculations in with his medical theories.

The medical systems of the age, particularly the more modern ones, which had renounced the chemical or mechanical explanation, often constituted a peculiar mixture of experimental research and abstruse metaphysical considerations. They shared the common characteristic of carelessly falling back on supernatural factors in the absence of scientific explanations. When Swedenborg abandoned his mathematical and mechanical pursuits to dedicate himself to medical and zoological studies, he in effect abandoned a field where exact science had advanced considerably for one where the most extravagant and most fanciful theories still flourished in complete freedom and in which a fully Aristotelian scholasticism and medieval medical magic were still honored in the name of science. Empirical science had not yet, in Sweden or abroad, broken the bonds that linked it with alchemy or astrology, and medicine was particularly flawed, as a rule, by superstition and quackery.

Even the most illustrious names in the contemporary field of medicine were no exceptions in this respect. Two of the most prominent representatives of German medicine of that day, Friedrich Hoffmann and Georg Ernst Stahl, whose works figured in the library of Swedenborg, were both decided mystics, believing that demons were involved in diseases and attributing to the stars a considerable influence on the development of maladies. The wearing of amulets figured in their therapeutic prescriptions. Alongside highly noteworthy and precise medical discoveries, we find in their works an astonishingly superstitious interpretation of certain clinical phenomena. Thus, for example, Hoffmann considers the abrupt appearance of harmful insects in the atmosphere, or of worms in the soil, as the work of the devil.[72]

Through his prior study of contemporary medical literature, then, Swedenborg found himself in contact with a philosophy of nature clearly tinged with mysticism; and, in his *Economy of the Animal Kingdom,* we can find numerous elements that can be directly traced to that philosophy.

Moreover at this time his purely philosophical studies naturally provided further nourishment for his mystical tendencies. Thanks to the careful interaction of references included in the *Economy of the Animal Kingdom*, we are very well instructed regarding his philosophical reading at that time. They are in themselves a kind of guide to the understanding of his spiritual orientation.

The author most frequently cited in this work is Aristotle. It is he whom Swedenborg invokes constantly as the supreme authority, and, like the scholastics, he distinguishes him most often not by name but as "the philosopher." Aristotle is, moreover, one of the few thinkers for whom Swedenborg reserves his admiration during his theosophical period. When he relates the conversations he has with

Aristotle in the spiritual world—for example in *Arcana Coelestia* §4658—he always ranks him among the most rational of spirits.

This predilection for Aristotle is not to be wondered at. The historiographers of mysticism have often mentioned the peculiar fact that the philosophy of Aristotle, however hostile it may be toward mystical sentiment, and though it strives toward exact and rigorous analysis, has always been, since the scholastic era, clearly allied with numerous mystical systems. The explanation has been found in Aristotle's definition of God as the absolute reality, acting upon the world in view of the fact that imperfect things aspire to divine perfection. To know the highest human capacity of thought, the spiritual vision (*theoria*), is to share pure thought, which is the very essence of deity and an enjoyment of beatitude.[73] We are to see that these Aristotelian notions appear also in Swedenborg's philosophy in the *Economy of the Animal Kingdom* and that they will be retained in Swedenborg's theological system.

The influence exercised upon Swedenborg by Plato and by Neoplatonism, the principal sources of Christian mysticism, is naturally even greater. Swedenborg was acquainted with the work of Plato, not only by Aristotle's exposition of it, but also directly. In his works dating from this period, we find quotations from many of Plato's Dialogues.

On the other hand, Swedenborg's works contain no quotations from Plotinus, a circumstance allowing Tafel to deny categorically that Swedenborg had ever studied that philosopher.[74] This statement can be disproven by the fact that Swedenborg, in 1705, had inscribed his name on the title page of a volume of the *Opera philosophica* of Plotinus, which had once belonged to Stjernhjelm, and which the latter called his *pabulum animi* (food of the soul).[75] Among the works cited in the *Economy of the Animal Kingdom*, we also find a purely Neoplatonic one that includes long extracts from Plotinus' *Enneads*. This is known as *The Theology of Aristotle*, of which we possess an Arabic text, dating from from around 840, but which is considered to date back to a lost Greek text; it is credited to a member of the Neoplatonic school, perhaps Porphyry. Swedenborg refers to it under the name of Aristotle, and the title that it bears in the Latin translation of 1572 (*De Secretiore Parte Divinae Sapientiae Secundum Aegyptios*). In a passage of his works in manuscript, he nevertheless questions whether the citations mentioned are of Aristotelian origin.[76] Swedenborg is familiar with a certain number of other mystics of antiquity, among whom Iamblichus, "Mercurius Trismegistus," and Philo are notably found cited in the *Economy of the Animal Kingdom.*

It is occasionally almost impossible to distinguish in Swedenborg's works between the influence traceable to the Church Fathers and that of the Neoplatonists. He appears to have been quite familiar with the former, a number of whom are referred to in his works. We find, for example, long quotations from Lactantius and Augustine, whom he greatly admired at that time for "the clarity of his judgment."

It is more difficult to establish Swedenborg's knowledge of medieval and modern mysticism. No reference whatsoever to German mystics is found in his works, and any parallels observable between their doctrines and his own may very well be based on a second-hand acquaintance through Arndt or van Helmont. I find it hardly likely, however, that the son of Jesper Swedberg had never read Thomas á Kempis or the *Theologia Germanica*.

Regarding French Quietism, there is every reason to suppose that Swedenborg had read Mme. Guyon and Mme. Bourignan, whose works were commonly read as edifying texts at that time. In any case, he had become acquainted with some of their basic views through the works of Nicolaus Malebranche, which were found in his library and which exercised an influence on his philosophy in the *Economy of the Animal Kingdom.*

Naturally, Swedenborg could not have avoided acquaintance with the medical systems of the Renaissance, such as those of Paracelsus and van Helmont, which were strongly colored by Kabbalistic philosophy. It is probable that he had read these two masters in the original.[77] But even if there were reason to doubt this, one could find enough medical works that he cites, or that he had in his library, that belong to this school to fully explain their reflections in Swedenborg's philosophy.

As for Jacob Boehme, Swedenborg himself stated, in a letter to Gabriel Beyer in 1767, that he had never read Boehme's writings, and added in connection therewith that he had been "forbidden to read authors on dogmatic and systematic theology before heaven was opened to me." On the strength of this declaration, Tafel, along with most of the orthodox researchers on Swedenborgianism, felt warranted in denying that Swedenborg was acquainted with any mystical writings or that he was influenced thereby.[78] Even granting that he had never read a work by Boehme, it is clear that he could not have been ignorant of Boehme's doctrine, which was professed at that time by numerous sects and which counted several leaders of the Pietist movement among its propagators, notably Gottfried Arnold. Swedenborg must at least have known the outlines of Boehme's system that were picked up by Dippel. Some of the latter's works, moreover, contain such a wealth of quotations from modern mystics and magicians that these citations alone would have sufficed to give Swedenborg an overview of contemporary mysticism.

I have already spoken of Swedenborg's early acquaintance with Fludd's disciple Rüdiger and have mentioned his relationship to the Neoplatonic Cambridge school. A glance at the catalog of his library shows that he owned books on magic, alchemy, and occultism, and surely knew of many others.

I have dealt at length upon what we know about the extensive mystical reading of Swedenborg in order to discredit once and for all the attempt, so frequently made by orthodox researchers on Swedenborg, to exonerate him from any reliance on other mystical writers or from any influence deriving from such a source. This effort is certainly well-intentioned but hopelessly unhistorical as well as psychologically invalid. During his theosophical period, Swedenborg appears to have refrained from any theological reading, but this was no doubt for the purpose of avoiding interference with his own thinking. Like most mystics, he was convinced that all his theosophical ideas were directly inspired by God, and he protests energetically when certain of his contemporaries—wrongly, I believe—regarded some of them as having been borrowed from Boehme. Yet Swedenborg never goes as far as his apologists in the denying all contacts with mysticism; had he done so, he would not have been believed.

There is an anachronism in claiming that such a cultured mind as Swedenborg's could have remained a stranger to mystical ideas during an era when mysticism occupied so preponderant a place in religion and science. Before leaving his paternal hearth, Swedenborg became acquainted with mystical doctrines; he came across them later in science clothed in alchemy and speculative medicine. During the period when he wrote the *Economy of the Animal Kingdom* and *Animal Kingdom*, a period of intense activity for the Swedish mystical sects, these doctrines were a daily topic of general conversation; and it was in the ranks of these sects, and more particularly in those of Dippelianism, that they were to find the greater number of disciples. When we add that Swedenborg was particularly engrossed in the solution of problems most hotly discussed by the mystics, the absurdity of arguing that he remained completely unaware of contemporary mysticism becomes plain.

But precisely because this knowledge of mystical systems has a long background in Swedenborg's life, I am not inclined to assume that the study of mystical literature was the main reason that he left the philosophy of *Principia*. For similar reasons, I cannot believe that the decisive role in Swedenborg's conversion should be attributed to the influence of Dippel, which the Swedenborgians likewise deny.

Naturally, we can in no way overlook the fact that Swedenborg's transition to mysticism took place precisely during the decade that marked the triumph of Swedish Pietism, that is, a time when religiosity sought to manifest itself in Sweden in its most ecstatic forms and with an energy known neither before or later there, when miraculous conversions, inspired dreams, revelations, prophesies, the speaking in tongues, and other manifestations of the same order were daily occurrences; when the consistories and tribunals sat in judgment on heresy; when every week witnessed the establishment of new conventicles or of new sects, often with fantastic doctrines, and of more or less extravagant cults. Such a highly charged religious atmosphere obviously could not fail to act upon even such a genuine closet-scholar as Swedenborg and to accelerate, in some measure, his religious conversion.

But nothing warrants a belief that he was ever a disciple of any of these sects. Holmquist and other theological researchers on Swedenborg presume that he had met Dippel during the latter's sojourn in Stockholm from 1726 to 1727, and attribute a great importance to this meeting in Swedenborg's conversion.[79] If he was actually exposed to the influence of Dippel at that time and if it is true that they met, which is far from being confirmed, it is rather astonishing that no trace of this influence is perceptible in the *Principia* or in his contemporary writings. Swedenborg declares that when he passed through Copenhagen in 1736, "he found the city still infected with Pietism, or Quakerism. In their folly they believe in making themselves agreeable to God through suicide or murder, numerous examples of which exist."[80] The least one can conclude from this declaration is that it indicates no sympathy for the sects referred to.

On the other hand, it appears incontestable in certain passages of the *Spiritual Diary* (§2890ff., §3485ff. and elsewhere) that Swedenborg had read Dippel's works, and we shall see that several specific points are important in the structure of his philosophical system of *Economy of the Animal Kingdom.* Still more significant is Dippel's influence on Swedenborg's theology such as it appears to us in its full state of development. Consequently, it seems to me very likely that Swedenborg, over a more or less extended period, had been subject to the influence of Dippel. Nothing allows us to pinpoint this influence, however. It does not appear to me likely to have had the range some have wanted to make out, and I see no reason to suppose that this influence may explain the departure from the philosophy of *Principia* to the mystical view of *Economy of the Animal Kingdom.* It is still less probable that such influence may have determined the violent religious crisis that followed later, and of which we learn from his *Journal of Dreams* for the years 1734–1744—a crisis, following which Swedenborg abandoned science for theology. Indeed, he seems to have begun that period while in contact with the English Moravian Church, which he briefly considered joining.

If I am little disposed to see the decisive factor for Swedenborg's conversion in his mystical readings or in his supposed association with the diverse religious sects, it is principally because the history of mysticism teaches us that it is neither by their reading nor through personal influences that the great mystics generally realize their mission. On a closer look, one finds that the beginning of their mystical commitment is more often related to a personal experience that they considered to be divine revelation. This is not necessarily the first mystical manifestation in their lives; they are often born visionaries, having had dreams or ecstasies of divine inspiration, in many cases during their childhoods. The kind of revelation that concerns us here is often produced initially at a mature age, following years of confused meditations regarding problems they appear powerless to resolve. An external stimulus, often of a rather banal character, seems to give them a kind of sudden internal clarity, an intuitive certainty that was previously lacking. This does not at all mean, on the other hand, that their systems are always clear from the start or that they become fully structured mystics in a moment. But their destinies from then on are determined. From the moment they receive this call they see that their thoughts are divinely inspired. The godhead having deigned in a moment of grace to make them participants in its own light, they are called henceforth to proclaim to ordinary human reason the things hidden from us.

To illustrate what has been said above, I want to remind the reader of the well-known experience of Jacob Boehme. During his wandering years as a shoemaker, he had felt the vague presentiment that some day he would be called to a rather extraordinary mission. But torn between contending Protestant sects, he was the prey of indecision, and the vision he had brought him no guidance. One day, after establishing himself as a shoemaker in Görlitz, his eyes fixed themselves on a light shining in a tin plate. He immediately experienced an elevation of soul, feeling he was suddenly suffused by an inner clarity so miraculous that he believed himself empowered to penetrate the very essence of things. Ten years passed before he dared to record the truth revealed to him. But his road is thenceforth mapped out; and, in his mind, the moment the reflection of the sun in the tin struck his eyes remained for him the time of initiation into higher knowledge.

From Swedenborg's *Principia*, we have been able to conclude the problem that particularly preoccupies his mind at this time. He wants to know whether a human being can again share the intuitive knowledge of Adam that our species had lost after the Fall. Neither physiology nor philosophy offers him an answer to this question. Knowledge of this nature is well beyond the reach of discursive reason; only from personal experience can one know whether it exists.

It is through such a revelation that van Helmont had learned that, at a God-granted moment, the *mens* can recover its original clarity and behold the divine. In his *Imago Mentis*, he relates that once, when weary after prolonged contemplation, he had felt his spirit was transported in slumber beyond the limitations of reason and perceived, through a cleft in the wall, a light of inexpressible clarity.[81] As a consequence of this vision, which was beyond the power of words to describe, van Helmont was seized by an overwhelming desire to know the soul, a longing that knew no respite during twenty-three long years. Only when he was allowed to see his *mens* in human form, streaming like a crystal-clear light of inexpressible and incomprehensible brilliance, was he able to understand the vanity of these twenty-three years of striving. Even this vision, as beautiful as it was, could not teach him about his *mens* intellectually; the vision could only reveal the existence of the *mens* without being able to add anything to its perfection. Was it perhaps an experience of the same order that first convinced Swedenborg of the possibility of an intuitive awareness, thus determining the orientation of his entire later thinking?

At first sight, the question appears impossible to answer. For the document that might have informed us in this respect, Swedenborg's account of his visions of 1736 to 1740, was detached by an officious hand from the manuscript (entrusted to the care of the Academy of Sciences) to be returned to the Swedenborg family; and it then disappeared without a trace. We can only rely upon one fact: that from 1736 on, the same years during which he began to write his *Economy of the Animal Kingdom,* Swedenborg also began to record his dreams and visions. This most significant coincidence allows us to suppose that these visions directly relate to the psychological and scientific speculations that occupied his mind at the time. Like the visions of the diaries for 1743–1744, as we shall see, they bear a close relationship with the scientific research that he pursued during the same period.[82]

In an overlooked passage in Swedenborg's diary for 1743–1744, we come across a recollection of one of his prior visions. We shall try to show that the first mention in the works of Swedenborg of his decisive initiation in divine intuition can be found here. Swedenborg records on October 27, 1743 (*Journal of Dreams* §282):

> In the morning, on awakening, I was overcome by such a dizziness or one such fading of consciousness or *deliquium* by which I had been seized previously six or seven years ago in Amsterdam, when I began to write my *Economy*; but this time more subtle, feeling myself near to death. And it then happened when I saw the light, but which dissipated little by little, because I fell into a brief slumber, so that this *deliquium* was internal and more profound, yet quietly passed; from which I understood that my head was cleared and truly relieved of all that could hinder these thoughts; which occurred as on the preceding occasion, and that this endowed me with the faculty of penetration.

This former occurrence must be related to Swedenborg's second sojourn in Amsterdam, August 17–20, 1736. He would return to that city only in December 1739, where he would finish his *Economy of the Animal Kingdom.*

It is apparent that this occurrence was no more than a loss of consciousness, following which Swedenborg had felt his thoughts "purified" and found himself endowed with "penetration." The assumption is based on the grounds that this state was provoked by that respiratory suspension to which Swedenborg, as he himself relates, was accustomed ever since his childhood (see chapter one above). Mention of this "internal breathing" is already found in *Economy of the Animal Kingdom.*[83] It constituted the basis of Swedenborg's physiological theory about the relation between the brain and the lungs. And in the detailed description of this phenomenon cited above, which we find in the *Spiritual Diary* §3464, Swedenborg relates that he had experienced this respiration while he was writing the works that were published later.[84] Since these records come from the year 1747, only the natural scientific works can come into question, as Tafel notes. Swedenborg here says, moreover, that this internal breathing usually occurred while he was studying the interaction between heart and lungs:

> In this way I was through my infancy accustomed to such respiration, especially by intense speculations, during which ordinary respiration ceased; for otherwise no intense speculation on the truth is possible. Afterwards also, when heaven had been opened to me, so that I could speak with spirits, I was so fully introduced into this respiration that for the space of almost an hour I did not draw any breath: there was only so much air inhaled that I was able to think.

Swedenborg believes this respiration can also be experienced while asleep, for he says, "I noticed again and again that after falling asleep [external] respiration was almost entirely withdrawn from me, so that on awakening I gasped for breath." And in closing he asserts: "By this means it was also granted me to be present with spirits."

In his theosophy, Swedenborg further develops the doctrine that internal respiration comes from heaven, while ordinary breathing comes from the world. When, at the moment of death, external respiration ceases, internal breathing continues. It varies according to our state of blessedness, so that the breathing of angels is internal, while that of the inhabitants of hell have a more external respiration. In the beginning, human beings were created for internal breathing, which they preserved while in their original state of integrity; it is from the moment when it ceases, that we lose all bonds with heaven.[85]

When we know about this theory of internal breathing, it is easy to understand how the *deliquium* of which Swedenborg speaks is produced. In the course of intense intellectual concentration, a respiratory inhibition intervenes, to which Swedenborg has been accustomed since childhood; this inhibition provokes a fainting fit with a sensation of imminent death. The breathing "continued while I saw the light," which helps explain a concomitant phenomenon. Certainly, it is here not a matter of sunlight, for the phenomenon took place at night, but of a mystic light. In the *Adversaria,* he tells us:

> Flames mean confirmation; such a flame has, by the grace of God-Messiah, appeared to me many times, and indeed of various sizes and different colors and brilliance; so that then I was

> writing a certain little work scarcely a day passed for several months without a flame appearing to me as bright as a chimney fire. This was at the time a sign of approbation, and it was before the time that spirits had begun to speak with me in an audible voice.[86]

On a manuscript sheet regarding his molecular philosophy, we find already in 1740 a characteristic notation by Swedenborg in these terms: *Haec vera sunt quia signum habeo* (These are truths because I have the sign).[87]

The type of vision described here by Swedenborg is one of the better-known among psychologists. They generally classify it as a phenomenon of hallucinatory or pseudohallucinatory sensory automatism and designate it under the technical name of "photism." It constitutes one of the customary mystic phenomena, and numerous examples have been collected, from the heavenly vision of Paul on the road to Damascus to the religious conversions of our day. I find it enough here to refer to the well-known work of William James,[88] the source of the above definition, and who provides several concrete examples of photism. The fact that it is here a matter of a confirmatory luminous appearance experienced by Swedenborg at the moment of undertaking his *Economy of the Animal Kingdom*, is plain from the always-overlooked preface to this work, which clearly explains how he passed over from science into mysticism. His travel journal shows that this preface was written around September 6 or 7, 1736, that is, only about three weeks after the revelation mentioned above occurred.[89]

The preface to *Economy of the Animal Kingdom* constitutes an introduction to Swedenborg's study of the composition of the blood, but in reality it deals mainly with the question of knowledge, and perhaps also includes a piece of self-confession.

The point of departure is the same as in the introduction to the *Principia*: "We are born into dense ignorance and insensibility. Our organs are opened only by degrees; the images and notions as first received are obscure and, so to speak, the whole universe is represented to the eye as a single indistinct thing, a formless chaos. In the course of time, however, its various parts become comparatively distinct and, at length, are presented to the tribunal of the rational mind, whence it is not till later in life that we become rational beings" (*Economy of the Animal Kingdom* I, §8). Experience alone can lead us to knowledge of the cause of things, that is, to the truths. For when the *mens* "*vis propria contemplativa*" ("with all the speculative force that belongs to it") is left to rove abroad by itself without this guide,

> how easy it is to fall into error from these into other errors and finally into the error of errors. . . . It is not possible to deduce experience from established principles, but to deduce principles themselves from experience. . . . When we are carried away by ratiocinations alone, we are somewhat like blindfolded children in their play, who, though they imagine they are walking straight forward, yet, when their eyes are unbound, plainly perceive that the have been following some roundabout path. (*Economy of the Animal Kingdom* I, §11)

As we see, Swedenborg's view is more empirical here even than in the *Principia.* He seems to perceive no other road to knowledge than that of experience which, personal at first, can gradually become general with the support of the experience of others. And he acknowledges that he has been too constructive in the course of his preceding scientific activity. Misled by his self-esteem and from isolated experiences, he had sought to draw general conclusions and establish definitive principles. This time he proposes to adhere more or less exclusively to the exposition of discoveries by other thinkers. Self-esteem and vanity, he tells us, are the worst enemies of science. Most scientists work without any true vocation for their calling. They build castles in the air that they then gravely offer to the admiration of the public. They believe that beyond their own muddy lake no more territory exists (cf. *Economy of the Animal Kingdom* I, §20).

Against these figures, Swedenborg sets the natural-born scientists, for special talents are necessary in order to deduce the causality of things from given phenomena, and these faculties are not given to everybody. We know that poets, musicians, singers, painters, architects, and sculptors are born with their respective gifts; it is the same with thinkers. From birth, they are endowed with a particular function of memory and a particular faculty of imagination and intuition (*Economy of the Animal Kingdom* I, 19).

When such a born thinker succeeds, after prolonged reasoning, in discovering a truth, he feels a sensation of vivifying light, a sort of cheering confirmatory flash that lights the sphere of his mind, a kind of secret radiation (*occulta radiatio*) that, in some way, brightens the sacred temple of the brain. By these signs, he recognizes the existence of a kind of rational instinct that tells him that the soul has been summoned into a kind of more intimate communion and has returned at that moment into the golden age of its original integrity (*Economy of the Animal Kingdom* I, §19). Swedenborg concludes by saying that the soul, having once known this joy, consecrates itself thenceforth exclusively to research, disdainful of all corporeal pleasures.

It appears to me beyond cavil that such is the confirmatory luminous vision of which Swedenborg is thinking here in the preface to *Economy of the Animal Kingdom*. This sensation of ecstatic bliss that he attributes to himself is found to be marked in all the examples of photism reported by James. James also adds that the descriptions of sensory photisms that he had occasion to study "end by being no longer anything more than metaphorical descriptions of the feeling of new internal illumination."[90] Such is precisely the case of the description provided by Swedenborg in the *Economy of the Animal Kingdom*.

Through this metaphorical transformation, Swedenborg comes to frame a kind of theory of intuition that hardly differs from that of Locke. In order to keep from skirting the outer limits of skepticism and being constrained to acknowledge the relativity of all knowledge, Locke had conceived of an intuitive knowledge beyond sensation and reflection. This intuitive knowledge is an irresistible certitude granted to us when our reason discovers the concordance or antinomy of two ideas as clearly as the eye perceives the light as soon as it is turned that way. There we have the clearest and surest knowledge of which our human fallibility is capable, and it is upon this that all certitude and all evidence in our understanding depend.[91]

Cassirer has observed that, in admitting the existence of intuitive knowledge, Locke entirely demolishes his psychological system.[92] It is in vain that he seeks to establish accord between the two avenues of knowledge by applying to them two different categories of objects. Intuition retains supremacy; it cannot be applied only in the domain of the physical and natural sciences. In this domain, we are constrained to resort to experience and can consequently achieve only a relative knowledge. "Locke, then, in this area, is an empiricist by resignation," so that the concordance observed between the Swedenborgian view and that of Locke is not the result of a pure coincidence. In a passage in *Economy of the Animal Kingdom* where he gives a detailed description of the *anima*, the organ of intuition, Swedenborg himself appeals to "the illustrious Locke" and cites, among others, the *Essay Concerning Human Understanding,* in which Locke proposes the thesis that the angels and spirits of the righteous are to enjoy, in a future life, a knowledge analogous to our intuition.[93]

If we recall the epistemological pessimism of *Principia*, Swedenborg's development becomes fairly clear. In his anguished meditations on trying to find an infallible criterion of truth and on the means by which humankind might rediscover the certain knowledge that it possessed before the Fall, he finds in Locke the concept of a knowledge that is not obliged to have recourse to the always uncertain discursive method. He could not have suspected that this theory, propounded by the universally recognized father of empiricism, would tend to include "occult qualities." But by his conception of intuitive knowledge, Swedenborg introduced a mystical element into his scientific world. It awakens all his congenital inclinations that had lain dormant for many years.

So when, during the course of an intellectual effort, a light suddenly appears before his eyes, he finds its explanation at hand. There is a "sacred temple" in the brain. It is the Deity himself who with his flaming light confirms Swedenborg's theory. The bond between the human creature and the infinite is not broken; the person reverts, so to speak, at that moment, to the "Golden Age of his primitive state." It is readily understandable that, from his faith in these intermittent flashes, Swedenborg should have passed on to the Neoplatonic conception of a permanent light that, proceeding from the Divinity, shines within us each time we no longer try to withdraw from it voluntarily. In its broad lines, the philosophy of the *Economy of the Animal Kingdom* is already found complete. But there is more. From that moment on, Swedenborg finds himself in permanent association with a superior power that offers confirmation whenever he comes upon a truth and that denies this confirmation when he is in error. From that moment on, Swedenborg writes and thinks, in a certain sense, under divine inspiration. His work from then on bears the stamp of a truth more profound than it had been before. Whatever modesty he displays to the public in the presentation of his scientific and philosophical works, it is clear that, to his mind, these are no longer hypotheses that are more or less established, but indisputable verities. "*Haec vera sunt quia signum habeo.*"

four

THE PHILOSOPHY OF *ECONOMY OF THE ANIMAL KINGDOM*

The characteristic that most clearly distinguishes the philosophy of the *Economy of the Animal Kingdom* and that of the works that are either contemporary with or immediately follow the *Principia* perhaps appears most strikingly in the fact that Swedenborg here strives to demonstrate the Aristotelian distinction between form and matter. All created things owe their qualitative determination and purpose to form. "Matter longs for form as the female longs for the male, and form cannot be abstracted from matter except in thought," he writes, quoting Aristotle (*Economy of the Animal Kingdom* II, §286).

With this doctrine, Swedenborg combines the theory, drawn from mystical philosophy, of a natural creative force, of an *archeus,* a mystic principle of life; flowing from the primitive substance of nature, the natural point, the *archeus* acts in everything as a creative, directive, and underlying principle:

> *Est quaedam Substantia aut Vis formatrix, quae a primo puncto vivente ducit stamen, et ductum usque ad ultimum vitae continuat; quae aliis vocatur Vis plastica, Archeus, et nonnullis simpliciter natura agens, sed intelligibilis magis, uti reor, si illa respective ad formationis opus, audiat vis aut substantia formatrix.*
>
> [There is a certain formative substance or force, that draws the thread from the first living point, and afterwards continues it to the last point of life. This is called by some the plastic force, and

> the Archeus; by others, simply nature in action; but I think it will be more intelligible if in reference to the work of formation we term it the formative force and stubstance.] (*Economy of the Animal Kingdom* I, §253)

The different terms used show that Swedenborg had come across this conception among several mystic natural philosophers. Indeed, the word *archeus* is used by Paracelsus and van Helmont, who apply it to the creative force; it is to the doctrine of these two philosophers that Swedenborg appears to be most intimately attached. The "plastic force" is the name for the *archeus* in Ralph Cudworth and Henry More. Certain philosophers resort to a terminology rather close to that of Swedenborg. Marcus Marci, "The Plato of Bohemia," gives the creative force the name of *idea formatrix* (formative idea). Like Swedenborg, he combines this formative idea with the Aristotelian conception of form. This is also picked up by other mystic philosophers known to Swedenborg, such as Rüdiger and Dippel. The closest definition is that of van Helmont, who characterizes the *archeus* as an "*aura vitalis, productor et sustentator omnium rerum*" (a living aura, protector and sustainer of all things). For van Helmont, this living aura is, in the animal species, represented by the most subtle component of the blood, which he calls *spiritus vitalis,* and which accords, to a certain degree, with the conception of Swedenborg, for whom the *vis formatrix* (formative power) is constituted in the animal kingdom by the *fluidum spirituosum.*

Swedenborg has the same mystic conception of this *vis formatrix* as his predecessors. In its quality as universal and perfect substance, it is beyond the sphere of articulate speech and ordinary formalities; no word is adequate to describe it. It reigns as sovereign mistress at the heart of the microcosm that it has created and of which it is in some way "*semidea, Lar tutelaris, genius*" (half-divine, tutelary deity, genius; *Economy of the Animal Kingdom* I, §259). It is the germ of the microcosm in which preexist all the stages through which the latter is to pass on the way to its final destination. But this mighty force is in turn only an emanation of the master of nature. It is only perfect to the extent that it remains its image. As we see, through this *vis formatrix* Swedenborg transforms the mechanical image of the universe as expounded in his *Principia* into an organic image. Everything in the universe, even what appears lifeless, is animate and organic.

By combining this doctrine of a *vis formatrix* with the Aristotelian notion of form, Swedenborg now establishes a relationship that is both causal and teleological, between all the organisms that constitute the universe. To this systematized transformation from higher substances to inferior ones, he gives the name of "the doctrine of series and degrees." In a certain sense, we find here a continuation of the conception of cosmological transformation that he expounded in the *Principia,* and one can observe in Swedenborg's prior works certain tendencies toward a general doctrine of organic progression in the universe. This doctrine, however, will be found completely developed in the definitive form that it will henceforth have in the theological system of Swedenborg (as the doctrine of discrete degrees) only in the eighth chapter of part I of the *Economy of the Animal Kingdom*.

Swedenborg clearly states that, by the term "degree" in this context, he in no way understands it as the difference between various quantities of a like quality, "*quantitates qualitatum" (Economy of the Animal Kingdom* I, §583). In that way, only "continuous" relative degrees are obtained (cf. his discussion of this subject in *Divine Love and Wisdom* §184ff.). The distinct degrees in question here are not perceptible by the help of the senses alone, as the other degrees are. They require a complete knowledge of the genesis and continuity of the universe and rest, in large part, on analogical conclusions. By means of these degrees, we can see how simple substances are transformed into more complex ones and, even in the course of their evolution, continue to be defined by them. They reveal to us the whole scale of created beings from the primary and simple substance of the universe.

Except for this primordial substance, the whole universe is in effect divided into "series," themselves combined into degrees, each of which combines a series of several degrees, and so on. The most extensive series is that of the six kingdoms of nature. As an illustrative example, Swedenborg compares the system to a tree composed of a series of branches, each of which includes a series of boughs, etc. The first substance of each series is the simplest, comprising in a sense the unique substance from which the series proceeds and which governs the series. It is the *vis formatrix* of the series. It is that from which all the other substances derive, and there exists among them all the same causal relationship, so that the substance directly determined by the primitive substance of the series gives birth to the following one, and so on. We find, then, a complete causal chain in each series (*Economy of the Animal Kingdom* I, §594ff.).

The prior substance in the series can be thought of as independent of the one that follows it, but not of the preceding one. The prior substances are more universal and of a more perfect quality than those that follow (*Economy of the Animal Kingdom* I, §612). Through the series, all relationships in the universe emerge. That is why the series do not govern visible existence exclusively, and all spiritual life has them to thank for its existence. All science, all forms of government are constituted by series. Through the series we understand, think, and act. In their absence, nature perishes (*Economy of the Animal Kingdom* I, §586).

Our entire spiritual life is to be explained only through considering the human organism as a series of diverse degrees, acting some upon the others and having causal relations between them. It is through the intermediate determinants that the highest faculty of the soul, the *anima,* finds itself in relationship with the body. This psychological thesis, destined to replace the *harmonia prestabilita* (preestablished harmony), without the necessity of resorting to *influxus physicus* or occasionalism, was given by Swedenborg the name of *harmonia constabilita* (established harmony).

Thanks to series and degrees, the universe acquires a sort of general uniformity. It governs the same *varietas harmonica* in the microcosm as in the macrocosm. Thereby this theory likewise gives us the possibility of acquiring, with the help of experience, an intimate knowledge of nature. From the study of the highest subsequent degrees of a series (the more complex designs constituting aggregates), we can in effect deduce the existence of more simple and earlier degrees of the series (*Economy of the Animal Kingdom* I, §628ff.).

It seems to me quite evident that, in elaborating this doctrine, Swedenborg principally had in mind the organic gradation of Aristotle. For the latter, things formed a continuous evolutionary chain in which each object provided the matter of a higher object and the form of a lower one. In one passage of his works, Swedenborg identifies his doctrine of series and degrees with that of the relations existing between form and matter.[94] In another passage (*Economy of the Animal Kingdom* II, §244), he describes the gradation of forms in the universe. In the lowest degree, form represents both the outer and the inner structure of a body. Thereby he also means the structure of other things that have no bodily form; thus, we speak of forms of government, forms of motion, forms of words, etc. At a higher degree, form means image (*imago*), that is, such as it appears to the *animus*, when abstracted from matter. At a still higher degree, it is pure form (*nuda forma*), or according to others, idea, for at this level it becomes abstracted from any figuration, dimension, motion, or limits.

If we follow this ascending scale, we reach the universal in all its complexity, that is, the *forma formarum naturalium*. All transcendence toward yet higher forms leads us above and beyond the universe to where the intuitive motion of the soul and the scope of the language cease. All description of these forms is only a vain juggling of words. When we apply the denomination of *forma formarum* to the *fluidum spirituosum*, we must assume that it is a matter of representation of the entire universe, including phenomena that our mind (*mens*) is incapable of visualizing. For nothing exists in the human body that does not answer to something higher in the universe.[95]

In the *Economy of the Animal Kingdom*, the number of degrees that comprise a series is arbitrary. Nevertheless, Swedenborg already declares (*Economy of the Animal Kingdom* I, §601) that a complete series has to include at least three degrees, one determinant (*agens*), one determined (*patiens*), and a degree intermediate between the two. Later on, each series is limited to three degrees, the first of which represents the end; the second, the cause; and the third, the effect. It is beyond doubt that this development of the doctrine of discrete degrees, which gives Swedenborg's theology its peculiarly triadic character, flows from the system he established through the firmly structured doctrine of correspondences, of three interrelated spheres of end, cause, and effect. This analogy with the doctrine of correspondences is directly indicated for the first time in the preface to *De*

Cerebro (The Brain) written about 1744, where the doctrine of degrees appears in its transmogrified form.[96]

Through the doctrine of series and degrees, then, nature becomes a giant organism in which each part is a reflection of the whole. All the organisms retain their relationships, their form, and their motion thanks to the four atmospheres or *auras* that surround the universe: air, ether, magnetic fluid, and the highest *aura*, from which the *fluidum spirituosum* emanates. By "a sane instinct of reason," Aristotle has said that the heavens had a soul, but an auxiliary one (*animam assistentem*) without intellect. These *auras* become truly alive, in the higher sense of the term, only when they flow into the microcosm (*Economy of the Animal Kingdom* II, §§199–200). But the life in which they then become participants is not the life of the microcosm itself, and no longer does it emanate from nature. *"Nam natura in se spectata est mortua, et modo inservit Vitae pro causa instrumentali"* (For nature, considered in itself, is dead, and only serves life as an instrumental cause; *Economy of the Animal Kingdom* II, §234). All life flows from God, the source of all wisdom, the eternal light. (*Economy of the Animal Kingdom* II, §238). It is through him that life and intelligence penetrate both the most rudimentary and the most perfect substances created to receive it. Consequently, life and intelligence also penetrate living beings in their most perfect substance, the *fluidum spirituosum,* and finally, through this medium, all other things according to the degree of their perfection (*Economy of the Animal Kingdom* II, §240). Analysis does not permit us to explain how this life and wisdom penetrate created substances; we can only formulate a representation by comparing it with light. Swedenborg recalls here that, in the Bible, God is frequently compared to the sun (*Economy of the Animal Kingdom* II, §254).

And it is here that the image of the Divinity appears compared with the spiritual sun that has been so beloved by the mystics since Plato. As the sun, in its universe, is the source of all light, likewise the Divinity is the sun of all life and of all wisdom. And as the sunlight flows into our world in a specific way without uniting with the illuminated things, so does the sun of life and wisdom (*Economy of the Animal Kingdom* II, §251).

Swedenborg does not permit himself to extend this comparison further, which illustrates but does not reveal the very nature of the object of comparison (*Economy of the Animal Kingdom* II, §254). But what he says about it largely suffices to convince us that he has adopted the Neoplatonic reasoning, This line of reasoning will orient his thinking progressively to the point where we find it raised to the level of a dogma in his theological doctrine; according to this, God created the world by means of a spiritual sun, of which the natural sun constitutes only a reflection (*Divine Love and Wisdom* §§151–157).

It is hardly worth the effort to seek the source of this Swedenborgian conception, which we have already seen broached in the *Prodromus.* He could have gotten it directly from *The Republic* of Plato (book 6, 508) or from Plotinus; he could have borrowed it from Saint Augustine, who often paraphrased it;[97] perhaps he owes it to numerous other mystics, in whose writings it frequently appears. It could also have come to him from the prologue of the Gospel according to John, the text of which Swedenborg never fails to quote in support of his view of the true light that illuminates the world. It is also evident that this conception could only find nourishment in the "supernatural" luminous visions referred to above.[98]

Swedenborg's predecessor, van Helmont, who himself also considered form-creating light (*lux formalis*) as the inmost essence of life, bases his view on the fact that all who, like him, have been called to perceive the inmost foundation of life in a moment of ecstasy, have conceived it as a light.[99] What is important is that Swedenborg comes thereby to accept the Neoplatonic emanationism which, for most of the Christian mystics, constitutes, consciously or unconsciously, the basic construct to which their visions, dreams, and speculations are attached. Already in his *Clavis Hieroglyphica* (§18), written in 1744 and posthumously published in London in 1784,[100] he develops the allegory of the sun in a Neoplatonic sense, thus trying to eliminate God's role in the existence of evil in the world. No more than the sun is deprived of light when worldly objects obstruct its rays—hence, creating darkness—can God be considered as the cause of ignorance, which is merely the lack of wisdom. "God is never deprived of wisdom, but the corporeal desires of the soul set themselves against the penetration of God and of his wisdom; and therefrom arises the folly (*insania*)." And, as with the Neoplatonists, evil is necessary in the universal plan: it is the shadow of good. "Light without shade would not appear to be light, as neither would perfection without the imperfect. . . . Wisdom without ignorance or insanity would not appear to be wisdom, as neither would the good without evil, for there would be nothing from which it [either one or the other] could be perceived" (*Clavis* §20).

We find in the doctrine of degrees and of forms, as it is expounded in *Introductio ad Psychologiam Rationalem* (Introduction to Rational Psychology),[101] which dates from 1740 or 1741, an interesting example of the metaphysical superstructure in the Neoplatonic manner that Swedenborg erects on the mathematical structure of the world that he formulated in the *Principia*. Just as in this later work, he here follows the evolution of motion phenomena from the simplest form, the rectilinear, to the circle, to the spiral and to the vortical, in order to arrive at the form he calls *perpetuo verticalis*, or heavenly, which he regards as belonging to the simple primary of nature.

But while in the *Economy of the Animal Kingdom* (see chapter three above), he still avoids all transcendence beyond the limits of the universe, here he lets his train of thought continue. Above this form which constitutes "pure" motion, the highest in the universe, we find the form that Swedenborg calls *perpetuo caelestis*, or *spiritualis* (*Economy of the Animal Kingdom* III, §267). This form is placed above all created nature and escapes all human analysis. It is beyond all determination, and from it all things of the universe exist. And at the highest point of the scale is the form Swedenborg calls *perpetuo spiritualis*, the inconceivable divine being, the Creator, origin and end of all things. It is in this form that everything infinite, undefinable, holy, resides. "It flows into the forms of the angels and of the heavens and into our souls through the intermediary of the *forma spiritualis* and of the Word. But these are arcana, which is why it is proper to remain silent, awed, reverent, and worshipful, than to speak of it profanely, that is, in natural terms."

From this divine, spirituality emanates; the spiritual creates the celestial; the vortical and the entire descending series flows from the celestial (*Economy of the Animal Kingdom* III, §268, §272). This graduated scale applies likewise to substances, forces, modes, qualities, and eventualities that only exist through form; and they also are gradually raised toward spheres that are more and more elevated and ever more perfect (*Economy of the Animal Kingdom* III, §271).

It is needless to emphasize the entirely Neoplatonic character of this conception. From this undefinable primitive, to which, according to Swedenborg, one cannot even give the name of form, and which thought has to conceive as abstract from all determination of time and space, of all variation or of all transformation, the entire universe issues through emanation. In the course of this process, however, this primitive being has lost none of its force and has not been the object of any transformation whatsoever. It is only by the intermediation of the spiritual form, the first sphere of divine activity, that this primitive being comes to penetrate the souls of angels and our own, created to receive from it life and intelligence just as all our bodies are created to receive motion (*Economy of the Animal Kingdom* III, §269). For Swedenborg, as for Plotinus, the totality of the universe is thus spiritualized. Matter is but a shadow, dead and soulless, which comes alive when penetrated by the divine light. It is not surprising that the citations borrowed from the dialogue of Plato or Aristotle's theology are more frequent here than in any other passage in his works.

Just as the cosmological system of the *Principia* is transformed under the influence of the idea of a spiritual sun, almost without notice as it were, into a purely Neoplatonic image of the universe, so the description Swedenborg gives of the human soul and its functions, in the final chapter of the second part of the *Economy of the Animal Kingdom*, constitutes an evolution of his prior psychological theories in a Neoplatonic manner.

We recall that Swedenborg, in the *Principia*, expounded the traditional twofold division of the soul, comprising the vegetative soul (*animus*) and the reason (*mens*). This division is now modified: above the *mens*, Swedenborg places the intuitive faculty of the soul, the *anima*. This is nothing other than the activity of the *fluidum spirituosum*, and can be considered as identical with it.[102] The functions of the *mens* are located in the cerebral cortex,[103] which is the first determination of the *fluidum spirituosum*. The *animus* acts throughout the entire brain. With the sensory and motor organs of the body, then, these diverse forms constitute a series of four degrees.

Swedenborg appears to be perfectly aware that, by locating intuition in an organism other than the reason and placing it above the latter, he flies in the face of general opinion. But all experience confirms his opinion entirely, he says (*Economy of the Animal Kingdom* II, §277). We know that our soul possesses a faculty of this nature, entirely apart from reason, from the fact that, in many cases, we are led towards events as though by one of the threads of the Fates. We learn about this thanks to our consciousness when remorse and anxieties emanate from principles unknown to us. And this is why we speak of happenstance, accident, and fortune. For the mind knows nothing of the way the *anima* governs and admonishes its empire (*Economy of the Animal Kingdom* II, §282). In its very essence, the *anima* is likewise unknown to us. It surpasses the intellectual mind and thereby our knowledge of the concepts and sphere of words (*Economy of the Animal Kingdom* II, §277). When we wish to speak of the *anima,* we are obliged to resort to terms and comparisons that are barely intelligible.

The *anima* is placed very much above all the other faculties of the soul; it is their law and their organization, the very condition of their activity. It is knowledge itself, the principle of all our science. "Unless the soul were science itself, there could be no sensation, no volition, that is, no affection. The fact that we possess a soul (*anima*) with more knowledge than we believe is obvious from the very nature of the mind, in which a kind of highly rational philosophy and a peculiar logic evolve, as it were connate from the first beginning of our sensations, and which is perfected in proportion to the growth of our understanding" (*Economy of the Animal Kingdom* II, §276). There must exist in us, then, something whose activity is knowledge itself and whose activity embraces everything. It is here that Swedenborg appeals to Locke's description of intuitive knowledge, the existence of which is beyond any doubt, which neither demands nor permits any proof, upon which rests the evidence of all the theses that are imposed on the human spirit as soon as they are propounded, as well as those subject to it, on which it impinges without the help of discursive reason.

The role of the *anima*, then, consists in representing the universe; and thanks to intuition, it is capable of enveloping the universe, not only in its present state, but also in its past and future states. The *anima* is likewise capable of attaining knowledge of ends, at least those which fall within the proper limits of the created universe. For the *anima* itself belongs to created nature; it is consequently only knowledge itself, and not wisdom, the exclusive attribute of God (*Economy of the Animal Kingdom* II, §276.) The *anima* is thus the light that fashions our perception of our consciousness. It flows in the same way as the light into the *mens* (*Economy of the Animal Kingdom* II, §274). The *anima* has spatial extension, being contained in bodily tissues, and can escape only by physical death. It also preserves the exact form of the body even after leaving it (*Economy of the Animal Kingdom* II, §348).

To the question of whether the *anima* is material or incorporeal, Swedenborg replies that it participates in both states. In its quality of fluidity, organically linked with the fibers and fluid of the body, it belongs to matter. But its own life is an emanation from the Holy Spirit; from this point of view, it cannot be viewed as material. Everything that is substantial or derived from a substance in the created universe is subject to dimension and can therefore be considered material. But to the same extent that it has being and life, the *anima* shares in the uncreated, the godly, and cannot be called material. The soul is not material to the degree that it receives its being and life from the Divine and cannot be called material, any more than the body can with respect to its life.

It can be said, then, that the soul is at once material and immaterial; and, on this circumstance, materialists and nonmaterialists both can rest their opinions (*Economy of the Animal Kingdom* II, §311). Just like the soul itself, its functions are at once material and nonmaterial. In themselves, they are only manifestations of motion, modifications identical to those we discern in the *auras,* of which they are the determinants. "All ideas, be they classified as material or nonmaterial,[104] are, then, real essences *(essentiae reales)* similar to the forms and diverse modifications of the *auras*; but as soon as they enter into a relationship with the vital or animated (*animatum*) fluid in any sensory manner whatsoever, their nature manifests itself, becoming from that moment participants in the essence and life of the *anima* (*Economy of the Animal Kingdom* II, §289).

Thanks to his Neoplatonic view, Swedenborg thus continues to elude the necessity of formally setting boundaries between the spiritual and material. To his mind, the body is no more than the envelope of the soul, the matter that only the mind can distinguish from form. It is this fundamental conception that, to a certain extent, allows Swedenborg, in the elaboration of his theological system, to spiritualize everything corporeal and materialize everything spiritual. From the foregoing, we have already seen that he looks upon the body as the shadow image of the soul to the extent that it shares the divine life, while he believes the soul to preserve the bodily form beyond the end of earthly life. When we come to his adaptation of the doctrine of correspondences, we shall see how he conceives, in more precise fashion, the relationship between sensory phenomena and spiritual reality, which constitutes sensory phenomena's origin and bathes them in its light.

Concerning the lower organs of consciousness, Swedenborg strictly applies the empiricism of Locke, with which he appears to have well familiarized himself. The more his empirical development is emphasized, the more he affirms that all knowledge of our reason derives from experience. In the prologue of *Animal Kingdom* (I,§10), he proclaims that it is not the province of man to divine true principles and deduce them from experience, but only of higher beings: spirits, angels, and of the Omniscient himself. Locke, who also studied the operations of our intellect as meticulously as anatomists scrutinize the human body, has definitely established that reason (*mens*) possesses no innate ideas. On the contrary, the *mens* is only tardily developed in the normal man and is lacking in infants and idiots (*Economy of the Animal Kingdom* II, §294).

Consequently, while the lower organs of the soul only appear over a period of years and develop tardily, the individual is endowed with an *anima* from birth. Adam alone received his soul directly from God. Thereafter, it was propagated through the human sperm and is, consequently, a paternal inheritance; it does not come from the mother.[105] Having a common origin, it possesses the same degree of intelligence in all human beings. It can neither degenerate nor sicken.

The infant, the adult, the idiot, all have the same intelligence in their *animas*. The only difference is that, in the idiot, the channel that consolidates the *anima*'s relations with the *mens* are destroyed, while with the infant, they are not yet open. In effect, it is only from the time when the *mens* is developed by experience acquired through the senses—experience that has been transmitted by the *animus*—that it can receive the light from the *anima*. We are born in a complete state of ignorance, and our organs respond only gradually. From its earliest germ, the *anima* is enveloped by fibrils and filaments, isolating itself, so to speak, behind veils and enclosures "as though it did not wish to touch or behold the world it has fallen into" (*Economy of the Animal Kingdom* II, §298). By this psychological theory, Swedenborg believes he has adopted a middle ground between the advocates and adversaries of innate ideas. The *mens* possesses no innate idea, but the *anima* is, from the mother's womb, in possession of all its intelligence, which can, nevertheless, validate itself only to the degree that the lower faculties of the soul are developed through the empirical channel.

From the foregoing, we can appreciate how understanding makes its appearance in the developing individual. Sensations emanate from the body through the intermediation of the *animus*, and collide, in the center of the *mens*, with the divine light shed by the *anima*. The *mens* is the center of rational life as well as the life of the will, for the light in the *anima* is beyond the reach of the intellect. To be grasped, it must descend. But there is only one means for it to rise anew toward life itself and towards certitude. To elevate itself thus is to rise above selfhood, above its egoism, from love of fatherland to love of God (*Economy of the Animal Kingdom* II, §287). Swedenborg concludes this chapter, in which he deals with the elevation of the soul toward higher ends, by picturing nature as a great circle enclosing an infinite variety of ever smaller circles, all of which emanate from a single and common center. Each point, in whatever circumference it is found, refers to the common center, failing which it is ejected from the circle.

This view of nature as a series of circles, expanding with decreasing perfection around a primal center, is not the only Neoplatonic element here. Swedenborg's psychological system, with his theory of irradiation, rising by degrees above the sphere of human reason, is, by its very construction, Neoplatonism. This does not in any way mean to say that Swedenborg would have drawn the particulars directly from Plotinus. The inspiration can well have come to him also from the Church Fathers, particularly from Augustine, whom he further invokes for his division of the soul, or from the Neoplatonists of the Renaissance and their successors. Here, to illustrate the interrelationship that unites all these mystico-psychological systems, I shall briefly relate van Helmont's conception of the spiritual life.[106]

We recall that van Helmont distinguishes a superior soul, the *mens,* image of God, from the *anima sensitiva*, which is only its earthly envelope. His *anima sensitiva* has the same functions that Swedenborg ascribes to the *animus* and the *mens* collectively: that is, it includes not only the lower faculties of the soul but also the reason *(ratio)*.[107] The *anima sensitiva* receives its content from the senses; it is material and perishes with the body. The *mens*, on the contrary, is immortal and unalterable. It is not the *mens,* but the *anima sensitiva* that is affected in illness or insanity. The *anima sensitiva* no doubt thinks by its own faculties, but the light necessary for it to attain clarity comes from the *mens,* as the light from the moon is a reflection from the sun. By the very reason of its imperfection, however, it is penetrated only imperfectly by that light. Because all our thought is mixed with sensory impressions, we can know nothing precise regarding the *mens,* which is beyond our sphere. But if we can free ourselves of all self-love and thereby from all activity of our own, eliminating every disturbing sense impression, we become capable of receiving the light of the *mens* in all its clarity.

It is easy to see that a psychological system of the type that Swedenborg constructs in the *Economy of the Animal Kingdom* divides personality into two parts: one "internal" and one "external," which regard each other as sworn enemies. That which, coming from the *anima*, penetrates the *mens*, constitutes the internal person; that which comes to it from the *animus*, the external. *"Ergo homo externus est idem ac animal; internus vero idem ac angelus"* (the external man is therefore the same as an animal, and the internal the same as an angel; *Animal Kingdom* VII, §166).[108] And this dualism is further complicated by the fact that it is the external person, that is, the lower person, who exhibits all the characteristics of the personality that are developed and evolved, while the internal person, the *anima*, remains immutable and constitutes the vessel that receives the heavenly light. This dualism is already found in Aristotle,[109] and Plotinus speaks of a double ego, a double soul, in man.[110]

This discrimination between an interior and an exterior being eventually appears in most theological systems. It is evident that this dualism was not born in Swedenborg's mind exclusively under the influence of ancient psychology. It is in answer to the antagonism that he experienced in his own personality, an antagonism that grew with the years. In his mind, the natural scientist wages a life-and-death combat against the mystic. He is motivated by a burning desire to learn and is suffused with scientific ambition. It is in the hope of definitively resolving the problems of spiritual life that he renounces his official functions and undertakes long journeys. But he feels in himself, on the other hand, a voice that warns that all his labor is fruitless and that the only thing that really matters for him to learn cannot be revealed to him on the empirical level. This knowledge is revealed only to the seeker who opens his inner being unreservedly to divine light; it is consequently as readily or even more readily accessible to the mystic dreamer. It is in vain that he seeks to establish a kind of collaboration between science and revelation, between the most intense intellectual activity of the researcher and the beatific contemplation of the Quietist. More and more clearly a collaboration of this nature appears to him as chimerical. From this point on, we perceive in Swedenborg the inner conflict that will assume a manifestly morbid tone in his *Journal of Dreams* for the years 1743–1744. From this point on, he is overwhelmed by the conviction that the only way to true knowledge consists of throwing aside all scientific research, with its temporal results, and choosing the *anima* as his sole guide, totally renouncing the will-o'-the wisp of sensory knowledge.

The unfolding of the personality appears in a particularly clear fashion, in its state at birth, in the description of life and volition that Swedenborg gives in the *Economy of the Animal Kingdom.*

In agreement with Leibniz,[111] Swedenborg characterizes the will as a tendency *(conatus)* to act. The will, then, is a potential act, or rather, as Swedenborg says, action is perpetual will; this is why the worthiness of the action should be judged according to the will (*Economy of the Animal Kingdom* II, §318). It is with the help of this conception that Swedenborg identifies saving faith with the moral life.

In a human being, the will proceeds parallel with the understanding (*Economy of the Animal Kingdom* II, §321), and Swedenborg conceived the source of a voluntary act in a manner analogous to that of knowledge. Each perception of the *animus* is accompanied by love (*amor),* which enkindles both its origin and is its very life (*Animal Kingdom* VII, §175). Simultaneously with divine light, divine heat—love—streams from the *anima*. The *mens* stands at the center. The desires of the *animus*, the temptations of the senses, try, from below, to hinder the *mens* from being led by that supreme love of good that flows from the *anima*. Thus, there exist in us an internal personality and an exterior one, perpetually at war (*Economy of the Animal Kingdom* II, §321). The same combat is waged within us by God and the devil (*Animal Kingdom* VII, §219).

In themselves, earthly instincts are in no way culpable; they become harmful only to the extent that they divert our thought from heavenly things; if the *mens* is left helpless to control their guidance, it risks seeing its kingdom succumb to licentiousness. These instincts prevail over the impulses of the *anima* because they are beyond the reach of our understanding. (*Economy of the Animal Kingdom* II, §§323–324).

The two plates of the scales are in the hands of the *mens*, and it is its judgment that determines every decision. And it is precisely within its faculty to affirm or deny all that enters its sphere that free will resides (*Animal Kingdom* VII, §158).

Nevertheless it becomes extremely difficult for Swedenborg, refusing, like Locke, to acknowledge practically any innate principle and considering that all knowledge derives from experience (*Economy of the Animal Kingdom* II, §326) to explain the possibility of this free will. It is, in effect, by the intermediation of *amores* ("loves") emanating from the body and the *animus* that the *mens* has been created. He likewise concedes that this *mens* finds it difficult to take advantage of the free will granted it and that it is more often "like a helpless captive of the heavier plate of the scale" (*Animal Kingdom* VII, §177).

No complete and unrestricted freedom has ever existed except with Adam, the most perfect of men, such as it was before the Fall. His *mens*, which had not been educated through the senses and which was not subject to temptation by any other *mens*, drew its heat exclusively from spiritual love and was a docile instrument of the *anima*. In like manner, the *anima* was the docile subject of the will of God (*Animal Kingdom* VII, §180; *Rational Psychology* §374).

Since this intimate relationship between God and the creature, between the *anima* and the *mens*, was destroyed by the Fall, we have been deprived of all true spiritual freedom. The higher love that has its seat in the *anima* is, in effect, beyond the bounds of our understanding. All our freedom consists in the fact that the *mens* is free to decide what it wishes or, on the other hand, to allow itself to be borne along by lower instincts, the *amores naturales* (natural loves; *Rational Psychology* §372; *Animal Kingdom* VII, §178). And once we have decided, we are allowed to submit it to a sort of court of appeals before we translate it into act. "In this respect the will seems to possess something like liberty" (*videtur hoc respectu ipsa Voluntas aliqua libertate donari; Economy of the Animal Kingdom* II, §328).

Our freedom, then, is, in reality, negative. It consists in freedom to sin or not to sin. And one can ask oneself why this freedom has been granted us, which led Adam to the Fall and which, even today, creates our torment and condemns us to hell (*Animal Kingdom* VII, §§180–181). One can reply that, in the absence of free will, no freedom of thought would exist, and consequently there would be no understanding. Neither men nor virtues would any longer exist, and creation would find itself incapable of attaining its ultimate goal, which is the kingdom of God, for which our earthly life is only a preparation.

As long as it is a matter of higher things and of divine things, the *mens* is capable of willing the means and of preventing us from following the impulsions of the *animus*; but, in respect to the end, it must let itself be guided by the *anima* which, in turn, is directed by the Holy Spirit. These things are above our comprehension, and we can acquire no exact knowledge of them by way of the senses. But with the help of our teachers, by study of the universe, and above all by the study of Holy Scripture, we can nevertheless learn what is necessary for our practical life, and we especially learn how worthy they are of ardent research (*Economy of the Animal Kingdom* II, §329).

By ourselves, we cannot, then, direct our will toward objectives beyond our comprehension. "We ourselves have no power to ignite this sacred fire; and scarcely to desire it with more than a wish that is not active of itself" (*ex quondam voto per se non activo; Economy of the Animal Kingdom* II, §330). But we can raise ourselves by degrees toward these ends by freeing ourselves from forces that tend to degrade us by combating the desires of our *animus*, thus opening the *mens* to the influences of the *anima*, and this to the light from above, to the "spirit of wisdom." God has sent the Savior to incline the scales to his side (*Economy of the Animal Kingdom* II, §332). If we strive to the utmost of our power, we perceive above us a higher power that bestows superhuman strength and thereby raises us to a higher state that resembles that liberty we have lost. For there appears to exist a divine law according to which our volition evokes the will of God (*Economy of the Animal Kingdom* II, §331).

Thus directing our love—fully aware of our impotence toward more noble ends that we only vaguely suspect—we come to realize a mystic union with the divine. For God is the spiritual essence of all things, and love constitutes the bond between him and all that is divine in creation. Love consists in loving, in another person, what one wants to see become like oneself, that with which one wishes to unite, loving us in order that we become an image of him or her. That is why the ultimate source of all love resides in the love of God for his creature, and in our love of God, who rules us. We are divine and possess life and understanding only in the measure of our love of God. Our love must strive toward infinitude. That is an end we cannot attain, our souls being finite, but God's love for us allows us to raise our own love toward this infinite (*Animal Kingdom* VII, §§213–214).

As we see, in his theory of free will, Swedenborg is led to purely theological considerations and, in the last of the above citations (drawn from *De Anima* [The Soul], written c. 1741), he arrives at a mysticism tinged with pantheism. His conception of man's free will in the work of redemption differs radically from the doctrine professed by Luther and by orthodox Protestantism, for whom the fallen man is totally deprived of liberty.

In reality, there is hardly a point on which, in the course of his theological period, Swedenborg argues more energetically against Lutheranism than this. For its religiosity deeply tinged with morality, the declaration of the Confession of Augsburg, according to which humanity, after the Fall, is by nature blind to spiritual things and can be converted only by grace, meant the impossibility of all moral aspiration (see, for example, *True Christian Religion* §464). Swedenborg's conception of humankind's cooperation with the work of redemption is significantly closer to certain Pelagian tendencies at the heart of Catholicism. It also has its equivalent in the doctrine of free will that the Pietists (Dippel, in particular) criticize as sharply as Swedenborg does, and on the same grounds: the orthodox negation of all free will. Nevertheless, Dippel's psychological theory of free will completely differs from that of Swedenborg, who, in defining free will in worldly matters as a faculty of denying or confirming the judgments of reason, simply reproduces Cartesian ideas. It seems to me more credible that Swedenborg came to his theory through Malebranche, who was to exercise a marked influence on him in the course of his theosophical period.

This attachment to the philosophy of Malebranche is only natural. The latter, like Swedenborg, felt the influence of Platonism and of Augustine. Although an adept of the Cartesian school, Malebranche represents, like the Platonists of the Cambridge School, a mystical reaction against the rationalism of Descartes. Swedenborg was acquainted with Malebranche, not only directly (he possessed in his library a Latin translation of *Recherche de la vérité*), but also through John Norris's *Reflection upon the Conduct of Human Life,* which recapitulates the moral theory of Malebranche. It appears from a letter by Swedenborg to Benzelius that he read this work during his sojourn in England.

For Malebranche, as for Swedenborg, human freedom is a mystery.[112] He found himself constrained to acknowledge it in order not to be obliged to draw from his conception of God as unique cause and unique activity of the universe the conclusion that God is likewise the cause of evil. It follows that for him, man's free will is essentially negative: the freedom to sin or not to sin. He is free with regard to "*les biens particuliers*." He can decide against personal goodness, but he can also "suspend his consent" (*suspendre son consentement)* to this natural tendency, which impels him against goodness.[113] And in this manner, from the fact that he does not restrict his love to created things but appreciates them in their true relation to God, man becomes capable of elevating imperfect desires toward the most perfect form of love of God, which consists in loving God as God loves himself.[114] To the degree that we raise ourselves toward God, we lose our freedom, for it is the divine force that draws us upward. And without the grace of God, we can persevere no further in the good. Nevertheless, without the personal contribution of self-liberation from the love of created things that threatens to divert us from the love of the supreme good—without the collaboration of our will—we cannot attain divine grace. For according to the immutable order he has established, God loves his creature to the extent that the latter rises toward perfection.

If we compare Malebranche's view with the thesis of Swedenborg described above, we perceive remarkable similarities between them. These become yet more marked in Swedenborg's theological system when it is more fully developed, for it is allied to Malebranche's conception of the relationship between God and the world, which is strongly colored with pantheism. In the *Economy of the Animal Kingdom,* Swedenborg still displays some hesitation with regard to certain doctrines of the French philosopher, notably in respect to those that submit God to the law of "immutable order." He writes: "This law of his ordaining appears to be that our willing should invoke God's willing, and that our power (*posse*) should invoke his." And he adds that God could naturally put himself above this law at his pleasure (*Economy of the Animal Kingdom* II, §331).

It is evident that this theory of free will and its relation to God leads Swedenborg to a conception of the process of salvation that is entirely different from that of Lutheranism. For Lutheranism, particularly in its then-predominantly orthodox form, proclaims the absolute liberty of God to accord or deny his grace and the absolute impotence of the sinful human creature to contribute directly to his or her own salvation. For Swedenborg, redemptive faith is not a gift of grace that humanity receives from on high without having done anything to deserve it, but it is, in a certain sense, the result of efforts of our free will and of the morality that flows therefrom into our activities. It is true that these efforts could not attain their goal—or even glimpse it—without God's cooperation, but the initiative comes from the individual person if God is to grant his help.

In *Economy of the Animal Kingdom*, Swedenborg had already concluded with regard to this thesis that it is all one "whether we say that we are judged by our faith, by our will, or by our acts." For every soul striving toward the Divine can do or will nothing that is not dictated by his or her love of the ultimate end. "Faith without will is faith without love, that is to say, mere knowledge and acknowledgment; in fact, it is faith without life, and thus dead faith." And a will of this nature implies an action, a goal for its efforts. "Thus we may know from the action itself, unless it is a pretense, whether there be faith or not, and if there be, what the faith is" (*Economy of the Animal Kingdom* II, §333).

Swedenborg's awareness that he is engaging in direct conflict with Lutheranism stands out very clearly in his treatise *De fide et bonis operibus* (Faith and Good Works, published in 1846 in *Opuscula Philosophica)*. This works dates from around 1738 and is consequently more or less contemporaneous with *Economy of the Animal Kingdom.* He declares here that the passage of the Epistle to the Romans, on which Luther based his doctrine of salvation by faith alone, has been falsified by him in his translation by the addition of the words "without works." "And I consider that, in this life, he has committed no greater sin than when he added these words himself" (*Faith and Good Works* §10).

In *Faith and Good Works*, Swedenborg seeks to establish the relationship between faith, will, and works in more detailed fashion, but in the same sense as the passage cited above from *Economy of the Animal Kingdom*. According to him a truly redemptive faith is a voluntary act. It is distinguished from "historical" faith, mere knowledge accessible to demons themselves, which does not deserve to be called faith. True faith cannot exist without love, and true love cannot exist without will; that is, without a will to act, it is absolutely contrary to all reason to proclaim salvation by faith alone apart from works. On the contrary, salvation can only be attained by a faith that is translated into works, *fides in operibus*. Naturally, one can conceive of a redemptive faith in the absence of the possibility of accomplishing good works. However, it is seldom that external obstacles should hinder us from showing our good will, and it is this good will that God takes account of. Moreover, the account of the sacrifice of Abraham and many other examples clearly attest that God himself provides us with the means to act in accordance with our faith.

The distinction that Swedenborg makes here between historical faith and living faith has earlier traditions in Catholic orthodoxy. It is identical with the distinction that Swedenborg's father affirmed between "cerebral and verbal" faith, on the one hand, in which demons themselves were participants, and on the other, "the faith of the heart and of works," which God requires of us.[115] Pietism contributed to expand still further the concept of this "living faith." Spener had already professed that the love of good, and good works, is born simultaneously with faith—*opera sunt in fide presentia*—although he did not believe that good works should be accounted for in humanity with respect to salvation.[116] Dippel goes a step farther: for him, faith is not at all a historical knowledge, but a voluntary act. To believe in Christ means to follow the Gospel in forsaking the world and its desires and to live for Jesus Christ.[117] In the elaboration of his doctrine, Swedenborg naturally felt, to a degree, the influence of Pietism, although it is not possible to assert that this doctrine is directly connected with that of any one of his predecessors. It is in direct rapport with his philosophical conceptions, being the necessary consequence of his profession of free will.

When we speak of "rationalism" in Swedenborg's system, we usually cite his doctrine of the necessity of good works for salvation as an example. This is, to a certain degree, correct. Without any doubt, it is first of all to that doctrine that Swedenborg's theology owes its pragmatic ethical stamp. This is what led him to abandon the doctrine of reconciliation, to reduce the significance of Christ in the cause of redemption and, to a certain extent, to transform this function into a purely moral process in which the conceptions of faith and of grace lose the major part of their mystic content.

From my outline, it nevertheless appears that it is not by the rationalistic method that Swedenborg has been led to this doctrine. If he abandons the Lutheran dogma of salvation by faith alone, it is not because this dogma appears too mystical to him. Nor does his point of view derive primarily from the interest that he may have inherited from his father regarding all moral matters, in which case it would have sufficed to proclaim, like his father, the role of works of Christian benevolence and the necessity of living in conformity with their teachings without directly breaking with Luther over the conception of salvation. Contrary to the opinion of a certain number of theologians, it is hardly likely that Swedenborg was unaware of Luther's own view of the importance of good works or of the orthodox views of the seventeenth century. In the writings of Jesper Swedberg, we find numerous quotations from Luther in which he insists on the necessity of an active Christian life, which he contrasts with the "great faith" of his century.

It is actually from a need for mysticism that Swedenborg's conception of salvation sprang. He refuses to believe that the Fall could have forever and completely destroyed this relationship between the Divine and humanity, which Luther considers to be reestablished at the moment the sinner receives redeeming faith as an act of grace. No more than he accepted that the Fall of Adam could have deprived humankind of the gift of intuitive perception did Swedenborg hold that our wills were forever lost, along with their freedom in the spiritual domain and their aspirations toward the infinite. Just as we reach the highest degree of our knowledge when our natural understanding receives a ray of light from the *anima*, so do our purest moral aspirations rise, with the help of divine power, toward ends that we cannot suspect. Our love meets with the divine love and becomes part of it.

Clearly, envisioned in this manner, the process of salvation as it appears to Swedenborg must take a different course from that conceived by Luther. It loses its central character and becomes a process of slow rebirth, in the course of which the individual gradually rises toward divinity. From here on Swedenborg professes in *De Anima*

(*Animal Kingdom* VII, §220) that a sudden conversion is a rare miracle, "for without a miraculous and singular favor an evil soul cannot at the same time at once be rendered forever good. There is need, however, of bringing force to bear on oneself and of the most ardent prayer and continual cultivation of that which is truly spiritual and Divine."

In the same treatise, Swedenborg shows how humankind thus arises gradually to attain an ever more perfect state of freedom. It becomes a kind of compensation for the orthodox doctrine of order and grace. The first stage of free will consists in the fact that the *mens* frees itself from desires of the flesh and makes the *animus* its servant. At the second stage, the *mens* is formed by study of the Word of God and other instructive works, receiving an intellectual faith. Finally, we reach the third state by having assiduous recourse to the means of grace: frequent worship, participation in the sacraments, adoration of God, and primarily in dedication to prayer. On the condition that a person gives himself to pious practices in a spirit of justice, the divine grace that inculcates faith and love in his heart never fails him.

It is then that the person comes to the fourth stage, that of true free will, which implies a kind of regeneration and spiritualization of intelligence, thanks to the spiritual zeal that animates him or her. At this stage, the person rediscovers the state of the innocence of children before their senses are awakened. The human soul forgets all that extinguishes spiritual things and expends no care upon them except to the degree that the individual may be able to live prudently as a dutiful participant in civil life. This state cannot attain absolute purity in the course of earthly life. But we can approach it closely enough to enjoy, in our corporeal life, an internal bliss and a heaven, and to aspire to our own dissolution (*Animal Kingdom* VII, §§178–180).

By arising gradually toward perfection, we contribute to the aims of creation, which is the kingdom of God, for which the terrestrial kingdom of God, the *civitas Dei,* is intended to be a preparation. This kingdom of God on earth is not confined to any particular religion or church. It is the legacy of all those who love

God above themselves and their neighbors as themselves (*Animal Kingdom* VII, §245).

Naturally, God in his omnipotence could have created his kingdom directly and directly peopled the heaven of souls without having them be born and multiply on this earth. But he has created the world with the purpose of perfecting that harmony and diversity that is to reign in a heavenly realm. For, as on earth, perfection in heaven consists of the different parts forming a whole. We are consequently obliged to conceive of the same diversities among the souls of the elect in heaven as exist among people on earth. In the absence of this, individuality would no longer exist. This difference, however could reside only in the state of souls, and thus we come to envisage the kingdom of God as composed of a number of different communities in the midst of which no soul finds itself exactly in the same state of salvation (*Animal Kingdom* VII, §§244–245).[118]

As we see it, for Swedenborg, the human being is the center of the universe. It is for humanity that creation was brought about. And, in their turn, human beings exist only for their souls, whose ends are beyond nature and can be known only by intuition. There we have a "society of souls in which God sees the end of creation and by which God may be regarded as the *"finis finium"* (*Economy of the Animal Kingdom* II, §365). The law that provides the means of attaining this end is none other than the Holy Scripture, whose teachings are never so obscure or so profound that any sincere soul that permits the spirit of God to govern it may not draw from this pure fountain, without violating any ecclesiastical discipline, the strength to serve the members of the kingdom of God scattered over the surface of the whole earth (*Economy of the Animal Kingdom* II, §366). And Swedenborg closes the second part of his *Economy of the Animal Kingdom* by reproducing, in slightly paraphrased form, Isaiah's description of the future millennial kingdom.

With this hope, that the ransomed of all religions will be able to unite in an active brotherhood to establish the kingdom of God on earth, independently of all confessional divergence, one may rightfully discern the influence of Pietism. We find, for example, an identical doctrine in Dippel, according to which all the churches are to unite in a single *Geisteskirche* ("church of the spirit"). Like

Swedenborg, the German Pietist grafts chiliastic hopes upon this concept. But what one does not find in Dippel, however, and what foreshadows Swedenborg's later theology, is the fact that this evolution of humanity is seen as being determined essentially by the study of the Bible. At any rate, we find here, although still in a rudimentary form, the first indication of Swedenborg's doctrine of the New Jerusalem.

five

THE DOCTRINE OF CORRESPONDENCES

The publication of *Economy of the Animal Kingdom* approximately coincides with the appearance of the most fundamental element of the Swedenborgian outlook: the doctrine of correspondences. This, perhaps by itself alone, may be considered as including, in embryo, not only Swedenborg's later biblical exegesis but also his spiritualistic system. Mentioned in some passages in the third part of *Economy of the Animal Kingdom* (1740), it is found outlined in a brief draft in 1741,[119] to reappear in developed form in a manuscript of the same year, entitled *Clavis Hieroglyphica arcanorum naturalium et spiritualium per viam Representationum et Correspondentiarum* (Hieroglyphic Key to Natural and Spiritual Arcana through the Way of Representation and Correspondences). This manuscript was published in London in 1784.

By "correspondence," Swedenborg means in this work the concordance between natural, spiritual, and divine things, particularly the concordance that exists between the verbal designations of these things. Their designations lie in the respective relationships of type, image, and shadow. "*Omnia enim Divina sunt exemplaria, intellectualia, moralia et civilia sunt typi et imagines, naturalia vero et physica sunt simulacra*" (Every natural thing is the representation of a spiritual thing, and this, in turn, is the representation of a divine thing).

There is no need to dwell further on the doctrine of correspondences to discover its Neoplatonic origins. With Plotinus, things perceived by the senses are the reflection of a form imperceptible to the senses, and this is itself the reflection of the archetype, the idea.

Previously, with his adherence to the Aristotelian conception of form and the related thesis of a *vis formatrix* as the creative and animating force of every natural thing, Swedenborg had introduced into his system an equivalent of the creative principles of forms acting in the germ of things, thanks to which, according to Plotinus, the soul of the universe forms matter. By his acceptance of the Neoplatonic notion that all life in the universe is the emanation of the spiritual sun, Swedenborg was naturally led to draw another Plotinian conclusion. The formative force of matter is itself only stuff for the real form; in the intelligible world, it is a mere reflection of the archetype. That Swedenborg actually arrived at his theory of correspondences in this manner is a circumstance that appears to me to find support in a passage of *The Worship and Love of God* (§65), where he declares that nothing in all nature exists that does not derive its body and its form from a kind of soul, of which it is the reflection. And these souls constitute ends preestablished by heaven where they have their origin. That is why earthly things necessarily accord with heavenly things, and from lower things, one should be able to infer the knowledge of higher things.

Based on the quotations taken from the *Theology of Aristotle* by which, in the third part of *Economy of the Animal Kingdom*, he seeks to justify his doctrine of the degrees of forms as I discussed in chapter four, it may be deduced that Swedenborg had already been attracted to the Neoplatonic doctrine of ideas, prior to the publication of the *Clavis*. In one passage, he advances the Neoplatonic doctrine of creation: "God first created the supreme world, in which he set up, without any thought, forms all pure and perfect . . . and then this sensory world as its image" (*Economy of the Animal Kingdom* III, §271). In another passage, still referring to the *Theology of Aristotle*, he states further: "The forms of the supreme world, says Aristotle, were called by the ancients *exemplaria*, wherein, according to Plato, is seated the substance of things inferior" (*Economy of the Animal Kingdom* III, §264). The relationship with the doctrine of correspondences appears more clearly yet in this third quotation: "Aristotle speaks beautifully of the *natura prima* and of the order in which one depends on the other, when he says that every natural form has in the supreme world some other and similar form corresponding (*respondentem*) to itself but more noble" (*Economy of the Animal Kingdom* III, §266).

Yet the most manifest proof that the doctrine of correspondences owes its origin to Neoplatonism is found in a direct affirmation made in the *Clavis* (19ff.): "The Egyptians, moreover, seem to have cultivated this doctrine, and to have signified these correspondences by hieroglyphic characters . . . whereby are expressed not only natural things but also and at the same time, spiritual things . . . on which there is a whole book written by Aristotle" (*Clavis* §53). The passage from the *Theology of Aristotle* to which allusion is made here is found in chapter fourteen of book fourteen, where it is said that the wise men of Egypt and Babylon succeeded, thanks to the acuity of their minds, in beholding the mysterious secrets of the higher world. Instead of writing what they had learned, they engraved in stone the images of the things they saw. These stones were preserved in the temples and served as books. They thus meant to indicate that the activity of the intelligence has created all things as reproductions of their own forms independently of all matter. The knowledge of these signs is accessible only to rare initiates.

We see, then, that according to the work cited, hieroglyphics represent not only natural phenomena but also the essence of things; for the Platonists, this is the aim of all language.[120] This exposition of Egyptian hieroglyphic science is found again in the works of Swedenborg whenever it is a matter of the history of correspondences. As an example, I quote a passage in the *True Christian Religion* (§205), which will show how the theory of Swedenborg agrees in the smallest detail with the exposition of the Aristotelian doctrine:

> The idolatries of nations in ancient times had their origin from a knowledge of correspondences because all things seen upon the earth correspond, thus not only trees but also beasts and birds of every kind, also fishes and all other things. The ancients who had a knowledge of correspondences made for themselves images which corresponded to heavenly things and were delighted with them because they signified such things as were of heaven and the church; and therefore they placed them not only in their

> temples but also in their homes, not to adore them but to call to mind the heavenly things which they signified. Therefore in Egypt and elsewhere there were images of calves, oxen, serpents, as well as of boys, old men and maidens; because calves and oxen signified the affections and powers of the natural man.

The attempt that Swedenborg makes throughout to relate the idolatry of ancient peoples to their knowledge of correspondences finds its complete parallel in the thesis of Plotinus, for whom all idolatry is understandable when one becomes aware that there exists an "empathy" between the idols themselves and the higher powers they represent. The same reasoning is again found, moreover, in the *Theology of Aristotle*.

Thus conceived, our entire physical world is only a symbol of the spiritual world (*symbolicum Mundi spiritualis; Animal Kingdom* I, §232, note u). And so this poses the question of how we are to interpret these symbols so that we can rise from the knowledge of natural things to that of the spiritual truths that they reflect but that, in themselves, are beyond our intellectual reach. Swedenborg starts from this premise: that the verbal representation of spiritual things and that of natural things share the same mystical relationship as these things themselves. In the *Animal Kingdom* (I, §232, note y), he says that, when we express any natural truth by the use of physical terms and when we substitute the corresponding spiritual terms for these physical terms, we bring to the surface, replacing the physical truth or physical principle, a spiritual truth or theological dogma, the appearance of which no mortal could have foreseen by simple transposition of terms. It is according to this method that Swedenborg illustrates the doctrine of correspondences in the *Clavis*.

I have already given a characteristic example of this reasoning by way of Swedenborg's comparison between the sun in our universe and the divine sun of wisdom and love. Just as the sun in the visible world is the source of all light, so God in heaven is the source of all wisdom. This is in line with his theory outlined above, according to which every natural thing has, in our own world, a spiritual correspondence, a form that unites it with its heavenly correspondent. In the *Clavis*, Swedenborg enunciates three connected theses that give us, first, the physical truths; second, "intellectual" or moral truths; and third, theological or divine truths.

One cannot avoid seeing the influence of the Kabbalah in this method, especially since, in his earlier manuscript notes, Swedenborg arrived at the doctrine of correspondences through an attempt at an allegorical exegesis of the Bible. It is hardly possible to distinguish what he owed to Neoplatonism from what he owes to the Kabbalah, since the latter was itself from its beginning closely related to Neoplatonism; moreover, this influence was emphasized among the philosophers of the Renaissance who constantly mingled Neoplatonic and Kabbalistic considerations with their doctrines.

So I shall confine myself to pointing out that the Kabbalah accepts the doctrine of ideas in its Neoplatonic form. Before the creation of our world, all its creatures preexisted in their true forms in the mind of God. The entire lower world is created in the image of the higher. All that exists in the higher world is translated to us as in the form of an image. All that comes within the reach of our senses, then, has a symbolic significance. The most material forms and phenomena can, therefore, inform us of what is happening either in the mind of God or in the human intellect.[121] Starting with this concept, the Kabbalah arrives at the doctrine of a heavenly alphabet and of the physiognomy that is also a proof of the intimate union between the inner and the outer, between the corporeal and the spiritual. And it is precisely this physiognomy that Swedenborg refers to when he seeks to illustrate his doctrine of correspondences in *Arcana Coelestia* (§§2988–2989).

This affiliation appears even clearer when Swedenborg is compared with certain natural philosophers of the Renaissance or the natural and Kabbalistic philosophies of the seventeenth century. In general, they start from the same principle of three superimposed worlds: the "sublunary" world of the elements, the celestial or "sidereal," and the "supercelestial." These three worlds are intimately related so that everything in the lower world has its equivalent, in more perfect form, in the higher world.

I have chosen a few examples from Pico della Mirandola to illustrate how his thought approaches Swedenborg's doctrine of correspondences:

> Among us, heat is an elementary quality; in the celestial domain, it is a calorific force; among the angels, it is the very idea of heat. . . . For us, fire is considered an element. In the sky, the sun is fire, and fire in the supramundane regions is seraphic intellect. . . . Elementary fire scorches, celestial fire vivifies, the supercelestial fire loves.[122]

Pico goes on to develop how this connection between all that is created finds confirmation in Holy Scripture, which gives rise to an allegorical exegesis of the Bible: *"Ab hoc principio . . . totius sensus allegorici disciplina manavit"* (From this principle has flowed the discipline of all allegorical sense):

> For the ancient fathers [and thereby he surely means the biblical authors] would have been incapable of representing each thing in the appropriate image (*figura*) had they themselves not known the relationships and the correspondences, secret, so to speak, which exist throughout all nature. In the absence of this knowledge, they would naturally have had no reason to represent things in one form rather than another. But knowing all things and led by the spirit who not only knows these things but even created them, they represented [*figurabant*] the things of one world in the form of those which they knew corresponded [*respondera*] in the higher spheres. And this is why whoever truly wishes to interpret their images (*figuras*) and to learn their allegorical significance must possess the same knowledge (unless assisted by the same spirit).[123]

By this long quotation from Pico della Mirandola, I do not mean to imply that Swedenborg was necessarily acquainted with him. It would have been as easy to confirm the concordance of the Swedenborgian doctrine with that of Cornelius Agrippa, who drew from the so-called Platonist his theory of concordance between the three worlds. If I have quoted Pico della Mirandola, it is because he was the first in modern times to have clearly formulated the Kabbalistic method of interpretation that was later adopted, almost unaltered, by so many exegetes and naturalist mystics; moreover, his exposition clearly accords with the doctrine of correspondences later formulated by Swedenborg and the exegesis that necessarily flowed therefrom.

At no time has Swedenborg pretended that he invented the doctrine of correspondences or that he was the first to apply it. On the contrary, he always emphasized that it is a matter of knowledge formerly possessed by humanity and later lost progressively as it turned away from God. In *True Christian Religion* (§§202–206), he declares that men of "the most ancient church," that is, those who lived before the Flood, "were of a genius so heavenly that they spoke with the angels of heaven and that they were able to speak with them through correspondences." They conceived, then, all that they saw on this earth not only in a natural way but also through the spiritual sense.

This doctrine, which was expressed in acts of worship, was transmuted little by little among the Jews into idolatry and ended, under divine providence, in total oblivion. It was conserved by Enoch, however, and, thanks to him, spread into a number of countries such as Canaan, Egypt, Assyria, Chaldea, Syria, Arabia, Tyre, Sidon, and Nineveh, where it persisted and was practiced, particularly among "those who were called diviners and sages and, by some, magi." From these oriental countries, it was carried over into Greece, "but there it evolved into fabulism, as it appears among the most ancient scribes of that country." This doctrine gradually fell into general oblivion everywhere and did not even reappear at the coming of Christ, which indicated that the Christians of the primitive church were so simple (*simplices*) that it would have been of no use to them. And after the Council of Nicea, which established the dogma of the Trinity, the world found itself invaded by such darkness that the doctrine of correspondences could not be revealed there. It is only thanks to Swedenborg's intervention that this doctrine and, with it, the spiritual sense of the Word were again revealed to the world by the grace of God. Such is Swedenborg's conviction, after he has received his religious mission.

In the *Clavis*, he does not yet pretend to possess the knowledge of the spiritual correspondences of all natural things. He often expresses himself with the greatest circumspection about the concordances he believes to have discovered and frequently invokes, as proof of this accord, the fact that such and such a word is used in an allegorical sense in the common tongue. In the brief preface of his first manuscript sketch on the correspondences, he declares that ignorance of the spiritual sense of a word is the cause of many controversies and false interpretations to which the study of holy writ in particular gives rise.

It is nevertheless evident that, from that time, Swedenborg considered the doctrine of correspondences as a secret one with ancient roots. This is notably proven in his above-cited allusion to the Egyptians and in his affirmation at the end of the *Clavis* that the ancients knew a form of correspondences which he classified as "*fabulosa*" and which are also found in the heroic poets. It is clear that Swedenborg here alludes, as in the declaration mentioned above regarding one Greek fabulist, to the allegorical explanation given by the Stoics to the mythology and works of Homerian explanation that Swedenborg knew very well from *De Rerum Natura* of Cicero, which he quotes in *Economy of the Animal Kingdom.* As we know, this allegorical interpretation of the Stoics became, by the intermediation of Philo, one of the primitive stages of the allegorical exegesis of the Bible.

Turning to the naturalistic philosophers of the Kabbalah, one recognizes, in the exposition of the origins of their doctrine, all the details Swedenborg gives on the history of the doctrine of correspondences. Even the Greek philosophers were accustomed to consider Egypt as the cradle of all wisdom; since the Hellenic period, tradition speaks of the treasures collected by Pythagoras, in the course of his fabled voyages in Egypt and the Orient, in the form of mysterious doctrines that were later transmitted from generation to generation. When the Kabbalists picked up these traditions, they naturally traced the doctrines of the Greeks and their oriental mentors back to Moses or the people before the Flood. One thus had an explanation for the manifest similarity between Neoplatonism and the Kabbalah without being constrained to have recourse to the inadmissible hypothesis according to which this Kabbalah would be a graft of Neoplatonism.

It would take us too far afield to show in any detail the similarity between the history that Swedenborg gives of his doctrine and that which the Kabbalists give of theirs. Like Swedenborg, the Kabbalists attribute a certain role to Enoch in the establishment of the tradition. As transmitters they list the same people as the Swedish philosopher and, like him, recognize the relationship of this mysterious doctrine to magic. Like Swedenborg, they stress the fact that the three wise men from the East who worshiped the newborn Christ were called "magi."

Swedenborg's concepts here nevertheless diverge from those of the Kabbalists in a way that should not be overlooked. For the Kabbalists, knowledge of the relations between the different worlds implies the mastery of occult forces. Earthly things have not only the form and the character of their supercelestial or sidereal correspondences, but additional occult forces that can be dealt with only by the knowledge of "natural magic"; the latter, in turn, must be distinguished from necromancy, which calls on the help of demons.[124] Pico della Mirandola tries to establish in a precise manner the differences between these two doctrines. He emphatically proclaims that natural magic, like that of the Kabbalah, can only convince us of the divinity of Christ and many other theological verities.[125] Swedenborg, on the other hand, condemns all magic, even "natural" magic, which cannot predict what is divine but only what is against the divine (*Arcana Coelestia* §3698). This evidently does not prevent him from openly acknowledging the possibility of this magic. In many passages of his works, he declares that magic actually comes from the abuse of correspondences and that it led to the oblivion into which, by the providence of God, this doctrine fell.

For Swedenborg, then, the doctrine of correspondences has value only as a key to knowledge; the gigantic effort of the Renaissance to dominate the aggregate of occult forces while extending this knowledge stirs no echo in him. For him, the doctrine of correspondences should lead us, first of all, to a more perfect understanding of Scripture. It is exceedingly significant that already in 1741 (the year when he drafted the first outline of the doctrine of correspondences and four years before he received from God his mission and interpreter of the Bible), Swedenborg had assembled a number of biblical passages and sought to interpret them allegorically.

He evidently found support in this from earlier attempts to discover a mystical sense in the divine Word, attempts quite common at that time not only among students of the Kabbalah but also in the most embedded ranks of orthodoxy. In his manuscripts, Swedenborg divides the various correspondences into five groups: *correspondentia harmonica, correspondentia parabolica, correspondentia typica, correspondentia fabulosa et somniorum* and *correspondentia actionum humanarum et divinarum*—a classification to be found in his *Clavis.* It is thus clear that Swedenborg felt the influence of contemporary biblical exegesis. Solomon Glassius, who, according to Diestel,[126] was the great orthodox hermeneutic authority of the time, distributed the spiritual or mystical sense of biblical text into three categories: *sensus allegoricus, sensus typicus,* and *sensus parabolicus.*[127] Glassius' explanation and examples of these three categories are quite close to the doctrine expounded by Swedenborg, and each of these categories include, in turn, subdivisions: there is notably a special chapter "*De allegoriis fabularum.*"[128] It is probably possible to trace the classification introduced by Swedenborg in his doctrine of correspondences to Glassius or some other exegete. That, however, seems to me a rather uninteresting task, since the distinctive characters of the diverse categories do not appear to have been formulated with a very rigorous logic either by Swedenborg or by his precursors.

Among the categories Swedenborg refers to there is one that nevertheless seems to me to merit some attention here: this is what he designates as *"correspondentia fabulosa et somniorum."* According to examples he cites in this connection, it appears that he is thinking of the dreams related in the Bible such as those of Pharaoh and Joseph. These very dreams are found in a subdivision of the *sensus typicus* of Glassius.[129] But it is equally certain that the personal dream Swedenborg had at that time had played a role in his elaboration of the doctrine of correspondences. From Swedenborg's later recovered *Journal of Dreams,* which he recorded from 1743–1744, it seems that he has symbolically interpreted all the oneiric visions to which he had been subject at the time. Everything leads us to suspect that the same applies to his preceding notes, which have been lost. Nor can one deny that part of the correspondences outlined in his *Clavis* closely parallel the folkloric tradition of dream interpretation.

But the significance of the correspondences does not reside merely in Swedenborg's biblical exegesis or in the symbolic interpretation of his dreams. What is at least as important is that this doctrine allows us to deduce the absolute congruence of the spiritual and sensory worlds. Swedenborg had already noted in the *Theology of Aristotle* that every earthly being has its original image in the higher world and that this higher world consequently offers us a perfect reproduction of our own world. Just as in this one, we find there plants, streams, aquatic animals, although they are of a superior essence *(De secr. parte,* 1, VIII, 3).

We shall see later how, for Swedenborg, the spiritual world becomes a duplicate of the visible world and how, during his theosophical years, he will affirm with increasing emphasis that this correspondence between the two worlds extends to the most minute details. In the two first works on the doctrine of correspondences, only one or two conclusions are found regarding the spiritual world. Thus, in the *Clavis,* he demonstrates the existence of "spiritual intelligences," of good angels and bad spirits. In the introduction of the draft manuscript, we find certain reflections on spiritual language, of which the angels make use for natural expressions, just as we recur to natural terms for spiritual phenomena. The angels are able to comprehend our language; they can receive a stronger impression of it to the extent that we strive to free our thoughts from material things, an effort in which we cannot entirely succeed in earthly life. The language of angels themselves is purely spiritual and cannot be expressed in sounds deriving from the motion of the tongue, or at any rate by sounds perceptible by us. As we see, Swedenborg did not yet believe he was in conversation with angels, and his notions of spiritual language emerged only from his doctrine of correspondences.

He found in this theory, then, the key that he believed would open to him the doors of the supersensory world. Thanks to the mystical relationship between words, it henceforth becomes possible for him to see a prophetic sign behind an apparently insignificant occurrence and to discover in an apparently insignificant affirmation a significant spiritual intervention. The world and its sensory phenomena will now be, for him, only the symbol of a higher life; the new verities of science are no longer significant except to the extent that they can be interpreted in a divine sense.

One can clearly foresee that, from this moment, Swedenborg is to renounce natural sciences as of minor importance in order to dedicate himself exclusively to the new mission toward which the theory of correspondences leads him: that of the biblical exegete and spirit seer. In every phenomenon, he discovers a deep significance. Every word he utters thereafter has an unconscious mystical sense. Above him, there exists a world whose details he is able to learn thanks to the links of analogy. The world in which he wanders is a world of shadows, images, resemblances. Whoever is incapable of interpreting these symbols walks like a blind man. "We are justified in believing," he writes at the end of the *Clavis,* "that the whole world is filled with types (*typi*) but that we know very few of them" (*Clavis* §67). It is to the clarification of these types that he is hereafter to consecrate his life.

The unfortunately all too brief review that I have given of the contents of *Economy of the Animal Kingdom* and the other works from the same period should make it clear to the reader that we can find in these works, *in nuce*, Swedenborg's whole theological system. In these treatises, whose plan is of purely natural-scientific and mainly physiological concern (replete with details I have no reason to examine here), Swedenborg has developed not only his philosophical ideas but also a complete system of theology that lacks only the certitude vouchsafed by divine inspiration to turn into religious preaching. On considering the works dealt with, it is difficult to accept the theory, put forth in most biographies of Swedenborg, that a conversion occurs suddenly in 1745 at the moment when he turns toward theosophy from a philosophy of nature tinged with materialism.

I believe that this conclusion, though supported by certain declarations by Swedenborg himself, is the result of erroneous generalization; the discovery of the *Journal of Dreams* for the years 1743–1744 should have discredited this view once and for all. Peculiarly, it has survived much longer outside Swedenborgian circles than in these circles themselves. Modern followers of Swedenborg have understood how to harmonize the results of more recent researches with their religious conceptions by acknowledging a progressive awakening of his "spiritual insight," a theory already found in Tafel and still more vigorously expounded by Stroh. On the contrary, the "profane" critics are generally obstinate in considering Swedenborg's theological system as the result of his visions. Even in the cases where this view has not been subservient to the effort to explain Swedenborg's entire teaching as the result of a putative mental illness (a hypothesis as unsatisfactory from the psychological as from the historical point of view, but which nevertheless has illustrious advocates), they have allowed themselves to be led, consciously or unconsciously, by a repugnance toward acknowledging that, even at the time he was making his great physiological discoveries, Swedenborg could have been haunted by mystical or theosophical conceptions, which today is considered incompatible with all exact scientific research. I have already shown how this manner of thinking is subject to the error of entirely overlooking the dominant spirit of the time in the natural sciences, particularly in medicine.

All in all, it does not appear that the philosophy of the *Economy of the Animal Kingdom* has been accorded its rightful stature among Swedenborg's published studies. In a large number of biographies, even those that are otherwise quite complete, this work is entirely neglected or simply attached to the *Principia.* This is notably the case with Hans Schlieper's exposition of Swedenborg's philosophy, which is also highly unsatisfactory.[130] Swedenborgian authors, such as Rudolph Tafel, J. J. G. Wilkinson, and Alfred H. Stroh, for example, have, on the other hand, established that, in *Economy of the Animal Kingdom*, Swedenborg gives a glimpse of certain aspects of his later system; but, for understandable reasons, these are held to be indications of details.

Thus, despite all the research to which Swedenborg has been subjected, no one has come to the conclusion that, in its essential lines, the whole system of Swedenborg was already elaborated, not merely prior to his visionary period proper but even before the religious crisis to which his *Journal of Dreams* testifies, and which found its poetic expression in *The Worship and Love of God.* And this applies just as well to theological theses as to his scientific and philosophical conceptions. It can be stated without exaggeration that, during his theosophical period, Swedenborg does no more than develop his system and draw from the structure of his earlier thought the conclusions imposed by logic.

People have always been astonished to find that a theosophy that professes to rest on things *visa et audita*, that is, on visions and apparitions, could have become a system so tightly coherent, every link of which seems to demand the next one, in which one finds so few traces of the capricious nature of dreams and where, finally, the most fantastic conceptions can be logically linked to one another. There is no need at all to establish Swedenborg's superiority by comparing him with the visionaries of his times who never tried to arrange their religious experiences into a speculative system. He perfectly withstands comparison with illustrious theosophists such as Boehme or Fludd, but no one will fail to be struck by the remarkable difference between these and Swedenborg with respect to the clarity and logic of his ordering of ideas. In the works of all these authors, whether their systems are structured on the *Areopagita*, on the Kabbalah, or on the mysticism of medieval Germany, we find odd superstructures that are impossible to harmonize with the architecture appropriate to the system. We also encounter badly assimilated reminiscences of prior theosophical systems which these philosophers have appropriated without bothering to relate them organically with their own world of thought; confused notions of an occultism born of magic, astrology, or alchemy; or mythological conceptions of angels and demons, which can generally be traced to the superstitions of antiquity. Their doctrines demand to be believed in order to be understood, and only the reader who resolutely suspends his mental processes and delivers himself up to his pure imagination has some chance of assimilating them.

How greatly the system of Swedenborg differs from these! On all points, he seeks to convince the reader by marshaling rational arguments. With a sometimes painful attention to detail, he tries to bring each point of his thesis to life in a logical manner; in Swedenborg's works, what most minds probably reject is precisely their character of reasoned abstractions. His system, the theory of correspondences, doubtless constitutes an element of occultism; but, in the methodical form he gives it, it loses every trace of magic. During his whole life, moreover, Swedenborg disdainfully kept at arm's length all the invokers of spirits, magnetizers, and individuals who sought to transform his theories into necromantic practices.

Nor does his exposition of the spiritual world rest on ancient demonological traditions. It is, like our own world, scrupulously structured on the theory of correspondences. Swedenborg always finds logical arguments to support the descriptions of angels and spirits he establishes and the explanation he gives for the diverse states of souls after death. Nor does his religious moral code offer any kind of spiritual medication. It does not occur to him to indicate to his readers any way whatsoever to enter into contemplation or to establish communication with the spiritual world. His practical revelation has no other purpose than to point out the ways leading to a pure life, and he does so at times in ways that seem very prosaic to us or even trivial, with such a cold precision does he trace the true limits of human activity.

Swedenborg's strangely logical construct can only be explained by the fact that his system was elaborated, in its essential lines, before the author's missionary period. It has been developed by a mechanician accustomed to abstract structures, by a scientist who held, even after his conversion to theosophy, to the necessity of exact methods. When impelled later by the same internal necessity that had caused him to abandon the mechanistic philosophy of the *Principia* for the mysticism of the *Economy of the Animal Kingdom,* he becomes the visionary and exegete. The fundamental doctrines of this system have taken root in his mind to the extent that he involuntarily reproduces them in his dreams and visions. We shall see later that Swedenborg's entire philosophical conceptions are again found in the visions described in his *Journal of Dreams;* accordingly, his apparitions are always related directly to his philosophical theories. In his *Spiritual Diary*, he notes day by day the spiritual phenomena of which he is the object with the same scrupulous exactitude that he has previously applied to his scientific observations. He accepts nothing that cannot be incorporated into his grand system. Thus, his biblical exegesis is for him only a means of providing divine authority for his previous theses. Thanks to an extraordinary faculty of combination, he succeeds in incorporating into the biblical text all the philosophy of *Economy of the Animal Kingdom* without discarding his exegetical principles.

I have already outlined the external and internal conditions that constitute the foundation of this philosophy; here I shall only summarize the results. In *Economy of the Animal Kingdom*, we find ourselves in the presence of a doctrine that one can, in general, relate to the stream of ideas from the English Cambridge Platonists and from the Frenchman Malebranche, a current that had its equivalent in

Germany among the adversaries of the rationalism of Leibniz and Wolff. Swedenborg's philosophy has, in common with these diverse movements and their ramifications, what constitutes a reaction, tinged with theology, against the materialistic conclusions the natural sciences threatened to impose. It also has a close dependence on the Neoplatonism that Swedenborg was familiar with, not only by direct study, but also through the Church Fathers and Renaissance philosophy.

What distinguishes the philosophy of *Economy of the Animal Kingdom* most clearly from the *Principia* is that, under the influence of Aristotle, Plotinus, Leibniz, and also of modern science, the mechanistic conception gives way to a clearly organic one. Nature is a system of ends that mutually condition each other; it is a living organism whose development is best explained by the analogies offered by the human anatomy. We already see dawning in Swedenborg's mind the representation of the universe as "the grand man," an idea he found in various places in the ancient philosophy and which he is to apply later in an entirely paradoxical fashion. This organic conception of nature is translated in his scientific mind by his systematic application of the doctrine according to which all that exists in the macrocosm is reflected in the microcosm. Not only humanity, but even the most minute particle of the universe constitutes a world in miniature, presenting the same organic structure and subject to the same laws as the macrocosm. For Swedenborg, the theory of series and degrees serves above all to illustrate the organic interconnectedness of everything in nature.

A consequence of this doctrine, connected with the specifically theological conception of *Economy of the Animal Kingdom*, is the idea that every being carries within itself the germ of its entire ulterior evolution and that in this germ, in potential form, are found not only the forces to which it will give actual existence later on but also the ends that are its mission to realize. Such is the meaning of the doctrine of a *vis formatrix* that exists in every creature.

Finally, the theory of correspondences permits us to penetrate the spiritual world of which our own world is but a reflection.

These are the bonds of continuity and analogy uniting the most humble things with the most exalted, which, for Swedenborg, constitute the very essence of his philosophy. In the *Principia* (19), he had already compared the immense mechanism of nature to a cobweb. Philosophy is the spider at the center of the web, sensing the slightest of motions, however peripheral they might be. In his imagination, the great natural mechanism had already made way for the great organism of nature; but the goal of his philosophy continued no less to be the discovery of the threads, tenuous and almost invisible, that form the immense tissue of creation.

With Swedenborg, the idea that regulates this cosmic network is, as we have already indicated, of an emanatory nature. Like his predecessors among the Church Fathers or the Renaissance Platonists, Swedenborg does not give voice to any systematized emanationistic doctrine. He notably declares that creation is a free act of God. But he conceives of every phenomenon, of each life in the bosom of the universe, as the result of a continuing emanation of divine energy. To make plain the fact that this emanation does not in the least diminish the energy inherent in God and that this energy is not the object of any substantial union with created things, he always returns, like Plotinus, to the allegory of the sun, which irradiates the universe across the celestial spaces without losing any of its own light and without engaging in any material union with the objects illuminated.

This comparison of divinity to the sun, which is at first a simile to concretize a phenomenon of which Swedenborg has no exact notion and which he considers beyond human comprehension, little by little becomes, as often happens with mystics, an entirely dogmatic thesis. In accordance with his cosmological conception in the *Principia,* Swedenborg proclaims that our universe was created by God from the natural sun. But things thus created are inert in themselves; they are only vessels destined to receive the love and wisdom that penetrates them with the light of the spiritual sun.

To be sure, in this precise and complete form, this doctrine is found only in Swedenborg's theological works. During his scientific period, he did not find time to formulate the *doctrina influxuum* that he had promised in the foreword to *Animal Kingdom*. But it is already found in draft form in works dating from that period. It is the dawn of what one sees in the theory of correspondences, in the idea of degrees proceeding downward from above, from perfect to imperfect to evil. But in Swedenborg's psychological view, it has already played a role of prime importance.

One corollary of the theory of the sun as the source of life and wisdom clearly should have led Swedenborg to deny to human beings any possibility of acting and achieving knowledge by our own efforts. Our thoughts and our acts belong to us no more than the sun's rays belong to the objects it illumines. It is obvious that Swedenborg does not dare to venture that far. On the one hand, he brings out, when he compares God to the sun, that he may by his spirit be essentially united with humankind as he was with Adam before the Fall (*Economy of the Animal Kingdom* II, §258). On the other hand, his empirical conception of the origin of consciousness, along with the fact that he maintains the freedom of the will, obliges him to seek a compromise. He is thus led to posit, above our ordinary spiritual life, an intermediary of the divine light, the *anima,* which, without possessing activity of its own, is enlightened by God and guided by his will. All our conscious acts should, then, tend to permit, through the *anima*, the penetration of the lower regions of our soul. This penetration evidently becomes possible if we reject all the influences and the seductions of the world that obstruct the light emanating from the *anima*. It is then a matter of a purely negative mission; pushed to its extreme consequences, it concludes in nothing less than the annihilation of our own personality, of our "external man," to use the expression of Swedenborg; in a word, "to the state of infancy before the awakening of the senses." In this state, the human being exclusively becomes the receptacle of divine light.

It is in this tendency toward effacement of the personality that the mystic character of Swedenborg becomes more and more evident in the works of this period. It is precisely this tendency that prevents him from adhering to the Lutheran doctrine of faith and salvation. For Luther, our spiritual freedom begins at the instant, by divine grace, we accept redeeming faith. For Swedenborg, on the contrary, as for most of the mystics, salvation consists precisely in the final alienation of our free will after a long period of ascetic self-education. We are to use our freedom to lose this free will step by step, to make of ourselves an instrument of divine activity. We shall see further that this reasoning will become the basic theme of his meditations in the course of the religious crisis described in his *Journal of Dreams*.

Before embarking upon the study of this period, when Swedenborg experiences true vision for the first time and lays the foundation for his theory of spirits, I want to call the reader's attention to certain passages of his previous works in which he delivers himself up to speculations on the future life and describes certain mystic states of the soul.

In my exposition of Swedenborg's philosophical conceptions, I have already referred to some passages in his works dating from his scientific period in which he reasons about the nature of spirits, their various modes of apparition, and the division of the heavens into a number of communities within which no soul enjoys exactly the same happiness as the others. In a chapter of *De Anima* that deals with destinies of the soul after death, we find a more complete exposition of these questions and some other related ones.

It is well to recall that Swedenborg does not yet consider himself as possessing more complete knowledge than others about life after death. At every turn, he invokes the Bible, the doctrines of the Church Fathers, the intuitions of those sages of paganism Pythagoras, Socrates, and Plato regarding the existence of a future life and dwells on the analogies that can be deduced from earthly conditions. He even describes these speculations as baseless fantasies that will perhaps appear ridiculous to him when he enters the future life. Nevertheless, they hold for us a real interest because they allow us to deduce the image Swedenborg had of the future life before his visionary period. In a general way, they harmonize with prevalent Christian notions. However, we already glimpse a certain number of personal traits that foreshadow Swedenborg's later eschatology.

We recall that, for Swedenborg, it is the *anima* alone that survives the body. The lower strata of the soul enjoy no immortality. The proofs he advances for the immortality of the *anima* are perceptibly identical to those we learn about through *De Infinito.* Endowed with a form superior to that of natural things, the *anima* may not be destroyed by these. For a time after bodily death, it continues on in a somber state of existence, devoid of intelligence; in fact, it cannot abandon the body until the latter has disintegrated, and it can thus free itself from its tissues. Here we have a remnant of Swedenborg's previous reflections on the same subject. It is an interesting carryover, for it demonstrates to what extent he remains convinced of his notions of the materiality of the soul. He finds there, among others, a confirmation in the fact that, in some cases, seamen have returned to life several days after they were believed to have drowned. During this interval, the *anima* possesses the same life as during the fetal period, and it is only from the moment that it finds itself freed from the body that it resumes an entirely individual life (*Animal Kingdom* VII, §§234–236).

Just as in his earlier works, Swedenborg seeks here to learn how the dispersed components of spiritual substance come together again after death. He believes that this reunion is perhaps due to the inner empathy that allies them. As proof of this hypothesis, he cites analogies drawn from nature. It is well known, he says, that bushes, plants, or flowers, when reduced to dust, are reborn when immersed in water. If, then, the various parts of these lower things are capable of renewal, how much more reason there must be for the same to apply to the substances of the soul? Swedenborg returns to the example used by his father to prove the resurrection (see chapter one). It is said that ghosts, after the last rites, can appear before their friends, which would be impossible if the vital spirits were not joined one with another and could not be brought together again. This reconstitution of the bonds that join spiritual substances finds new confirmation in paternal love; this love has its source in the father's sense that the offspring has been drawn from his own soul and that it consequently tends to rejoin it (*Animal Kingdom* VII, §237).

It might be feared that, under such conditions, one soul might be confused with another. Swedenborg believes, nevertheless, that divine providence has arranged everything so that no soul is ever absolutely identical to another (*Animal Kingdom* VII, 238). One soul is distinguished from all others by the degree of wisdom it has attained. This is developed during the earthly life in one direction or another and after physical death is not susceptible to mutation in its individual essence (*Animal Kingdom* VII, §§241–242).[131] To the question of knowing in what manner the soul becomes an angel when it enters into the celestial life, Swedenborg replies that, for his part, he does not think that it will get a corporeal form, since in heaven angels don't need hands and feet, viscera, and sense organs. It is also possible that we shall assume, in the heavenly life, not the imperfect corporeal form but a heavenly one (*Animal Kingdom* VII, §238). Souls know about the present and the past through a permanent sense of intuition; without the help of sense organs, they perceive everything that happens on earth as well as in heaven. They can communicate in the language of angels who, in a single thought, express what would require thousands of words and material ideas in the language of the world (*Animal Kingdom* VII, §247).[132]

In another passage (*Animal Kingdom* VII, §95ff.), Swedenborg proposes the hypothesis that marriages, happy or unhappy, persist after death, the former as heavenly recompense and the latter as infernal punishment. Here we find a rough draft of his later doctrine on spiritual marriage. Thus it is that souls live in heaven a life fully consecrated to the love of him who is life itself, in respect to which earthly life is but a shadow and a dream (*Animal Kingdom* VII, §247). As for Swedenborg's conception of hell, this still appears to me, in its general lines, to conform with the orthodox one, as is his description of the Last Judgment (*Animal Kingdom* VII, §§248–249). It is evident that Swedenborg has not yet arrived at the concrete views that he adopts later about the body of the angels and about the functions of this body. These hosts of the spiritual world acquire a corporeal reality only little by little in the course of his theosophical period.

This does not diminish Swedenborg's disposition to acknowledge from now on the possibility that the souls of the dead can appear to us in visible form. He supports the belief that, from the moment it is freed from the body, the soul has the faculty of assuming any form it pleases, so that "if it descends to earth it can take on the human form momentarily." For the whole of nature was created to serve as an instrument of the spiritual life. Just as, in the course of earthly life, the body executes the orders that reach it from the soul and, likewise, during uterine life, thoughts of the mother can be transmitted to the infant in the form of birthmarks, so it must be admitted that in the heavens a soul possesses the faculty of assuming any human or animal form whatsoever by a simple act of will. For the soul in the heavenly environment is entirely free in its decisions, and its free will is no longer restricted as it was in its life on earth (*Animal Kingdom* VII, §§239–240). All these determinations seated in the soul after the end of earthly life nevertheless depend on its active and spiritual principle; in consequence, they can only serve necessary ends. In fact, it would be inadmissible that these determinations should be the result of a feeling of pure curiosity or a desire for novelty, since these instruments belong only to the *mens* and the *animus* (*Animal Kingdom* VII, §240).

From this time on, then, Swedenborg appears convinced that the souls of the dead can appear to the living under diverse forms and can exercise a certain influence upon them. But nothing in his exposition of the matter indicates that he considers himself to have experienced an apparition of that nature. However, one clearly sees the interest he shows in the topic. It can be easily foreseen that, in the day when he himself will be the object of visions, he will entertain no doubt of their reality.

One comes to the same conclusion when reading Swedenborg's exposition of the "Diseases of the Fiber" in the third part of the *Economy of the Animal Kingdom.* Here it is a matter of various maladies of the soul and supernatural states of the soul. This passage holds a special interest when one seeks to comprehend the terminology of the *Journal of Dreams* and the *Spiritual Diary,* and it is strange that none of the psychiatrists who have undertaken to elucidate the nature of mental illness which they have suspected in Swedenborg has studied in detail his own theories on the diverse maladies of the soul and their symptomatology. My own interest is here focused on the views Swedenborg had at that time of the specifically mystical states of the soul as well as his explanation of them.

First of all, it is notable that to Swedenborg these psychic states constitute real diseases that are due in large part to states of physical weakness. He generally connects them with features of his psychological system. Most often he considers them to be provoked by a splitting of an external personality from an internal personality. Thus, in somnambulism *(noctambulatio),* the external personality wanders about like a machine, while the internal personality is submerged in deep rest (*Economy of the Animal Kingdom* III, §531).

During ecstasy, the contrary takes place. The soul separates itself from the corporeal body while it is still alive

> and one can believe that the soul (*anima*) has escaped from the body or that, at least, though admitting that it remains associated with its body, all relations between them have been interrupted. Certain individuals enter into ecstasy at the moment of agony and their soul is, so to speak, exalted above the world, but returns to its home, or its prison. . . . In northern regions certain persons skilled in the art of magic are credited with being able to fall spontaneously into a kind of ecstasy, in which they are deprived of the external senses and of all motion, and with being engaged meanwhile in the operations of the soul alone, in order that after resuscitation they may reveal thefts and declare desired secrets. (*Economy of the Animal Kingdom* III, §537)

At the end of the same chapter, Swedenborg repeats that there is nothing contrary to reason in believing that certain individuals are capable of entering into ecstasy; belief in magic has its origin in just this circumstance. Among the external symptoms of ecstasy, he notes the suspension of respiration.

As we see, Swedenborg considers ecstasy to be a lethargic state of the body and of the lower faculties of the soul in which the *anima*, in consequence, enjoys a supernatural illumination. This is the explanation he later gives of his own ecstasies, and it is beyond doubt that he thus interprets his former *deliquia,* accompanied by suspension of respiration and interior light. Nevertheless, in this chapter, he gives no indication that he has himself experienced such ecstatic states.

On the other hand, it appears that his descriptions of hallucinations contain an implicit avowal of this nature. The phenomenon he describes under the title *"Imaginatio Fanatica,"* and to which he dedicates a whole chapter, clearly appears to his mind to be nothing else than hallucination, properly speaking. He characterizes this phenomenon as a sort of inner vision coinciding with a weakening and at times a complete suppression of ocular sight. He subdivides it into "*hemeralopia*" and "*nyctalopia,*" according to whether it has been produced by day or by night.[133]

Among the causes that can provoke this "fanatical imagination" Swedenborg mentions, in addition to disease and excesses, is an intense intellectual concentration. And he especially emphasizes that case when thoughts are jumbled and the mind finds itself projected into a flood of light surrounded by darkness. Such is the case especially with persons who strive to meditate *(contemplari)* on the state of the soul after physical death, "that is, when intellectual faith studies to attribute the greatest part to itself" (*Economy of the Animal Kingdom* III, §526).

It is hardly possible that, in giving such detailed examples of this phenomenon, Swedenborg had in mind any other personality than his own. The question of the destinies of souls after death of the body was indeed one of those which he set himself the task of resolving: it was the problem whose definitive solution the *Animal Kingdom* was to provide. He may have wished it to be understood, in the quoted passage, that this problem is of such an exalted nature that to try to resolve it by the sole force of reason (see chapter three regarding his conception of *fides intellectualis*) involved great risk of succumbing to overwork and becoming the victim of fallacious visions.

From the above exposition, then, it appears that Swedenborg had already at that time experienced hallucinatory states. But he remained undecided about how he should interpret these hallucinations: are they divine indications, revelations of new truths, or are they misleading lights, mental disturbances representing chastisement of the researcher who has ventured to pierce the veils providence had intended to keep closed?

A reading of the speculative passages of *Animal Kingdom,* written just before the critical period revealed in the *Journal of Dreams,* leaves the same impression. The serene certitude, proclaimed in the first parts of *Economy of the Animal Kingdom* regarding the divine inspiration of his theory, the nature of the soul, and the consequent certain truth of that theory, has completely vanished. In the prologue (§19), he reproaches himself for having undertaken too hastily, drawn by this ardent thirst for knowledge *(ardor sciendi)* a description of the soul after having merely studied the blood and its circulatory system. His firm intention henceforth is to approach the soul, which is immaterial, progressively, and to expound its relations with the body as well as its state after physical death only after he has first studied the anatomy of the human body in full and explored the brain, nervous system, and muscular structure in the light of his new theory of degrees, forms, and correspondences. And this can be done only with the permission of God.

In reality, in *Animal Kingdom,* he underscores more insistently than ever the necessity of the analytical method, the only avenue accessible to the human creature. It is reserved to superior beings, angels, and to the Omniscient himself to investigate the true principles with the help of *mens* alone, and to draw the consequences therefrom (*Animal Kingdom* I, prologue, §10). Swedenborg claims to be the first to have resorted, in a systematic fashion, to the analytic method to explain the very essence of the soul (*Animal Kingdom* I, prologue, §15). Even though one has arrived at the principles of things by a similar analysis and can begin making deductions, the truths arrived at are, nevertheless, blended with ignorance and shadows, and are only illusions of the truth *(Veritatum simulachra).* For as long as the *mens* is united with the body, it can never be free of the deception of the senses (*Animal Kingdom* I, prologue, §13).

He complains that we are so infatuated with ourselves that we consider ourselves as moving, not on the periphery, but at the center, not on earth but on the heights, not in darkness and error but in the rays of the most brilliant light and in heaven itself (*Animal Kingdom* I, prologue, §10). In the epilogue of the second part of *Animal Kingdom,* written during his visionary period,[134] Swedenborg seems to indicate still more clearly that the luminous visions, to which he had hitherto directed his research, are perhaps will-o'-the-wisps. In effect, he declares (*Animal Kingdom* II, §401) that corporeal ideas are accompanied by phosphorescent fires deprived of energy *(fatui quidam ignes et quasi phosphori)* but which fallaciously represent themselves as the very light of life. Such are the fires of the body, the *animus*, and the *mens*.

Without doubt, Swedenborg remains faithful to the main lines of the psychological system we came to know in the *Economy of the Animal Kingdom.* But the intuition which, under the influence of Locke, he receives into the system becomes more and more a superior form of sentiment and no longer only superior reasoning. In a word, this intuition is completely confused with mystic ecstasy, that union with the Divinity which can only be consummated by faith and by contemplation completely submerged in God. When he describes the highest form of human awareness in the prologue of *Animal Kingdom*, he declares:

> It is important above all that the mind be pure and that it apply itself to universal matters for the happiness of humanity and the glory of God; then, from his heavenly abode Truth penetrates our reason, for it is from heaven that truth emanates. Plato used frequently to say, as the philosopher tells it, that when his soul was in a state of contemplation, he seemed to enjoy the supreme good and incredible delight; that he felt himself petrified in admiration, he participated in the higher world and, inundated by a dazzling light, felt assured of immortal life; his intelligence, fatigued by that contemplation, ended, nevertheless, by falling back into pure imagination, and he felt himself, when that light was again lacking, overcome by sadness. When he again separated himself from his body to return to the light, his soul seemed to him inundated with clarity, and this state reacted upon the body. And Plato says elsewhere: the soul rises as though freed from the body and clarifies itself; when it descends once more it becomes obscure again, to rise anew after becoming purified.

Swedenborg adds: *"Verum hoc ignotis forsitan ut fabula narratur"* (But perhaps this will be taken by the ignorant to be a mere fable; *Animal Kingdom* I, prologue, §12).

The above citation attributed to Plato is extracted from the so-called *Theology of Aristotle* and, in reality, constitutes only a reproduction of Plotinus' description in the *Enneads* of the ascension of the "I" towards the ideal world.[135] The fact that here Swedenborg likens the highest form of awareness to mystic ecstasy in its classical sense shows more clearly than any other argument the interior evolution that takes place in his thought during the course of the few years that had passed since he wrote the first chapters of the *Economy of the Animal Kingdom*.

It might appear useless, or even dangerous, to try to penetrate the supreme verities by way of analysis if they are inaccessible to reason and if they can be known only through ecstatic contemplation and faith. Swedenborg in no way disregards this objection, and he tries to respond in the closing lines of his prologue. He realizes that whosoever succeeds in learning these high truths by faith alone without the use of intelligence is to be considered the happiest of mortals. He should abstain from reading Swedenborg's book and from seeking to understand these things by his intelligence alone. There is no need to talk of light when one has vision (*Animal Kingdom* I, prologue, §§21–22). This book has been written solely for those who can believe only what their intelligence conceives and who consequently deny everything beyond the reach of their understanding. It is to them that Swedenborg dedicates his work, in the hope that it will open the way to faith.

It is easy to read between the lines that Swedenborg does not yet venture to include himself among those privileged mortals who are capable of learning the highest truths by faith alone. It is to forever extinguish his own doubts that he embarks upon the gigantic task of penetrating the very essence of the soul by scientific analysis. It is only during the period of crisis revealed in his *Journal of Dreams* that "by the grace of the Spirit" he will attain the "faith without reasoning" (*Journal of Dreams* §149). He then recalls his prior declarations, which he judges to have been inspired by God, even though he was not yet capable at that time of grasping their scope entirely:

> Happy are they who believe and do not see: I have repeated these words in numbers 21 and 22 of my prologue, but I could not have remembered them by myself or come to them by deduction: the grace of God alone acted in my favor, and I learned these things later from their very effect and by the change that took place throughout my inner being, for such is God's grace—eternal glory be to it—and thereby I understand how much greater efforts the wise make than the ignorant to come to their faith and rise above themselves to the point of smiling at their own weakness; for the adoration of their own reason should first

> of all be abolished and annihilated, which is the work of God and not of men. (*Journal of Dreams* §§150–151)

But it is clear that once this conception of faith is achieved, Swedenborg considers his own scientific activity not only as useless but also as likely to impede the attainment of true faith. Henceforth, his way will no longer be that of a scientist, but that of a religious teacher. It is this evolution that we will observe in his *Journal of Dreams*.

six

THE RELIGIOUS CRISIS

In the life stories of several great mystics, we find a strange period of depression following the first period of ecstasy and before the final "apostolic" period when the individual feels himself solely as the instrument of God.[136] The mystics who have theoretically described the different stages of the way to union with God, such as Mme. Guyon in her fine psychological study, *Les Torrents,* look upon this period as one of purification. The ecstasy of the first stage is not sufficiently pure. The subject enjoys and is proud of the grace vouchsafed and forgets his own weakness; he lives in a state of "*gourmandise spirituelle*." The second stage consequently becomes a time of ordeal during which God lets the soul feel the humility of its condition, leaving it to struggle against temptations and to aspire to the divine grace it believes it has lost. This state, characterized by physical suffering, is a progressive downward spiral. The ego is annihilated: all personal traits are effaced. This is what Mme. Guyon calls "*la mort mystique*." The soul no longer lives its own life; it is God who lives and moves within it.

In general, it is precisely this second stage of mystical evolution that is rife with pathological manifestations. Drained by privations and penitences, frequently passing from the deepest despondency to a state of ecstatic bliss with a touch of megalomania, the subject exhibits symptoms that psychiatrists know too well not to be tempted to identify with their own clinical observations. Unfortunately, they are not content to point out the existence of these pathological signs: they regard them often as explaining not merely the mystical states, but all the individual's subsequent development as well.

Delacroix appears to me to have dealt very judiciously with this point of view. He finds it warranted in many cases relating to inferior mystics, so to speak, whose celebrity rests exclusively on their success in crystallizing their symptoms around a religious idea. But it is not the same thing with respect to the great figures of mysticism. It is true that great mystics, almost without exception, have displayed symptoms characterized as neurotic; in certain cases, their mysticism is related to the neurosis by which they are afflicted. But behind these morbid phenomena, one observes magnificent intuitions and a kind of homogeneous impulse that guides their lives. "For were there not a distinct mental state underlying the neuroses there would be no artistic genius any more than religious genius."[137]

It seems to me evident that the period in the life of Swedenborg (with which we are acquainted through the strange journal published by Gustaf Klemming under the title *Swedenborg's Drömmar,* reviews step by step the state of depression seen in mystical development.[138] Until now the mystic apparitions of which Swedenborg has been the object have brought him only joy. Thereafter, even in full ecstasy, he suffers an affliction he attributes to his unworthiness. For the first time, he discovers "that one can be a prey to spiritual suffering even though certain in his mind of having achieved the remission of his sins." He feels selfhood to be deeply rooted in his being; therefore, from time to time, he despairs of divine grace (Tafel II, Doc. 209, 60). He strives to free himself from earthly desires, and when temptations threaten to triumph, he submits to penances. He entreats God for the grace "to belong to you and not be left to myself." And little by little, he feels himself freed from his own selfhood to become "the instrument to be used by God at his pleasure" (Tafel II, Doc. 209, 54).

From this journal, it also appears very clearly that Swedenborg has not been free of the neuropathological symptoms that most mystics experience during this period. To judge by the testimonies of some contemporaries (which are actually rather divergent), these symptoms would take such an intense form in him that people around him would consider him to be mentally deranged. The thesis of Swedenborg's insanity, which was widespread in the eighteenth century and which later found numerous propagators, apparently originated from rumors that spread at the time. They were not based on the rationalistic view that any man who believes himself in communication with the supersensory world must necessarily be mentally imbalanced. I am not competent to pronounce on the nature of the hypersensitivity Swedenborg had acquired at that time and shall only revert to this in the following pages to the extent that it is pertinent in explaining his mystical state.

The first pages of his journal merely contain commonplace travel notations. In the spring of 1743, Swedenborg had obtained a two-year leave of absence from his functions as assessor in order to finish the *Animal Kingdom* and have it printed abroad. In rapid sequence, he describes his voyage via Stralsund, Hamburg, and Bremen to Holland, where he seems to have spent the closing months of the year. Here the journal presents a hiatus; the pages following the final notes on August 20, 1743, have been torn out.

When he resumes his jottings, apparently in December 1743, they are of an entirely different character. Now they are dedicated to his dreams, the beginning of which certainly goes back to a month or two earlier. Tafel[139] calls attention to the fact that in the notes of April 17–18, 1744, Swedenborg says he has had "with God's grace a preternatural sleep" and this has been the case for an entire half year. This traces the beginning of his critical dream period back to October 1743.

It is clear that this "preternatural sleep" was accompanied by dreams relating to his scientific works. We have noted that already in 1736, on the occasion of the intense labor required by the definitive edition of the *Economy of the Animal Kingdom,* Swedenborg had experienced similar dreams and ecstatic luminous sensations in which he saw a divine confirmation of the theories he was about to expound. Here too it appears that concentrated intellectual labor may have awakened his former predispositions. Later, when he interprets his dreams in the journal, he will frequently seek to relate them to the chapter that he is currently in the course of writing in *Animal Kingdom*. And in the *Spiritual Diary*, he relates also (§2951)[140] that "before my mind was opened, so that I could speak with spirits, and so be persuaded by living experience; for many years previous, . . . not only were there dreams . . . concerning those things which were written, but there were, also, changes of state, when I wrote." It is evident, however, that these dreams were not the only mystical phenomena of that period. Swedenborg feels that a radical change has been produced in him, the cause of which he is not entirely able to explain. In his notes of December 8 (*Journal of Dreams* §12), he writes that he "wondered at myself for having nothing left to do for my own honor, so that I was even touched. Also at not being at all inclined towards the sex, as I had previously been all my life." Three days later, he summarizes the changes of which he conceives himself the object:

> How, after I arrived at The Hague, that my interest, and self love in my work, had passed away; at which I wondered.
>
> How the inclination to the other sex so suddenly ceased, which had been my strongest passion.
>
> How I had, during the whole time, the best sleep at nights, which was more than kind.
>
> How my trances were, before and after sleep.
>
> My clear thoughts about things.

Here we have all we know of the crises that preceded the date of these notes. Although scanty, this material nonetheless suffices to establish a general concordance of the phenomena noted by Swedenborg with the symptoms usually observed at the onset of religious conversions. William James, who deals with an abundance of psychological material, has underscored, as characteristics of these crises, the fact that the individual suddenly feels, without conscious effort, that he is transformed and freed from the temptation that previously assailed him. "Such a rapid liberation," he says, "from old tendencies and dispositions recalls with such fidelity the authentications which have been established on the results of hypnotic suggestion that one cannot help thinking that subconscious influences play as decisive a role in the brusque changes of character as in hypnotism."[141] Among the examples of this phenomena that James cites, there is reason to note the case in which individuals of marked erotic temperament feel instantly delivered from all sexual temptations.

One may ask oneself, then, what psychological factors provoked this character metamorphosis in Swedenborg. I do not believe that one runs a great risk of error in acknowledging that these factors are closely related to his scientific output. The attention awakened abroad by the works of Swedenborg has quite naturally given him a fully justified awareness of his own worth. This feeling is further enhanced by the thought of the great work he proposes to draw up in its definitive form and for which he has accumulated rich material during the last decades in his anatomical researches. This work should, to his mind, permit him to acquire a sure knowledge of the life of the soul during its stay in the body and of its destiny after physical death. The exalted idea that he entertains of this work is shown in the supercilious terms in which he demands a leave from the Board of Mines and in which he declares in the preface of *Animal Kingdom* that he is the first to have the audacity to seek to acquire knowledge of the soul by this means.

On the other hand, however, he is clearly aware that it is not by his own strength that he has achieved this result. At every step taken in his field of research, he feels the need for a sign of divine confirmation. It is to these luminous visions, accompanied by suspension of respiration and loss of consciousness, that he attributes what he calls his "clear thoughts." But it is not enough to desire this divine confirmation. Now and then he even has the very distinct feeling that the more strongly he insists on God's help the more it escapes him. It is this feeling he expresses in his notes on the tenth of December:

> How I opposed myself to the Spirit; And how I then enjoyed this, but afterwards found that it was nonsense, without life and coherence;
>
> And that, consequently, a great deal of what I had written, in proportion as I had denied the power of the Spirit, was of that description; and, indeed, that thus all the faults are my own, but the truths are not.
>
> Sometimes, indeed, I became impatient and thought I would rebel, if all did not progress with the ease I desired, after I no longer did anything for my own sake. I found my unworthiness less, and gave thanks for the grace.[142]

And on the following day he tells how, on having opposed "the power of the Holy Spirit," he saw "hideous specters . . . without life."

It is not difficult to see the spiritual conflict concealed in these incoherent notes. It is the same kind of conflict that we recognize in almost all Christian mystics, torn between their urgent need for activity and the passivity that is the necessary condition for receiving divine grace. Since Swedenborg's researches sought the glorification of God, it sometimes seems to him cruel to have to wait so long for the solution of enigmas he has undertaken to unravel. And in his impatience, he seeks from time to time to take the lead and attain to truth without the help of divine light. But these attempts unfailingly end in his humiliation, and he is forced to acknowledge his error.

Why has the Divine abandoned him in this way? Undoubtedly it is because his soul is not yet sufficiently purified, is not yet free enough from earthly desires and the vanity of a man of science. "The power of the Spirit" can only come down into a vessel completely cleansed of all filth so that it can be completely filled by this power. Like most mystics, Swedenborg awaits this purification by a divine miracle, by a sudden gift of grace. In his journal, we constantly see him assuring himself that he has finally triumphed over his "external being." But time and again, the temptations of the senses and the vanity of the scientist renew their unceasing assaults, and he endlessly finds himself again the prey of despair and deprived of divine grace.

Before entering upon the various phases of Swedenborg's inner development as they appear to us in his *Journal of* Dreams, I shall say a few words regarding the forms of mystic phenomena to be found there. Without a brief study of these features, the quotations that I shall include from Swedenborg's journal would risk remaining rather obscure. Unfortunately, Swedenborg's own descriptions of his apparitions are by no means clear, and I am obliged to beg in advance to be excused for the errors that might insinuate themselves into my exegesis.

There is no need here to explain the nature of the apparitions that Swedenborg himself classifies as dreams. He consistently regards them as symbolic; they have been sent by God to help him in his scientific works, to point out the way to follow and to let him know what the future holds for him. In general, he tries to interpret them by applying the theory of correspondences. At times, nevertheless, his methods remain unworkable, and he must acknowledge that he has not yet penetrated the intentions of God, for there are "representations, of which as yet I understand very little" (*Journal of Dreams* §175).

Certain visions that Swedenborg claims to have had are very close to dreams as when he reports that he has "been neither asleep nor awake, in a strange trance (*Journal of Dreams* §174). This state seems to leave him a degree of consciousness. "I knew everything that I dreamed and my thoughts remained captive," he says in the same passage. The visions discussed here appear to agree in their main lines with the experiences that are purely oneiric; nevertheless, to a certain extent, they seem to exercise a more marked influence on his mind. Apparently, as Herrlin indicates,[143] it is a kind of hypnagogic hallucination, a common type of vision even in normal mental states. On the other hand, the apparitions that Swedenborg himself classifies as visions also seem to occur in a state of wakefulness. What is characteristic is that they take place almost exclusively immediately before or after the state of torpor. The particular receptivity of these two periods to hallucinatory phenomena is considered to be one of the most frequent initial signs of mental disturbance.

Among these hallucinations, some are of a more elementary nature. It is thus that Swedenborg sees "gold," or on another occasion, the vision is "of a coal fire, burning strongly" (*Journal of Dreams* 261). It is evident that photisms, the first mystic manifestations of which he is the object, belong in the same category as visions. Certain expressions in the journal clearly indicate that Swedenborg continues to have visions of this nature from time to time, and under conditions perceptibly identical. Notably when he says (*Journal of Dreams* §116) that his thoughts "became ruddy in light," it is clear that he considers this luminous phenomenon to be a divine confirmation of his inspiration.

There is reason to compare these visions with those in which Swedenborg's thoughts are "represented" by "a kind of illuminated spiritual writing" (*Journal of Dreams* §111). The most remarkable visions he records at that time are incontestably the apparitions of Christ. In several of them, he is allowed to contemplate Christ face to face; in others, he simply has a vision of the crucifix. It is very probable that these visions, like those observed with most mystics, should be regarded as pseudohallucinations. Unlike psychosensory hallucinations, pseudohallucinations are not localized within the subject's normal field of vision. Swedenborg declares that his apparitions are perceived by his "internal sight," by "his spiritual eyes." Such is, at least, the sense to which it seems necessary to attribute the passage in which he notes that "in the same instant Jesus Christ was presented vividly before my internal eyes" (*Journal of Dreams* §168).

It is no less probable that the auditory perceptions noted by Swedenborg in his journal are also of a pseudohallucinatory nature. The journal does not display any precision in this respect, however; most often, Swedenborg limits himself to writing, "It was told me," etc. In his account of his conversation with Christ during his grand vision, he says absolutely nothing of the fashion in which the words of Jesus reached him. But in *The Worship and Love of God,* which he has already begun to write at the time, as well as in his first exegetical work, the *Historia Creationis a Mose Tradita* (The History of Creation as Related by Moses), which he will write the next year, one finds the mention of a language of spirits, as sonorous as that externally articulated by the lips and tongue, although it is not transmitted by sounds but is rather perceived by the mind or by "the internal sight" (*Adversaria* I, §§15–16). This description agrees entirely with that which psychiatrists give of verbal pseudohallucinations: the subject does not localize these by ear, even though they otherwise have the nature of an auditory perception as well as, sometimes, a certain sonority.

If, despite the insufficiency of material, I consider it reasonable to accept the visionary phenomena of which Swedenborg speaks in his *Journal of Dreams* as pseudohallucinatory and not as hallucinations properly speaking, it is not only because we see there the ordinary instrumentality by which Swedenborg communicates with the world of spirits since the day his "spiritual sight" was opened. The manner in which he reacts to these mystic apparitions also indicates that they can hardly be of a psychosensory nature. A true hallucination, with the characteristics of a complete sensory perception, provokes in the subject an impression of terror—whatever content it may have—especially when it makes its appearance for the first time.[144] This observation will be confirmed by the grand vision in London, which was apparently psychosensory in character.

A pseudohallucination, on the other hand, does not produce this immediate impression of external reality. The subject conceives of it as something objective, independent of his will; but he does not at any moment, during the course of the hallucination, confuse these "inner" visions or these "internal" voices with real visions or voices. On the contrary, most often he considers himself as the object of a psychic influence; maleficent or beneficent forces come into association with him through these visions or voices and dominate his inner life.

It is the same with Swedenborg. He himself characterizes his own mystic states of that period as "being in the spirit." It is evident that he associates these states with the psychology of the *Economy of the Animal Kingdom* and that he understands thereby a state in which only the *anima* is active. It also stands out in Swedenborg's journal that he induces this state by suspending his respiration. In a passage of the *Journal of Dreams* (§111), he expounds his respiration theory, which he will often repeat later. According to him, thoughts "fly into the body" at the moment of inhalation and are expelled in exhalation. It suffices, then, to suspend breathing when one is assailed by "evil thoughts." Moreover, he observes that, during a period of ecstasy, a respiratory suspension was also produced and "the thoughts then seemed to have vanished. On the other hand, during sleep, when inhalation and exhalation are natural phenomena, then that is represented which flows into us from a higher world." In another passage, he notes further, "I had something like a vision—I suspended my own thoughts and was seized, as usual, by a trembling, which signified that I should not keep on like that for long, especially on Sunday or in the evening."

These physical symptoms—suspension of respiration and the shivering—play a particularly important role in the ecstasies, numerous descriptions of which are contained in the *Journal of Dreams*. The are accompanied at times by visions, photisms, or more complex hallucinatory phenomena. However, they present this common characteristic: by concentrating his awareness on a single focus—most often God or Jesus Christ—Swedenborg attains to a state of beatitude that he describes as a union of the deepest spiritual and sensory delight. He says that he is able to experience this inner *"jucunditet,"* which he equates "with a heavenly joy on this earth," at any hour of the day or night but more particularly in the morning or the evening (*Journal of Dreams* §201). It is "the spirit . . . the inflowing of the spirit of God" which "causes me to rise higher and higher, so that had I continued my assent I would be dissolved in this very *"vita gaudii"* (*Journal of Dreams* §127).

To illustrate the nature of these experiences, we shall relate here the first of the ecstasies of which Swedenborg gives a rather detailed description. He declares that since December 9 he has found himself "almost continuously in *extasibus vigilibus"* ("waking ecstasies"). The night following Easter day, after having taken communion that same day, he found himself at dawn immersed "in an indescribable heavenly ecstasy." He says, "I felt within me a sheaf of rays, feeling that martyrdom would be the supreme joy, for, due to the indescribable grace associated with the love of God, one longs for this torture which is as nothing compared with eternal torment, and the least is to lay down one's own life; and I felt in my mind and body such inexpressible beatitude that, had it been more intense, my entire body would have dissolved into pure joy" (*Journal of Dreams* §§47–48).

The form of ecstasy described here by Swedenborg recalls at every point the kind we encounter in the confessions of most of the mystics. It is a trance that does not much differ from a hypnotic state. The subject who, by a concentration of his thoughts and feelings on God and infinite love, withdraws himself from all the impressions, representations, or ideas alien to the Divinity, feels himself entirely suffused by divine love and is nothing but a oneness in God (cf. the Plotinian description of ecstasy in chapter five). This sensation, for most mystics as for Swedenborg, consists of a mixture of enjoyment and pain;[145] again like most of the mystics, Swedenborg specifies that this pleasure is itself also of a purely physical character.

Psychologists of religion have established by definitive examples that the "delicious martyrdom" of which the mystics claim to be the prey most often includes a sexual element of which the subject himself is not always clearly conscious. As often observed in religious manifestations, the love of God does not remain content here with drawing on the vocabulary of profane love but also has recourse to the physical correlates of this love.[146] For Swedenborg, who is an informed physiologist himself, these relationships are fully conscious, and he is much too true to himself to attempt to disguise them. Instead of the half-veiled allusions of other mystics, he gives us the most explicit description of the actual process. It is thus that he writes, with regard to an ecstasy that he experienced some nights later (*Journal of Dreams* §88), "This *amor* in the flesh of the mortal body, by which I was then suffused, recalled the pleasure which a chaste man experiences when he finds himself in a state of true love *in ipso actu* with his spouse; for such was the *amaenitas extrema* ["extreme pleasantness"] that penetrated my whole body." In other passages, he is even more explicit.

In his description of this later ecstasy, he likewise analyzes in detail the condition necessary for its appearance, that is, mental concentration upon a single object. He relates how he found himself submerged in the ecstasy shortly preceding drowsiness or immediately after awakening; for half an hour or an hour, it sufficed to open or close his eyes to escape that ecstatic state or to prolong it. He then understands that this ecstatic state is evoked by the concentration of his love on Jesus Christ and that "the moment I attached myself to another object of love, I was immediately diverted from my way; so that all my self-love or all love incapable of concentration withdrew me from the ecstasy, and I felt within me a kind of slight chill, like a shiver that accompanies nausea."

This brief outline of the states of ecstasy reported in the *Journal of Dreams* allows us to undertake, without much discussion, an examination of the crises of which the journal gives a glimpse.

The focal point around which this phase of Swedenborg's life and meditations revolves is, naturally, the mystic union of man with the divine. Despite all his efforts, he feels himself "so profoundly apart from God [that I am] unable as yet to think of him in such a living manner" (*Journal of Dreams* §164). The obstacles in the way of this union are in part the same as those he indicated in the *Economy of the Animal Kingdom*, particularly the constant struggle the inner man has to sustain against the external man. These are the drives of the *animus* and temptations of the senses that prevent the *anima* from shedding its light. Swedenborg believes he has observed "that in each of our thoughts, even in those we consider the purest, an infinity of sin and filth intrudes, just as in every desire emanating from our body where they are so deeply rooted." And he has likewise experienced "that the whole of the will with which we are endowed, a will governed by the body and giving birth to thought, is the enemy of the spirit. . . . The reason why: a continual battle is waged; and we are in no way able to unite with the spirit, but the spirit unites with us by grace. For we are as dead to all that is good, being our own masters only with regard to evil" (*Journal of Dreams* §110).

As we see, Swedenborg here emphasizes still more categorically than in the *Economy of the Animal Kingdom* the negative character of our free will, which can assert itself positively only with regard to sin. More than ever Swedenborg, during this religious crisis, has a clear awareness of his own powerlessness to save himself by his own strength and of the necessity of divine grace. The distance that here separates him from his previous conceptions appears, perhaps, with the greatest clarity in those passages of his journal where he comes closest to the reasonings of his earlier philosophy. Thus, he relates, for example, having struggled in vain one day against the thoughts that take hold of his spirit against his will and escape his control. He then understands that the grace of God alone can save him from these thoughts.

> I can compare it to two scales of a balance, in the one of which is our own will and perverse nature; in the other, God's power, which our Lord so places in temptation that he sometimes lets it come to an equilibrium, but so soon as ever it will weigh down one side, he helps it up. So I have found it, to speak in ordinary language. From this it follows that our power that presses down that scale is little, and that it rather opposes than assists the power of the spirit; and thus it is only our Lord's work, which he disposes. (*Journal of Dreams* §66)

Swedenborg himself observes that he resumes here his old conception of the *Economy of the Animal Kingdom* and adds (*Journal of Dreams* §67): "I felt that many things appeared in my thoughts which had been previously inspired and recognized as the truths of the

Word of God; that there exists in us neither the least word nor the least thought which God does not know and for which we are responsible if we do not have God's grace." And he concludes that, in this state, the only recourse that remains to us is, fully aware of our own unworthiness, to pray God to grant us his grace and to glorify us.

Certainly, the difference between this passage and that in the *Economy of the Animal Kingdom* to which Swedenborg makes special allusion is rather marked. In the latter, he expresses the conviction that, despite the limitation of his free will, human beings can and should take the initiative in investigating the area of divine grace. The will of God could not be made to operate otherwise than through our own will. Here, on the contrary, it seems to him, as it does to most of the mystics, that our own will constitutes only an obstacle to our salvation. We should seek to annihilate it completely and to abandon ourselves in a completely passive manner to the divine force that tends to raise us up. This reasoning, which we have at times glimpsed in his mind, acquires its most complete form at the actual moment of crisis. He considers that "Christ should be all in all, or God through Christ; so that we cannot ourselves do the very least; still less strive; for it is best to give oneself up in surrender at discretion: and still further, could a man therein be quite passive, it were the most perfect" (*Journal of Dreams* §266).

But it is not merely important for Swedenborg to annihilate his will in order to obtain divine grace. Reason itself constitutes an obstacle to the achievement of "strong faith." When Swedenborg plunges into reading the Bible or when he attends a service, he notes that his thoughts, even if they are "confirmatory," project a disturbance into his spirit and "open the way to contrary thoughts one is helpless to reject." The true faith, which one acquires only by grace, is the "faith without reason." It differs from and surpasses reason. "It is the *pura fides*: the other faith remains impure as long as it is mixed with reason: reason must be subjected to faith and one consequently should believe that He, who is God and is everywhere, expresses the truth itself" (*Journal of Dreams* §152). As we shall see later, this is the concept that is to lead Swedenborg to abandon his philosophical scientific works in order to give himself entirely to the religious apostolate.

We have outlined above the reasoning and the spiritual states that in a way comprise the leitmotif of Swedenborg's religious crises. These are in the main identical to those met with in the majority of mystics in the corresponding critical phases of their lives. It is to this reasoning and to these states that the psychic occurrences he records in his *Journal of Dreams* are related.

The most important of these occurrences is undoubtedly his grand vision of Christ at Easter 1744. That is the first call from God. To a certain degree it presages the great vision of 1745, following which Swedenborg will definitely renounce his scientific career to consecrate himself exclusively to his religious mission.

It is clear that, during the days preceding the Easter holiday, Swedenborg found himself in a state of particularly marked nervous hypertension. He had been warned by a dream that, if he took flight, he would be subjected to severe punishment on Maundy Thursday [§33]. He had also been seized by a violent fit of weeping, lamenting that he had not loved God and, on the contrary, had offended him when God wished to show Swedenborg the ways to the kingdom of grace [§36]. On Easter day, he continues to be the prey of the "anguish of the reprobate" which is translated into an excess of "trembling." Having taken communion, he feels a bit calmer in the certainty that his sins are forgiven, but he is no less assailed by temptations; deprived of confidence and love, he feels incapable of controlling his "fugitive" thoughts [§39]. During the night, temptation appears in the person of Erland Broman (a famous bon vivant, a favorite of King Frederick I, whom he served as a go-between for "the minor diversions"). On awakening, Swedenborg has the impression of having been delivered "by the intervention of Christ and the action of the Holy Spirit" [§42]. Going back to sleep, he feels himself subject of a sort of purification during which he is "enveloped by wonderful and indescribable circumvolutions . . . of which I know not how to speak, being a series of mystical action" [§43]. On reawakening, he is plunged into the ecstasy described above, an ecstasy that is maintained during the whole day, culminating in a spiritual calm [§44].

Toward the evening of the same day, nevertheless, he is subjected to "a new temptation." He has just read in the Bible "the miracles accomplished by God through Moses." He observes that his reason participates in this reading and that he lacks "the mutable faith which should be mine." Involuntarily he asks himself a series of questions: "Why did Moses appeal to the wind when the grasshoppers teemed; why did he harden the Pharaoh; why did he not act immediately and many other questions" [§49]. To be sure, he smiles to himself at these questions, but he nonetheless recognizes that they trouble him and that his "faith was not firm. . . . I looked into the fire, saying to myself that I should not believe that it existed, being the testimony of the senses more deceitful than the Work of God, the *ipsa veritas* which is proper to believe rather than trust in oneself" [§50]. After these thoughts, he smiled to the tempter. We quote the sequel of his relation *in extenso:*

> At ten o'clock I went to bed and felt a little better. Half an hour after, I heard a noise under my head. I thought that the tempter was then going away. Straightway there came over me a shuddering, so strong from the head downwards and over the whole body, with a noise of thunder, and this happened several times. I found that something holy was upon me.
>
> I then fell into a sleep; and at about 12:00, 1:00, or 2:00 in the night, there came over me a strong shuddering from head to foot, with a thundering noise as if many winds beat together, which shook me; it was indescribable and prostrated me on my face. Then at the time I was prostrated, at that very moment, I was wide awake, and saw that I was cast down.
>
> Wondered what it meant. And I spoke as if I were awake; but found nevertheless that the words were put into my mouth. "And oh! Almighty Jesus Christ, that thou, of thy so great mercy, deignest to come to so great a sinner. Make me worthy of thy grace." I held my hands together hard.
>
> Straightaway thereupon, I continued my prayer, and said, "Thou hast promised to take to grace all sinners; thou canst nothing else than keep thy word." At that same moment, I sat in his bosom, and saw him face to face; it was a face of holy mien, and in all it was indescribable, and he smiled so that I believe that his face had indeed been like this when he lived on earth. He spoke to me and asked if I had a clear bill of health. I

> answered, "Lord, thou knowest better than I." "Well, do so," said he; that is, as I found it in my mind to signify; love me in reality; or do what thou hast promised. God give me grace thereto; I found that it was not in my power. Wakened, with shudderings. (*Journal of Dreams* §§51–54)

Not long afterward Swedenborg finds himself "again in a state that was neither sleep nor awake." He reflected on what he had just experienced; for a few moments he doubts that it was truly the Son of God who has thus appeared and come down to him. He nevertheless concludes that his vision is real and "asked forgiveness for having so long doubted and for having asked a miracle, a thought it was not proper for me to have" [§56]

Since this apparition is the earliest of Swedenborg's grand visions, which in a certain sense has a decisive influence on his life, it warrants brief pause.

We note that, as in the first vision, here it is a matter of wakefulness or partial wakefulness, and not, as Tafel appears to believe, a dream.[147] In that case, there would have been nothing extraordinary, and the experience would surely not have had such a great influence on Swedenborg's later development. He himself declares that, at the moment of prostration, he was "wide awake," and it is evident that he is in full awareness when Christ appears to him. The reflection and prayers that follow the apparition likewise suppose a conscious state, even though Swedenborg himself states that he found himself "neither asleep not awake." It is noteworthy too that this vision is obviously produced at the very moment of awakening. During his sleep, Swedenborg perceives a loud noise; he awakens trembling and finds himself prostrate in his bed. With a feeling of inexplicable anguish, he prays to Christ, in a purely automatic manner, to appear to him. It is then that he perceives the first apparition, the sensation of a hand strongly pressing his clasped hands.

In the light of research undertaken during the course of the last twenty or thirty years on the mystic states of soul, it does not seem to me impossible to analyze the above vision somewhat more closely. It obviously has its origin in the "feeling of presence" that has given rise to so many visions. I shall here follow the description of this feeling and of intellectual vision emanating therefrom given by Delacroix in his *Études d'histoire et de psychologie du mysticisme,* where he gathers results discovered by psychiatrists and religious psychologists in their studies of this phenomenon.[148]

This "feeling of presence" is frequently observed on awakening: most of us have certainly experienced it in attenuated form. It consists of awakening with a start and imagining there is someone in the room. Delacroix supposes that these brusque and anguished awakenings are often influenced by a dream or nightmare that has already been forgotten at the moment of awakening. From the very fact that the subject finds himself "at the transition point between dream and the awakening, his mental control is partially suspended and he is easily led to give his emotion a defined subject."[149] This objectification is naturally more marked in subjects with hallucinatory tendencies. Delacroix cites several cases drawn from his own practice, in which this feeling of presence produces a veritable dialogue between the subject and the invisible spirit whose presence he senses.

As Delacroix justly claims, the question becomes more complex when dealing with mystics. Among these, the sensing of presence is manifested by an object in the form of a determined personality: Jesus Christ, demons, angels, all personalities with whom they have not had previously any direct acquaintance. One seeks to explain this phenomenon as the hallucinatory reproduction of a group of emotions conceived by the subject as likely to accompany the presence of the respective being. In the case Delacroix deals with here, especially the first Christ vision of St. Teresa (which at many points resembles that of Swedenborg), the subject has long sought to picture to herself the emotion she would experience if she found herself face to face with the Savior. Tormented by doubt, St. Teresa has for a long time begged Jesus Christ to grant a confirmation of her faith. And in the course of prayer, of mystic crisis, a form of ecstasy where words come automatically to the mouth of the person speaking, we see reproduced the entire emotional content that the saint has for so long cherished in her heart: "the impression of objective presence." And St. Teresa has no difficulty in identifying the person of Jesus Christ.

All the above phases are again found in Swedenborg's vision. He also has been tormented by grave doubts, and it is only after the same night that he succeeds in freeing himself from the devil. While he waits impatiently to see his faith strengthened by a manifest revelation, he ardently appeals for an assurance of divine grace. The whole of Easter day, his partaking of communion, and his strange dream of "purification" by grace of the Holy Spirit awakens in him a kind of presentiment of occurrences that will be decisive. From his first awakening, when "the tempter" departs with loud noise, he believes he feels within him "something holy." When he awakens for the second time, feeling he has heard thunder, and finds himself lying in his bed, this sense of presence becomes naturally more intense. In the prayer, he pronounces, directly after his awakening, the words of which are put into his mouth. He already believes it is the Christ who comes to him, and he fervently begs to be made worthy of this great grace. So it is that the hallucination develops gradually: it is at first sensory (he feels a hand press his), then visual, and finally auditory, when in the course of a fervent prayer the apparition addresses him. The enigmatic and entirely unexpected form of these words confirms in his mind the reality of the vision. For Swedenborg, it is a new proof that it was Jesus Christ who has appeared to him.[150]

It is in the vision of that night that it is proper to seek the original of the religious meditation by which Swedenborg is besieged during the weeks that follow. It seems clear to him that he has been the object of a special divine grace because he has been permitted to see the Savior. And his mind does not cease from thinking that, after an experience of that nature, he might well be considered a saint. The following night he writes:

> When, as was often the case, I was in my thoughts about these very subjects, and anyone accounted me a holy man and on this account offered me dignity—as indeed it happens among certain simple people that they not only venerate but even adore some supposedly holy man as a saint—I then found that, in the earnestness which then possessed me, I desired to do him all the ill I could to the highest degree, in order that nothing at all of the sin should stick to him, and that with earnest prayers I ought to appease our Lord, in order that I might never have any part of so damning a sin to stick to me.

> For Christ, in whom all the Godhead is perfect, ought alone to be prayed to. (*Journal of Dreams* §§72–73)

From now on, Swedenborg deplores his vain efforts to recover the inspired state of the preceding night. "At times I could by no means get my thoughts to contemplate the Christ that I had seen for that short moment. The movement and the power of the spirit came to me, and I felt that I would rather go mad" (*Journal of Dreams* 65). He considers himself as "more unworthy than others and the greatest of sinners, as our Lord has permitted me to go deeper into certain things with my thoughts than many people" (*Journal of Dreams* §74). And when, the following day, he hears one of his table companions ask one of the others present "if one could be really melancholic when he had an abundance of money," he sadly smiles to himself. He believes he knows better than anyone else that the sadness and melancholy arising from the lack of all "means" could not be equal to the melancholy arising from inner torments.

From that instant, he begins to feel himself as an exceptional being, having experienced more than has been granted to any man. In a well-erased and almost illegible passage in his notes of the same date, he relates that he continues to move in his normal social circles without anyone being able to observe the least change in him. He also knows that he has become another person "not daring to say that so high grace has been vouchsafed me" [§80]. Indeed, he wonders what his friends would think if they were informed of his new state and, on the other hand, he fears that an announcement of his new state might inspire "a love of self" in him. His designation as an instrument of God has happened so suddenly and under such unexpected circumstances that he has some difficulty imagining the reality of his mission. "I found no better comparison for myself than when a peasant is raised to power as a chief or king and can command all that his heart desired; but who yet had something in him that caused him to wish to learn that of which he himself knew nothing" (*Journal of Dreams* §81).

Swedenborg dedicated the following days to the reading of the "confession of sins, prayer, and fasting." He awaits a new appearance of Jesus Christ. Now and then, he believes that he is close to his goal.

On the night of April 10–11 he feels himself to be fully awake, "seized by an irresistible desire to prostrate himself, to clasp his hands and beg mercy for his unworthiness." He then notes that he is in a state of ecstasy but, being fully awake, he has no vision (*Journal of Dreams* §99). And when, on the following night, "thoughts come to him about his excess of dignity in his relations with others," he begs with clasped hands to be delivered from them; moreover, his prayer is heard.

A few nights later he is prey to "double thoughts" and experiences violent temptation. "Through the grace of the Spirit, I was brought to fasten my thoughts on a tree, then upon Christ's cross and on Christ crucified. As often as I did this, the other thoughts as of themselves fell flat. I pressed with the same thought so forcibly that I seemed with the cross to press down the tempter and drive him away" (*Journal of Dreams* §§121–122). He asks God for the grace to constantly behold his crucified Savior before his eyes, "for I dared by no means look upon my Jesus, him that I have seen; for I am an unworthy sinner; but rather I ought to fall upon my face; and Jesus it is that takes me up to look upon him; for thus I am enabled to look upon Christ crucified" (*Journal of Dreams* §122). From this exposition, it is clear that here it is not a case of a hallucinatory phenomenon, but an imaginative image evoked voluntarily, which ends in acquiring such intensity that Swedenborg truly believes that he is seeing in spirit the crucified one himself.

This ecstatic cult of the crucifix, of a nearly Catholic ardor, nevertheless appeared presumptuous and sinful to Swedenborg the next day. His father appeared to him in a dream, his face reflecting anger, saying, "'You are creating alarm, Emanuel.' . . . It meant that yesterday I had made too bold a use of Christ's cross." Nevertheless, on awakening, he again has before his eyes "the crucifixion and cross of Jesus." A little later, however, the resemblance of these phenomena with the Catholic worship of the cross enters his mind. In thought, he has "embraced Christ on the cross. Then I kissed his feet and afterwards removed myself away; then falling upon my knees I prayed to him crucified." And it occurs to him "that I could have the same thing before the eyes of my body in an image; but I found was far from right and was a great sin" (*Journal of Dreams* §128).

How much he has changed since his great Christ vision becomes progressively more clear to him. His external man ends by being conquered by his internal man. In his dream the following night, he hears the two words "*Nicolaus Nicolai*" pronounced. "I do not know," he says, " if that is my new name."

During the Easter holidays, he has the feeling of a fragmentation of personality. He is astonished to be able to have "two entirely different thoughts at the same time." This separation has now occurred. "The most remarkable thing was this: that I now represented the inner man and was as another person than myself, so that I made salutation to my own thoughts, frightening them; saluted my own stores of memory; accused another person; which shows that the change has come. I represent one who is against another; that is to say, the inner man, for I have prayed God that I in no wise may be mine but that God may be pleased to let me be his" (*Journal of Dreams* §133). And he adds, "This has now lasted for twenty-one days."

From then on, all his efforts are to free himself from the external man, that is from his own personality, in order to become an instrument entirely in the hands of God. He constantly prays God to make him his and to withdraw him from his selfhood. With equal fervor he asks for that "all-powerful" faith, "without reasonings." But he is not yet convinced that this new personality will be compatible with the scientific researches that have hitherto occupied him. At times, he is disposed to believe that this is the case. In one of his visions he is reminded that King Charles XII, after having suffered an initial repulse by Saxons, won the battle in a second engagement, "which signifies that with God's grace I have won the fight, and that Jesus' blood and merits helped me, and that I in my studies shall win in the end" (*Journal of Dreams* §156). The next day, after having dreamed of returning to Sweden, in an attack of discouragement, he composes himself "and found that I am come to do the best of all and to promote God's honor; got the talent; all helped thereto. The Spirit was with me from youth to this end" (*Journal of Dreams* §164).

But, from the days that follow, he feels warranted in concluding from his visions that the will of God is "that I ought to employ my remaining time upon matters that are higher; and not to write upon worldly themes any more, themes which are comparatively very low;

but upon that which regards the very center of all, and indeed, Christ. God be so gracious and enlighten me further about what my duty is; for I am still in some darkness as to whither I should turn" (*Journal of Dreams* §185). The preceding night it appeared to him "in a certain way that I ought not to contaminate myself with other books which concern theological and similar propositions; for this I have in God's Word and from the Holy Spirit" (*Journal of Dreams* §180). Now he seems to imagine that it is the will of God that he publish the work he has undertaken and with regard to which it has been revealed to him that "he will obtain approval," but he thinks that he should undertake another work of an entirely different nature later. He learns that his "speculation should turn *ad priora* which were formerly *in posterioribus*" (*Journal of Dreams* §195). By this somewhat obscure formula, Swedenborg understands without any doubt that God will henceforth grant him the faculty of attaining knowledge *a priori,* a faculty that he considers in his previous works as having been lost to humanity after the Fall and was reserved to angels. In a note from the same day, he likewise relates that he has learned from a dream that he ought to refrain from eating and drinking too much, "for such is the life of pigs, which is forbidden by Paul." He should live like a "*novus homo in Christo.*"

It is in this strange state of exaltation that Swedenborg arrives in England in the month of May. Very soon after his arrival, he seems to be in contact with the Moravian Bretheren, whose services he attends in Fetter Lane. From his first visit, he declares that they call themselves "true Lutherans and recognize the work of the Hold Ghost, as they tell each other, and only regard God's grace and Christ's blood and merits and simply go to work." He relates also that their church had been "represented" to him three months previously (*Journal of Dreams* §202).

That the "religion of the heart" of Zinzendorf, with its aversion to any metaphysical subtleties and its concentration on the inner life in Christ, had had, precisely at that time, certain elements in common with the religiosity of Swedenborg is easy to understand; moreover, it is clear from the above quotation. "One has to raise the cross of God before people, thus arousing in them a vision of the splendor of God's majesty"[151] was one of Zinzendorf's foremost rules of life.

Swedenborg adds, however, that "I shall no doubt be denied permission to fraternize with them." And five months later he finds "that he is not received there." The terms of Swedenborg's journal do not permit us to conclude with certainty whether it is a result of external circumstances or by instruction from God that he refrains from his manifest intention of joining the Moravian church. The latter of these alternatives is probably the case.

I have been unable to find in Swedenborg's later theology the slightest trace of his brief relations with the Moravian Brethren. This love of Christ, strongly colored by Catholicism, which characterizes the state of Swedenborg's soul during this period of crisis, disappears later on so completely that there barely remains any place in his theological system for the historical figure of Jesus Christ. At most points, he later finds himself in unmitigated conflict with Zinzendorf's teachings, whose Christocentric doctrine and exegetic liberalism are to hold a special antipathy for him. Of all the contemporary sects, it is the Moravian that is the most criticized in Swedenborg's later works. As a result of the aversion he showed to Zinzendorf and his followers, Swedenborg was the object of a marked antipathy among the Brethren, both in Sweden and abroad.

Due to the aversion the Moravians showed him, Swedenborg's biographers have tried to explain the rumors of insanity that finally reached Sweden. These gained such intensity that, according to one of his contemporaries,[152] there might have been a serious question of having Swedenborg declared "mentally disturbed as a result of religious dreams" by the Diet of 1769. One can establish with certitude the origin of these rumors in Swedenborg's sojourn in London during his period of crisis. The author could well be the Moravian Brother Brockmer, who was Swedenborg's landlord for some time.

It is absolutely impossible, however, to determine the historical accuracy of his declarations, which were largely transmitted second-hand, and are contradictory besides.[153] In brief, they are substantially that Swedenborg had displayed most eccentric behavior; proclaimed himself the Savior come to be crucified by the Jews; stripped himself in the marketplace and rolled in the mud; was given to strange rites of washing of feet; and suffered fits of delirium.

A careful and competent analysis of Swedenborg's journal would no doubt disentangle what truth there might be in these pieces of information. It would also perhaps throw light on the psychic crisis Swedenborg experienced at that time.[154] But it is not possible for me personally to pronounce on the matter, and the experts have reached contradictory conclusions in their attempts to establish a rather imprecise diagnosis of psychosis, so I can only pass over these problems as unresolved.[155] From the information we can extract from his journal, it does not appear that Swedenborg's psychic or physical condition had undergone any notable modification during the preceding months. He stayed in England to work all summer long on his *Animal Kingdom*, the first two parts of which appeared at The Hague, and the third part of which was printed in London in the spring of 1745. A large part of his dreams continue to relate to his scientific occupations and are supplemented by the brief notes or allusions in the works published at this time.

His religious crisis appears to follow a more or less uniform development. He continues to complain that "his body rebels unceasingly." He is exposed to the same temptations as before and aspires to return to the state "in which Christ accords his divine grace." What appears to be lacking above all is the true spirit of childlike innocence. In various manifestations, God has taught him that "one must be like a child before the Lord" and that God will grant everything he needs, both profane and spiritual, "from the moment when, like a child, I entrust all my cares to him" (*Journal of Dreams* §222). One night, he dreams that he finds himself in "the kingdom of innocence." He sees below him "the loveliest garden that could be seen. On every tree white roses were set in succession. Went afterwards into a long room. There were beautiful white dishes with milk and bread in them, so appetizing that nothing more appetizing could be imagined." He meets there "a lovely innocent child" who seemed to him "innocence itself" (*Journal of Dreams* §257). Only then does he understand that he can directly receive all knowledge of God, "having now reached the state of understanding that I know nothing, that all *praeconcepta judicia* [prejudices] have been taken from me, which is the beginning of learning to know that one must first become as a child and then be nursed into knowledge as is now taking place with me" (*Journal of Dreams* §267).

However, what predominates in the latter part of the journal is the question of whether Swedenborg should abandon his scientific labors. As we have seen, during the earliest stages of this crisis, he has already shown some intention of abandoning science altogether, because it attracted him to the world and led him into complacency. He now reproaches himself as before for having felt vanity in his work in the eyes of his contemporaries (*Journal of Dreams* §231). His dreams and visions evidently do not enable him to be certain of God's will in this respect; it seems to him at times that they are encouraging him to pursue his researches. Thus, during the night of September 29–30, he sees an apparition that confirms for him that what "with God's help, I have written lately about forms is such that it shall carry me on still further to that which is still more glorious" (*Journal of Dreams* §244). But he becomes aware several nights later that this has been inspired by evil spirits.

Nevertheless, during the night of October 6 or 7, he receives an indication of the road he should follow. He understands that "all love of anything whatever, for instance, to my works I have in had, when one loves them and not as a medium to the only love that is to God and Jesus Christ, is a meretricious love." At the same time, he receives a revelation of a divine book which has the mission to write: "Otherwise, it is something told me about my book. One said that it was a divine book on the worship and love of God (*Liber divinus de Dei cultu et amore*). I believe it was also something about spirits. I believed I had something about this in my book *De Infinito*. But, to this, no answer was made" (*Journal of Dreams* §250).

It is naturally the supreme sacrifice for Swedenborg to thus abandon, after so many years, the work he hoped to bring to a grand conclusion, and it is evident how that thought tortures him. Some nights afterward in a dream, he believes he is being punished for having been "busy with my work, which is quite different from the other and quite another love if it should prevail, and is not to be regarded as a matter of words or as a plaything in regard to the other." And upon awakening, he resolved to abandon this work. But he goes back to sleep and has a new dream that relates precisely to the chapter in

Animal Kingdom that he is in the course of writing. "By this, I was strengthened in continuing my work. God grant that it be not against His good pleasure" (*Journal of Dreams* §262–263).

The night of October 26–27, when he speaks in a dream with Jesus Christ, he learns that he should begin, on the following day, the new divine book regarding which he has already had a revelation. He is told that he "should not occupy himself with other affairs than my own. . . . May God guide me in the right way. Christ said that I should undertake nothing without Him" (*Journal of Dreams* §278).

That night ends in a *deliquium* of the same nature as the one he had experienced seven years previously in Amsterdam, when he began work on the *Economy of the Animal Kingdom* (see above, chapter three), "but much more subtle, so that I appeared to be near death." Like its predecessor, this phenomenon signifies for him "that my head is actually swept and cleansed from that which would hinder these thoughts." The "penetration" that he has just acquired is also reflected by the fact that "I seemed to write a fine hand" (*Journal of Dreams* §262).

Swedenborg's entries end here.

He then believes he has attained the goal, pursued consciously or unconsciously during that whole crisis, of killing his selfhood and abandoning himself as a passive instrument in the hands of God. He believes he has renounced, not only his scientific preoccupations and his scientific ambitions, but all his knowledge as well, to become a child again, in order that divine light might suffuse his soul without hindrance. He has attained the most inaccessible of objects, "unreasoning faith." And this change also appears to him in certain external signs. In the entry for October 9, he relates that he has become so sharp-sighted that he is able to read the small-print Bible without the least difficulty" (*Journal of Dreams* §260). Several days later he is informed in a dream that "for the last fourteen days my appearance has been growing much handsomer, and to be like that of an angel" (*Journal of Dreams* §268).

It is also toward the end of this crisis that Swedenborg finds the explanation for why the apparitions and visions he has experienced have at times seemed contradictory. In an entry spanning several days (October 3–6) he declares, "Several times I have remarked that there are spirits of all descriptions. The one spirit which is Christ's is the only spirit which has all blessedness with it. By the others man is enticed in a thousand ways to go with them; but unhappy is he that does so. . . . Therefore, it is necessary to distinguish the spirits, which is a thing man cannot do except through Christ Himself and His Spirit."

It is evident from the very form of the above entry that Swedenborg is here alluding to the well-known exhortation to distinguish between spirits based on the idea, found in primitive Christianity,[156] that demons can act upon man under forms resembling, and mistaken for, the spirit of God: "Beloved, do not believe every spirit, but test the spirits to see whether they are from God, for many false prophets have come into the world. By this you know the spirit of God: every spirit which confesses that Jesus Christ has come in the flesh is of God, and every spirit which does not confess Jesus is not of God. This is the spirit of antichrist, of which you heard that it was coming, and now it is in the world already" (1 John 4:1–3).

The primary origin of Swedenborg's experience of the existence of different kinds of spirits appears to have been a "representation" of which he was the object during a midday nap on October 3. The entry recording this (*Journal of Dreams* §246) is rather difficult to interpret because several words have been omitted, but it is to the effect that our thoughts, in themselves, "bear within them no other end and reason than that which comes into them from the Spirit of God (*spiritu Dei),* or the spirit of the body *(spiritu corporis*). If from the body, then all is sin from the innermost; for we aim after nothing else than that which strives against the spiritual." And Swedenborg adds: "Which rules we ourselves may observe if we reflect from our loves, which, in fact, accompany [us]."

It is clear that these are the loves dominated either by the "Spirit of God" or by the "spirit of the body" which, in Swedenborg's mind, appear to be provoked by spirits. We find direct confirmation of this in the journal entry dated October 6–7 (*Journal of Dreams* §252), where it is said, "From this and the foregoing we find how soon and how easily a human being is deceived by other spirits, which represent themselves according to the love of each and every person, for loves are represented by spirits, indeed, in fact, by women" (the text ends here).

This reasoning is later developed in *The Worship and Love of God*, which dates from that crisis. Human beings are subjected to two contrary influences, one emanating from God and the other from the Prince of the World: one, love of supreme good, the other, love for the greatest evil. Celestial beings, *amores* or "loves," act by way of the *anima*, while the genii of evil, our sensual passions, reach the *anima* by way of the body. Everyone has an infinitude of loves within him- or herself. But by reason of their very number, they escape our control, and each of them can disguise itself as the supreme love; in other words, we can be led to grant supremacy to a love that is sensual by nature and belongs to the *animus* (*The Worship and Love of God* §68).

During Swedenborg's theosophical years, this conception was, as we know, elevated to the rank of a perfectly characterized doctrine of spirits. Humanity is not led directly by God, but by angels and spirits. Every person is associated with two heavenly and two infernal spirits, who exercise their influence on all his or her thoughts and feelings. Every temptation emanates from spirits in matters of faith and from genii in manifestations of will. The spirits externalize themselves in visible form, but genii manifest themselves only by the influence they exert on the desires and passions of the individual. And this action is exercised so secretly and in such a malicious fashion that the person cannot imagine it is from them that temptations come, and believes that he or she is acting spontaneously (cf. *Arcana Coelestia* §751, §5035ff.)

I have already pointed out several times how much Swedenborg's system, with its dualism between divine and worldly influences, between the internal and external person, was apt to provoke a demonological development of this nature. Well before his crisis, he believed in the influence of supersensory beings on a person's will (see chapter two above). This belief finds fresh confirmation in the visions he has during the period of the *Journal of Dreams*. He himself has felt that the devil has penetrated to the very core of his being, seeking to lead him into temptation and that he has rejected it by the intervention of the Christ. Faced by the contradictions that he has observed in his visions, he ends by formulating certain suspicions; he feels he is the prey of malicious spirits who disguise themselves in an effort to appear in his eyes as the very spirit of Jesus Christ, the only true love.

We have noted that in the unfortunately truncated passages of his journal where he declares that the angels intervene in our "*amores*," Swedenborg comes to speak of women. It is clear that he interprets these feminine forms, which appear to him in the erotic dreams that are so frequent in his journal, as apparitions of angels and spirits. In the first woman who appears to him in dreams (*Journal of Dreams* §17), he believes he recognizes his "guardian angel."

One can scarcely avoid seeing the psychological cause of these ever more erotic dreams in which amorous relations with various women appear to him. In the introduction to his journal, Swedenborg informs us himself that his "liking for women" which up to that time had been his "dominant passion," had suddenly disappeared. To judge by the journal entries, it appears that he may have been restrained by a kind of asceticism.[157] For during the dream the subdued instincts regain their ascendancy with a violence which, in a man approaching his sixtieth year, suggests more than ordinary sexuality. A. Lehmann, the well-known psychologist, has even concluded from this that Swedenborg's nervous system was "thrown into complete confusion by sexual excesses."[158]

I have no competence to decide if Swedenborg's notes, by themselves alone, warrant a hypothesis of this nature. It is, nevertheless, at variance with all that we know of his private life and personality. However that may be, it is evident that the sexual factor after that time plays a considerable role in his imagined religious environment. I shall limit myself, in this respect, to recalling the descriptions he gives on several occasions of the state of supreme ecstatic bliss, which he identifies with erotic intoxication.

It is not correct, however, as Lehmann and other biographers attempt to do, to emphasize the abnormal nature of Swedenborg's sexuality and represent him as a kind of St. Anthony who by ardent prayer sought to free himself from the feminine apparitions that pursue him in his dreams. On the contrary, he welcomes the apparitions with the same satisfaction as his erotic ecstasies. Physical love appears to him, then and later, as something heavenly, as a stage leading to the supreme love, the love of God. At the close of one of his most detailed descriptions of his erotic dreams, he notes in his journal for April 23–24 (*Journal of Dreams* §174): "This denotes the uttermost love for the holy; for all love has its origin therefrom; is a series; in the body, it consists in its actuality in the projection of the semen (*projectione seminis*)." Nevertheless, he decides not to reveal this dream to anyone "for, in the minds of the world it is impure, though pure in itself."

It follows that the feminine figures he meets in his dreams are often, for him, heavenly appearances. They represent "objects of knowledge," "wisdom," "truth," "piety," etc. His sexual relations with the apparitions express his love of wisdom and so on. At times (for example, in the entry for April 28–29), he dreams that he moves away from a woman who has slipped into his bed. She then symbolizes his profane activities as an author, which he ought to abandon for more elevated matters (*Journal of Dreams* §185). As we see, he regards the women perceived in dreams as the spirits of various essences; because of the frequency with which they recur in his journal, it is not impossible that they may have inspired his first notion of the doctrine of spirits. We observe likewise, that in *The Worship and Love of God*, he envisages Adam as being in relations with spirits in the forms of women. Even during his theosophical period, Swedenborg interprets the visions of nude women as signs of love for spiritual objects (cf. *Spiritual Diary* §3856). In his biblical exegesis, the term *woman* signifies "propensities for truth" (*affectiones veri).*

The brief description I have just given of the *Journal of Dreams* has perhaps not made the role of the system of correspondences in this context sufficiently evident. Most of the dreams or visions that Swedenborg records assume a symbolic form and have to be reinterpreted by him to attain the nature of divine apparitions. Tafel has explained at length that these new interpretations almost always accord with those found later in his biblical exegesis and in his *Spiritual Diary*.[159] The visionary period thus becomes a preparatory school for the later supernatural relations and for Swedenborg's biblical exegesis.

The sudden interruption of the *Journal of Dreams* does not allow us to follow Swedenborg's internal evolution during this period of crisis to the end. We learn only by secondhand accounts of the grand vision that was the decisive confirmation of the mission God commanded him to fulfill.

The most detailed description is that provided by Carl Robsahm, a bank manager, who collected in his memoirs a number of interesting notes on his relations with Swedenborg during the last years of the latter's life.[160] He claims to reproduce textually what Swedenborg himself revealed to him about his vision. One day, Robsahm tells us, he demanded of him "where and how it had been given to him to see and to hear what takes place in the world of spirits, in heaven and in hell." Swedenborg replied:

> I was in London and dined rather late at an inn where I was in the habit of dining, and where I had my own room. My thoughts were engaged on the subjects we have been discussing. I was hungry and ate with a good appetite. Towards the close of the meal I noticed a sort of dimness before my eyes; this became denser, and I then saw the floor covered with the most horrid crawling reptiles, such as snakes, frogs, and similar creatures. I was amazed; for I was perfectly conscious, and my thoughts were clear. At last the darkness increased still more; but it disappeared all at once, and I then saw a man sitting in a corner of the room. As I was then alone, I was very much frightened at his words, for he said: "Eat not so much." All became black again before my eyes, but immediately it cleared away, and I found myself alone in the room.
>
> Such an unexpected terror hastened my return home; I did not let the landlord notice anything; but I considered well what had happened, and could not look upon it as a matter of mere chance, or as if it had been produced by a physical cause.
>
> I went home; and during the night the same man revealed himself to me again, but I was not frightened now. He then said that He was the Lord God, the Creator and Redeemer of the world, and that He had chosen me to explain to men the spiritual sense of Scripture; and that He himself would explain to me what I should write on this subject. That same night were also opened to me, so that I became thoroughly convinced of their reality, the world of spirits, heaven, and hell, and I recognized there many acquaintances from many conditions of life. From that day I gave up the study of all worldly science, and labored

> in spiritual things, according as the Lord had commanded me to write. Afterwards the Lord opened, daily very often, my bodily eyes so that in the middle of the day I could see into the other world and in a state of perfect wakefulness converse with angels and spirits.

A letter addressed by Gabriel Beyer to C.F. Nordenskjöld on March 25, 1776, adds some details to Robsahm's description of the second appearance by God on the same night. Beyer writes:

> The account of the personal appearance of God to Assessor Swedenborg, who saw him clad in purple and bathed in a majestic clarity, seated near the bed while he assigned his mission to Assessor Swedenborg, was made to me by the latter himself, and during a luncheon at the home of Dr. Rosen, where I saw the old man for the first time. I recall asking him how long the vision lasted to which he replied, "about a quarter of an hour"; and asked also if that brilliant light had not hurt his eyes, to which he answered in the negative.[161]

Swedenborg's first great biblical commentary (*Adversaria* IV, §§1956–1957) alludes to the same occasion, as Tafel indicates.[162] In his exegesis of Exodus 8, where God subjects Egypt to an invasion of frogs, Swedenborg states that these represent the most impure spirits who rule the lowest in man and arouse the lusts of the body and blood, particularly the voluptuosity of taste. They are of different aspects:

> creatures of this sort appeared to me one day arising [from myself] and thus so distinctly that I saw them crawling before my eyes. They suddenly compacted together and turned into flames, collapsing with a crackling that sounded in my ears like the noise of their explosion. After which the area appeared cleansed. This happened to me in London in April 1745. A kind of fog exuded from my pores, and the floor was covered by a multitude of crawling reptiles.

This notation, manifestly referring to the great vision, allows us first to fix the date of April 1745 with certainty. It was also at that time when Swedenborg reports the opening of his "spiritual sight."[163]

But this also adds considerable interest to an another viewpoint. It clarifies the quite confused relations in Robsahm's account between the vision of crawling things on the floor and the vision that orders Swedenborg not to eat so much. We now perceive much more clearly the agreement of this vision with the appearance of Jesus Christ that Swedenborg had experienced a year earlier. Here also the vision begins with the flight of the tempter with a loud noise. Herrlin seeks to explain in part the deep impression made on Swedenborg by this vision by the fact that it constitutes "his first true hallucination."[164]

It is naturally difficult to draw any solid conclusions from these secondhand accounts, but they seem to me to confirm Herrlin's view. Swedenborg insists that he was absolutely conscious and in full possession of his senses, although he usually relates in his journal that his visions occur in an intermediate state between sleep and wakefulness. He seems to locate the apparition in his external sense organs. Robsahm's account mentions Swedenborg's "bodily eyes," and the fact that Beyer asks if his eyes were not dazzled by the radiant apparition shows that Swedenborg had described his vision to them in analogous terms. What is even more remarkable is that Swedenborg sees the objects in their true spatial environment; the reptiles crawl over the floor, the human figure appears in a corner of the room. To these typical characteristics, which indicate that it is truly a matter of a psychosensory hallucination, is added the terror that the apparition provokes in Swedenborg. As I have already indicated, this powerful emotive reaction is characteristic of true hallucination, especially on its first occurrence.

It is precisely the clearly characterized nature of perception and the manifest reality of this vision that explains why Swedenborg found in it the definitive confirmation of his relations with a higher world and of his religious mission. The very words spoken by the apparition, however trivial they may have seemed to certain psychiatrists who have often made fun of them, were of a character appropriate to preparing him for the call that was to follow in the course of the nocturnal vision. We have already seen that Swedenborg had previously experienced visions that commanded him to "master" his appetite in order to live as a "new man in Christ." Like most visionaries, he considered asceticism as a necessary condition for all contacts with the world of spirits, and he adhered to a truly spartan simplicity during the rest of his life.

This vision, then, was for Swedenborg the external sign marking the end of the inner struggle within him. In a form that seemed to him to leave no room for doubt, he acquired a conviction about God's intentions for him. All the realms of the spirit were opened to his eyes. He learned that his mission would be henceforth to apply the internal sense of the biblical word and that God would help him in that attempt. And what is perhaps the most important is that he thereby renounced the exercise of "all worldly learning" in order to devote himself to labor *"in spiritualibus."* From that moment, he is certain of the way he will follow.

It is this final certitude that furnishes the theological period of Swedenborg, the last of his life, with its character of conscious calm and harmony. No doubt he is still the prey of temptations emanating from malicious spirits during this period, but these are transitory trials he feels are in order because he is the chosen instrument of God. The visions and apparitions continue, but they have entirely lost the ecstatic and violently emotional character that they had in his *Journal of Dreams*.

There is an infinite abyss between the calm narration Swedenborg gives of his tribulations in the world of spirits in his *Spiritual Diary*, in the *Arcana Coelestia,* and other works of his theological period, and the feverish descriptions in the *Journal of Dreams*. Doubt and anguish have given way to a serene faith and to its own dogmas, a faith that risks seeming to most of his readers all too categorical and sure of itself. The weak mystic at times seems transformed into an aggressive theologian who brandishes the bolts of anathema and condemnation in passionate polemic. At times when he seeks to guide his fellow man in the right way, he appears to forget the struggles he experienced during his own religious crisis. There is hardly place, in the account of his conversion and of his "new birth," for the factor that appeared essential to him during the period recorded in the *Journal of Dreams*: the complete renunciation of selfhood, aspiration toward an "unreasoning faith," the passive trust in the grace of God that banishes all care, since our own will impedes rather than contributes to salvation. From this view, deeply tinged with Quietism, he is to return to the doctrine, already expounded in the *Economy of the Animal Kingdom,* of the possibility—and obligation—for each person to contribute to the work of salvation by his or her own strength. Swedenborg's notion of "new birth" as a victory over sins and vices acquired by a slow and purposeful regeneration of character and by a virtuous life is in absolute contradiction with the situation that he describes in the *Journal of Dreams*: for here he reaches a stage where he continually awaits transformation into another man by a sudden influx of grace from God and where his ardent desire is to become an instrument of which God will make use at his good pleasure.

In reality, this development is quite explicable psychologically, and it has been observed by a good number of mystics. In his work, which I cited previously, Leuba regards it as characteristic of Christian mysticism and has confirmed its existence in St. Teresa, Tauler, Mme. Guyon, and others. He claims that the common trait of the great Christian mystics is not merely a tendency toward passive renunciation of selfhood, but also a tendency that seems directly antagonistic to the former—an expansive and practical drive toward a moral ideal. It is true that mystics seek to annihilate their own egos and isolate themselves from the external world. But these are tendencies that especially dominate in periods of crisis. For them, there is a need to combat the "natural" within themselves, in other words, to free themselves from physical needs and desires and therefore also from all the external impressions that threaten to distract them from the supreme goal they pursue: the mystic union with divinity. But once this goal is achieved, and from the day when they feel themselves to have become instruments of God and consider that they have finally killed their own "I," they have, in reality, resurrected it. Their isolation ceases and they rejoin social life with all their energy as reformers or religious organizers. The spiritual process they have undergone has killed all egocentric instincts and imbued them with altruistic tendencies. "*Passer de la volonté propre à la volonté divine signifie passer de la volonté particulière à la volonté collective*" (Passing from self-will to the divine will means passing from the individual will to the collective will).[165]

Leuba's psychological interpretation, only an extremely succinct account of which, regrettably, is all I am able to give here, appears to me applicable to Swedenborg point by point. I would even say that it applies perhaps better to Swedenborg than to any of the other mystics Leuba studied. For this practical and expansive aspect of mysticism was rightly and distinctively marked in the temperament of the great Swedish mystic. During his scientific period, there is not a single one of his works that fails to indicate in its introduction the practical end he pursues and that does not aim to provide a useful moral doctrine for humankind. Even in the moral crisis of the *Journal of Dreams,* one sees the dawn of a desire to let humanity know what he himself has experienced and to share with his kind the unshakable faith that fills his heart. And when he has surmounted his inner combat, it appears evident to him that he must consecrate the rest of his life to the religious apostolate.

It is only natural that, from the day he considers himself obliged to guide the world towards the way of the "new birth," Swedenborg should resort to the account of his own conversion. This conversion seemingly appeared to him in a different light after he had recovered his interior harmony. Besides, he hardly had any impulse to compare his own religious experiences with others like him. On the contrary, he never ceases to affirm that he has been a special object of divine grace. In his memoir, Robsahm relates that he asked him one day whether it were possible for anyone else to attain "the degree of spirituality" that he had acquired, to which Swedenborg replied, "Take care; that is a direct road to insanity: for when a man pores over spiritual and hidden things, he cannot protect himself against the delusions of hell." And he adds that he himself had never thought that he would reach "that spiritual state in which I am now."[166]

This is why he recommends to others the way of salvation that he considers the shortest and most practical: the path of conscious education of the will. His basic view remains the one he has inherited from his father and that he later defended in one of his works: to know that the essence of Christianity resides, not in the dogmas of faith, but in a pure life. That is, moreover, a conception that, despite his tentative steps toward a Quietist passivity, remained intact during the crisis itself. In one of his notes (*Journal of Dreams* §166) Swedenborg states he has noticed "that faith, in fact, consists in a sure confidence one gets from God, but yet consists in the work that one does in doing what is good to his neighbor, each according to his talent, and this more and more; and that one does it of faith that God so commanded and does not reason any further about it. . . . So therefore a faith without deeds is no right faith. A man must actually forsake himself." And during his great vision Christ responded to his ardent prayer for grace by saying, "Then do!" Already at the time, Swedenborg translated this as "Love me truly" or "Do what thou hast promised." Such is the true and positive love that is to become the focal point of all his subsequent teachings.

s e v e n

The Worship and Love of God

As we have seen, toward the end of his religious crisis as outlined in the preceding chapter, Swedenborg received a summons from God to renounce his lay writings and devote himself to "more elevated matters." He progressively came to feel that it was the will of God that he write a "divine book on the worship and love of God," in which he would take nothing of the "trumpery of others." He would adhere to his own inspiration, for God would show the right way.

He set himself to the realization of this divine command on October 27, 1744; and the following year, in London, he published the first two parts of his work. Of the third part, a few pages are preserved in galleys and some in manuscript.[167] The fact that this work remained incomplete is certainly connected with the great vision of April 1745, following which Swedenborg abandoned the "exercise of all worldly erudition" to dedicate himself exclusively to the explication of the inner sense of Scripture. When he mentions *The Worship and Love of God* in his first book—*Historia creationis a Mose tradita*—subsequent to the vision, he calls attention to the fact that this was written solely from his own reasoning and that it consequently merits credibility only in the parts that accord with the revelations of Holy Writ itself (*Adversaria* I, §7).

His *Worship and Love of God*, then, belongs to the interval between Swedenborg's scientific and theological periods, which, moreover, is clearly evident from the text. In this work, we find again, in a brief summary, the cosmology of the *Principia* and the psychology of the *Economy of the Animal Kingdom*, expanded by some new elements that came to light during his visionary period and are presented in the form of biblical myth. There is no question here of an allegorical commentary on the creation story found in Genesis, but rather of a partly scientific and partly poetical paraphrase of that creation—a sort of creational fiction; as such, it is the incomparably most beautiful we have.

The mythical mode of representation had always been dear to Swedenborg. An innate tendency to anthropomorphize all things, to clothe them in a sensory form, was supplemented by his knowledge of classical mythology, of Ovid and Plato; fundamentally, it is an expression of that poetic bent that contributed to Swedenborg's belief in a spiritual realm. This poetic bent was to be transferred by his overflowing imagination to the structure of the various worlds of spirit and to his explorations of the planets of our solar system. The brief exposition I have given of the philosophy of the *Principia* cannot provide an appreciation of the extent to which Swedenborg had recourse to the mythical style of narration.

Merely raising the question of whether Swedenborg had drawn his first idea of the creation of the moon and of the planets at the expense of the solar nebula from Ovid's *Metamorphoses* is sufficiently eloquent in itself.[168] In any case, this theory was expounded in the *Principia* in direct relation with the cosmogonic myths of antiquity. Using a quotation from *The Birds* of Aristophanes—the famous account of how the black-winged Night lays a wind egg from which Eros, the creator of the universe, was born—and by an account of the creation in the *Metamorphoses*, Swedenborg seeks, in the ancient fable of the universal egg, a historical precedent for his own theory. According to this concept, the sun was originally surrounded by a crust whose debris, projected into space, formed the various planets at the time the sun itself broke out of its chaotic state (*Principia* III, §395).

Further on, when he shows how the universe is born from the sun, Swedenborg turns to the same mythological concept. The infants to whom Phoebus gave life begin by frolicking around their parent; but, upon attaining the age of youth, they break away from him, each to settle into his own orbit. They nonetheless remain under the scepter of their father, the sun, and revere him as such. They pay him homage at dawn and at dusk, for it is from him that they have received their life and that they continue to receive it day by day; and he likewise always retains a paternal authority over them (*Principia* III, §398). We then follow the evolution of the earth, a naked infant at first, to become a radiant virgin, clothed in ether, and to break away from her father Phoebus in her turn (*Principia* III, §411). We finally leave her, in adulthood and completely clothed, during the course of the Golden Age, the era of Paradise. For Swedenborg returns to his favorite notion in the last chapter: when she was closest to the sun, the earth was a veritable paradise. The entire terrestrial globe constituted an immense garden. The empire of the sun, of which Plato spoke in *Phaedo*, the garden of the Hesperides beyond the seas, the Eden of the Bible, were then realities. Nature was in its infancy, playful and smiling. Flora and Ceres rested upon their couches of herbs; Diana ranged the forests followed by her nymphs. Jupiter, Phoebus, and the other gods lived among humans and kept gallant rendezvous in every grove. Pluto himself from the darkness of Tartarus rose to earth to kidnap Proserpine; Venus and her son were constantly at war (*Principia* III, §448).

Almost all of the mythical passages of the *Principia* have been used, as we shall see, in *The Worship and Love of God*. Even the elegiac description of the sojourn of the ancient gods on earth in ancient Greece in human form is found again in the introduction of the work.

It was more difficult to find a place for the element of fable in the psychological analysis of the *Economy of the Animal Kingdom*. Even here, however, Swedenborg's poetic tendency to crystallize his spiritual concepts into vivid mythological scenarios appears from time to time. And this propensity for mythical transformation finds a theoretical basis in the doctrine of correspondences and representatives. The spiritual only becomes intelligible to us when it is presented in a form within reach of our senses. Every earthly phenomenon is a mere symbol of a spiritual phenomenon, a kind of allegorical drama that acquires its deep significance only for the person able to interpret the symbols.

We have already observed, in the closing lines of the *Clavis*, that, for Swedenborg, the Bible was just such a symbolic text with a deeper spiritual meaning concealed under the letter, and he had other reasons for choosing the Mosaic story of creation as the subject of his book. We have already seen that, in the *Principia*, Swedenborg allowed himself to ponder mystical considerations on the integrity of Adam's psychic functions before the Fall. This theory of the continuity of our psychic life, of a bond that unites us with the Divinity and permits us to behold the supersensory world, a bond broken at the moment of the Fall, is glimpsed through the psychological structure of the *Economy of the Animal Kingdom*. During the entire latter half of his scientific period, Swedenborg had persevered in trying to reconstruct this bond to achieve intuitive knowledge and that awareness of union with divinity characteristic of the first humans. This aspiration led to his first mystic experiences, the moments of "penetrations" coming to him by flashes. And this whole period of penitence that we have followed through the *Journal of Dreams* is an extended effort to recover, while combating the allure of the senses and renouncing all intellectual travail, the innocence of the first man and to become worthy to receive the irradiation of divine light.

Swedenborg finally attained his goal. The extent to which he identifies his new state with that of Adam before the fall appears in a particularly clear fashion in his initial comments on the story of creation in *Historia creationis a Mose tradita* (1743) where he explains the state of Adam, the latter's conversations with God and angels, etc., by the experiences Swedenborg claims to have had himself. I cite as examples only the terms he uses in explaining that, in eating of the fruit of the Tree of Knowledge of Good and Evil, the first couple ceased to live by heavenly influx and became the toys of their senses, constrained to seek knowledge by empirical experience: "From the state which is ours when we are led by divine influx, and that not merely in thought but also in act and in the movements of the body, and how it is no longer permissible to act under the influence of caprices stimulated by our lower psychic faculties, are things I have learned by the grace of God" (*Adversaria* I, §18).

The tableau of the first human couple in their original state of integrity consequently became, in large measure, a picture of his own internal state at that time. One easily perceives this close relationship in the fact that Swedenborg attributes to Adam and Eve several mystical occurrences that he himself had experienced during his period of purification. Thus, Adam is seen to be the object of a state of ecstasy identical to that described in the *Journal of Dreams*; and Eve relates to the suspension of respiration in Swedenborg in order to not disturb her own thoughts and to give his *anima* full and entire freedom. Swedenborg's recent experience—that we are subject to the influence of spirits who insinuate themselves into our most intimate feelings and with whom we can exchange thoughts—is reflected in the conversations of Adam and Eve and in their psychic faculties, translated into the form of spirits, by the certitudes and heavenly intelligences that occupy the major part of the completed work. And the first human couple is likewise admitted, in the form of representative accounts and expositions, to the knowledge of spirits of inferior quality in the service of the Prince of the World and of the *animus*. Here we find, reflected in a orderly but basically identical form, the dream life of the journal.

It is evident that the work, in pursuit of such a vast objective, cannot adhere to the narrow range of biblical narration. Swedenborg was convinced that the Scriptures aimed at expounding how man, instead of eating of the Tree of Life which offered him this knowledge that penetrates the *anima* from on high, ate of the Tree of Knowledge, that is, sought knowledge to be acquired through the senses and science (cf. *Historia Creationis* I, §17). Therefore, it obviously became necessary to precede this account with an explanation of the psychic life of humanity like that in the *Economy of the Animal Kingdom*. And this exposition, in turn, is not intelligible unless one understands the cosmological system structured by Swedenborg in the *Principia*. So, it was entirely natural that the latter work should intervene in the new one to a considerable degree, especially since, in the *Principia,* Swedenborg had expounded upon the creation of the world; in most respects, he remains faithful to his earlier views.

It is characteristic of Swedenborg that, even after his conversion during the period of the *Journal of Dreams*, he continues to regard his prior scientific works with real sympathy. Indeed, he believes that God has prepared him from the start for the mission he is destined to fulfill and that his scientific activity was only a stage of this preparation. In a letter addressed to Oetinger in 1766, he declares that he was first of all introduced by the Lord to natural science and that he thus underwent a preparation from 1710–1744, when the heavens were opened to his eyes.[169] It is this intermediate stand between scientific exposition and pure poetry that makes it so difficult to give a general picture of the structure of *The Worship and Love of God.* I propose here, as an indispensable sequel, to give a brief glance at its contents, in the absence of which one could not form an idea of the true aims of the work and even less of its poetic values.

In a grandiloquent introduction, the author relates that one autumn day, walking lost in thought through a pleasant grove, he had seen dead leaves fall and was overcome by melancholy while musing on the succession of seasons. It had seemed to him that the earth itself had already outlived its infancy and adolescence—the ages of gold and silver—and now entered its last period, the age of iron. He recalls that the ancient sages, "whose soul was more distinct from the body than ours, and thus nearer to heaven," had realized that ages nobler than their own had preceded them. They had known that, in the first age after creation, the gods had come down from their astral abode to enter into friendly relations with humans, that in that age the earth was only a great garden where perpetual springtime ruled and breathed its soft western breezes. It is in this setting that the ancients raised the curtain on the stage of our sensory world. For in the diverse series of acts on this theater, they saw in the living and the dead a clear image of universal order, according to which everything begins its existence in the spring or in infancy. And it is in this same way that the author seeks here to consider the very figure of the universe in the reflection of the things themselves and to sense the destiny of times and ages.

As we have previously pointed out, this exposition is taken whole from the closing chapter of the *Principia*, but the notions that provide the basis of the reasoning, the knowledge that the earth was once nearer to the sun and the home of eternal spring, were notably more ancient and reappear in the chronologically earliest works of Swedenborg (see chapter one).

In the first chapter, when he takes up the creation of the world and describes the great universal egg, the yolk of which constitutes the sun, while the white germinates the earths that are later to form the various worlds, there is only a poetic paraphrase—adhering to Greek mythology—of the thesis he postulates in the *Principia* that all the planets and moons were formed by eruption of the solar nebula. And, in fact, we find here restated, in its smallest details, the cosmological mechanism of the *Principia*. Animal life issues from the vegetable, which arises in turn from the mineral, just as here he has the different kingdoms descending, one from the others, like so many eggs hatched in the heat of the sun.

I shall not proceed further here into these cosmological theories, since, in the above-mentioned work, Stroh has most thoroughly established their relationships with the *Principia*. But with ingenious imagination and with purely ancient coloration, Swedenborg expounds the various phases of the evolution of the universe. We watch the earth appear, after the creation of the vegetable kingdom, like a young bride adorned with the softest of budding roses, wearing a chaplet of the choicest blossoms, and inviting the heavenly guests to partake in her own boudoir of the first fruits she has brought. And we then see the crowns of the trees and the herbs of the soil achieve new generative power from the light of the sun and produce eggs, from which all the animal species are later born. It is by the same process, in even more solemn forms, that the first man is given birth.

At that time, the entire earth was a paradise, lacking only a conscious being to enjoy its beauty, a creature able to perceive the heavenly paradise from the earth and gratefully worship the creator in acknowledgment (*Worship and Love of God* §30). In the most temperate region of the terrestrial globe, there was an orchard of fruits so dense that the oblique rays of the sun were shaded. The orchard was traversed by numerous streams, whose evaporation was deposited on the undersides of the foliage and maintained a perpetual dew on the surface of the turf. At the center of this "paradise within paradise" arose a fruit tree, the Tree of Life, bearing an egg in which nature had concealed its most precious treasures (*The Worship and Love of God* §32). When nature had finished creating this egg, it was fertilized by the supreme mind (*suprema mens)*; indeed, this supreme mind, the true vital sun, had itself embodied the superheavenly form in this egg, the *anima*, which partakes of the infinite. In this *anima*, emanating from the supreme mind, a spark of sacred fire burned, a spark desiring to be let down on its wings from the cloudy citadel on which it was seated towards the lowest things of the earth. From here, after having sensorily tasted the joys of earth and transformed these into beatitudes (*felicitates*), it would return to its heavenly domicile to tell of these delights (*Worship and Love of God* §§33–34).

Let me note, in passing, how clear the Neoplatonic stamp is in this view. The soul who, in its supersensory world, was a part of the universal soul, is driven by an internal force to lower itself into the world below. But it is only to reascend to a higher world that her knowledge of a lower one has taught her to appreciate.[170] The very concept of the wings of the soul is found several times in Plotinus, who had it from Plato. Nevertheless, in Swedenborg, this motivation relates only to the first human soul. This soul has engendered the other souls. And here Swedenborg alludes, as before, to his acceptance of pre-existence.

The *anima*, itself the effigy of the supreme mind, by its radiation undertakes to form a microcosm in the bosom of this egg structured from the macrocosm. In this process, all nature was a docile auxiliary. The egg receives its sap, not only from the Tree of Life, but also from all the trees of the orchard. The sun dares not cast its rays directly on this egg, which radiate from spiritual light, but must let it be first moderated through the fruits. The vernal west wind blows without reaching the egg, lest the beginning of tissue formation be aborted. The surrounding vegetation spreads its branches like so many arms to lighten the burden on the leaf-sheltered mother, while other branches prepare a cradle cushioned by tufts gathered from the cotton plants. And nature is not alone in cooperating in this creation of humanity; heaven-dwelling spiritual minds (*mentes spirituales*) have been sent to the aid of nature. They guard the access to the sacred wood; and when wild beasts overstep the prescribed boundary, they are seized with a sudden terror and flee or kneel as though to worship their Lord and King. As the hour approaches, the parturient branch inclines by degrees toward the earth; the newborn frees itself from its blanket and draws its first breath (*Worship and Love of God* §§33–48).

The birth is at midnight, and all nature celebrates. Flowers exhale their softest perfumes; heavenly choirs let the delicate vibrations of their effulgence shimmer in the infant's eyes to prevent any other light than theirs from kindling the first spark of the light of his life. And at the first rays of the sun, they begin a paradisiacal dance of joy in honor of the newborn (*Worship and Love of God* §§39–40). The narrative proceeds in the same symbolic manner, with the creation and development of the human body, of its senses and its intellectual faculties under the guidance of the *anima*: a passage it is unnecessary to elaborate upon further, since we already know Swedenborg's theories on the formation of knowledge; these are found here without any variant. The images that receive their forms from solar light transform the soul and direct it first toward material ideas and finally toward intellectual ideas. It retains these thoughts in the memory and creates intelligence therefrom. It raises its own daughters to make them participants in its light and love. To the degree that they understand and assimilate this life, they become "certitudes." These intelligences and these certitudes form the *mens* of the newborn. Once Adam reaches adulthood, the *anima* lays down its scepter, however, and retires into the cerebellum, which is its normal seat.

The newborn awakens one fine day to find himself no longer an infant but an adolescent, able to converse with his "intelligences." He is appointed king by these intelligences and arranges a contest of wisdom among them (*Worship and Love of God* §§50–54). However, he does not succeed in learning from them the source of all the good and useful which, independent of the truths, flows into his brain. He realizes that this does not reach him by way of the senses but by an internal and mysterious route.

He meditates on these things almost to the point of seeing the doors of his reason torn from their hinges and chaos introduced into the places where his "intelligences" reside. Then he is suddenly snatched from himself and perceives his certitudes in the bosom of supreme love and his intelligences in conversation with divine beings. As though he awakens from a dream, he becomes aware that he has looked into the sanctuary from which all good emanates. At that instant, he becomes aware that he is, thanks to his intelligences, in relations with the Highest himself, and he expresses the desire to be united with him in love perpetually.

Once these words are pronounced, burning with the ardent desire to know what his human intelligences have learned from their heavenly intelligences, he feels as if he is being suddenly torn from himself and transported to the very heart of love amidst a choir of celestial beings. When he seeks in vain to cast himself to earth, he hears words uttered in his deepest self (*Worship and Love of God* §§54–55. This ecstatic manifestation conforms, point by point, to the visions of Jesus Christ experienced by Swedenborg, as detailed in the preceding chapter. Love—for it is Love that speaks—then announces to Adam that it is the source of all good, that the love, of which he is the object, is a reflux of his own love and reflection of divine love. He is warned that he must not drink from the fount of selfhood. In order that he may distinguish what belongs to him, a tree has been planted in the center of the garden, whose initial root issued from a heavenly germ, but which later put down its own roots. Adam is urged by Love not to eat of the fruit of this tree, but to seek his nourishment in love. And finally a paradise opens to the eyes of the first man, compared to which his own paradise is but a shadow. When the vision ends, a cloud covers Adam's eyes, his sight fails just as when we pass suddenly from the most brilliant light to darkness (*Worship and Love of God* §§54–55).

Distracted, the first man awakens in the same place as he was in before his vision and imagines that he has fallen from his heights and lost all contact with heaven. Nevertheless, one of his wisdoms consoles him. He still dwells in the bosom of God, and only the veil that covers his eyes impedes him from seeing heaven. It is within ourselves that heaven is found, in our *anima*, but we can be aware of this only when the light of the *anima* penetrates to our *mens* (*Worship and Love of God* §56).

In the following chapter, Swedenborg shows us the first-born being visited by heavenly beings in whose company he has previously seen his intelligences. They approach him in the form of nude damsels, their tresses held by golden clasps, their foreheads circled by precious stones and garlands of flowers that join them together. They circle around him in a dance of gently sinuous contours like those of the banks of the Euripus (*Worship and Love of God* §57).

During his conversation with his intelligences, Adam learns that our soul is exposed to two influences, one from the heavenly sun and the other from the natural sun; and that there are two kinds of love, one emanating directly from God, which draws us upward, and one coming from the world, which separates us from divinity. These two loves confront each other in the *mens*, which becomes the arena of their combat.

We recognize these theories, having found them already in *Economy of the Animal Kingdom*. The sole difference is that they are here clothed in a mythological Christian form. God himself, who created heaven and earth and sustains their various degrees, gave rise on our earth to a source of life of infinite flow; in other words, he created a ruler of the world and of spirits subject to him. This Prince of the World became so proud of the power conferred upon him by God that he rebelled against God and against his only Son. The Prince has two chiefs under his orders, *Amor sui* and *Amor mundi* (the love of self and love of the world), who, in turn, command their satraps, subalterns, and centurions, each of whom are surrounded by innumerable lictors. They command diverse kingdoms, provinces, or dominions.

The Supreme would have been able to destroy the universe by a single nod of his will and thrust the tyrants into Tartarus along with all the souls of their subjects. Inflamed in righteous anger, he was armed with thunderbolts. But the very moment when about to hurl these bolts, his only-begotten Son interposed himself between the adversaries, embracing those human minds and barely escaping being torn in pieces by the fury of the infernal dog. Fearing to hit his only Son, the Supreme laid aside his bolts and, on the plea of his Son to spare these ignorant and guiltless beings or allow him to perish along with them, the Most Holy Parent promised to indulge the world until it has passed through its sequence of seasons and falls into its sleep of eternal winter. He also gave the Savior power to loose or bind his enemy at his pleasure. Since that moment, the latter's power has been restricted within narrow boundaries, and the children of humanity enjoy a life naturally mingled with death (*Worship and Love of God* §§69–78).

By this mythological exposition, Swedenborg seeks, as he also explicitly declares in his work, to symbolize the internal struggle that is pursued in the depth of the human being, between worldly lust and heavenly love and the struggle between the external and internal person. The *anima* represents the Almighty (*Mens Suprema*) and rules as a goddess in its tiny sphere; it is from her that all life proceeds. The *mens*, with its understanding and its will represents Love itself, or the only Son of the Most High, whose image it is. The animus represents the Prince of the World (*Worship and Love of God* §70).

This is not just a matter of symbolism. Here we are little worlds and consequently carry the earth and the heavens within us, that is, the kingdom of God. God the Father truly exists in our *anima*, with his life; his only Son and his love, in our *mens*; and Prince of the World with his own life, in our *animus*. The latter is chained by our love, which closes the door of our *mens* to it; and as far as we are led by this love, not only can the Evil One not act upon us, but is entirely in our power. In reality, the Prince of the World is forced to present himself before Adam and, at his behest, take on the various disguises under which he is in the habit of deceiving humanity. Now he appears as a dog, now in the form of a dragon, of a flame, etc. (*Worship and Love of God* §81). In sum, these are the same forms under which the devil appeared to Swedenborg in his dreams.

In the second part of the book, Swedenborg writes similarly of Eve and her education and marriage. The first man was asleep in a grove, several furlongs distant from the one in which he had seen daylight himself, at the center of which there was also an apple tree, as beautiful as the Tree of Life. Resting upon his flowery bed, he perceives in a dream a radiantly beautiful nymph, at the sight of whom he feels himself suffused with glowing warmth. But when, smitten with love, he attempts to enfold her in his arms, she eludes his embrace like a bright cloud. Vehemently inflamed, he tries to catch her, but the area of his rib cage is distended to the point that it seemed to him that one of his ribs has just been fractured. Finally, when he succeeds in grasping her and covering her lips with kisses, he awakens and to his great chagrin perceives that all was but a dream. He was not aware that the tree under which he had slept bore an egg similar to the one from which he had been born, and that it was the branch of the tree he had embraced in his dream and the egg that he had covered with kisses, infusing into it a soul (*anima*) of his own. Nevertheless, he has a vague impression of having been led to this place by a divine impulse, and he has a presentiment that what he has seen in a dream will finally appear to him (*Worship and Love of God* §§87–88).

From this fertilized egg Eve is born. Under the tutelage of heaven, she grows into a maiden whose face radiates the purest innocence so that she seems to be a celestial grace in human form. All the motions of her soul are reflected in her features in colorations from white to purplish shades; for during this period of innocence, her *animus* is entirely submissive to the dominance of the *mens*, and her body is consequently a faithful mirror of her soul (*Worship and Love of God* §89).

One day, during her adolescence, she finds herself near a fountain. As she bends over its crystalline surface, she perceives, to her amazement, an image, a face that reproduces her motions, and her own ivory-white breasts, arms, and hands. She is astonished to see in this countenance the tracings of the image of her thoughts that have crossed her own mind. She betakes herself quickly to her celestial governesses and asks for an explanation of this phenomenon. The heavenly being who conducts the choir reveals that the face is only the mirror of the soul (*Worship and Love of God* §90).

Eve now learns, as Adam did, the inner and outer qualities of the human creature and the use to which it is assigned in the universe. (I pass over these considerations, which we have already found in Swedenborg's earlier philosophy.) She is finally instructed about her future husband. The celestial nuptial attendants unbind her hair, which falls to her shoulders in ringlets, there forming a golden ring. They affix a crown of diamonds. When the young bride, who does not yet realize her vocation very clearly, perceives him who is her destiny, her cheeks turn purple with a flame of love, and she is transformed into a naked heavenly Grace. When the first man who, since his vision, has been unable to divert his thoughts from the adorable nymph, perceives her amid the angelic choir, he realizes with joy the one whom heaven had shown him in his dream as wife and conjugal companion (*Worship and Love of God* §§109–110).

The third, unfinished part narrates the conjugal life of the first couple. It begins with a very beautiful description of the wedding night, during which nature, herself in full spring blossom, appears to invite the young couple to bind their new ties. Warmed by the same flame, both mutually confirm their faith with kisses and their young love grows into a consuming flame. This love is a rebirth for them, the beginnings of a new life. From that moment they realize all their pleasures in common; all that charms the senses of one of this pair likewise charms the senses of the other. This intimate communion purifies and exalts their joy, "so that the vein of all delights inflowed into a heart as it were united, but divided into two chambers" (*Worship and Love of God* §111).

But then,

> In the early morn when Aurora sent forth on high into the atmosphere of heaven the rays of the rising sun like arrows tinged with gold, they both awoke from a most sweet sleep in the conjugal couch which they had shared; for a kind of heavenly lightening glanced over their eyes, driving away rest and drawing the attention of both away from each other and to itself. (*Worship and Love of God* §112)

A vision of the universe and of its evolution is offered to their eyes as clear as the light of day. Here Swedenborg perspicuously condenses his entire philosophy of nature and his theory of creation. It is at first a vision of the spiritual sun, whose light is so brilliant that the two spouses are constrained to close their eyes. Through their closed eyelids, they nevertheless perceive that this sun has spread its rays, in decreasing splendor, across the entire universe. And they then see the birth of all creation up to the moment where, at the center of the sun, the human form rises and is swept up into heaven.

Following this vision, the young couple discusses what interpretation they should form about it. Here we find, for the most part, still in a more concentrated form, what we know from the preceding description of the creation. We find expressed here, as Stroh observed in his above-mentioned study, the key concept of the work that provided his title: that one draws near to God in the measure that one conjoins with him in love. In the middle of the interpretation of this marvelous vision, the narrative is cut off.

We can, however, form an idea of the fundamental traits under which Swedenborg had conceived the sequence of this work, by his first attempt at allegorical commentaries on Genesis published in 1745—the same year as *Worship and Love of God*—under the title *Historia creationis a Mose tradita*.[171] As I have already pointed out, he there in effect compares his preceding book to Holy Scripture and confirms the concordance between the two. It does not seem venturesome, then, to conclude that the interpretation of the creation sequence given by Swedenborg here also accords with the exposition he had intended to make in *The Worship and Love of God.*

In the *Historia Creationis,* the Fall of humankind is regarded as arising from the fact that Adam and Eve, who up to that point had received all their knowledge from the *anima*—that is *a priori*—turned away, under the sway of the serpent, representing the Prince of the World, from divine influx. Thereafter, they sought knowledge *a posteriori* and opened themselves to the influx from nature and were animated by self-love. This is symbolized by the eating of the fruit of the Tree of Knowledge, for this tree and its fruit represent the intelligence acquired through the senses.

From the day Adam and Eve taste the fruit of this tree, then, they cease to live a heavenly life and begin to live a natural one. They become aware of their nakedness—that is, they perceive the gaps in natural intellect. In the words regarding the future pains of women, Swedenborg sees a prediction of the struggle between heavenly and natural instincts, which began in us at that moment. To prevent the fallen humanity from tasting the fruits of the Tree of Life, that is, to keep nature and its desires from intruding into the *anima*, God banishes Adam and Eve from paradise; in other words, he closes the *anima* to the influences of the lower faculties of the mind. The cherubim who guard the tree have the mission to oppose the intrusion of the natural into the spiritual. The flaming sword symbolizes worldly desires; while their flame burns within human nature, we cannot enter heaven. It is only by the coming of the Messiah—a prophecy of which, with the Apocalypse, Swedenborg sees in the words announcing that the posterity of the woman will crush the head of the serpent—that the devil will be definitively conquered and humanity can again be united with God.

In an addendum, Swedenborg gives us to understand that Genesis should be more particularly related to the Messiah and his future realm, the celestial Jerusalem. For our entire earth was created only for heaven, and God wished that our terrestrial life should be a preparation for the kingdom of the heavens. It is necessary, then, that the first creation represent the supreme end for our earth and our race.

From the finished parts of *The Worship and Love of God,* it seems clear to me that Swedenborg had the idea of a plan analogous to that of the *Historia Creationis.* A number of passages in *The Worship and Love of God* surely indicate that it is thus that he had conceived the explanation of the Fall. And the analogy of conception of the original, which we find again in the preface to *Principia* and later in *Economy of the Animal Kingdom,* with works of the same period becomes strikingly manifest. But it is also beyond doubt that, when he wrote *The Worship and Love of God,* he already intended to expound not only how humankind lost our earthly paradise and severed relations with the Divinity, but also how the restoration of these relations would be made possible by the intervention of Jesus Christ; moreover, how humanity, in the New Jerusalem, achieves the supreme purpose of creation, the reunion with God. The very title *The Worship and Love of God* would be grossly inadequate had Swedenborg wished only to describe the original creation and the Fall.

To give an idea of the fundamental significance of *The Worship and Love of God,* I have had to neglect the long dialogues between the first human couple and the spirits, although these take up the major part of the book. Their detailed study could only lead to repetition. From *Economy of the Animal Kingdom* and other contemporary works, in fact, we know almost all the teachings already; indeed, certain phrases are even reproduced textually. Nevertheless, on certain points, Swedenborg enlarges his conceptions in a sense that foreshadows his theology.

It is thus that he clearly develops the thesis of God as the sole living being acting in the universe, a thesis already expounded in

Economy of the Animal Kingdom with its symbol of the spiritual sun, "There is only One who lives, and inasmuch as we live from Him, we also act from the Same; and if we live and act from Him we are in Him" (*Worship and Love of God* §58). No more than the eye can see unless it is lighted by the sun is our mind capable of understanding if it is not irradiated by the spiritual sun. All things created are only organs without activity of their own, unless an external force acts upon them. The divine Wisdom declares to Adam that

> nothing is thine own which thou supposest to be thine own. Thou are only a power potential, which from itself or from its own, never performs any action. But thou art a power more noble than all created powers. . . . Both heaven and earth inflow into thee with their treasures and gifts, but they are outside of thee; thou receivest these things, and actest as from borrowed forces. (*Worship and Love of God* §58)

When Adam objects that he seems to have freedom of will, the Wisdom replies that this will itself is, in each of his acts, governed by the end of our love. He adds in a beautiful analogy:

> Didst thou not observe lately the cock-dove up above the tops of our trees and how violently he beat the air with his wings? He beheld his consort dove and the nest which contained her young: This was the reason for his swift flight. It seemed to him that he himself vibrated his wings and chose the shortest way home, but in reality his loves, his fledged young and his mistress excited his mind and his mind moved his wings. . . . The case is similar in ourselves; our loves, whatever their number, hold the reins and excite and govern our minds; by them we are drawn and them we follow; and inasmuch as we follow we seem to act, because we vibrate the wings of our mind accordingly, and use the winged feet of our body. . . . We suppose the decisions to be our own. Love is, as it were, the charioteer who holds the reins and governs it as horsemen do horses and darken our minds, and persuades us that we sit as chieftains or leaders in the chariot. (*Worship and Love of God* §59)

Clearly, this exaggeration of the feeling of impotence, in which the human will finds itself, is related to Swedenborg's religious speculations during his period of crisis. He ends by expressing in the mouth of Adam an ardent desire "to no longer belong to myself, but to give myself to him." This is the prayer that often rises to Swedenborg's lips at the time of his journal.

However dependent the will of our love may be at times, it is this, and not our mind, that fashions our destiny, not only on this earth but also in the future life. Already at the time of his *Journal of Dreams,* Swedenborg was becoming more and more attracted to the concept (which is to appear later in such a marked form in his theology) that it is not intellect that guides the will, but the will that guides intellect. Will is the primary factor while intellect is secondary (cf. *Divine Love and Wisdom* §244 and *Arcana Coelestia* §1515).

In *The Worship and Love of God,* Swedenborg illustrates these relationships between mind and will when developing his symbol of the spiritual sun. From the light shed from this sun, the intellectual sight, comprehension of truth, is born, while the heat this same sun radiates is love, the origin of all sentiment of good (*Worship and Love of God* §63). Light and heat are distinct from each other and can exist separately. We are capable of understanding truth and thereby of distinguishing good; but the faculty of feeling and of being affected thereby does not proceed from light, but from heat. Our mind is like a garden. If sunlight does not accompany its heat, it remains as powerless as the winter sun. Leaves wither and fruits fall, the mind is plunged into darkness, and our will is reduced to impotence. On the other hand, if heat is joined with light, it is spring and summer; everything revivifies, germinates, and flourishes. These are the blossoms of verities and goods that expand in the *mens* (*Worship and Love of God* §§62, 63, 67). As Stroh remarks, this description is found again point by point in Swedenborg's theological works.[172]

Thus, all the stages of our life depend exclusively on the state of our love. And this state depends on which of the *amores* of our mind is preponderant (see chapter six). Like a divinity, or like the very soul of our energies, it directs our little world completely, at times with an unsteady hand. Once this love has instructed our *mens*, everything proceeds indirectly from this. Since this love is destined to provide the decisive factor of our entire life and of all our destinies, it is of capital importance for us to know the quality of our own love. For every love that becomes predominant with humankind is counted as the supreme love and thus gathers the mind into its snares (*Worship and Love of God* §68). We see here clearly pointed up the doctrine of *De Anima* and of the *Journal of Dreams* (see chapter six) on the *amor regnans,* which later is to play such a great role in the theological works, particularly in the descriptions of the future life. The conclusion, then, is that "it is the life of our love that we live, and that our life is such as love is" (*Worship and Love of God* §80).

By a tentative systematic introduction of Christian mythology with his conceptions of the universe, Swedenborg deviates to a certain extent from the doctrines of *Economy of the Animal Kingdom* and contemporary works. We have seen that, when he speaks in his journal, for the first time, of the divine mission given to him to write a "divine book on the worship and love of God" he has already begun to understand something about spirits; "believed I had something about this in my book *De Infinito*. But, to this, no answer was made" (*Journal of Dreams* §250; cf. chapter six above).

I have previously indicated that, in the work in question and in the works of the same period, Swedenborg had already given to understand that he wanted to pursue the scale of beings created beyond the limits of our natural universe and had acknowledged the existence of angels and spirits as mediators of divine providence. In reality, one can be sure that belief in these supernatural beings had always been a part of his views, as it was with most of his contemporaries. Many statements on the nature of angels are found in *Economy of the Animal Kingdom* as he developed his theory of correspondences, which gave him the certitude of a spiritual world analogous to ours; and he was led to speculate more and more on the existence of supersensory beings and their relations with ourselves. I shall limit myself to referring the reader in this connection to my exposition of Swedenborg's conceptions, still very rudimentary in his earlier works, about conditions of life in the future world where we are to live as angels or spirits (see chapter five). As we have seen, it is only at the time of his religious crisis that Swedenborg considered himself to have entered personally into contact with the spiritual world. He himself had experienced that we are tempted by spirits "who appear to each according to his loves" and that God sends his angels to fight within man against Satan and his legions. I have indicated, when quoting these declarations (see chapter six) that Swedenborg has already entered into the order of ideas that are to follow him later during his theosophical period: that angels and spirits act upon our thoughts and sentiments and that we carry in our most intimate selves a whole spiritual world where God and Satan strive against each other through their emissaries.

This conception is more developed in *Worship and Love of God,* and here we find a formal doctrine of spirits. The knowledges and intelligences that comprise Adam's will and mind and together form the *mens* have a higher correspondence in the knowledges and intelligences of heaven, as well as an inferior correspondence among the genii and spirits of the Prince of the World. These spirits of diverse nature have the faculty of penetrating into the person himself and acting on his functions: "For heavenly beings, because they are spiritual, have power of penetrating even into our inmosts, since nothing of nature can prevent it; for as they are in supreme things, so also they are in inmosts, yea, they even enter into a certain kind of association and discourse with the *anima* and the *mens"* (*Worship and Love of God* §41). And likewise the spirits and genii of the Prince of the World can penetrate the physical desires of each person. Adam learns that, when the Prince of the World succeeds in enticing to his side the intelligences of the lowest sort of any mind, the gates of this soul are opened wide before him and he makes his entrance followed by his genii, expelling the knowledges and intelligences who betake themselves to flight like doves at the sight of a hawk. He then appoints a leader for his genii, whom he calls *animus* (*Worship and Love of God* §72).

The subdivision of the world of spirits that Swedenborg establishes here accords precisely with that which we again discover in his theology, although the terminology differs somewhat. Thus, in *Arcana Coelestia* we read: "The angels who act into what is of man's will are called celestial, and they who act into what is of his understanding are called spiritual. To the celestial are opposed genii, and to the spiritual the spirits" (*Arcana Coelestia* §5878).

But one is equally struck by the concordance that exists here with Swedenborg's previous psychological system. The intelligences and certitudes that belong properly to Adam are expressly identified with the *mens,* with its will and its understanding. On the other hand, the heavenly knowledges and intelligences blend to a certain degree with the divine heat and light received through the mediation of the *anima*. Likewise, spirits and genii are to some extent identical with sensory knowledges and sensual desires.

It is probably this fact that led Stroh, in his above-mentioned work,[173] to object to the opinion according to which Swedenborg would have regarded his knowledges and intelligences as real spiritual beings. The American author does not develop his thoughts; but, to judge from the references by which he seeks to refute their reality as spirits, it seems that he would consider the certitudes and the intelligences of Adam as human faculties of the soul and their celestial correspondences as abstractions. Swedenborg's personification of them would, then, have only a poetical aim.

This view seems to be confirmed to a certain extent by the fact that, in *The Worship and Love of God*, the psychic operations are personified. Yet Stroh's understanding is defensible only concerning the knowledges and intelligences that are designated as belonging to Adam. It is said expressly of these (*Worship and Love of God* §68, note m) that together they constitute the *mens* and that they are identical to the will and the understanding. And regarding another passage cited by Stroh (*Worship and Love of God* §53, note p), it is said that by Adam's conversation with his intelligences it should be understood that he talked with himself; that is, he was thinking. Other declarations by Swedenborg could no doubt give rise to the belief that, in the latter's imagination, these entities had become in part independent spiritual beings, but the proof that he would consider them basically as faculties of the human soul is that he portrays them as being born from the *anima*.

It is nevertheless impossible to deny that, in Swedenborg's mind, the knowledges and intelligences represent angels. He expressly declares so in several passages, notably in the sequence of citations made by Stroh. Besides, he characterizes them as inhabitants of heaven, as servants of the only Son of God. They are from God, live in a heavenly light, and radiate a light of the same nature into the soul of man. They differ from humans in that they have no body (*Worship and Love of God* §106). However, Swedenborg does not doubt that they can appear to human beings in visible form. "I take on the human form when I please and leave it alike," says one of the celestial beings to Eve (*Worship and Love of God* §95). Just like angels, spirits and genii are born by the very fact of creation. To create a bond between heaven and earth, God himself had a source of life born in the world. "Such was the cause of the creation of a multitude of spirits and genii." (*"Haec Causa fuit creationis plurium spirituum ac geniorum, seu plurium essentiarum quae hic vivunt; Worship and Love of God* §69). The whole description of the revolt of these spirits and genii against God under the leadership of the Prince of the World is, moreover, based on the biblical doctrine of the fall of the angels.

To this interpretation it could be objected that, in a number of passages, Swedenborg speaks of celestial beings as divine forces, thoughts, and ends. It is superfluous to point out here, after the study we have made in the chapter regarding correspondences, the absolute concordance of this conception with the Neoplatonic ideas of Swedenborg.[174] But this in no way implies that, in his mind, they do not possess any reality as supersensory beings. These ideas already had the benefit of this double situation among the ancient philosophers by whom Swedenborg was inspired. We see the divine forces become spirits in Philo, who identifies them with the Mosaic angels. Plotinus pursues this thought and converts Platonic ideas into thinking spirits (*voï*). He describes demons who belong to a world intermediate between ours and the intelligible world as entirely individualized living beings. They have a body of intelligible matter; they have sensory perceptions and language. But they are also confused to a certain extent with human faculties. From among the demons who dominate human beings, each person chooses one as a guide.

Allow me to point to the striking analogy of this conception with Swedenborg's doctrine, according to which we choose as our guide one of the "*amores*" which are found within each of us. We find even more manifest similarities between the Swedenborgian doctrine of the *anima* begetting its intelligences and the Plotinian doctrine of diverse partial souls, each of whom has received a part of this Eros that belongs to the universal soul. "Demons who are erotic are born from the fact that the soul tends toward good and toward what there is of the highest, and all souls in this world beget from this demon."[175]

It is even possible to show with considerable certitude that the spirits conceived by Swedenborg in *The Worship and Love of God* are not unrelated to Neoplatonic demonology. One chapter of *The Theology of Aristotle* speaks of different kinds of spirits and their characteristics. In the edition of this work that Swedenborg possessed, the commentator calls to mind that by "spirits" the author appears to refer to the celestial intelligences of which Aristotle speaks in his *Metaphysics*[176] and that these heavenly intelligences are hardly different from our angels or demons. Our minds, hardly capable of conceiving a bodiless thing, attribute the quality of spirits to entirely immaterial objects, as does popular belief. As we see, there is here not only an identification of celestial intelligences with the spirits of Christian mythology, but also a direct defense of the custom, common in every popular demonology, to objectify every spiritual potency in the form of spirits.

What appears even more to support the direct relationship of the Swedenborgian conception with *The Theology of Aristotle* is the fact that several years prior to *The Worship and Love of God* Swedenborg makes reference to celestial intelligence with particular regard to *The Theology of Aristotle*. In the *Clavis*, which dates from 1741, it is indeed a matter of "spiritual intelligences, or of angels and souls" who, because of their supernatural character, are born in possession of their full intelligence (*Clavis* §19). (This appears in the passage immediately following the one previously cited—see chapter five above—where it is said that the ancient Egyptians already cultivated the doctrine of correspondences and that we have an entire book on the subject attributed to Aristotle.)

We see thereby how, beginning with his visionary experiences, Swedenborg was naturally led to bring diverse kinds of spirits into his psychological system, laying ahead of time the essential foundations of his spiritual doctrine.

There is, however, a radical difference between this theory of spirits and the one we find in *The Worship and Love of God.* In Swedenborg's theological system, the angels, as well as good or evil spirits, represent the dead; since there were no dead in the time of Adam and Eve, it is evident that in *The Worship and Love of God* celestial beings, as well as spirits and genii, must be considered as having been born from creation itself.

There is a further consequence from this: evil spirits cannot be considered as having been created by God. Swedenborg is obliged to acknowledge a heavenly fall prior to ours. In his doctrine on the Prince of the World, he tries to reconcile the Christian belief in a personal devil with his Neoplatonic ideas and arrives at a conception which recalls, from rather far back, that of certain Church Fathers. The Prince of the World and his genii were created to serve as an intermediate link between heaven and earth, between the purely spiritual life and inert nature. For there is no more of a relationship between the purely spiritual life and nature than there is between light and shade. Subjected by nature to divine orders, the Evil One gradually became captive of his love of self and of the world that had been subjected to his domination. And he developed the ambition to conquer heaven also; he rebelled against the Omnipotent. This revolt broke the bonds that united the Most High to nature (*Worship and Love of God* §129). From that time, the unique love emanating from the Most High and embracing the whole universe was replaced by two loves: the love of good, which seeks to unite the things of heaven with those of the earth, and the love of evil, which arises from hate and the desire to divide heaven and earth (*Worship and Love of God* §69).

We thus have two original falls, and Jesus Christ was there to intervene twice as mediator. The whole Neoplatonic thesis of the rupture and reunion of nature with the infinite is consequently somewhat effaced, and the emanationist principle of God as the only living and acting substance, as spiritual sun, whose light constitutes the life and activity of the universe, loses something of its importance. It is found to be obscured, on the one hand, by the existence of the only Son, born from eternity (whose relationship with the Father Swedenborg has some difficulty in defining clearly), and on the other hand, by that of the Prince of the World, who, after having served as intermediary between God and nature, has become the principle of evil of this same nature.

One can easily see that in order to unify his conception, Swedenborg is forced to eliminate the elements drawn from theological tradition to come closer to the emanationist doctrine of Neoplatonism. And that is why, in the course of his theological period, he resolutely abandons the doctrine of the Trinity in its orthodox form and makes Jesus Christ an incarnation of God himself intervening at the beginning of the evolution. It is for this same reason that he eliminates the dogma of a Fall prior to creation of the universe as well as the doctrine of a personal devil. Evil then arises consequent to the Fall of humanity, a fall that gives birth to hell. Humankind's apostasy and eventual reunion with the Divinity thus become the focus of his whole philosophy, during Swedenborg's theological period much more than previously, and becomes the fundamental problem around which all his theology crystallizes.

Nevertheless, I believe I have established by my previous expositions that one may not consider *The Worship and Love of God* as a work intended exclusively to expound Swedenborg's philosophical and theological point of view in the form that he had adopted at that time. I have already indicated at the beginning of the present chapter that this work constitutes a desired new allegorical exposition of Genesis and that, in the first exegetical work that he wrote after the decisive vision in London, Swedenborg disclaimed any validity in the passages that were at variance with revealed Scripture.

From this point of view, it is clear that, although it is written in prose, we are justified in considering *The Worship and Love of God* as belonging to the series of poems about creation that became fashionable toward the end of the Renaissance, and of which Haquin Spegel was, in Sweden, the most characteristic representative. It is unnecessary to dwell upon the work which served as model: this was certainly Milton's *Paradise Lost.*

We have no material proof that Swedenborg knew Milton's work. The fact that in a letter to Benzelius dating from 1711, he mentions Milton among the most celebrated writers in England does not in itself prove much.[177] It is hardly likely that he had read all these authors, Shakespeare among them. It is more probable that he compiled his list from some scholarly study. But on the other hand, it is quite likely that he read Milton during his stay in England, or that he became acquainted with him in Sweden. The venerable Spegel had already quoted passages from *Paradise Lost*; and Dalin exhibits, in his poem "Swedish Liberty," which is almost contemporary with *Worship and Love of God*, manifest Miltonic influences. A comparison between the two works, moreover, confirms that Swedenborg was acquainted with Milton and was influenced by him.

First of all, one is struck by a certain similarity between the structures of the two works. They both give the same importance to the struggle between Satan and God as they do to creation itself and to the destinies of the first human couple. For both, it is the human being who constitutes the final setting of the struggle between the two universal principles. They both have the purpose of expounding, within the framework of the biblical account, a doctrine that is at once philosophical and theological, and the means to which they have recourse are partly the same. In *The Worship and Love of God,* Adam's long conversations with the intelligences have their equivalent in Adam's long conversations with the archangel Raphael that occupy several books of *Paradise Lost* and by which we are instructed about the creation of the earth, of heaven and of its angels, and about the aims of God regarding the human creature.

The descriptions of the creation of Eve are also similar. Genesis simply states that God sank Adam in deep sleep, during which he extracted a rib out of which he created Eve. In *Paradise Lost,* book 8, ll.478–480, Adam already sees in his dream the woman who will become his consort. Her aspect, which exceeds in beauty everything he had seen up to that moment, awakens in him a new sentiment and, on awakening, he is disconsolate at the vanishing of his dream:

> Shee disappear'd, and left me dark, I wak'd
> To find her, or for ever to deplore
> Her loss, and other pleasures all abjure.

The moment he lost hope of ever seeing her again, he sees her approaching in her living form, conducted by her invisible Creator.

This is precisely the idea Swedenborg grasps, an idea he develops in the same manner. In the dream, during the course of which God takes his rib, Adam sees a nymph appear, so beautiful that he is immediately inspired by an ardent love for her and wishes to take her into his arms. She tries to escape his embrace; and at the very moment he succeeds in grasping her, he awakens and perceives, to his great chagrin, that it was only a dream. He is unable to console himself for her loss and unceasingly evokes the memory of the gracious apparition. The day finally arrives when he finds her again, just as she appeared to him in a dream, when the heavenly intelligences lead her to him.

Even though this appearance of the first woman to her future husband might seem a natural invention, and the similarity of the two episodes might therefore be fortuitous, the same explication cannot be applied to the scene I have related above, when Eve sees herself mirrored in the water for the first time and perceives her own visage with astonishment. The analogy with the famous narration of Milton (*Paradise Lost,* book 4, ll. 460–469) is truly striking, and one seeks in vain in Genesis the equivalent of this episode, which Milton is presumed to have borrowed from the myth of Narcissus in Ovid's *Metamorphoses*. This analogy is even found in details.

With Milton, Eve perceives that the face which appears in the mirror of water alters and changes in expression just as she herself does:

> As I bent down to look, just opposite,
> A Shape within the watery gleam appear'd
> Bending to look on me. I started back,
> It started back, but pleas'd I soon return'd,
> Pleasd it returnd as soon with answering looks
> Of sympathy and love; there I had fixt
> Mine eyes till now, and pin'd with vain desire,
> Had not a voice thus warn'd me, What thou seest,
> What there thou seest fair Creature is thyself,
> With thee it came and goes. . . .

The development of the episode is exactly the same in Swedenborg. Eve perceives that the image in the water reproduces the movements of her own body, and that, when this apparition evokes in her a charmed expression, the image likewise reflects the changing play in her own features. She then speaks to her "celestial companions" and seeks to learn from them why the face thus reflects the motion of the soul.

The narration of the nuptial night of the first couple seems to me to recall in its chaste nudity the famous description by Adam to the Archangel Raphael in *Paradise Lost,* book 8, ll. 510–517.:

> To the Nuptial Bow'r
> I led her blushing like the Morn, all Heav'n,
> And happy Constellations on that hour
> Shed thir selectest influence; the Earth
> Gave sign of gratulation, and each Hill;
> Joyous the Birds; fresh Gales and gentle Airs
> Whisper'd it to the Woods, and from thir wings
> Flung Rose, flung Odors from the spicy Shrub, . . .

Swedenborg is, of course, far from having the extraordinary sentiment of nature that Milton has, and his description seems devoid of color compared to that of the English poet. It is nonetheless obvious that the two descriptions can be precisely superimposed upon each other. The two lovers make their bridal bed in a grove, and all nature, in all its springtime splendor, rejoices in their union, while the constellations of heaven presage their happiness: *"Omnia enim in vernali flore, et geniali erant lusu, et sicut unionis documenta subblandiebantur amori, qui consociae mentis unitionem secum accelerare ardebat; nihil non etiam obsecundabat votis, afflavente ipso Coelo; quare non intercessit mora, quin etiam Sponsa pari et mutua redardesceret amoris face"* (For all things were in vernal flower and genial sport, and as it were enticed the pledges of union with the love which burned to hasten the union of the associate mind. Everything was auspicious, heaven itself favoring; wherefore no delay interposed until the bride also burned with a like torch of mutual love) *(Worship and Love of God* §111).

Moreover, it is easy to find in Swedenborg other tableaux of paradise whose tone recalls that of Milton. Like him, Swedenborg systematically seeks to give his biblical narrative a sheen of antiquity. The book swarms with allusions to classical myths and fables—to the point that, in two modern translations, a mythological glossary has been annexed.[178] Also as in Milton, the incidents are frequently illustrated by Homeric images, where names of classical localities predominate. Perhaps this Miltonic character is most apparent in the description Swedenborg gives of the Prince of the World, clad in resplendent armor like an ancient commander at the head of his legions. This is exactly like the form in which Milton loves to portray Satan. In *Worship and Love of God* as in *Paradise Lost,* we find the story of a great battle of which Jesus Christ provokes the final decision between those loyal to God and those loyal to Satan.[179]

If the conception of God and his relation to the world that emerge from *Paradise Lost* is studied a little more closely, it seems there is some reason to suppose that the Miltonic influence has made itself perceptible not only on the literary style of *Worship and Love of God* but that it has also had an effect on Swedenborg's theological period. The Puritanism of Milton is indeed strongly mixed with a Neoplatonic doctrine of emanation, which we have already detected in Swedenborg, but which led up to conclusions that Swedenborg was to draw only during his theological period. It is not yet known exactly, to my knowledge, where Milton got this concept. What is known, however, is that he was very familiar with Plato and most certainly also with Plotinus. The influence of Renaissance Platonism can also be acknowledged.

This Miltonic doctrine is known to us today, not only from *Paradise Lost,* but also from *De Doctrina Christiana,* which was not published until 1825. The view here is generally characterized by English scholars as a kind of modified pantheism.[180] In reality, it constitutes a typical Neoplatonic system of emanation. God is an incomprehensible unity, the only real existence. It is from God that all creation emanates and which is one day to return to God. All created things are matter in more or less refined form:

> O Adam, one Almighty is, from whom
> All things proceed, and up to him return,

If not deprav'd from good, created all
Such to perfection, one first matter all
Indu'd with various forms, various degrees
Of substance, and in things that live, of life;
But more refin'd, more spiritous, and pure,
As nearer to him plac't or nearer tending
Each in thir several active Spheres assign'd
Till body up to spirit work, in bounds
Proportion'd to each kind. . . .

Beneath these words of the archangel Raphael to Adam (*Paradise Lost,* book 5, ll. 469–479) we also see, in its smallest details, the image of the universe that Swedenborg imagined.

From this starting point, Milton fearlessly draws all the consequences it implies without worrying about orthodox dogma. Above all he is a certified antitrinitarian. The Son is not coeternal with the Father; he is born by the will of God and lives from his substance. Milton rejects the thesis that the world was created from nothing and believes that it issues from the very substance of God. He denies the existence of any antinomy between the soul and matter. The soul is only of a more refined matter and cannot be separated from the body, with which it forms a whole. "The whole man is soul, and the soul man."[181] He also believes the unit is composed of soul and body—which, according to Genesis, was made of the dust of the earth—and that it is a mistake to believe that the soul was "the spirit of life" that was immediately breathed by God into the human creature.

Like Swedenborg, Milton adheres to the traducian doctrine, according to which the soul is transmitted to the son in the sperm of the father. It is not only the soul that survives after death but also the body, in a more refined and spiritualized form. Without doubt, human beings support the life of the body by means of material nourishment; but since matter is inferior to the soul only by degree, there is no contradiction in the sublimation of the body into spirit. In the above-cited conversation with Adam, the archangel Raphael says:

> Your bodies may at last turn all to spirit,
> Improv'd by tract of time, and wing'd ascend
> Etherial as wee. . . .

This is a point on which this disguised "materialism" of Milton may be especially presumed to have influenced Swedenborg; it is in the application of this materialism to angels and to the world of spirits. We have seen that Swedenborg's initial conception of the spiritual world was far from being as realistic as it became in his theosophy (cf. above, chapter 5). Even in *Worship and Love of God*, one of the heavenly intelligences tells Eve that she has the faculty of assuming and abandoning the human form at will (*Worship and Love of God* §95). The forms in which these celestial beings appear to us are merely representations. In themselves, they are incorporeal and free from all human affection (*Worship and Love of God* §44). It is naturally in full agreement with his Neoplatonism that Swedenborg, during his theological period, comes to attribute to his angels not only bodies composed of a kind of "substantial" refined matter, but all the physiological functions as well. And his visions have naturally contributed to concretize his conception of the spiritual world. But one can hardly refrain from supposing that Milton's extremely audacious conjectures about the physical functions of the angels have exercised a certain influence on Swedenborg. It is perhaps in the often-quoted passage where the archangel Raphael visits the first couple and where Adam asks him, not without hesitation, if he wishes to share their frugal repast, that the Miltonic conception stands forth the most clearly. At Adam's invitation, the archangel responds that the nourishment given man by God, nourishment in part spiritual, should equally suit the purest spirits (*Paradise Lost,* book 5, ll. 407–413):

> and food alike those pure
> Intelligential substances require
> As doth your Rational; and both contain
> Within them every lower faculty
> Of sense, whereby they hear, see, smell, touch, taste,
> Tasting concoct, digest, assimilate
> And corporeal to incorporeal turn.

He then expounds how every creature has to be sustained and nourished, even heavenly bodies. After this, he seats himself at the side of his hosts and eats with good appetite:

> So down they sat,
> And to thir viands fell, nor seemingly
> The Angel, nor in mist, the common gloss
> Of Theologians, but with keen dispatch
> Of real hunger, and concoctive heat
> To transsubstantiate; what redounds, transpires
> Through Spirits with ease. . . .

What is even more characteristic is that in his tendency to materialize the spiritual world, Milton has in a way given expression in advance to one of Swedenborg's favorite ideas during his theological period, that of heavenly marriages. When in *Paradise Lost* book 8, l. 592ff., the archangel Raphael says to Adam that true conjugal love ennobles man and constitutes the step by which he raises himself toward heavenly love, Adam then asks (ll. 615–617):

> Love not the heav'nly Spirits, and how thir Love
> Express they, by looks only, or do they mix
> Irradiance, virtual or immediate touch?

To which the archangel replies, blushing:

> Let it suffice thee that thou know'st
> Us happy, and without Love no happiness.
> Whatever pure thou in the body enjoy'st
> (And pure thou wert created) we enjoy
> In eminence, and obstacle find none
> Of membrane, joint, or limb, exclusive bars:
> Easier then Air with Air, if Spirits embrace,
> Total they mix, Union of Pure with Pure
> Desiring; nor restrain'd conveyance need
> As Flesh to mix with Flesh, or Soul with Soul.

As we see, although he has not clearly developed his idea, Milton assumes conjugal relationships among the angels.

The most important role played by the author of *Paradise Lost* for Swedenborg is beyond any doubt that the Swedish mystic learned from Milton to transform and modernize the biblical text, making the most of its poetic content while giving entry to his own conceptions. Like Swedenborg, Milton had transformed the naive account of the creation according to the cosmological ideas of his day and expounded his own philosophical and theological views. This tendency had already given Milton's work something abstract, at least in comparison with that of Dante. Not for nothing was he called the last adept of the abstractly allegorical school of Spenser. In any case, the primary interest of his work lies in its poetic element; the didactic and religious aspect of his spirit are only secondary.

To the contrary, Swedenborg undertakes to create a "*liber divinus*," summarizing his philosophical and religious concepts as he has elaborated them in the course of his scientific studies and later developed during his religious crisis. At the moment he first sets his hand to his new work, he is convinced that he does not have to grope among the shopworn ideas of others, but that God will inspire him to write what he should. It was half against his will that the poetic element had slipped into his work. When, toward the end of his life, he was asked whether *The Worship and Love of God* should be included among his canonical works, he was accustomed to reply that it was based on the truth, but a bit of his egoism had slipped in and he had made a somewhat playful use of Latin.[182] It is most certainly through fear of allowing himself to be seduced by "egoistic" artistic interests that he was so cautious to give no place in his work to anything that could not be explained allegorically as part of his philosophical system. Even what appears to us as the most palpable reality is to be interpreted as an abstract truth.

It follows that Swedenborg's work never achieves the concrete character of *Paradise Lost.* The figures of the Swedish mystic never cease to be symbols of the faculties of the human soul; their activity is always destined to be transposed from the material domain to the spiritual. Consequently, it can happen that the reader can become bored in being obliged to decipher new enigmas on every page. For the reader who wishes to penetrate the recesses of Swedenborg, it is beyond cavil that his scientific and theological works constitute a much more accessible avenue.

On the other hand, there is no work whose study can be more fruitful for those who want to acquaint themselves with the poet Swedenborg. There no doubt exists in his later works many passages comparable, for their poetic grandeur and artistic style, to *Worship and Love of God* particularly the memorabilia found in *Conjugial Love.* But in the theological works, these poetic beauties are frequently wrapped in dogmatic reasonings, whose sound and at times fastidious development dismay most readers.

The Worship and Love of God escapes this rigid dogmatism. Here it is not with the revelator of a new religion that we have to deal, who has his dogmas crystallized at every point, but with the religious dreamer, the mystic who for the first time clothes in a poetic form the thoughts that have been the subject of his meditations for a long time. At the moment when, after his crisis, he rejects his books and his science, never again to allow his thoughts to be guided but by the hand of God, he feels himself reborn; he returns to the state of innocence which was that of the first human couple before tasting the fruit of the Tree of Knowledge. He has just rediscovered the lost paradise.

He nonetheless continues to envisage the problem of the origin of the universe and of humankind from a scientific angle, and it may be said that, to a certain extent, his work is a continuation of his repeated efforts since his youth to reconcile the biblical myth of creation with his own cosmological and psychological theories. But the religious experiences he had during the period of his *Journal of Dreams* have definitely convinced him that scientific analysis based on sensory testimony is, by itself alone, incapable of resolving the problem. He has been allowed to see the light that emanates from the spiritual sun, he feels conjoined to the Divinity in his blissful ecstasies, and he has acquired, through his dreams and visions, the certitude that supersensory beings exist beyond our universe.

It is in this new essence of life that he wishes, in *Worship and Love of God,* to have the reader participate. But he does not do so by way of confession. The biblical fable of creation and of our first ancestors will serve as a disguise for his own experiences. Even when he describes the spirits who appeared to him during his religious crises, he usually pretends to personify the faculties of the human soul but for a poetic purpose and he gives parallel psychological explications of them in the form of notes. It is difficult to decide to what extent Swedenborg adopts this procedure with a view to the public or in the hope of reconciling the two interpretations, the scientific or "natural" and the supernatural.

But it is precisely because, in *The Worship and Love of God,* Swedenborg doesn't yet believe himself constrained to reproduce his own experiences directly and because he does not yet appear convinced of their verity that he gives his poetic imagination a freedom he will not venture to grant it in the future. Conceived in a spirit that is intermediate between the scientific commentary and biblical paraphrase, his work comes strangely close to the symbolic tales of Romanticism. And one understands the naive assertion of the Swedish poet Atterbom, for whom *The Worship and Love of God* is written "with a poetic inspiration which, if divided among a dozen poets, would suffice to fix them all in the firmament of poetry as so many stars of the first magnitude."

e i g h t

THE SPIRIT SEER

Walking one day on a garden path in the spiritual world, Swedenborg meets with strolling young men who enjoy themselves with conversation on matters of wisdom. One of these asks him how it happened that, while approaching along the path leading toward them, at one moment he was visible and at another moment he dropped out of sight. "Smiling at this I said, 'I am neither a stage player, nor a Vertumnus, but I am alternately in your light and in your shade; thus here I am both a foreigner and a native'" (*True Christian Religion* §280).

These words could serve as an epigraph for Swedenborg during his twenty-eight final years. He feels he belongs only half to the world he treads and appears to most people he meets as a strange and inexplicable being. Despite the curiosity of which he was the object among his contemporaries, the numerous and detailed descriptions of his life during the course of his last decades of existence hardly provide us with any real clue to his personality.

"In winter he wore a reindeerskin coat and in summer a likewise well-worn dressing gown recalling the wardrobe of a philosopher," reports Robsahm in his memoir.[183] Robsahm hastens to add that Swedenborg was simple but adequate in his grooming, except when he happened through distraction to overlook some detail of his dress or to wear shoe buckles that did not match. Less charitable observers declared that, at least in his declining years, his clothing was quite negligent. Lidén, who had met him in London in 1769, says, "His clothing was soiled and even sordid; his face and hands appeared not to have been washed for several years."[184] The Pastor Ferelius of the Swedish Legation tells us that Swedenborg never washed his face or hands and never brushed his clothes, "saying that neither dust nor filth stuck to him." Cuno, a citizen of Amsterdam who in his autobiography has given us the best portrait we have of Swedenborg, intimates that the Dutch landlord of the great mystic had reported to him in confidence startling details on the filthiness of his tenant.[185]

His domestic habits were most simple, doubtless by taste rather than avarice as Lidén would have us believe. In Stockholm, his meal was composed only of a piece of wheat bread dipped in warm milk;[186] when he was abroad, he contented himself with a cup of chocolate and dry biscuit.[187] He never had supper, but frequently during the day he would drink a cup of heavily sugared coffee that he prepared himself in the tiled stove.

He had no real intimates. At his home at Hornsgatan, he was served by the elderly wife of the gardener, whose sole duty appears to have been to make his bed and bring to his chamber a large kettle of hot water every morning. It seems that, during his journeys, he saw very few people, and it is rather odd that, despite his long sojourns in London, he found it very difficult to express himself in English.

This voluntary isolation, however, was in no way due to misanthropy. Swedenborg appeared to suffer from a certain timidity that was partly provoked by an acute stutter. Here it is perhaps also necessary to consider the consequences of his labors as a writer and of his habit of going to bed every evening at seven o'clock. When, during his last years, he returned to Stockholm, an odd character whom everybody wanted to see, he seemed to take pleasure in these visits, which contributed a bit of the unexpected to the monotony of his daily life. It was to receive all these curious visitors, Robsahm relates, that Swedenborg had built, in 1767, two pavilions, whose agreeable decor contrasted with the severe simplicity of his apartment.[188] One of these pavilions sheltered his library; in his study, he placed only the Bible in its original languages as well as his own manuscripts. In one corner of the garden, he had constructed "a maze exclusively for the entertainment of the good people who came to see his garden, and more particularly their children whom he received with gaiety, enjoying the pleasure they found in his arrangements." Swedenborg loved children very much and it is told of his early stays abroad that he never went out without returning with sweetmeats for the children of his hosts.[189]

Among the other "inventions" which Swedenborg, somewhat awkward in his amiability, conceived for the entertainment of his visitors, Robsahm cites a fake door to the pavilion. Behind this there was another door furnished with a mirror, in which a green hedge and a birdcage were reflected, "a pleasant effect intended to surprise those who opened the door of the second garden, which he declared more beautiful than the old one. This surprise particularly amused Swedenborg whenever he received the visits of inquisitive young ladies."[190] It is certainly before this mirror that one should visualize the delicious scene related by Fryxell, in which a young girl asked Swedenborg to show her a spirit.

In front of the house, there was a group of Holland boxwood shaped "to represent animals and many other things." According to Robsahm, Swedenborg must have spent considerable sums on the development of this artistry, no doubt also intended to amuse visitors.

It appears that, when visiting other people's homes, Swedenborg displayed that same naive and rather childish gaiety. For he willingly accepted invitations, provided they did not interfere with his early evening habits. Despite the spartan simplicity of his ordinary life, Robsahm tells us that he did not disdain "spreading good cheer in society and to shed a *poculum hilaritatis* [cup of good cheer] in moderation."[191] At such times, he would abandon his old chestnut doublet and, to the amazement of his hosts, appeared "*ganz propre und wohlanständig in schwarzem Sammt gekleidet*" (entirely proper and becomingly clothed in black velvet), as Cuno tells us.[192] An interesting and instructive conversationalist, very gallant with the ladies, he gave the impression of an old gentleman, friendly and worldly wise. After dinner, he would delay a short time to play l'hombre, which he greatly enjoyed, or preferably to listen to music. He had inherited a real passion for music from his father. "Believe me," he said to Cuno at eighty-one years of age, "if I knew that God would call me to himself tomorrow, today itself I would call musicians to rejoice me for the last time on this earth."[193]

Whenever the conversation on these occasions turned to his relations with the spiritual world—and that was the subject that was almost always finally discussed—Swedenborg never refused to satisfy the curiosity of his interlocutors. In his journal, Cuno strikingly describes the impression the great mystic left on his hearers, with his low and stammering voice and his dreamy light-blue eyes confidingly fixed upon the inquirer "as if they radiated truth itself."[194] In the numerous assemblies of persons who came with the firm intention of ridiculing him as a visionary, it was not unusual to see the smiles fade from their lips as they listened open-mouthed to "the marvels which Swedenborg related to them regarding the spiritual world with the frankness of a child. . . . It appeared that his eyes had the faculty of imposing silence on each one." (We observe that Cuno himself had not the slightest belief in Swedenborg's visions.)

It would seem that Swedenborg was less fortunate when he tried to defend his theological doctrine. His stammer made him ill-equipped for discussion, and he appears most often to have limited himself to referring his questioners to his books. He was absolutely averse to all proselytizing, and the rare disciples he made during his life appear to have come to him less from the effect of his personal influence than by the reading of his books.

And undoubtedly very rare were those who sought him on account of an interest in his teaching. Most of his visitors came to see him because they were curious to meet a man who was known as a seer having the gift of prophecy. At that time, Swedenborg's celebrity both at home and abroad was due to his "telepathic" vision of the conflagration at Stockholm, the discovery of the lost receipt of Mme. de Marteville, and the interview with the late brother of Queen Louisa Ulrika.

Swedenborg was personally quite upset by the popularity he derived from these occurrences, feeling that it overshadowed his true mission. No doubt he did not contradict their authenticity, but he regarded them as of very small importance compared to his other visions.[195] The result of this propagation of his "miracles" was that Swedenborg was overwhelmed by the requests "of desolate widows wanting to learn the destiny of their late husbands, or of other persons who, taking him for a medium, sought from Swedenborg the revelation of secrets, thefts, etc."[196] A certain number of letters written to Swedenborg by his contemporaries and strangers, Swedish and foreign (collected and published by Tafel), had no other purpose. And it appears from Swedenborg's responses to these demands that he had no intention of competing with Arfvidsson, a famous fortuneteller in contemporary Stockholm.[197]

I have summarized these episodes from the last decades of Swedenborg's life, most of them well-known, for the purpose of showing how peaceful and idyllic this life appeared to be. The great dreamer felt himself already to be halfway a participant in the life of the other world. "Whoever has experienced conjunction with the Lord," he told Cuno, "has already a foretaste of eternal life and whoever has this foretaste puts little value on this ephemeral life."[198]

All his contemporaries, even those openly hostile toward him, are in accord in proclaiming the rectitude of his judgment in respect to matters of this world. "The old man talks most reasonably on all other subjects," say Lidén in his notes on their meeting in London in 1769, "but the moment one starts to talk about spirits, he becomes crazy; and my belief and my conviction are that the old man is not entirely same." And Tessin records his recollection of Swedenborg as follows: "My faith and my reason being solid, thank God, it is easy to imagine the opinion I could have of this man. He is otherwise of agreeable conversation, without obstinacy, susceptibility or conceit, amiable, courteous, and frank; judging men and the times with distinction, interpreting everything with kindness and appearing as a philanthropist who passes his days agreeably and takes pleasure in his fantasies, for which there is probably no remedy." Tessin adds, "I can't say whether I consider a weak character who enjoys his imagination as happy or unhappy."[199]

If I have recorded two of the most unfavorable opinions that have been adduced regarding Swedenborg, it is because some of the psychiatrists who have affirmed the madness of the great Swedish mystic have cited as proof the fact that all his contemporaries looked upon him as deranged. It appears quite clearly that these contemporaries of Swedenborg postulated from the start the principle—elevated to a dogma—that whoever did not share their "sound faith" could only be a more or less unbalanced dreamer. Except for the possibly apocryphal reports that Brockmer records regarding Swedenborg's crisis, no one, to my knowledge, has claimed that he manifested any signs of mental deficiencies. Indeed, quite to the contrary, his contemporaries agree in acknowledging, not without a certain surprise, the impression of calm and good sense arising from his conversations on any other topic. He undoubtedly appeared to be a most uncommon character exhibiting a somewhat youthful innocence and naivete, above all during his latter years, but no abnormality was ever apparent as long as he did not talk about his religious ideas. Furthermore, his visitors had only highly confused ideas about Swedenborg's religion, having, for the most part, drawn their notions from his replies to their questions.

I do not intend to deny that Swedenborg, during this period, may have been subject to some kind of mental illness. But the testimony of his contemporaries cannot be accepted as proof. To them, all religious dreamers whose teachings were at variance with the established church were as mentally deranged as Swedenborg was. At this time there were only two ways of explaining heterodox doctrines: conscious fraud or madness.

Furthermore, the external circumstances accompanying Swedenborg's visions have been endowed with a supernatural aura they probably did not have in reality. An influential example is the anecdote related by Atterbom regarding Swedenborg's interview with Virgil.[200] As was his custom, Atterbom, who cites Porthan as his informant, has not failed to embellish with his own imagination what has been reported to him.

According to Atterbom, Porthan, when visiting Swedenborg, had to wait a moment in the salon and listen to his host converse fluently in Latin "on the antiquities of Rome" with an imaginary individual whom he escorted to the door with all gestures of the most exquisite courtesy, with a friendly nod to Porthan in passing. After taking leave of his visitor following further effusions, Swedenborg returns toward Porthan and tells him he has just had a visit from Virgil, "a very charming man." Swedenborg's disciples have vainly tried to demonstrate that the episode has no historical validity. Swedenborg never regarded spirits as moving in the earthly environment, and the idea certainly never entered his mind to offer them chairs and escort them to the door. As Tafel points out, it is still more implausible that, while Swedenborg was having a visit with Virgil, he could have recognized and greeted his Finnish guest.[201] Finally, the very topic of his alleged conversation with Virgil is hardly plausible. Thanks to its simplistic style, this legend has nevertheless acquired a popularity that has overshadowed the truly authentic accounts of the external circumstances surrounding Swedenborg's visions.

These accounts are in accord with the evidence that, on the occasion of these visions, Swedenborg found himself in a kind of trance and was entirely unconscious of the presence of others. The Danish General Tuxen relates that he surprised him one day in such a state, finding him with his elbows on a table and head in his hands. His eyes were open, looking upwards. When Tuxen spoke to him, he awoke, but it took him some time to recover his animation.[202] The same account was given to Robsahm by the wife of Swedenborg's gardener, who naively added "that the pupils of his eyes shone with the clearest fine light and that this glow only faded after half an hour."[203]

It appears that at times in his states of trance Swedenborg spoke aloud, especially when he was being tempted by evil spirits. The old gardener couple confirms having heard him in crises of this nature weeping and invoking the help of God's mercy.[204] A similar account is found in Ferelius.[205]

These trances seem to have the same external form as Swedenborg's first visions. It is probable that they were, like these, released by a critical inhibition of respiration. Indeed, in his *Spiritual Diary,* Swedenborg declares that, thanks to "internal breathing," he could establish communication with angels and spirits (cf. chapter one above). By having recourse to indications that Swedenborg himself gives, notably in his *Spiritual Diary,* it is possible to penetrate the diverse forms of his visionary states in detail.

Swedenborg himself characterizes the onset of his communication with spirits as an awakening of his "inner sight." This expression is worth dwelling upon for a moment.

In *Arcana Coelestia* §994, he wrote the following:

> Except that there is interior sight, no eye can ever see. The sight of the eye exists from interior sight, and for this reason after the

> death of the body man sees equally as well and even better than when he lived in the body—not indeed worldly and corporeal things, but those of the other life. . . . So too, when man sleeps, he sees in his dreams as clearly as when awake. It has been given me to see by internal sight the things in the other life more clearly than I see the things in the world.

We will encounter this explanation again whenever it is a question of visions. It is thus that in another passage (*Arcana Coelestia* §1532), speaking of the heavenly splendors described by the prophets and through the Apocalypse, he writes: "With the bodily eyes no man can possibly see [heavenly things], but the moment the interior sight or that of the spirit is opened by the Lord, such things become visible. The visions of the prophets were nothing else than openings of their interior sight."

A retrospective glance at Swedenborg's psychological theories in *Economy of the Animal Kingdom* makes it possible to grasp his thought more precisely. In our ordinary perceptions, it is the *anima* that feels, sees, hears, etc., thanks to inner organs of perception that constitute the cerebral cortex; the external sensory organs are intermediaries.[206] That it is precisely this vision by the *anima* that Swedenborg calls "inner sight" is certain, since it is this vision we enjoy after physical death. It is in complete accord with this concept that, during his theological period, he speaks of it as of a "vision of our spirit" (*visus spiritus*) and clearly distinguishes it from the sight we enjoy through our corporal eyes. To possess this inner sight in the present life is thus to see without the help of the eyes or the cerebral optical centers (the "internal organs of sight")—to have, by the sole activity of the soul and in a waking state, visions as perfect as those we have in dreams.

The fact that Swedenborg makes such a marked discrimination between "inner sight" and the perceptions of our "corporeal eyes" seems to me to prove that his visions, like those of most mystics, were of a pseudohallucinatory nature. In reality, it is precisely through mystics' revelations about their "intellectual" visions emanating from "internal eyes" that psychiatrists have acquired the notion of hallucinatory phenomena that, unlike true psychosensory hallucinations, do not have the character of sensory perceptions, but come still closer to imagination. While in visual hallucination, properly speaking, the visionary localizes his vision in space or, if his eyes are closed, upon an obscure field, pseudohallucinations have no spatial exteriorization. The subject is thus never tempted to confuse them with external reality. They are distinguished from purely imaginative images by the feeling of psychic objectivity which they provide to the one experiencing them; moreover, they seem to be independent of the will.

It is evident that Swedenborg himself distinguishes these visions from psychosensory hallucinations, which, as we have already seen (cf. chapter six above), he had also experienced. Among the strange forms of visions of which he has been the object, one consists in a kind of extraction of the man from his own body; he thus finds himself in an intermediate state between dreaming and waking. Personally, he feels as if he is fully awake.

> All the senses are as fully awake as in the highest wakefulness of the body; the sight, the hearing, and wonderful to say, the touch, which is then more exquisite than it can ever be in the wakefulness of the body. In this state also spirits and angels have been seen to the very life, and also heard, and, wonderful to say, have been touched, and almost nothing of the body intervened. (*Arcana Coelestia* §1883)

He compares this kind of vision with the one related by St. Paul in the 2 Corinthians 12:2–3, where he suggests that he was "caught up to the third heaven—whether in the body or out of the body I do not know, God knows." Swedenborg reports having been in that state only three or four times, and then only to experience its nature and be convinced that angels enjoy all the senses as well as a tactile sensitivity more exquisite than ours (*Arcana Coelestia* §1883; *Spiritual Diary* §651; *Heaven and Hell* §440).

It is difficult to establish whether Swedenborg is in a waking state at the moments when he had visions of this nature. It is possible that, although he may feel as if he is awake, he may not consider himself to be because his doctrine is opposed to the possibility that man, while awake, can see and touch the spirits physically. This also explains his statement that "almost nothing" of the body intervened. It is further useful to recall that the great vision in London also begins by the apparition before his eyes of a darkness that dissipates thereafter.

What matters to us is, nevertheless, the marked difference between these rare forms of visions, with their clearly pronounced sensory character, and the visions that Swedenborg qualifies as ordinary in this respect. In the *Arcana Coelestia,* he even refuses to give them the name of visions. Rather he is communicating and conversing with angels and spirits in a state of complete wakefulness as though he were one of them (*Arcana Coelestia* §1884; *Heaven and Hell* §442).

In the *Spiritual Diary* §651, he designates this category of visions with which he is the most familiar under the name of "representative visions" received with open eyes (*in aperti oculi statu*) and by which heavenly things are represented—spirits or other manifestations. This kind of vision is more confused than the "living" vision previously described, but is clearly distinguished from common human imagination (*imaginatio*). In the *Arcana Coelestia* (§§1966–1973), Swedenborg establishes a marked distinction between these visions and illusions. He gives a detailed description of the latter, which he ascribes to a state of weakness of the *animus* that renders the visionaries credulous. He also seeks to separate out the visions that "enthusiasts" have in matters of faith, visions that emanate from evil spirits.

> By genuine visions are meant visions or sights of such things in the other life as have real existence, and are nothing but actual things that can be seen by the eyes of the spirit and not by the eyes of the body, and that appear to a man when his interior sight is opened by the Lord (that is, the sight which his spirit has), and into which he comes when, separated from the body, he passes into the other life; for a man is a spirit clothed with a body. Such were the visions of the prophets. When the sight is opened, then those things which have actual existence with spirits are seen in clearer day than that of noon in this world, not only the representatives, but also the spirits themselves, together with a perception of what they are, also of what essence they are, whence they come, whither they are going; also of what

> tenderness, what conditions, even of what faith they are, all confirmed by living speech, exactly as if it were human speech, and this free from all fallacy. (*Arcana Coelestia* §1970)

Further on, Swedenborg declares that these visions, which are apparent to the eyes of the soul but not to those of the body, become progressively more "internal" and obscure according to the degree of one's perception of a higher world. Thus, the visions Swedenborg had of the spiritual world shone with a clear light, while the apparitions emanating from the heavens were much more vague. In many cases, one can only discover what is talked about in heaven through the intermediation of spirits.

Finally, he mentions two visions he considers particularly apt for illustrating the characteristics of these experiences. They seem to me worth referring to here, as Swedenborg most often explains the nature of his visions by way of analogous examples:

> After a troubled sleep, about the first watch, I had a pleasant vision. There were wreaths, as if of laurel, quite fresh, in most beautiful order, with motion as if alive; of such form and elegance of arrangement that description fails to express their beauty and harmony, and the affection of bliss that flowed forth from them. They were in a double series, at a little distance from each other, and running on together to a considerable length, and constantly varying the state of their beauty. This was plainly seen by spirits, even by evil ones. This was afterwards followed by another sight still more beautiful, in which there was heavenly happiness, but it was only dimly visible; there were infants in their heavenly sports, that affected the mind in an inexpressible manner. (*Arcana Coelestia* §1974)

Swedenborg talked afterward with spirits of various categories. We recall the striking analogy between this vision and the description found of heavenly games in *The Worship and Love of God.*

We have already seen that Swedenborg's association with spirits has been, in large part, by way of conversation. If we examine his apparitions more closely, we find that the majority are of a verbal nature. One will remember that already, in his first grand vision of Christ, he had had verbal perceptions. However, the *Journal of Dreams* does not provide us with a more detailed description of the nature of these visions. Nonetheless, one may suppose that here, according to all appearances, it is not a matter of auditory hallucinations, but of these "inner words," of which mystics often speak and which constitute an equivalent of the "view within," the topic of our preceding exploration. A little later, we find very precise descriptions of this phenomenon in his accounts regarding the language of spirits.

The question has already been touched upon in *The Worship and Love of God.* There Swedenborg describes the conversation between Adam and his intelligences; and in §53, note p, he explains this phenomenon: "The fact that Adam discoursed with his intelligences is to be understood as follows: he discoursed with himself, or with his intellect, that is, that he thought; for thought is a certain kind of discourse with oneself, the operations of our mind being veritable actions (*reales activitates*) or changes of state by variations of form. It follows that they also constitute a kind of interior speech." He then develops his old theory: thoughts are fluid undulations transformed by the organs of speech into atmospheric vibrations and thereby into sounds:

> If it were otherwise, and were it not the same with eyesight, it would be impossible to perceive what we think and even more so to talk to ourselves, to utter the same thoughts, to transform them into sounds or articulated words. . . . Thought, then, being a real speech, and more perfect than that of our larynx, at the same time including more simultaneous and successive elements, it follows that it is heard and understood by the celestial souls, called angels, entirely as well and even better than oral speech is understood by our companions and by our interlocutors.

As we see, here Swedenborg conceives the language of angels as a pure transmission of thought. He is not yet speaking of inner voices. It is evident, however, that his conception of thought as an inner language involves a certain predisposition towards this kind of verbal pseudohallucination.

It is beyond doubt that it is a matter of hallucinations of this category in *Historia Creationis a Mose tradita*, written in 1745. With regard to the conversation between the serpent and Adam, Swedenborg, by invoking his own experience with the language of spirits, gives us several indications of high value, probably recalling above all the occurrences of the preceding years. He declares here that the language of celestial beings issues from marvelous circles of heavenly form and is so universal that it corresponds to any spoken language.

> This language enters first into the thought or the inner sight and there gives birth to barely conceivable elevated ideas, thereafter to evolve into the habitual tongue of the hearer. . . . There exists, therefore, a language common with spirits and men who live in the state of our first ancestors, just as among earthly interlocutors: but this language is an internal one. Also, this language is even as sonorous as if it proceeded from the mouth and tongue, although it is not transformed into any sound. (*Adversaria* I, §§15–16)

Swedenborg adds that no mortal can have knowledge of this language if it has not been given to him or her, as a spiritual being, by the grace of God.

It is this same language of the spirits that later, during the course of his theological phase, Swedenborg says he understands. In the detailed descriptions that he gives in the *Arcana Coelestia* (§§1634–1650, §§1757–1764) and elsewhere, he makes it plain that this language is the mother tongue of the initiate and that it is as distinct and as clearly understood as the ordinary speech of human beings. It is not, however, transmitted by air or through the ear, but carried in an inner way to the very organs of the head and brain. This is why it is perceived in the same fashion. In reality, the language of spirits is composed not of words, but of thoughts. Spirits possess only internal memory and are consequently incapable of pronouncing a single word. But when they communicate with a person, their thoughts are transformed into words in the corporeal memory of the latter and are thereby translated into the very language of the listener (*Arcana*

Coelestia §1638, §4342). These words, pronounced by spirits or rather evoked by them in the memory of the listener, are distinguished by being particularly well-chosen, clear, and clearly articulated. They are particularly adapted to the thought they are to express, just as when a person, without thinking of the words, leaves them to be dictated by the internal phrasing itself. Swedenborg says he has conversed with angels by means of his internal memory too, that is to say in their own language, the language of thought (*Arcana Coelestia* §§1638–1639).

During Swedenborg's conversation with spirits, he has a sense of their spatial location. He perceives them in various parts of the body: in the head, in one of his ribs, one of his elbows, or within his organism, according to the seat of various spirits in the "Grand Man." He thus comes to know their spiritual state and their nature. He even deduces their character from the tones of their voices (*Arcana Coelestia* §1640).

Swedenborg's minute descriptions allow us to link this perception of the language of spirits with the "internal speech" of which all mystics often speak and which modern psychiatry identifies with "verbal pseudohallucinations." I believe it useful to analyze here in some detail the explanation Séglas gives of the origin and nature of these hallucinations.[207] It is, of course, impossible for me to judge the exactitude of his theory, but we shall see that it strangely accords with Swedenborg's attempts to explain the phenomenon.

"We think with the help of words," says Séglas. "Each item of thought is translated in our mind into a verbal formula. This is what is called the inner language." As we see, we have there a point of departure identical with that of Swedenborg in *The Worship and Love of God*. Our awareness of this internal language is in general rather unclear. However, there have been cases in which this language becomes, without effort on our part, spontaneously more alive in a way that the subject comes to hear in himself his own thoughts transformed into verbal form. This phenomenon is at times so intense that not only the words become clearly perceptible, but they acquire a kind of tone, a true internal resonance that is clearly different from the external sound of a word as perceived in the ear. Psychiatrists note an analogous phenomenon in the fact that, in certain persons who are particularly sensitive to music, a melody heard some time previously comes to mind suddenly and involuntarily in the consciousness with a manifestly sensory precision that at times has such clarity that the various instrumental parts and notes are distinguishable. As Kandinsky remarks, this phenomenon already partially presents the compulsive quality of pathological hallucinations.[208] The musical motif "rings" in the ear, and the hearer cannot shut it out.

Verbal pseudohallucinations assume the form of monologues or dialogues. Most often the subject is immediately aware of hearing his or her own thoughts.

There have been cases, nevertheless, when this is not at all so: the speech appears enigmatic, in contradiction with one's own will and one's own desires. They do not come from him, and he exercises no control over them. Here, a psychic automatism intervenes, accompanying objectivization. Séglas, whose explication I here follow point for point, maintains that the moment when the subject finds himself thus in conversation with his inner voices, he distinguishes them from his own mental responses by the fact that they are notably clearer than and completely independent of his own will. Like several other researchers who have studied this phenomenon, Séglas notes that the subject usually localizes these voices, not in his auditory organs, but in other parts of his body. It is thus that they frequently seem to emanate from his chest, epigastrium, etc.[209]

It seems to me quite interesting that it is possible to establish that Swedenborg's visions and revelations—like those of most mystics—are basically of a pseudohallucinatory character. Of course, this does not explain their meaning or their significance to the evolution of Swedenborg's worldview. As I have already pointed out, psychiatric diagnoses that pretend to explain historical phenomena from some pathological trait are inadequate and unscientific; in reality, numerous other factors also have to be taken into account. This kind of approach appears exceptionally absurd in this case, when we are dealing with such a uniquely intelligent mind as that of Swedenborg, who had intuited profound religious views from his far-reaching philosophical speculations long before he had experienced any hallucinatory states.

In this case, it can even be seen *a priori* that the role of his hallucinatory states in his religious system will be limited in large measure to confirm the results already attained by his conscious thought, and, at times, to lead him to conclusions before which he would perhaps have hesitated. Swedenborg's doctrine, then, is not as it is portrayed by the psychiatrists who have studied him; it is not a sort of "conglomerate" of his hallucinations. It would be more accurate to say that, after the period of crisis revealed in the *Journal of Dreams* and up to his last years, Swedenborg's visions and appearances are no more than objectivized manifestations of his own world of thought, a continuation of his conscious speculations in the form of dreams and hallucinations. In a way, Swedenborg himself was convinced that this was so, and he repeatedly declares that the doctrines he proclaims have not come to him "from any angel," that is to say, by a vision, but that he had them "exclusively from God while reading the Bible" (*True Christian Religion* §779).

With this quite natural reservation, it appears to us that, in accepting the analogy between Swedenborg's visions and the pseudohallucinations so well-known to modern psychiatry, we arrive at certain conclusions of the highest interest about the external forms of Swedenborg's "relationship with spirits."

First of all, the pseudohallucinatory character of Swedenborg's visions seems to a certain extent to answer the question posed by all commentators on his theosophical phase: how was it possible for him for years and years to be the daily object of visions—which were at times highly fantastic—without showing any observable sign of mental imbalance and without causing his theological work to lose anything of its penetrating character? It is easy to demonstrate that his theological doctrine, such as he expounds it at the age of eighty-two in *True Christian Religion,* notably surpasses in logic and clarity the scientific doctrines of his *Economy of the Animal Kingdom* and contemporary works.

In effect, it appears to be well-established that pseudohallucinations neither suppose nor involve mental disturbances that are as marked as true psychosensory hallucinations. They appear with incredible ease and are frequently encountered among absolutely normal people, usually just before sleep or after awakening. There is only one step to pseudohallucination from mental images. Many psychiatrists even refuse to admit the hallucinatory character of these phenomena and believe that here it is a question of inner images that the subject interprets as apparitions.

In Séglas's study, he avers that pseudohallucinations, particularly verbal ones, frequently coincide with a belief in telepathy and spiritism or that they appear in individuals who believe they are the objects of magnetism or suggestion. "The particular ideas of *direct* influence, that is to say, without sensory intermediaries, amounts to a march toward verbal pseudohallucination."[210] Needless to say, this conception responds very well to the case of Swedenborg. It was precisely this belief in an influence independent of any sensory element that led him to mysticism. In reality, the majority of mystics give explanations of their visions and their spiritual conversations that are very similar to those Swedenborg has given of his. I have even found, in a case referred to by modern psychiatrists, a representation of an interior memory similar to that related above: "Mme. Kr. declared that she had two memories: one which enabled her, like anyone else, to remember everything at will, the other which recalled to her awareness voices and internal images without intermediary. She also distinguished between internal voices and external ones."[211]

I do not in any way wish to restrict the visions of Swedenborg to those apparitions and inner voices that rank in psychiatry as mental hallucinations. From his own declarations, it is evident that he had been the object of clearly characterized psychosensory hallucinations, visions during which he has seen spirits with his "corporeal" eyes and in which he has even touched them (*Arcana Coelestia* §1883). He has, furthermore, had auditory perceptions that he has localized in the acoustic organs, and he has even, without any doubt, been the object of complex hallucinations that Ballet qualifies as "oneiric" and which one might classify as a sort of waking dream, comprising coherent scenes in which all the senses of the subject appear to participate. Swedenborg's relations with the spiritual world are in no way limited to these various categories of hallucinations. He enters into contact with this world not only in dreams of various kinds (a description of which would take us too far afield), but also in a state of consciousness that he describes as between sleep and wakefulness. And as we shall see, he little by little comes to attribute the source of all his perceptions and his corporeal and spiritual functions to spirits.

In any case, it seems to me that Swedenborg's strange conception of the spiritual world, as well as his description of it, becomes more readily explicable if one bears in mind that most of the apparitions of which he has been the object were manifested in the form of visions and inner voices.

His minute descriptions of the spiritual world, its inhabitants, and their life, however particular in their details, do not bear the scrutiny of reason. We rarely find in Swedenborg these picturesque and colorful scenes so frequent in the accounts that popular visionaries provide of their apparitions. Swedenborg's descriptions of the world of spirits, which are the most detailed and the most concrete, are often the most servile reproduction of terrestrial conditions. He rarely describes a landscape in a concrete fashion or points to such and such an individual character of a spirit, even though he furnishes the environments of these spirits with forests, groves and lakes, and causes the spirits to share in the material structure of man. Even in his abundant descriptions of the Last Judgment as it was given to him to witness in 1757 in the spiritual world, we find not the slightest picturesque detail; these are indeed endowed with a certain living drama, but they give the impression of secondhand accounts.

To a certain extent this remark also applies to the most fantastic of his works, *Earths in the Universe* in which he realized a dream that had haunted him since his scientific period. It is about a voyage across sundry planets with whose inhabitants and spirits he became acquainted. The picturesque details there are at once very rare, and they present stereotypical characters. It is thus that Swedenborg repeatedly speaks of birds with golden wings which take flight across the azure sky. This lack of the picturesque is evidently explicable by the somewhat abstract nature of his imagination. It can also be explained by the theory of correspondences, which does not allow the author to mention any concrete detail that fails to respond to something spiritual.

But the fundamental cause of this characteristic appears to be that most often these visions have not had for Swedenborg the character of entirely externalized hallucinations, but fall in the class of pseudohallucinations. By all evidence, it is possible that these pseudohallucinations are as clearly perceptible and as alive as true hallucinations, but their kinship with mental imagery implies that they do not have the same illusory visual character. Since the subject does not localize these pseudohallucinations in external reality, they are frequently distinguished from spatial conditions and from the proportions of this environment. From numerous statements in the *Spiritual Diary*, it is evident that he often had difficulties in describing them distinctly.

Furthermore, a large portion of Swedenborg's knowledge of the spiritual world manifestly comes from his interviews with the spirits. And it is readily perceived, in a general way, that his contacts with angels and spirits are the object of a notably clearer description and are of a higher literary standard than his own eyewitness reports.

Beyond a doubt, his most splendid descriptions of spirits are found in the memorabilia of his later works. They expound his philosophical and theological discussions with the spirits, some of whom are specifically named, while others are anonymous. These brief scenes, which he frequently locates in an ancient setting, furnished with a few characteristic accessories, take place under the arcades of the Atheneum or in the octagonal palace built on Parnassus where the great philosophers of yore, wearing hyacinth-colored togas, are seated on stone benches, are crowned with laurel, and hold palm leaves in their hands. The conversations delivered in these schools of wisdom have a certain ancient style and recall the Dialogues of Plato, which were certainly present in Swedenborg's mind.

In the closing chapter of *True Christian Religion*, he predicts that many readers will consider these reminiscences "inventions of the imaginative faculties," but he assures us that he has reported only what he has seen and heard when completely awake. It does not seem to me that there could be cause to suspect the sincerity of that declaration. For example, in one of his better-known reminiscences, he records that one day he had asked the Lord to grant him an interview with the disciples of Aristotle, Descartes, and Leibniz. Following this prayer, he had a vision in which he was visited by nine persons, three from each school, with whom he discusses the relation of the soul to the body. There is no need here to argue for the hallucinatory character of this vision from the fact that the subject had already fixed the object. It appears to be well established that an individual who is predisposed to pseudohallucinations can, in certain cases, consciously assign a determined content to them.[212]

In any case, it is beyond doubt that Swedenborg has interpreted this vision—which only repeats his old theories on the interrelations between soul and body—not as a product of his own intellectual activity, but as an emanation of inner voices independent of his will. The close kinship between a particularly vivid mental image and a verbal pseudohallucination suffices to explain the fact that these two phenomena can at times seem nearly identical in their exterior manifestations. In many cases, the psychiatrists themselves do not know whether they are dealing with a pseudohallucinatory phenomenon or a case of poetic inspiration.

Finally, assuming that the greater number of Swedenborg's visions may have had a pseudohallucinatory character, it is possible to state that this spiritual world with which he believes himself to be in contact does not appear to him as an objective reality entirely exterior to his own being, but as partially an aspect of his own mind. As Séglas has pointed out, the psychosensory hallucination, with its illusory sense of an empirical reality, does not encourage the representation of spirits acting in the interior of the subject in the same way as does the pseudohallucination. To completely understand Swedenborg's views in this regard, it is first necessary to take into account his general theory on the action exercised by spirits on man.

This theory rests on the foundation of the psychological system with which we have become acquainted in *Economy of the Animal Kingdom* and in *The Worship and Love of God*. As in the latter, Swedenborg puts man into contact with heaven through the intermediary of the *anima* and with hell through the senses. But while he previously thought that the heavenly light was irradiated directly into the *anima*, just as the sensory desires came directly from hell through the *animus*, he has now become convinced that these influences manifest themselves through the mediation of angels and of spirits, that is to say, through the souls of the dead. Animals alone are ruled by a general influence from the spiritual world, because they are born with instincts that are essential to them, and they have no need for instruction. Man, however, who has separated himself from heaven, no longer finds himself in the order of nature for which he has been created and must consequently be subject to the special guidance of God. If human beings did not receive influx from angels and spirits, they would throw themselves blindly into the deepest hell (*Arcana Coelestia* §5850; *Heaven and Hell* §247).

This doctrine of spirits is found clearly characterized already in the first part of the *Adversaria* and in volume one of the *Spiritual Diary.* It can be traced back to 1745 or 1746. We find it in the *Arcana Coelestia* in a completely systematized form.

"Man cannot think or will anything by himself, but everything flows in; good and truth from the Lord through the heaven, thus through the angels who are with the man; evil and falsity from hell, thus through the evil spirits who are with the man" (*Arcana Coelestia* §5846). Everyone is linked with two angels and two infernal spirits. If the human being did not find himself thus in contact with heaven and with hell, he could not survive for an instant (*Arcana Coelestia* §§5848–5849). The fact that people find themselves accompanied by two spirits of each category arises from the existence of two sorts of angels in heaven and two sorts of spirits in hell, to which the two faculties of the mind correspond: the will and the reason. A heavenly angel and an infernal genius contend for the will of the individual, while a spiritual angel and an infernal spirit act upon the person's intelligence (*Arcana Coelestia* §§5977–5978).

The evil spirits and genii who are within the person indeed come from hell; but during their presence in the human creature, they are relocated into the world of spirits, intermediate between heaven and hell. They therefore suffer no infernal penalty, but experience the same love of self and of the world as the person to whom they have been sent. These spirits, who are associated with the human being who is their recipient, penetrate into his memory and into all his thoughts and feelings. They therefore share the same character as that person; they are miserly if the person is miserly, proud if he is proud, etc. And it is why, to the extent that his own interior is modified, the person acquires new spirits, supplanting those that haunted him before (*Arcana Coelestia* §§5850–5852).

The spirits present in the human being are not at all aware of this association; only the angels know it, because they are exclusively associated with the person's soul and not with his body. Likewise, people are ignorant of their union with the spirits and with the angels. Just as we imagine that we think and will of ourselves, so do the spirits associated with us consider as their own the thoughts and feelings of the one they inhabit. Only the awakening of the "inner sight" of human beings allows them to become aware that they are led by angels and by spirits, and the latter then become aware of their consociation with humanity. This state implies great danger for humankind, for the spirits hold us in mortal hatred. Once they become conscious of their association with a man, they try by all means to destroy him, body and soul. Such is the origin of the terrible temptations suffered by Swedenborg (*Arcana Coelestia* §§5862–5863).

Through these *tienstandar,* "spirit servants," a term used by Jesper Swedberg and at times by his son (*Spiritual Diary* §3985), a person finds himself, without his knowledge, in permanent association with the spiritual world. For in their turn, these spirits are influenced by other spirits. They in some way constitute ambassadors of the various societies in the spiritual world; indeed, there exist in this spiritual world societies concerning everything that can be the subject of human thought and desire (*Spiritual Diary* §4154).

Thus, humankind becomes the focus of an infinity of spirits who influence our thoughts and sentiments. Since 1747, Swedenborg declares in his *Spiritual Diary* (§254), as myriads of muscles and fibers cooperate in an action, the elaboration of a thought demands the cooperation of thousands of angels and spirits. He is very careful to be able to localize the seat of various spirits with reference to his anatomy. Their situation is determined by the place that they inhabit in heaven and in hell, both of which have the human form. The benevolent spirits appear to him to reside in large part around the head; spirits who provoke anxieties sit in the abdomen; the avaricious, a little higher, etc. Spirits act, not only on a human being's thoughts and feelings, but also upon his physical functions; for all natural phenomena is only the effect of spiritual action.

There is, then, nothing surprising in Swedenborg's declaration, which appears already in his first exegetical works (*Adversaria* 1149ff.)

that spirits direct his steps, preside over the movements of his hands, his fingers, head, and eyes, and that they guide his hand when he writes. In one chapter of the *Arcana Coelestia* (§§5711–5727), he even gives a detailed description of the fashion in which spirits cause maladies. In effect, they have their origin in the desires and passions of the *animus,* which, in turn, emanates from infernal spirits. It is thus, as Swedenborg tells us, that a spirit who was an adulterer in the course of his life on earth appeared after his death under Swedenborg's feet and provoked a violent pain in his toe.

Swedenborg goes as far as attributing to spirits the most trivial occurrences. He relates that having enjoyed an excellent butter one day in the presence of a celestial angel, he was then nauseated by it. It was then the spiritual angels who had caused a disagreeable odor of the butter to penetrate his nostrils. On the other hand, having one day tasted some milk in the presence of these same spirits, he experienced indescribable pleasure. He concludes therefrom that butter relates to the celestial angels and milk to spiritual angels, who detest butter. By this he understands not that angels consume these foods, but that the butter and the milk are representations of the angels (*Spiritual Diary* §§1161–1163). Evil spirits can play some very malicious tricks in the course of a meal. They can give sugar the taste of salt (*Spiritual Diary* §645). On the other hand, the good spirits watch him carefully so that there is no excess at the table. It was thus one evening when he had just finished his frugal repast of bread and milk the spirits found that he had eaten exaggeratedly and gave the food the odor of excrements and urine, from which he realized that he had committed the sin of gluttony (*Spiritual Diary* §618). He narrates elsewhere, no doubt remembering an old popular Swedish prejudice, that the spirits did not allow him to think of pointed or sharp articles (*Spiritual Diary* §208).

Like all people predisposed to obsession with demons, Swedenborg often finds himself painfully uncertain of the good or evil nature of spirits who influence him. He uses many means of distinguishing the infernal spirits from the celestial, but none of these appears to be infallible. He declares at times that he recognizes the infernal spirits by the chill he perceives at their approach (*Spiritual Diary* §406). But in a number of such cases, he is not sure whether the impulse he experiences comes to him from God or the demon. So it is that he repeatedly senses during the night (*Spiritual Diary* §399, §755) a voluptuous sensation that simultaneously brings a feeling of the highest celestial beatitude and one of the most intense conjugal pleasure, and the help of God alone has allowed him to recognize this as an illusion emanating from the devil. For the infernal horde is so cunning in its aptitude for impersonating angels and simulating objects of human imagination that a person would succumb to temptation at any moment if the Lord Jesus Christ did not himself restrain the demon (*Spiritual Diary* §617). As we see, the marvelous ecstasies dating from the crisis of the *Journal of Dreams* have already lost their divine character for Swedenborg.

I have selected several examples from the *Spiritual Diary* at random to provide the reader with some idea of the range of Swedenborg's intercourse with spirits. In every human thought, in each voluntary act, in every sensation, he sees the influence of good or evil spirits. They are even his mute collaborators in his descriptions of them. Thus he writes (*Spiritual Diary* §4154) that, reflecting one day on the secrets hidden in the account of Noah's Ark in the Scripture, he became aware of the presence of certain spirits who were discussing these secrets. Some were talking about the opportunity for revealing these secrets, others about the truth of the account, and still others about the possibility of disseminating them. And in a brief note on the origin of the *Spiritual Diary* (§2894), Swedenborg declares that all that he has written in this work derives from "living experience," from conversations with angels and spirits, and that these inspire his thoughts and his words at the very moment he is writing; they have even guided his hand. In concluding, he says, "Even this (which I am now writing) is directed by the spirits closest to my head, for I have often perceived their presence."

It is not sufficient, however, to reach an understanding of the ties that link humanity with the spiritual world or for us to visualize ourselves as the center of an infinity of spirits who act upon the life of our souls. It is also necessary to understand that within, through his *anima*, each person is a spirit and belongs to the spiritual world. As Swedenborg states in *Heaven and Hell* §436,

> That in respect to his interiors man is a spirit I have been permitted to learn from much experience, which, to employ a common saying, would fill volumes if I were to describe it all. I have talked with spirits as a spirit, and I have talked with them as a man in the body; and when I talked with them as a spirit, they knew no otherwise than that I myself was a spirit and in a human form as they were. Thus did my interiors appear before them, for when talking with them as a spirit my material body was not seen.

In comparing Swedenborg's visions with his theory of spirits, as I have tried to do above, one easily comes to understand that he came to consider all his psychic functions as being inspired by the angels and the spirits; at the same time, these spiritual influences became familiar phenomena for him. Like himself, all men are dependent on spirits and angels in their thoughts and in their feelings. What distinguishes Swedenborg from his fellow creatures is that he has received from God the gift of seeing the spirits. "It has been given me to witness, by an experience so clear that it leaves no room for doubt," he states in a passage in *Arcana Coelestia* (§6191), "that man is, by God's grace, directed by angels and spirits." He relates in this respect that it has been given him for several years to feel that all his thoughts and all his feelings enter into him through the intermediation of angels and spirits. He has received the gift of conversing with them, of identifying them, of recognizing to what "society" they belonged and even of engaging in conversation with their societies themselves. "And though all the thoughts and all the feelings were emanations of angels and spirits, I thought and felt the same as previously, I spoke with men as in the past without anyone observing any difference between my current lifestyle and my preceding one, I expect that nobody will believe me, nevertheless, what I am saying is the eternal truth."

Swedenborg believes, then, that in spite of his constant intercommunication with spirits, he enjoys the same relative freedom in his thoughts and in his decisions as other people. When he finds himself in the street, in a crowd, and consequently he is no longer thinking of spirits, they are no longer aware of their presence within him. They are plunged, he says, into a sort of lethargy and can only act from his memory and his rationality without being able to see through his eyes or to converse with him. It is only while he looks at them with his inner sight that they wake up and resume consciousness.

The Swedenborgian doctrine of spirits is therefore not the product of a disordered imagination that justifies his biographers in dealing nonchalantly with his theology. It constitutes a systematic development of psychological theories that he expounds in *Economy of the Animal Kingdom*. Among the figures who appeared to him in sleep or in a state of wakefulness, he believes he recognizes dead friends and acquaintances. The inner voices he has heard have at times confirmed him in his belief and have at times tempted him to follow his earthly desires. Already during the period of his *Journal of Dreams*, these voices have been objectivized into good and evil spirits and have been made into intermediaries of two powers who dispute the domination of his soul: the sun of the divinity with its light and heat, and, on the other side, the world with its desires and temptations. In *The Worship and Love of God,* this conflict between the inner and outer man finds a universal correspondence in the struggle between God and the Devil.

During his theological period, Swedenborg feels that the same combat is taking place within him, even though hell and the infernal spirits no longer have their origin in the revolt of the devil against God, but in the Fall of humanity itself. Created to live in the divine light and warmth, we have allowed ourselves to be seduced by the world and by the desire to be our own master. We tasted the fruit of the Tree of Knowledge; that is, we opened our inner being to the seduction of the senses. From that moment, we lost all direct contact with the Divinity. Having violated divine order, humans became incapable of obeying the direct influence of God. Upon us, the children of the new generations, rests the burden of repeated apostasies of our fathers in the form, not of an ineluctable hereditary sin that predestines us to hell, but of a congenital inclination for evil. This is what is symbolized by the action exerted by the souls of the dead on our thoughts and feelings. God sees to it that the equilibrium between angels and evil spirits is always maintained in us, so that the choice may lie within our own will. We thus become quite as responsible for our own fall as the first man was.

I shall return to this reasoning in a more detailed fashion in regard to Swedenborg's theology. I have discussed it here to show that, although it is built on visions and even on manifest reminiscences of the popular faith, the traditions of which reached him over so many routes, notably through his father, Swedenborg's doctrine of the spiritual world did not in any way constitute a loose appendage to his system or a derogation of the structural principles of this system. The goal of this doctrine is to emphasize the fundamental notion that we have been able to follow from his first philosophical works, according to which God is the one and only life and the sole activity of the universe, and that all beings, whether of the spiritual or natural world, are only an emanation of his divine goodness and wisdom. The entire theological system of Swedenborg, as well as all of his visions, in reality goes back to the day when, for the first time, he felt his interior penetrated by the divine light.

If one wishes to see similarity between the experiences of his theological period and his first contacts with a higher world, it is useful to read the description in *Arcana Coelestia* (§§168–186), where he relates that he learned "by a living experience" how a person passes from corporal to eternal life: "I found myself in a state of physical insensibility, in a state analogous to that of a dying man, while keeping intact my inner life and faculty of thought, so that I could observe and recall what happens to those who are dead and who have been resuscitated. I kept breathing to the extent necessary to maintain life and then breathed in silent respiration."

As we see, this is precisely the state in which Swedenborg had already found himself in the fainting *deliquia* he had experienced while writing the preface of the *Economy of the Animal Kingdom,* and which he later suffered and described at the close of the *Journal of Dreams.* We recall that he had then been seized by one of his respiratory suspensions during a fainting spell when he "had appeared to be close to death" (cf. chapters three and six above). Later, in the *Arcana Coelestia,* he recounts that he found himself, in that state, completely isolated from the spirits of the world of spirits and entirely abandoned to the influence of celestial angels, two of whom take up place in his heart and two in his head. He comes to perceive their aphonic "cogitative language" from modifications their influence stimulates in the positions of his lips. Thanks to the sensation of a kind of balsamic perfume, the presence of the angels gave an aromatic character to what had been a cadaverous odor. Then the angels proceed with a rite that consists of peeling a membrane from his eyes. The first effect of this operation is a vague luminous sensation like that one senses through the eyelids when awakening. When he is resuscitated and later enters into eternal life, the passage is represented in the form of a white light, embellished by yellowish reflections. We note that this apparent state of death, here, as with Swedenborg previously, engenders the vision of a supernatural light.

We therefore find again the same basic elements of the phenomena Swedenborg sees as the definitive confirmation of the resurrection of the human being in the form of an angel and of his first vision that apprized him of the transrational existence of a faculty of the soul—of a glass into which the divine light could penetrate directly from its original source.

Since that time, we may well ask ourselves if Swedenborg himself has not observed this analogy, and if, during his theological period, he has not accorded greater importance to these luminous visions that are accompanied by respiratory suspension than at the very moment when he experienced them. It is easy to prove that this is the case. In *Heaven and Hell* (§438) he declares that, in the course of corporeal life, a person becomes a member of a community by his soul. His *anima* becomes part of a heavenly community if he is good, and of an infernal community if he is evil. Swedenborg affirms without any doubt that the human being is not visible in this "society" during his terrestrial life, from the fact that he thinks naturally. "But," he adds, "those who free their thoughts from their body *(qui autem abstracte a corpore cogitant)* show themselves on occasion in this society, for they are then in spirit; and when they are visible they are clearly perceived by the spirits there, for they are absorbed in their reflections, keeping silent without regard to those around them. Everything occurs as though they did not see them and, once a spirit speaks to them, they disappear." Thinking *abstracte a corpore* is, for Swedenborg, to eliminate all impressions arising from the senses and to allow the *anima* to bathe the soul in its light; one reaches this state by internal respiration. "It has also by these means been granted me to associate with angels and with spirits," he says in his *Spiritual Diary* (§3465, cf. above, chapter three). And it now dawns on Swedenborg that he has also been present in the spiritual world long before becoming aware of it. On every occasion when, during his scientific period, he found himself sharing the divine light, he had been unconsciously absorbed in his thoughts, walking like a spirit—an object of astonishment to other spirits without being able to see or converse with them. Well before the awakening of his "inner sight" he had been both "an alien and a citizen" in the spiritual world; and it is thereby that the relation between his theological system and the philosophy he expounds in his later scientific period are to be explained.

nine

The Exegete

Swedenborg's earliest attempts at an allegorical explication of the Bible go back to 1741, as I have previously pointed out, contemporaneous with the doctrine of correspondence and manifestly contributing in large measure to the elaboration of this doctrine. When he receives from God the order to abandon his scientific writing and to devote himself instead to religious studies, it is also by a kind of allegorical exposition of the Creation that he inaugurates his new activity. *The Worship and Love of God* corresponds in a certain measure to the Kabbalistic and natural-philosophic paraphrases of the early chapters of Genesis, similar to those that were so numerous during the Renaissance and following centuries, beginning with the *Heptaplus* of Pico della Mirandola. Through the vision I have analyzed in previous chapters, however, Swedenborg received a further divine injunction to limit himself to comment on the inner sense of Scripture and write under the guidance of God. And it is to this exegesis that he dedicated the rest of his life.

It would be an alluring task to relate in detail the evolution of Swedenborg's exegetic method up to its full development in *Arcana Coelestia*. A study of this nature would certainly be realizable, since Tafel published the largest part of the material under the title of *Adversaria,* while the rest exists in manuscript and in photolithographic reproductions. Nevertheless, this subject is beyond what I have proposed to undertake, so I shall limit myself to relating briefly Swedenborg's conception of Scripture and its inner meaning.

When Swedenborg seeks, in his *Historia Creationis a Mose tradita* of 1745, to explain the story of the Creation for the first time, he proceeds with the greatest circumspection. On the basis of two Latin versions, he only gives allegorical explications of the passages in which the biblical text seems obscure to him or which appear to contradict his own cosmological principles. However, he often appeals to his visions and leaves it to be understood, at the end of the work, that the Bible text has a deeper meaning and that it shows that God has created the world to advance the kingdom of heaven, the heavenly Jerusalem. This thought is found consistently developed in his second commentary on Genesis, *Explicatio in Verbum Historicum Veteris Testamenti.* Here he considers the first chapter of Genesis throughout, not only as a description of the creation of the natural world, but also of the establishment of the kingdom of God. Paradise represents heaven; and the union of Adam and Eve, the union of the Messiah and the kingdom of God.[213]

In the course of this work, Swedenborg observes no fewer than three hidden senses behind the historical letter of Scripture. The nearest to the letter of Scripture is a universal one, generalizing what the Bible describes and applying it to the future. It is thus that the history of Jacob encloses that of the Jewish people as a whole. Beneath this universal level of meaning is found a second, of an even more extensive universality, by which the biblical text allegorizes the destinies of the entire human race. According to this sense, Jacob and Israel symbolize not only the Jewish people but the whole human species. Finally, the third, the most profound and the all-embracing of these deeper senses, applies exclusively to the Messiah and his future kingdom. The Bible thus comes to present a certain analogy with humankind, its letter corresponding to the human body and the three hidden senses to the three degrees of the human soul (*Adversaria* I, 505).

This latter line of thought is quite frequent in the history of biblical allegoric exegesis. Earlier, Philo of Alexandria considered the literal sense as the body, enveloping the allegoric inner sense as its soul.[214] We find also an analogous interpretation in the Kabbalah, in which the literal sense becomes the apparel that covers the body. Origen, along with a great number of allegorical exegetes after him, designates the historical sense of the letter as the body of Scripture, the moral content as the soul, and the mystic sense as the spirit of the Scriptures.[215] But I have been unable to discover in any author an equivalent to Swedenborg's classification.

This classification is simplified during the theological period, in the course of which Swedenborg generally reverts to the biblical trinity of body, soul, and mind in humans. In his *New Jerusalem and Its Heavenly Doctrine* §80, he declares that two other deeper senses exist behind the literal sense of Holy Scripture: one spiritual sense applies more particularly to the Church, and a still higher sense, the celestial, applies to God. These two layers of meaning in particular provide the object of his studies. Behind the historic narration in the Mosaic books, he traces a kind of spiritualized biblical history that relates how humanity has withdrawn itself more and more from the Divinity and thereby has also departed more and more from that state of integrity in which Adam found himself created in the image of God. Accordingly, new revelations of the Divinity and of new churches are needed.

We shall return later to this strange allegorical transformation of biblical history, to which Swedenborg has newly arrived through a combination of the biblical account with the ancient myths of the four ages of the earth. But he also discovers one inmost heavenly sense. Although it takes the form of historical accounts, it reveals to us a truth that is independent of all time and absolutely universal, where it is a question of God in his differing appearances and the relations of man with the Divinity. To make this a little more intelligible to the reader, it is necessary to examine Swedenborg's method of interpretation more closely. It rests directly on the doctrine of correspondences, in a form almost identical to the one described previously. Each word of the Bible being sacred and inspired, one should be able to substitute all the words representing natural things by spiritual concepts that correspond to them and that thus reveal an entirely new hidden sense. Anyone who is ignorant of the doctrine of correspondences, said Swedenborg (*Doctrine of Sacred Scripture* §18), gets the impression that the Bible speaks much of terrestrial matters and very little of celestial things. But when it speaks about Egypt, Assyria, and Edom, it must be understood thereby to refer to science, reason, and the natural mind. When gardens, groves, and forests are mentioned, wisdom, intelligence, and knowledge must be understood. The olive, vine, cedar, poplar, and oak trees correspond to heavenly, spiritual, rational, natural and sensory truth and goodness, respectively. The lamb, goat, and cow signify innocence, love, and natural bents; mountains, hills, and valleys signify elevated matters, less elevated things, and the lower things of the Church.

The method here applied is exactly the one Philo of Alexandria and Origen followed in their allegorical exegeses. I cannot here enter into the detail of comparative examples, which would lead us afar. Readers interested in the matter will find it dealt with in Siegfried's study of the commentaries on the Old Testament by Philo. From the summaries presented in this work in the form of tables of the allegorical equivalents established by Philo and by Origen of the names of peoples, animals, trees, etc., it is evident that each author, despite individual differences in the results of their interpretation, operates on the same basis as Swedenborg. Both admit *a priori* "that God expresses himself like a man, without, however, speaking as a man."[216]

This starting point is identical to that of Swedenborg in the *Clavis,* where he affirms that, in the Bible, the spirit speaks both naturally and spiritually at the same time. In his later works, he expounds in more detail how everything in Scripture is expressed by correspondences. In the Bible, God speaks of his divine Being and of all that has a divine character, which is manifested in nature in the form of correspondences (*True Christian Religion* §201). It is evident that, with Swedenborg as with his predecessors, this concept is based upon the belief that the authors of the Bible were verbally inspired. Philo is of the opinion that it is God himself who speaks through the Bible, whether in a direct manner or in making his spirit speak through the mouth of the prophets, who thereby are not expressing their own thoughts but are merely instruments of revelation of eternal verities. Philo does not recognize any differences between the various biblical scribes in this respect; they are conceived of as prophets, disciples of Moses. This concept, which is common in late Judaism and which one finds in the Epistle to the Hebrews, makes him consider the Bible as the source of the rule, not only of religious truth, but also of all truth.[217]

This is precisely Swedenborg's point of view. For him, it is Jehovah himself, the God of heaven and earth, who speaks in the Bible through the mouth of Moses and of the prophets. The Bible, then, is the divine truth, for the words of Jehovah cannot be but the truth (*Doctrine of Sacred Scripture* §2). In various passages, Swedenborg describes how the inspiration of the prophets comes about. Thus, inspiration consists of an influx emanating from the world of spirits and from heaven in the form of dreams, visions, or spiritual speech, so that in moments of inspiration, they did not write their own words but the thoughts breathed into them by the spirits who possessed them (*Arcana Coelestia* §6212). The words they took down were directly dictated to them by the spirits (*Heaven and Hell* §254). And this is why the Scripture is the very life of God, the light of God that enlightens the world. It is in this sense that we must understand the words of the Gospel of St. John: "What I say to you is spirit and life" (*Doctrine of Sacred Scripture* §2). The style of Scripture is, consequently, the style appropriate to Divinity; each sentence and at times each word enclose a sanctuary. The Word conjoins humankind with God and opens heaven to us (*Doctrine of Sacred Scripture* §3).

One can then ask why this source of truth is not equally accessible to all people and why the inner meaning of the Scriptures constitutes an arcanum. Echoing the explanation of mythology pronounced by Plato, Philo proclaimed that it was because the Divinity had to place it within reach of the weak intelligence of humanity. Since most of humanity is incapable of understanding the Divinity in all its purity, God must have recourse to anthropomorphism.[218]

In substance, Swedenborg's view is the same. He even maintains that, when the Word was given by God to the people of Israel through the mediation of Moses and the prophets, there existed a more ancient Word, written in correspondences that were extremely difficult to interpret. This Word, to which allusion is made in the books of Moses, was disseminated throughout Asia and, according to the revelations Swedenborg received from spirits, still existed in "Great Tartary" (*True Christian Religion* §279). It is in this Bible, the most ancient of humanity, that the ancients found their religious notions. When the sages of antiquity, such as Aristotle, Cicero, Seneca, and others, wrote of God and the immortality of the soul, they drew these notions not from their own intelligence, but from the tradition that had been transmitted to them by those who had been capable of reading the most ancient Word (*True Christian Religion* §273). Those who had an intimate knowledge of the correspondences of this Word were later to be called divines and magi.

To the degree that anyone separated him- or herself from God, however, these correspondences became more obscure for that individual. The Word began to be falsified; and from these correspondences, falsely interpreted, various forms of idolatry arose among different nations.[219] This initial Word according to the will of God was therefore lost and was replaced through the mediation of the prophets of Israel with a Word composed of more intelligible correspondences (*Doctrine of Sacred Scripture* §102). As we recall, however, the doctrine of correspondences fell little by little into complete oblivion and could not even be revealed to the early Christians because of the weakness of their spirit. Thus, the spiritual sense of the Bible remained unknown. For this reason, only in a few cases the inner meaning of Scripture is known, namely what God himself revealed to the prophets.

To succeed in discovering this internal sense anew, even in order to be conscious of its existence, it is necessary for the Divinity to intervene. By the grace granted to Swedenborg to maintain an association with angels over a period of several years, God has desired to reveal it to humanity through him (*Arcana Coelestia* §5 passim). The mission of the exegete is, consequently, for Swedenborg, entirely as dependent on divine inspiration as is that of the sacred scribes—a matter about which he is equally in accord with Philo. For the latter believes that his own interpretation of the Bible has only been possible through a direct collaboration of the Divinity and he relates that, finding himself in a state of "enthusiasm," he has had divine visions about the hidden sense of the Scriptures.[220]

The marked concordance we have observed between Swedenborg and preceding allegorists, both in their assumptions about their rationale and in their methods, facilitates an explanation of the analogies one notes in their conclusions, although there is no reason to suppose that Swedenborg has borrowed directly from his predecessors. I have not had occasion to research the extent of these concordances, but a superficial comparison leads me to assert that a number of the most widely known of the biblical accounts have been the object of rather similar commentaries. A few examples will suffice to illustrate these analogies and at the same time to give an idea of Swedenborg's exegesis.

When God says to Abraham, "Go from your country and your kindred and your father's house" (Gen. 12:1), Philo interprets these words as a command given to humankind to break away from our body, senses, and language; for the body is only a parcel of the earth we are condemned to inhabit, the senses are the servants and brothers of thought, and language is no more than the envelope and dwelling of the intelligence that is our true father.[221] In his eyes, Abraham represents the initial type of virtue acquired from teaching, just as Isaac represents the innate virtue and Jacob the virtue acquired by the practices of asceticism.[222] For Swedenborg (*Arcana Coelestia* §1404), Abraham represents the celestial man, Isaac the spiritual man, and Jacob the natural man. God's command to Abraham signifies that he must renounce corporeal things and the things of the world; the command to leave his family implies a renunciation of external things, while the command to abandon "the house of his father" means to renounce interior things (*Arcana Coelestia* §§1411–1412). If we proceed to the story of Hagar, we observe that, with Philo, the Egyptian servant girl represents encyclical knowledge, while Sarah represents integral virtue. Before being able to fertilize Sarah, Abraham will have to "know" Hagar. That is to say, before addressing theology, he must practice Chaldean meteorology.[223] When he exiles Hagar, it is then human science, which claims preeminence, that he discards to dedicate himself to higher science.

In Swedenborg, we find an identical commentary. Sarah is intellectual verity; the Egyptian servant represents the love of knowledge. In effect, Egypt means the sciences. The purpose of Abraham's liaison with Hagar is to permit the patriarch to attain to intellectual truth in cultivating his reason (*ratio*). "Intellectual truth, which appertains to the inmost is altogether barren, or like a childless mother, when as yet there is not any rational into which and through which it may inflow" (*Arcana Coelestia* §1901). Swedenborg returns to the theory expounded in the *Economy of the Animal Kingdom,* according to which knowledge is acquired empirically during the growing years; it is only later, when the intelligence has been cultivated, that the highest faculty of the soul can irradiate its light. Moreover, he pursues his reasoning as Philo does. The newborn becomes presumptuous and finds him- or herself exiled by intellectual truth.

I repeat that it is not at all my intention to establish, by this comparison, that Swedenborg would have borrowed the preceding commentaries on the biblical accounts directly from Philo. To judge from the exposition by Siegfried, it appears that this transposition of the story of Abraham and of his liaison with Hagar had been taken, under a more or less identical form, from later commentaries such as those of Origen and Ambrose.[224] I believe that I have found these same analogies among other authors of whom I have made comparative studies. Clearly, here we are dealing with an uninterrupted tradition of which Swedenborg is the late inheritor. A more profound study would undoubtedly reveal to us the works that have put him into contact with this tradition and which of the former allegorical exegetes to whom he was closest. For my purposes, it suffices to establish that he relies on this tradition not only in the method but also in its application.

This fact explains in a certain measure the infallible certainty with which Swedenborg proceeds; it also helps explain the ease with which he succeeds in formulating a logical assessment of the biblical account without being forced to have recourse to extended modifications of the text or to revise previous explications of the correspondences applicable in the context. On the other hand, the narrow dependence on the prior tradition would appear to me to deprive Swedenborg's biblical exegesis of its principal interest.

Although he constantly assures us of the contrary, he has not discovered a new way of interpreting the Bible. The only difference between his results and those of his predecessors is, all in all, that his results have been adapted to his philosophical system, whereas the latter have allowed their explications to illustrate their respective systems. Like his forerunners, Swedenborg so freely used allegorical interpretation to reshape the meaning of Scripture that it became possible for him to incorporate his whole philosophical system in his exegesis and to form a logically consistent theological doctrine out of this hermeneutic operation. When he repeatedly stresses in his theological works that he has learned all the teachings of his church from reading the Word (see for instance *True Christian Religion* §779), he is certainly sincere. All the same, it is quite the opposite. He has independently formed a philosophical-theological view that he then point for point finds corroborated in his biblical studies.

To show how this was possible, and at the same time to give the reader an idea of how much more radical his reinterpretation of the Bible was in the *Arcana Coelestia* than in his previous attempts in *The Worship and Love of God* and the *Historia Creationis a Mose tradita,* I will in the following give an account of the inner meaning of the Mosaic creation narrative (explicated by Swedenborg in *Arcana Coelestia* §§6–313).

The first three chapters of Genesis relate to the most ancient Church, whose descendants perished in the flood. This Church had received in the Bible the name of *Homo* or "Adam," which informs us that the latter was drawn from the dust *(humus)* and was made by God and born to the quality of a human being. It is this creation of humankind to which the first chapter of Genesis refers. More particularly, it applies to the birth of the original Church, but the six days of creation likewise symbolize the six stages in the regeneration of humanity. The work of regeneration was perfected on the seventh day, and the human, who was born from dead matter, has become spiritual and finally celestial. The Sabbath consequently refers to celestial man. When it is said that God created man out of the dust of the earth, it is to be understood thereby that the external man who formerly found himself in a struggle with the internal man, and who thereby was not a man in the proper sense of the word, acquired human stature and is placed at the service of the internal man.

The following description of the earthly paradise also has an entirely symbolic significance. "Garden" means intelligence, "Eden" love, and so forth. Up to that time, the biblical story described the most ancient Church in the age of its splendor.

With the verses concerning the creation of woman (Gen. 2:18), we enter into an account of the apostasy of the descendants of the original Church. When God perceived that the humans no longer wanted to live from him alone, but oriented their desires toward themselves and toward the world, he gave them a *proprium*, that is, a personality or selfhood. This proprium is symbolized by the story in which God created woman from a rib of the man. There then followed the temptation and the Fall. The serpent, that is, the sensuality of humans, persuades the woman, that is to say, the proprium of the humans, to taste the forbidden fruit—in other words, to seek to elucidate the articles of faith through the senses.

Led astray by love of self, humans henceforth refuse to believe what is revealed to them unless this revelation is confirmed by their senses and empirical science. And humankind, properly speaking, the human reason, also allows itself to be persuaded to taste the forbidden fruit. Before this rupture of relations between God and humanity, the latter possessed the faculty of seeing sensory things through heavenly things. Every object, at the moment of assuming a visible form, had evoked the perception of the heavenly and divine realities that it represents; human external sight was only the instrument of inner life. After the Fall, sense perceptions became the essential phenomena. Judging heavenly things from earthly matters, humanity found itself struck by spiritual blindness.

The following chapters of Genesis apprise us of the fate of the oldest Church up to the epoch of the Flood, when it was annihilated. The curse God laid on the serpent signifies that the sensory part of humanity, by its refusal to believe what the senses cannot confirm, condemned itself and became infernal. To avoid leading the whole of humankind into hell, God promised to come to earth himself. This promise is expressed by the passage that says the posterity of the woman will crush the head of the serpent. Finally, the exclusion from the earthly paradise symbolically shows how the later generations of the primordial Church saw themselves deprived of all inclination toward the good and the true and were abandoned to their abject thoughts and gross desires so that they would no longer be capable of profaning the holy matters of faith.

As we see, Swedenborg's symbolic representation of the story of creation is, in its broad lines, that which we find in *The Worship and Love of God*. But although he comments here on Genesis point by point, Swedenborg has managed to free himself from the biblical myth in a noticeably wider measure than previously. The story of creation is no longer that of the origin of the universe; it represents the ascent of the human species toward union with God, while the myth of the Fall no longer applies exclusively to the first humans, but reveals the elimination of a whole series of generations with regard to the Divinity. Moreover, the historic element plays only a very attenuated role here. Swedenborg himself declares (*Arcana Coelestia* §66) that the original Church, from among whose descendants Moses took all that he had written in Genesis up to the time of Abraham, did not limit itself to expressing these thoughts by representations, but also arranged them in a quasi-historic series, all to give more life to them.

The naive story of the Bible, then, has given place to an abstract account of the essential problem that has not ceased to preoccupy Swedenborg since the *Principia*; that of knowing how humankind has been reduced to the uncertain road of empiricism while it possesses, in the inner core of its being, an organ created to receive the divine light directly.

We shall see later how Swedenborg envisaged the solution of this problem. I have sought here only to establish, by a concrete example, that this solution is the fruit of Swedenborg's own thought and not the result of his biblical studies. It is obvious to any reader that the factors Swedenborg tries to eliminate—the momentary Fall of Adam, the factual existence of evil, etc.—are clearly found in the biblical text. Only the implacable method that governs this transcription permits Swedenborg to discover in the Scripture a hidden sense that is in part entirely contradictory to the text itself. It is beyond doubt that he himself was firmly convinced that each point in the Bible confirmed his own conceptions; and if one studies more closely the evolution of his speculations on the state of integrity in humanity, beginning from the *Principia* to the psychological explications of *Economy of the Animal Kingdom* and up to the notably more circumspect *Worship and Love of God*, one has no difficulty understanding how he has been led to introduce his own views into the history of creation.

From the passage referred to above, it is plain that Swedenborg denies the historical character of the narration in Genesis for the whole period preceding the Fall. Beginning with the story of Abraham, however, he believes the text of the books of Moses relate truly historical events, just like the historic books of the Old Testament. But their concealed sense is applicable to everything else (*Arcana Coelestia* §66). Judging from the examples I have cited above, it is permissible to think this hidden sense illustrates Swedenborg's own theological conceptions.

The real content of the Scripture, as conceived by Swedenborg, differs notably, then, from what the majority of Bible readers see there. In short, it is his own doctrine dressed in allegorical form and in the form of historical narrative. The parts of Scripture in which he does not succeed in finding this doctrine, such as Chronicles, Proverbs, Ecclesiastes, the book of Job, and the Epistles, are declared to be barren of inner significance and to form no part whatsoever of the Word of God, properly speaking. It is this point that has led Sundelin to conclude "that the real charter of religion must be found in the works of Swedenborg, and not in Holy Scripture."[225] He justifies this conclusion by pointing to the doctrine of Swedenborg according to which "the prophets and the apostles wrote without knowing themselves what they wrote." This same conclusion, Sundelin adds, "is in no way weakened by the declaration of Swedenborg himself that his biblical exegesis is based upon or emanates directly from the letter of the Word."

This way of thinking, which we find echoed in a number of variants among several theological authors in their studies of Swedenborg, is fallacious in the sense that they risk suggesting that, by a kind of rationalistic biblical critique, Swedenborg sought to undermine the authority of the Scripture to the advantage of his own doctrines. On the contrary, for Swedenborg the Bible is not only "the true charter of religion," but even the only "authorized charter" of this religion. The essential critique he levels against the existing Christian churches is that they have assimilated their own professions of faith into the Bible and insinuated their own accepted dogmas, such as that of the Trinity, which are not found in the Scriptures. Swedenborg is not an adherent of the doctrine of inspiration in its most verbally servile form, and he must therefore admit that, behind the written words as dictated by God through the prophets and the apostles, more profound verities lie concealed than they themselves suspected.

This doctrine of inspiration seems to me close to the view that flourished in the days of orthodoxy in Lutheranism, particularly in the Reformed Church. People generally sustained a mechanical theory of biblical inspiration, according to which God had dictated the contents of Scriptures word for word to the prophets, who were thus only the "amanuenses" of the Holy Spirit. And it was acknowledged that many words of the prophets and the apostles exceeded human understanding.[226]

If one wishes to have a correct idea of Swedenborg's position with regard to the Bible, it is necessary to understand that he considers every word belonging to this world to be a reflection of a celestial word. The celestial word, which corresponds to our word, is written in characters every one of which encapsulates a particular meaning. In the realm of the spiritual angels, these characters resemble our printed ones, while in that of celestial angels, they resemble the ancient Hebrew alphabet with characters crowned by figures oddly curved and surmounted or accented by signs. One does not find in these words either names of persons or names of places as in our own language; nor do numerals exist. These are both replaced by the things that correspond with the words. All angelic communities possess an example of this Word written by the angels, inspired by God in their turn, and it is in this Word that the angels find their wisdom. In the sanctuary that shelters this Word, there is a white and flaming light surpassing in brilliance every other celestial light. For God himself resides in the Word (*Doctrine of Sacred Scripture* §§72–74).

The inconsistencies Sundelin tries to find in the Swedenborg's position on the literal sense of the Word disappear if one bears in mind this doctrine of its celestial correspondence. Even in its literal meaning, the Word is the divine truth. It possesses its holiness and power in fullness because at the same time it embraces a hidden celestial sense. The verities of the literal sense are not all naked truths, but only appearances of truths, images, and comparisons borrowed from natural things, and consequently adapted to the understanding of the simple and of children. But when they become correspondences, they embrace primary verities, just as a crystal bowl holds wine (*Doctrine of Sacred Scripture* §§36–40). The truths that are more important to our faith are clearly enunciated in Scripture itself. The others shine with a brilliance ever more pure through their disguise to the degree that the Bible reader is suffused by love of divine truth (*Doctrine of Sacred Scripture* §55).

Therefore, a person is capable, without knowing anything about the doctrine of correspondences, of establishing contact with God and with angels through reading the Word of God. Every time the Scriptures are read by a lover of God and that person is living a life of love, God and the angels perceive the Word as alive, even if the reader, in his or her simplicity, merely believes in what is written. In a passage of great beauty, Swedenborg informs us that the angels understand the hidden sense of the Word when it is read by children who find themselves in a state of innocence and love and who consequently are more receptive to the inner light. These humble readers are themselves incapable of discovering the hidden sense of the Word and do not know that the angels reveal it through their mediation; but they feel a kind of inner joy in their spiritual state. That is why the angels affirm that the Word of God is in itself a dead letter, but that it comes alive, by the grace of God, in him who reads according to the state of innocence and love in which he finds himself (*Arcana Coelestia* §1767, §1776).

In the words of this world, then, the measureless wisdom of the angels lies hidden. We attain to that wisdom when, after death, we are transformed into an angel by God's grace (*Doctrine of Sacred Scripture* §75). It appears superfluous to me to appeal to other citations to establish the central role that Swedenborg attributes to the Word. It gathers the divine light into itself; it constitutes the link between humanity and angels, between the angels and God. But this divine light is only accessible to the person who turns in love toward God. For every other reader, the Word remains a dead letter.

ten

God and the World

The theological concept that Swedenborg himself called the doctrine of the New Church already received the popular appellation of "Swedenborgianism" during his lifetime. Yet it was only officially fixed in its dogma by his *True Christian Religion,* which appeared in 1771, the year preceding his death. All of Swedenborg's prior works only give us fragments or brief overviews of its essential dogmas without detailed argumentation.

As we have seen, Swedenborg initially believed that his mission consisted of explaining the hidden sense of the holy Word to humanity. This mission was extended only step by step toward the institution of a New Church and the proclamation of a new doctrine. It finished by identifying this mission with the announced return of the Messiah to the earth, a return that would take place this time, not in a personal form, but by the explication of the Word. Swedenborg himself would serve as the human instrument.

This explains why a number of the dogmas of the New Church found their definitive formulation relatively late in the works of its founder. In Swedenborg's first exegesis, edited by Tafel under the title of *Adversaria,* most of the dogmatic questions are still at the same point as in *The Worship and Love of God.* Beginning with the *Arcana Coelestia,* however, Swedenborg starts to expound his unorthodox doctrines on the Trinity, the doctrine of redemption, etc. These doctrines reappear in a more developed form in the systematic later works.

There would be great interest in following step by step the evolution of Swedenborg's dogmatic system. Naturally, only in a study of that nature would one find the integral explication of the stages that led him to his definitive concept. But research of this nature would require an entire volume in itself, so I must limit myself here to the study of Swedenborgian theology in its definitive form. Even in this limited domain, I shall address only the doctrines that appear to me to be characteristic of Swedenborg's mysticism and that can be considered as the culmination of his prior speculations. It would be useless to give a summary of the theology of the New Church here, since Swedenborg expounded its fundamental dogmas with all desirable clarity. A truly fruitful study of his historical and dogmatic point of view can, of course, be done only by a specialist in this field.

Passing on from his philosophy of nature to his theological writings, one is struck by the concordance between them in the minutest details. There is hardly a single thesis in *Economy of the Animal Kingdom* that has not been used in the theological works. Already in the commentaries on the first chapters of Genesis in the *Arcana Coelestia*, we find a veritable recapitulation of Swedenborg's old psychological schema. A more attentive examination, however, confirms that the system has acquired more unity, that it attaches itself more closely to some fundamental ideas that have always predominated in Swedenborg's mind, and that it ends in bolder conclusions. The point of view one frequently finds among lay commentators—that during his theological period Swedenborg reasoned in a less liberal fashion than previously, since he had to subordinate his thinking to the Bible—neglects the central fact that Swedenborg had always considered the Bible as the ultimate authority.

In fact, while he was previously obliged to reconcile his own ideas with biblical teachings, thanks to his allegorical exegesis, he becomes independent of the sacred text. No doubt it is necessary that his doctrine agree with the "hidden sense" of the Bible, but we have seen to what extent this hidden sense takes the form of his own views. The more he is convinced that he has been given a mission to proclaim a new religion, the more he naturally feels himself free from orthodox dogma. And this is why we find in his theology, much more than in the philosophy of *Economy of the Animal Kingdom,* the guiding tendencies of his thought.

I shall first address the problem that had been most prominent in his mind since his philosophical period: that of God and of his relationship with the world, as well as his spiritual relationship with humankind. We recall that, in his first work of religious philosophy, the *Prodromus,* Swedenborg, like the Neoplatonic mystics, already tended to conceive of God as beyond all determination and existing above all human thought. He had on the whole preserved this view of the Divinity during his intermediate period and had even developed it by connecting it with the Neoplatonic emanationist doctrine. During his period of crisis, however, he met the Deity under quite another form—more concretely. He believed he saw Christ himself and that he had conversed with him. On several occasions, he had felt that his thoughts and feelings were influenced by the "power of the spirit." These are the personal experiences that, to a certain degree, have determined the new doctrine he proclaims regarding the Trinity.

Swedenborg begins by denying all determinability to God. He distinguishes between the divine Being *(esse)* and the divine Essence *(essentia)*; the former is more universal than, and the necessary condition of, the latter. In its absolute sense, "the divine being, which is Jehovah," is beyond all thought and every conceivable thing:

> The *esse* of God . . . is impossible to define, because it transcends every idea of human thought, since this can take in only what is created and finite, and not what is uncreate and infinite, . . . the Divine *esse*. The Divine *esse* is Being itself, from which all things are, and which must be in all things in order that they may have being.(*True Christian Religion* §18)

The divine Being constitutes the very substance and the very form. Angels and humans are of the substances and of the forms of God and are his image in the measure that they are in him and he is in them (*True Christian Religion* §20). The divine Being is being and existence in itself. It cannot be said to be being *by* itself, the expression "by itself" implying the idea of duration. That would amount to saying that another God exists proceeding from God or that God created himself. He would then be neither infinite nor uncreated (*True Christian Religion* §21). Indeed, according to Swedenborg, this is the source of the absurdity of the orthodox dogma of the Trinity. The divine Being could not create another deity who would be both being and existence in himself, and hence the dogma of three equal persons within the Divinity is necessarily false (*True Christian Religion* §23).

Needless to say, much of this conception of divine Being accords with the declarations of Plotinus on the first principle. For him also, God is, in his absolute importance, above all thought and all being. He is himself uncaused and the absolute cause of everything finite.

The sole attribute that one can ascribe to the divine Being, then, is absolute "infinitude," an infinitude that surpasses all finite reason. The "ancients tell us the story of a philosopher who threw himself into the sea because he could neither see nor conceive, in the light of his reason, of the eternity of the world; what would he then have done if he had tried to conceive the eternity of God?" It is consequently vain to seek to learn the nature of God in his being or in his substance: it is enough to know him according to created things in the bosom of which he exists in an eternal form (*True Christian Religion* §28).

From the moment one renounces the search for the divine being, to try to create a concept of the essence of God, the attributes that are recognized in him become infinite. The infinite that exists in God and emanates from him relate above all to two attributes: love and wisdom. Divine love and divine wisdom are life itself, "the sun of spiritual life at the center of which Jehovah is found" (see *True Christian Religion* §§36–39).

We thus return to Swedenborg's fundamental philosophical concept. I shall show below how it develops during the theological period. But before this demonstration, I shall comment briefly on the notion of the Trinity.

In his absolute being, Jehovah is not even conceivable for the angels of the highest heaven; for the angels are finite, and no finite being can conceive of the infinite. The first manifestation of God consists in that, in pronouncing the Word, he penetrated heaven, and this penetration by Jehovah gave heaven a human form. By means of this "divine-human," God found himself, prior to the Incarnation, in contact with angels and humans; and when he manifested himself to human beings, it was in the form of a "Man-God," that is to say, in the form of an angel. But when humanity came to the point of turning from God, the Deity, in the form of the "Man-God," lost his influence. God then assumed the purely human form by birth from a woman, just like an ordinary human (*Arcana Coelestia* §3062, §6280, §10579).

Thus, Jehovah himself descended toward the earth and took on the human form to ransom and save humankind. It is a mistake to believe that God, Creator of the universe, should have, from all eternity, engendered a Son. His objective is the annihilation of the hells, the ordering of the heavens, and the establishment of the Church. "And this work, God could realize only, in his omnipotence, through the human being, in that no one could do anything if he had no arm" (*True Christian Religion* §84). For the omnipotence of God operates according to the law of divine order, to which he has subjected himself (see the following chapter).

And this is why, to become truly a man, he must be conceived, carried in the womb of a woman, be born, and grow little by little in intelligence and wisdom, just like other humans. The human being through whom God himself descended to earth is called the Son of God. He took from his mother her purely human quality, while his soul (*anima)* was of divine origin. Here Swedenborg appeals to his old traducianist theory that the human body emanates from the woman, while the soul is transmitted in the sperm of the father (*True Christian Religion* §89, §92). The fact that in the Bible the Lord calls Jehovah God his Father, and the latter calls him Son, only confirms that the divine being of the Father is his soul and life, just as each infant has his life and his soul from his father (*True Christian Religion* §82). By the temptations to which he submitted himself and over which he triumphed, the Lord transformed his human self into a divine being during his incarnation. He thus cleansed successively the human being he had from his mother and clothed a human form with the divinity he had within him. "And in this manner God became man, and the man became God in a single person" (*True Christian Religion* §101). It is in this glorification of the human essence of

God, and not the suffering on the cross, that the redemption consists (*True Christian Religion* §95). The doctrine of salvation by faith alone has masked the essential point of the doctrine of the Church: that Jehovah descended to earth and took human form. Nonetheless, it is only by this conjunction that a human being can enter into a relationship with God and thus realize his salvation.

It is evident that this strange conception of God is a mixture of Christian and Kabbalistic doctrines. In the Kabbalah, God is, in his pure essence, absolutely undetermined and inconceivable. "Before he had created a form in this world, before he had produced an image, he was alone, formless, without resemblance to anything whatsoever. And how could anyone, before the creation, conceive him as he was, since he had no form?" To reveal itself, the divine light that filled all things had to concentrate itself in the human form, the norm of every created thing. The first emanation from God is the primitive man, Adam Kadmon, who is also called Logos, or the Son of God. He is the prototype of the entire creation. The heavenly man is the vehicle by which Jehovah descends into the universe which has emanated from him. And the earthly man has been created in the image of this celestial man.[227] Consequently, the Kabbalists join a purely abstract concept of God, like that of the Neoplatonists, with an extremely concrete notion of the divine manifestation in human form. Like Swedenborg, they speak of different parts of God's body. Kabbalistic philosophers of nature in the Renaissance accepted these two concepts of God and did their best to reconcile them with orthodox Christian dogma. Such is notably the case with Pico della Mirandola.

Swedenborg, then, rejects the doctrine according to which God would be, from all eternity, given a son, a doctrine he considers as contrary to all reason as that of the Platonic doctrine of preexistence, which he has never been able to accept despite his marked adherence to Platonism. "That a Son of God begotten from eternity descended and assumed a human [form] may be compared to the fables of the ancients, that human souls created at the beginning of the world enter into bodies and become men" (*True Christian Religion* §171). And it is by the same reasoning that he also eliminates the third person of the Trinity. The Holy Spirit is the divine truth and divine power that emanates from the "Lord God the Savior" (*True Christian Religion* §138).

Instead of the orthodox conception of the Trinity, which, according to Swedenborg, makes us worship three gods when we confess our faith in one, Swedenborg teaches that the holy Trinity is composed of three parts *(essentialia)* of a single and identical Being, parts joined among themselves, such as soul, body, and activity in humans, to which they correspond (*True Christian Religion* §166). This Trinity did not preexist at the creation of the world; it only appeared later when God himself came down to earth in human form, and was, by the will of God, realized in the Lord God, the Redeemer and Savior Jesus Christ (*True Christian Religion* §170). It is, then, to him alone that Christians should turn.

The analogies between the Swedenborgian conception of the Trinity and the Monarchian modalism of the second century C.E. has often been underscored by the theologians who have studied Swedenborg. It is thus partly similar to teachings of Praxeas, according to which the Father himself was born of the virgin and suffered on the cross. With the Son, then, he constitutes a single identical person and bears the name of Son by reason of his body and Father by reason of his spirit. The doctrine also presents certain analogies with Sabellianism, according to which the Deity manifests itself successively as Father, as Son, and as Spirit. A certain concordance has also been pointed out between the Christology of Swedenborg and the doctrine proclaimed during the fourth century by the heretic bishop Apollinaris of Laodicea, who sustained the belief that, with the Christ, only the body and the vegetative soul were of human nature, while the spirit was represented by Logos himself.[228]

As far as I can judge, there exists no systematic concordance between the Swedenborgian doctrine and these diverse doctrines. It appears plausible, however, that Swedenborg had some knowledge of them and that he may have received some inspiration from these sources. That this might actually be the case is further indicated by the fact that Swedenborg constantly pointed out that the dogma of the Trinity in three persons was inaugurated by the Council of Nicea and that the former apostolic Church had no knowledge of it. He regards this thesis as being proven by the apostolic symbolism in which he sees a reflection of his own concepts.

But even while admitting that, in the construction of his doctrine of the Trinity, Swedenborg may have allowed himself to be inspired partly by the heterodox doctrines of the first Christians, it is evident that, independent of this eventual influence, his own tendencies would orient him in the same direction.

Since his first work, it is toward the divine infinite that he directs his adoration. His religious impulse consisted, in a more or less conscious fashion, in a pantheistic tendency to conjoin himself with the Divinity, to lose himself in the universal All, to feel himself to be a spark of the divine sun. The visions of his period of crisis had largely failed to draw him more closely to the historical personality of Jesus Christ. They had simply imposed upon him the obligation of representing the Divinity to himself in a human form. This need could in no way be satisfied by the orthodox doctrine of the Trinity, which disappointed the requirements of his imagination for a clear and concrete image. "Whoever seeks to visualize this triarchy or create for himself a visual image in the eyes of reason (*coram visu mentis)*, at the same time invoking this unity of three persons, fails to fix this concept in his contemplation otherwise than in the form of a three-headed body or a head with three bodies."

It is in these terms that in *True Christian Religion* (§171) Swedenborg expounds his critique of the Athanasian Creed regarding the Trinity. His own doctrine allows him, in full accord with his visionary requirements, to conceive of God as a perfectly visible human figure:

> . . . being a man, [God] has a body and everything pertaining to it, . . . a face, breast, abdomen, loins and feet; for without these he would not be a man. And having these, he also has eyes, ears, nose, mouth, and tongue; also the parts within man, as the heart and lungs, and their dependencies, all of which taken together make man to be a man. (*Divine Love and Wisdom* §18)

God is the only true human, and it is only by him that human beings, created in his image, know that he is a man (*Arcana Coelestia* §3061).

If one recoils at visualizing God in a bodily form, it is because one has not grasped that spiritual bodies exist as well as natural ones.

It has been objected against this solution of the problem of the Trinity that the dilemma that Swedenborg had hoped to avoid in refusing to admit the doctrine of three persons in the Divinity continues to arise as long as it is a matter of incorporating the distinct parts of the Being into one sole person.[229] Such reasoning, however, neglects the fact that the dualism between the divine soul and the human being of God incarnate finds its precise correspondence in Swedenborg's customary psychological system. In the Man-God, there exists the same antagonism between the inner being and the external being as among all humans, with the difference that, in his human form, God triumphs without yielding to any temptations and finally glorifies his human being, of which humans are incapable. This is the process that unites us with God and which, at the same time, constitutes the inimitable model for the regeneration of humanity.

On the other hand, Swedenborg's critics are right in maintaining that his doctrine completely effaces the personal traits of the figure of Christ and that his redemptive mission loses all the significance it possesses in the traditional Christian conception. But this is precisely one of the themes that has determined Swedenborg's rejection of the orthodox doctrine of the Trinity. Following his marked opposition to the dogma of salvation by faith alone, he was led step by step to condemn all the Christian dogmas related to it, notably original sin, divine wrath, and particularly the entire Christian doctrine of redemption. Jesus Christ did not come to this earth to appease divine wrath and redeem humanity by an expiatory sacrifice, and no one can count on salvation by invoking the intervention of Christ.[230] He descended to earth in human form to combat the forces of hell, which had attained a frightful power as a consequence of generations of human sin, and to renew the relationship between man and God. The human being achieves salvation only after Christ's ascension, just as he previously attained it: by a life of self-purification. But now the way is smoothed by the fact that the evil spirits' hold on humankind has weakened and the equilibrium between heaven and hell has been reestablished. Humanity, however, will, as a result of new apostasies, repopulate the world of spirits with evil spirits, and a new Last Judgment will thus become necessary in the realms of the spiritual world. We shall return to these ideas in dealing with Swedenborg's eschatology.

Swedenborg's God, then, becomes the absolute infinity from which all things have proceeded and by which all things subsist. Humankind cannot, nor should it, represent this Being to themselves in any form other than that in which he manifested himself to them; that is, in the form of the original man, the universal man, whose soul is none other than the indeterminate divine Being and whose activity is the Holy Spirit.

The consequences of this view, which has innumerable equivalents in mystical and Gnostic doctrines, appear in a particularly striking manner in Swedenborg's doctrine of the creation and in his theories on the relationships between humans and God.

Since God is the true and only substance, it is evident that there could not have coexisted with God any eternal matter from which he could have created the universe. Moreover, the universe could not have been created from nothing, since nothing can only produce nothing, and the notion of creating something from nothing is a contradiction (*True Christian Religion* §76). There remains only one possibility: that God may have created the world from his own Being:

> The universe, . . . which is God's image, and consequently full of God, could be created only in God from God; for God is *esse* itself, and from *esse* must be whatever is. . . . But still, that which is created in God from God is not continuous from him; for God is *esse* in itself, and in created things there is not any *esse* in itself. (*Divine Love and Wisdom* §55)

As we see, Swedenborg persists in maintaining the transcendence of God. He is fully aware that his doctrine reeks dangerously of pantheism. He says, "Many have seen this, because reason causes them to see it; and yet they have not dared to confirm it, fearing lest they might thereby be led to think that the created universe is God, because from God, or that nature is from itself, and consequently that the inmost of nature is what is called God" (*Divine Love and Wisdom*

§283). If they fail to decipher this enigma, it is because they have considered both creation and God himself on the basis of time and space, which are qualities of nature.[231] The world was not at all created by God in time, "but time has been instituted by God by the fact of Creation" (*True Christian Religion* §31). That is the very doctrine that St. Augustine professes.[232] In God and before God prior to the creation, neither space nor time existed; they appeared after this creation. Creation, then, cannot be considered as having been created from space to space or from time to time, that is, progressively and successively, but from eternity and infinity (*Divine Love and Wisdom* §156). After the creation, God himself is present in space without space and in time without time (*True Christian Religion* §30).

To explain how the universe could emanate from God, the absolute and indivisible unity, Swedenborg employs his doctrine of the divine-human essence of God. As with humans, in whom a multitude of organs and body parts concur in forming a unity, "the God-Man" constitutes a unity of infinite things at a still more elevated degree (*Divine Love and Wisdom* §17, §22). Desiring to put an end once again to all contradiction, Swedenborg considers creation not as a direct work of God, but as an operation mediately accomplished through the spiritual sun, which is not God himself but an emanation (*procedens*) proceeding from his wisdom and from his divine love. This sun contains innumerable things (*indefinita)* that ultimately, "in their form of images, assume existence in the created universe" (*Divine Love and Wisdom* §155). Swedenborg thus attempts to realize a transition between absolute unity and the multiplicity of created things.

The process itself by which the love and wisdom of God proceed in the spiritual sun, however, appears inexplicable, as Swedenborg acknowledges. He affirms that he has conversed with angels about this who said they had precise information regarding their spiritual light, but that this knowledge was difficult to communicate to the natural light of the human being. They tell us that, just as God is enveloped by the spiritual sun, they are themselves deep within a sphere of affections and spiritual thoughts that emanate from their own being (*Divine Love and Wisdom* §291). This spiritual sun, in turn, irradiates the divine light and heat with an intensity that decreases across the three spiritual atmospheres. To these three atmospheres correspond the three atmospheres of the natural world, and this is why everything natural has its spiritual equivalent.

Natural things have also been created by the spiritual sun, although not directly but through the mediation of the natural sun. This natural sun is in reality a dead sun, and all matter created by it is consequently dead. For the atmospheres lose their light and heat to the extent that they are distant from their original source. They end up becoming so condensed and inert that they are no longer atmospheres but immobile and fixed, of the same nature as the terrestrial atmospheres, and are given the name of matter (*Divine Love and Wisdom* §§173–176, §302).

Vegetation and animal life, following in order, have their distant origin in the spiritual sun. It is to the spiritual that they owe their form, and it is the spiritual that "condenses" (*constipat*) them, on the basis of earthly matter, to give them consistence and stability (*Divine Love and Wisdom* §340). Or, as Swedenborg says elsewhere, the spiritual clothes itself with the natural. But for its existence, this spiritual has need of a permanent irradiation from the spiritual sun. And if the living power of this spiritual sun should fail them, the natural sun, of which the spiritual sun is the center, would immediately dissipate, and with it the entire solar world (*Divine Love and Wisdom* §157).

Natural things, then, are only vessels that receive the light of the spiritual sun. Likewise the spiritual world, with its own sun, is in turn only a reflection of the divine Being itself:

> But although the Divine is in each and all things of the created universe, there is in their *esse* nothing of the Divine in itself; for the created universe is not God, but is from God; and since it is from God, there is in it an image of him like the image of a man in a mirror, wherein indeed the man appears, but still there is nothing of the man in it. (*Divine Love and Wisdom* §59)

It is hardly necessary to point out here that this conception of the world, which is only the logical development of the conception expounded in *Economy of the Animal Kingdom* and *The Worship and Love of God,* comes very close to the Plotinian doctrine. In Plotinus, it is also the original Being who creates the universe from his inexhaustible richnesses without diminishing himself or abandoning his own substance to the creation. And Plotinus explains the relationship between the original Being and its emanation using the same images as Swedenborg—as a sun that irradiates the luminous atmospheres to lose itself finally in the darkness, as a mirror that reproduces the being without partaking of it. The immanence of the things in God should not be conceived as spatial. It consists exclusively in this: that these things are among the effects of the Divinity. God is everywhere and nowhere.[233]

God is present in the intelligible world through the *nous* and in the sensory world through the soul, the way that the light penetrates the sun and through it the moon.[234] One sees how this reasoning coincides, in its essential lines, with Swedenborg's conception of the interrelationship between God, the spiritual sun, and the natural sun, although the parallel should not be pushed too far.

But one could then ask, if Swedenborg denies the preexistence of matter that might serve as material for the divine creation and if he refuses to conceive a creation from nothing, how does he succeed in explaining the manifestation of a universe apart from the Creator? How are the atmospheres formed that gradually diminish the light and heat of the spiritual sun? How can the light from this spiritual sun really be attenuated when there is no matter to traverse and when it cannot even lose itself in the darkness, which, according to Plotinus and his innumerable successors, is equivalent to nothing in the absence of light? How can mortal vessels be created in which the divinity will ultimately be reflected?

Swedenborg believes the response to these questions is found in his doctrine of degrees, which, in the philosophy of his later years, assumes a more constitutive significance than earlier. As I have indicated above, this doctrine is modified in the sense that the number of degrees, which was originally arbitrary in each series, is now limited to three mutually related ones: those of end, cause, and effect. Even more important than this modification, which already appears in the last part of his scientific period, is the fact that these degrees which, in *Economy of the Animal Kingdom,* had the exclusive goal of demonstrating the evolution of nature, here take on a universal application.

In *Economy of the Animal Kingdom,* every stage of the series and degrees has its origin in the primitive substance of the world, which itself belongs to no series. But Swedenborg later denies the existence of an absolutely simple created substance:

> It is asserted by some that there is a substance so simple as not to be composed of lesser forms and that from conglomerations (*coacervationes*) of this substance are produced derivative or composite substances, and finally those which are called material. But no such absolutely simple substances exist. Indeed, what would substance be without a form? (*Divine Love and Wisdom* §229)

To find a substance that has no relation to higher and more simple substances, we must follow the chain to God himself. Nevertheless, even with God, the divine Being alone is of pure form. Unity and multiplicity coexist in God. He is not only infinite from the fact that he is being and existence in himself, he is equally so because he contains the infinite in himself (*quia infinita in Ipso sunt; Divine Love and Wisdom* §17). Swedenborg does not hesitate thereafter to make a series of the Divinity—the highest of all the series. Of his uncreated degrees, the third, the natural degree, only existed in a potential state until God clothed himself in a purely human form and became thereby "a man similar to the men of this world" (*Divine Love and Wisdom* §233).

Since the end, cause, and effect exist in God, they must also exist in everything in the universe, in the least as in the greatest (*Divine Love and Wisdom* §169). Both the spiritual world and the natural world owe their origin and existence to these degrees (*Divine Love and Wisdom* §155). In any case, these degrees are "discrete" and not continuous, for the cause cannot be identical with its effect. They are distinct, one being identical with its effect. They are distinct, one from the other, like prior and posterior degrees, like the creation of the form and the form itself (*Divine Love and Wisdom* §185). For Swedenborg, this evolution also implies an evolution from the simple to the composite, and consequently from the higher to the lower degree. For primitive objects, as more simple, are more "naked" and less surrounded by substance and inert matter (*Divine Love and Wisdom* §204).

All composite things thus form a kind of trinity. A muscle is composed of grosser motor fibers that are formed in turn of fasces of finer fibers. This triune order is also found in every domain of nature; we can, then, conclude that it equally governs the things that escape our eyes (*Divine Love and Wisdom* §190–191).

The end thus engenders the cause and thereby the effect, which must manifest the end (*Divine Love and Wisdom* §189). It is evident, then, that the end governs the cause and the effect, or, as Swedenborg says, "that the end is wholly in the cause and wholly in the effect." One can, therefore, just as well designate end, cause, and effect as the initial, mediate, and ultimate end. But in order that the end may also inhere in the cause and effect, it is necessary that these contain something of this end in which it might operate (*Divine Love and Wisdom* §168). We thus see that the creative act of God reproduces itself on every level of creation. Just as the spiritual sun surrounds itself with atmospheres in order to be able to extend its heat and light through their intermediation, likewise each end seeks to create a cause and an effect to attain its own realization. "For every end without a cause, or independent of any cause, would have no existence, being no more than a word" (*Divine Love and Wisdom* §167). When we classify matter as inert, we conceive it as an effect. But every effect becomes again a cause in another series or, as Swedenborg says, all *"fines ultimi"* return as new *"fines primi"*; accordingly, there is nothing so inert and dead that it does not possess an active force. *"Etiam ex arena exspirat tale, quod confert opem ad aliquid producendum, ita ad aliquid efficiendum"* (*Divine Love and Wisdom* §172).[235]

But while the created ends unconsciously pursue the creative act, the creative act itself is a conscious one. And that is why the universal end of the creation (*Finis universalis seu omnium creationis)* can only be realized by the creation of conscious beings, in whom the Divinity can elect to reside "as by itself." Such beings can receive the love and wisdom of God "as from themselves" and can raise themselves towards the Creator and conjoin themselves with him "as of themselves." This conjunction of human beings with God is the ultimate goal of creation, and it follows that the creation exists for humanity. Just as every higher thing is the goal of a lower one, so every inferior thing serves to be of use (*usus)* for the superior thing. Thus, creation is elevated by degrees from the lowest things up to humankind, and through us to God, from whom we emanate (*Divine Love and Wisdom* §85).

This situation of humankind as the supreme goal of the universe explains the evolution that the ancient doctrine of the microcosm and macrocosm has undergone in Swedenborg's theology. "Man was called a microcosm by the ancients because he reflected the macrocosm, representing the universe in all its extent." But at present it is not known why humankind is so called, for there is nothing of the macrocosm in us except the fact that we are born from the animal and vegetable kingdoms, that by our bodies we live in this macrocosm, perceive its light, and breathe its atmospheres; but these reasons are insufficient to qualify us as a microcosm. This name had been given humankind by the ancients because they were aware of the doctrine of correspondences and found themselves in contact with celestial angels. "For the angels of heaven know, from all they see around them, that every thing in the universe, considered from the point of view of its utility, reflects the man in a single image" (*quod omnia universi quoad usus spectata, referant in imagine hominem*; *Divine Love and Wisdom* §319).

Because the entire universe is at the service of humanity, the human organism becomes a norm for all created things. All the kingdoms of nature offer analogies with human beings: animals by their anatomical structure, their drives and their tendencies; vegetation by its development from a germ and by its reproduction; minerals, finally, by the fact that they nurture the germ and permit it to sprout. This tendency of nature toward the human form is only vaguely perceptible to us during our earthly lives, but we perceive it clearly once we are elevated to the spiritual world. For this spiritual world reflects the representations of the three kingdoms, and the new angel who finds himself in the midst of them perceives them around him. When the deepest levels of his own reasoning open up to them, he recognizes himself therein and sees his own image as in a mirror (*Divine Love and Wisdom* §63).

Every society of spirits, like every infernal society, is of perfect form. Hell and the world of spirits, seen as a whole, have the form of a human being. Thus, it is that, finally, all the heavens together form "the greatest man" (*maximus homo).* But terrestrial souls do not at all suffice to form this "greatest man." All the planets of our solar system are peopled by humans who later enter the heavens in the form of angels, and this is the reason each planet corresponds to a part of this *maximus homo.*

In nature, we find at each level organic forms, great and small, and their structure and activity present certain analogies with humankind. It is in the human being, the ultimate end of creation, that God realizes his own image. He is the microcosm, not only because all other created substances are in his service and mediately contribute to his formation, but also because, with the human being, every part of the body, every organ, every faculty has its correspondence in the *maximus homo* in the kingdom of God and, consequently, its still higher correspondence in the Man-God himself. And this is possible because "in God-man there are infinite things which appear in heaven, in angel, and in man, as in a mirror" (*Divine Love and Wisdom* §21).

This concept of the human figure as the norm of every created thing and the very form of the Eternal is found, in Swedenborg's theology, applied with the systematic minuteness that characterizes him. He refuses to hesitate before any consequences, however paradoxical they may appear to be. He gives a detailed description of the sites in the heavenly or infernal person that are occupied by the diverse spiritual societies; in his work on the role of the terrestrial globe in our solar system, the spirits on each planet represent a part of the body or a faculty of the *maximus homo.* Like the doctrine of correspondences and heavenly marriage, this teaching has become one of the most remarkable parts of the Swedenborgian system. Kant early gave a caricatural exposition of it and qualified it as a "monstrous and extravagant fantasy" (*eine ungeheure und reisenmässige Phantasie*). It was later invoked as proof of Swedenborg's mental derangement. Partisans as well as adversaries of the Swedish mystic seem to admit that he himself came to it as a kind of inversion of the microcosmic man thesis. It is nothing of the sort. Swedenborg certainly picked up this doctrine from ancient sources or from the nature philosophers of the Renaissance.

Plato and Aristotle had previously represented the world as a living entity; among the Stoics, this doctrine, which certainly has extremely ancient origins, was joined to that of microcosmic man. Philo declared that the Stoics called the human being the "little universe" and the universe the "grand man."[236] In Hermes Trismegistus, the complete world resides in the form of a man provided with a body, a soul, and of all their constituent parts, physical and psychic.[237] This conception is found later in the Kabbalistic doctrine of Adam Kadmon. For the Kabbalists, the original divine being is also the macrocosm that includes all created things: "The Form of man contains all that exists in heaven and on earth, superior beings as well as inferior. . . . No form, no world, could preexist the human form; for it includes everything; all that is, only exists by it, without it the universe would not exist."[238]

The combination of these two elements—the ancient concept of the universe as a living being and the Kabbalistic doctrine of Adam Kadmon—is found already realized in a fully conscious manner in the Renaissance philosopher Cornelius Agrippa. He expounds in detail the different parts of the body of God mentioned in the Bible and by the Kabbalists as constituting the primitive images, the "ideas" of corresponding parts of the human body. Aligning himself directly with Hermes Trismegistus, he maintains that not only humankind but also the entire universe has been created in the image of God and that, consequently, this universe constitutes a living being endowed with reason.[239]

Certain other Kabbalistic philosophers apply the name of *maximus homo* directly to the universe. Such is the case, for example, with Pico della Mirandola, who proclaims the audacious thesis that Moses has made use of this expression already in Genesis and who expounds in abundant detail how the heaven of the angels corresponds to the head of the *maximus homo*, the firmament to the part of the trunk from the neck to the navel, while our sublunary world constitutes the lower half of the trunk and the extremities.[240] Likewise, Paracelsus maintains that, since all earthly matter has contributed to form the human organism, the human being is the microcosm and, inversely, the universe is the grand man: "*Dann die gross Welt hatt alle menschliche Proportiones, Diuisiones, Partes, Membra, etc., wie der Mensch. . . . Darauff folgt nuhn, dass Himmel und Erden, Lufft und Wasser ein Mensch ist in der Scientia*" (For the great world has all human proportions: divisions, parts, members, like a man. . . . Thus it follows that man is heaven and earth, air and water in knowledge).[241]

However, even admitting that elements of this doctrine can be found more or less everywhere, with astrological or magical applications, in the philosophy of nature, ancient or modern, and in the doctrine of correspondences, we cannot deny Swedenborg a certain originality in his handling of ancient ideas. With him, these elements become, in their systematic doctrinal development, a means of satisfying his tendency to conceive of everything in an organic form. Everything in nature has relation to humanity; all tends, with a greater or lesser measure of perfection, towards the human form. This is true, not only for the animal and vegetable kingdoms, but also for minerals. The earth receives the seed in its bosom and makes it germinate, the ocean depths nourish the corals, and the minerals of the mines nourish the flowers. Every kingdom of nature tends toward the realm directly above it, because the human image exists in every natural form (*Divine Love and Wisdom* §§61–62, §317).

It follows that all natural processes should be considered by analogy with human processes. Every tendency becomes love, all cosmic conjunction becomes marriage. There is nothing that does not have a place assigned to it as part of the human body. Above our visible universe, the human form attains proportions that are more and more gigantic. Angels and spirits, heaven and hell, all display the human form; finally, all the terrestrial globes of our solar world and all the societies of the heavens are united to constitute the greatest of created forms, the *maximus homo*. In this manner, all creation, from the highest to the lowest, forms a mirror image of God's proper humanness. Each form reflects the Infinite and the Eternal (*Divine Love and Wisdom* §318). Swedenborg has indeed traveled a long way since the time when he considered the earth as a great machine.

As we have seen, Swedenborg refused to admit the existence of any matter that did not have its origin in God; he cannot identify matter with evil, as Plotinus has done. We know that Plotinus supposes that light ends by losing itself in the darkness; the spirit becomes matter and the good, evil. It is manifestly against this contradictory reasoning[242] that Swedenborg says, in a conversation with two angels (*Conjugial Love* §444):

> Do you not know that there is good and evil, that good and not evil is from creation, and yet evil, viewed in itself, is not nothing although it is nothing of good. Good has existed since the creation, a good of a higher degree and a good of a lower degree as well; and when this inferior good becomes nothing, the evil arises [*exsurgit*] from the other side. There is therefore no relation between good and evil, nor progression of good to the evil but a progression of goodness and one of evil, for they are throughout in constant opposition.

The two angels then ask him how evil could have originated since it did not proceed from the creation and the good decrease to the point of becoming evil, Swedenborg replies:

> That is a secret which cannot be revealed unless one knows that nothing is good but the Lord alone, that apart from God there is no good that is good in itself; that is why anyone who looks to God and wishes to let himself be led by God is in good, but he who turns from God and wishes to lead himself is not in good; for the good he does is either done for himself or for the world; this good is either meritorious or simulated and hypocritical, from which it is plain that the man himself is the origin of evil, not that this origin is inherent in man from creation, but that he has imposed it on himself by turning from God.

So Swedenborg categorically rejects the doctrine of an evil existing in the creation itself before the Fall. "It is criminal to think that God himself created evil" (*True Christian Religion* §490). And he equally denies that evil is only an imperfection of the good and even that this imperfection is a condition of the birth of evil. All the evil that exists in the creation has its first source in the original sin that man committed from his own will.

The Fall gave birth to hell, which is the source of all evil. Animals harmful to humankind, tigers, serpents, crocodiles, harmful insects, poisonous minerals or plants, do not proceed from God and are not part of the original creation; they have issued from hell and are distant progeny of the Fall of Man (*Divine Love and Wisdom* §§338–339). All these harmful animals and poisonous plants correspond in hell to the putrefied substances of urine and excrement.

However, as humanity, by persevering in sin and evil, must be supposed to exercise free will, without which we would be led by the omnipotent Divine, so also harmful animals and inanimate substances are to be considered as having a kind of freedom of choice that equips them to do harm. Swedenborg declares in *True Christian Religion* (§491):

> The fact that God has granted freedom, not only to man, but also to animals and, even to a certain extent, to inanimate things, in the sense that he has given every thing the faculty of receiving this liberty conformingly with its nature and that he has implanted good in everything, and this good having, nevertheless, been turned into evil, is easily explained by the following comparisons: . . . The oceans provide asylum in their kingdom for all the fish, but they cannot be responsible because one fish eats another, nor that the crocodile transforms his nourishment into a poison which enables him to kill a man. The sun dispenses its light and heat to all creatures, but these things, which are the diverse vegetation of the earth, receive them in different ways; a useful tree or bush receives this light and heat otherwise than do the thorny brambles, an inoffensive plant otherwise than a poisonous plant.

We see, then, that in his ardor to deny God any part in the existence of evil in the world, Swedenborg paradoxically has the birth of evil from original sin committed by virtue of free will—of a free will that is above all the lot of humankind, but which in a certain measure has been also given to every created thing, even inanimate things. It is quite evident that the problem is not resolved thereby in any way. It remains to be shown how humans could sin although they have been born good and there was no evil in the whole universe that might seduce them. It is interesting to observe that Swedenborg here finds himself constrained to return to the reasonings of Plotinus. He pictures the Fall as less of a revolt against God or a positive willful act than as a slow detachment, a progressive estrangement from the Divinity. This explains why Swedenborg interpreted the account of the Fall given in Genesis as applying, not to the first human pair, but to the progressive decay of the human species until the Flood (cf. chapter seven).

It stands out in one of his most beautiful memorabilia that Swedenborg was fully aware of finding himself, by this reasoning, on Neoplatonic ground. The scene takes place in the Atheneum in the spiritual world, where all the sages of antiquity are gathered and, where, crowned with laurels, they discuss the gravest questions of philosophy in the octagonal salon of the Palladium.

> One of the philosophers, standing in the center of the Palladium, with a palm leaf in his hand, then said: Explain, I beg you, by what mystery man, created in the image of God, is able to see his form transformed into that of a demon. I know that the angels of heaven are forms of God and those of hell forms of the demon. I also know that these two forms are antagonists, these latter being folly and the former wisdom. Tell me, then, how man, created as a form of God, has been able to pass from light to such darkness that he has renounced his God and the life eternal? The teachers responded in order, first the Pythagoreans, then the disciples of Socrates, and finally the rest of the philosophers. But among them there was a certain Platonist who was the last to speak: It is his explication that prevailed and this was as follows: During the Saturnian, or the golden age, men knew that they were forms receptive of life from God; also that wisdom was inscribed in their hearts and in their souls, so that by the light of the truth, they perceived what is true and that, through verities, they perceived the good from the delight pertaining to the love of good. But, in the measure that the human species ceased, in the course of time, to recognize that all truth and wisdom, and consequently all the good which love requires,

> was an unceasing emanation from God, they ceased to be the dwelling place of God; at the same time conversations with God and association with the angels came to an end. For the interior of their sentiments which was initially elevated toward God by God, deviated more and more obliquely toward the world, thus going to God from God by way of the world to take finally the opposite direction, which is toward what is lower and towards oneself. And as God could not be perceived by a man turned away from the divinity and perverted in the recesses of his mind, men detached themselves from God and became forms of hell, and thus forms of the devil. (*True Christian Religion* §692)

When Swedenborg put these words in the mouth of a Platonist, he was probably thinking of Plotinus's celebrated description of the Fall. "From whence," he asks, "comes it that the souls who have their being in the upper world and belong definitively to this world, have forgotten God, their Father, and have thus come to know him no longer, and no longer know themselves?" Plotinus finds the origin of evil in their excessive pride and in their desire to belong to themselves. "They thus rejoice in their own glory, from the fact that they move outside themselves. While on the opposite road, separating themselves a long way, they lost the notion of their celestial origin; like children early separated from their parents and raised far from them for a long time, coming to know neither themselves nor their fathers."[243] And Plotinus shows how, after having lost the sense of their origin and their own selfhood, these souls attach themselves more and more to things of the sensory world. As we see, this reasoning is identical to that of Swedenborg: the fall of the soul consists in attaching itself to earthly existence, forgetting its celestial origin.

Swedenborg thus believes he can explain the appearance of evil without God's participation. But it remains for him to explain the persistence of this evil. The old question remains: does God permit evil? Or does he not have the power to erase it? To a certain degree, Swedenborg responds affirmatively to the second of these questions. But he hopes to rescue the dogma of omnipotence of God by adhering to the doctrine of Malebranche on divine order.

According to Malebranche, the omnipotence of God is not in accord with the way our human reason generally understands it. God cannot, like a capricious tyrant, act arbitrarily, contrary to all reason and all justice. Being himself reason and justice, he is committed to a law he rigorously observes. This is the immutable law of order. God himself is the order.[244] This is precisely Swedenborg's view. "It is generally considered today that the omnipotence of God is analogous to the absolute authority exercised by a king in this world, who can act as he pleases at will, absolve or condemn whoever he wishes, etc." (*True Christian Religion* §57). But God being the very substance, love and wisdom themselves, is at the same time order itself (*True Christian Religion* §53). Power and will are only one in him, and God being unable to wish otherwise than good can only do good (*True Christian Religion* §56).

This thought will exercise a considerable influence on Swedenborg's view of God's relation to creation. The cause of the creation of the universe lies in the nature of divine love, which is to love others and to render each happy from oneself (*True Christian Religion* §§43–46). This, then, is the execution of the immutable law of the being of him who has created the world. His omnipotence is manifest and operates in everyone and in everything according to the preestablished laws of order (*True Christian Religion* §56). He has endowed humanity with free will in order that we make use of it to conjoin ourselves with him. Although we have turned away from him, God, remaining faithful to the preestablished order, cannot lead us to him without our cooperation.

> From this absurd concept of the omnipotence of God it would follow that he would have the power to transform every goat into a sheep, according to his fancy could move someone from his left to his right; to transform spirits of the dragon into angels of St. Michael, to give to the understanding of the mole the vision of the eagle, to make a dove from an owl. These things are not in the power of God because they are contrary to preestablished order, although he unceasingly wills to effect them. Had he been able to do these things, he would not have permitted Adam to listen to the counsel of the serpent, to take the fruit

> from the tree of Knowledge and put it in his mouth . . . Indeed if he had been able to do these things, he would, by the redemption of his son, saved all humanity and extirpated all hell (*True Christian Religion* §58).

Furthermore, God cannot act contrary to his own order: he cannot condemn a person, throw anyone into hell, predestine a soul to eternal death, avenge inequities, allow himself to become angry or to punish. He cannot even turn himself away from a human being and look upon him or her with severity (*True Christian Religion* §56).

The Creator follows the immutable divine order, the operating plan of creation, in its minutest details. And this plan implies that every created thing shall one day return to God, and there shall exist an eternal bond between the Creator and the universe he has created. This plan requires the existence of beings in whom this Divinity may dwell as in his own self. And this is why these beings receive his love and his wisdom as though coming from themselves; they are to raise themselves toward the Creator as of themselves and conjoin themselves with him. No union is possible without this reciprocity. Only human beings possess this faculty, and this is why the entire creation exists only for humankind. The earth is destined to be a seminary where angels prepare themselves for heaven, which is the end of creation (*Divine Love and Wisdom* §§167–170, §§329–330).

God approaches each person to the degree that the latter approaches God. He shines his light on humanity to the degree that we acquire truth. He loves us to the degree that we raise ourselves to him in love. Such is the law of divine order, which the Divinity himself cannot contravene. "God can, in conformity with his own laws, only pardon a man for his sins to the extent that man renounces them in conformity with his own laws. God can only regenerate a man spiritually insofar as the man regenerates himself naturally in accordance with his own laws" (*True Christian Religion* §73).

As one sees, Swedenborg's conception of the purpose of creation is, in substance, that which he expounds in *Economy of the Animal Kingdom* and the *De Anima*; we also find in these two works his description of the cooperation necessary between the Creator and the creature for the realization of these purposes. But the system has acquired more cohesion through the introduction of the concept of divine order, which Swedenborg had hardly dared to touch upon in his previous works for fear of limiting thereby the divine omnipotence. At the same time, he has simplified this system by eliminating the fall of the evil one who, in the philosophical works as well as in *The Worship and Love of God,* shared with humankind the responsibility for having introduced evil into the world. There exists absolutely no Satan in revolt against God, as the orthodox doctrine teaches. All the souls who populate hell and heaven are human souls, and by Satan the Bible simply means hell (*Heaven and Hell* §544).

We find an identical development in Swedenborg's psychological dissertations during his theosophical period. In itself, the fundamental construction is the same as previously; but while Swedenborg previously sought to conciliate the diverse philosophical schools and pursued a precarious reconciliation of his doctrine with the orthodox dogma, he now courageously draws all the consequences of his premises. He no longer needs the support of other doctrines; he has no longer any need to make himself the apologist of some already established religious philosophy. It is directly from God that he has the revelation of the truth.

The fundamental schema of his psychology remains, on the whole, visibly the same during the theological period. Nonetheless, the *anima* becomes more and more subordinated to the *mens*, of which it constitutes only a lower element. Like all the other series of the Swedenborgian doctrine, the human being includes three degrees: the *anima*, the *mens*, and the body. The *anima* receives divine influx directly from the spiritual sun, the *mens* receives it by way of the spiritual world, while it reaches the body through the intermediation of the natural world (*Interaction between the Soul and Body* §8). In discussing Swedenborg's visions, I have already indicated how the *mens*, which includes the will and the reason, is exposed to the influence of good and evil spirits. I pass over the further subdivisions found in Swedenborg's theological system of Swedenborg, as they are of only small importance in its conceptual totality.

As before, Swedenborg interests himself particularly in the reciprocal relationships of the various degrees of the human being. He has dealt with this problem in a special volume, *The Interaction between the Soul and Body.* As we recall, he had early rejected the three hypotheses by which contemporary philosophers sought to explain the relationships between soul and body: physical influx, occasionalism, and the preestablished harmony of Leibniz. His own psychological theory, expounded in the *Economy of the Animal Kingdom,* had justly been imagined to explain these relations. This theory, which rests upon the doctrine of degrees and which he calls the "co-established harmony" (*constabilitas),* posits in principle that the lower degrees of soul and body are only determinations of the *anima,* which, as the primary substance of the human organism, governs the whole series. The soul is the form and life of the body, and this is why all the human functions have their origin in it. The body is only the instrument of the soul. "It follows that it is the soul (*anima)* which understands, thinks, judges, desires, represents, aspires, remembers, sees, hears, perceives odors, feels, speaks, and acts" (*Economy of the Animal Kingdom* II, §285). Swedenborg attempts by this declaration only to establish that the soul is present in the whole body. On the other hand, it allows no communication between the *anima* and the body (*Animal Kingdom* VII, §83). He conceives, however, a certain alternate direct rapport between *mens*, *animus*, and body which he calls "correspondence" rather than "influx."

During his theosophical period, Swedenborg seeks to go a step further: he denies all influence of the body upon the soul and makes all knowledge of the *anima* emanate immediately from God. He says in *Arcana Coelestia* §6322:

> It appears to everyone as though the external senses, such as sight and hearing, flow into the thought and excite ideas there, for it seems that objects touch the senses, first the external and thereby the inner; . . . but this appearance, however conclusive it may seem, is nevertheless an illusion, for what is external, material and gross, cannot flow into and move the inner, pure and spiritual senses. That is contrary to nature. It is the inner senses, the very sense of the soul, which sensates through the external sense, and which dispose the external sensorium to receive the objects at its good pleasure.

It is seen from a discussion between disciples of Aristotle, Descartes, and Leibniz, which is found at the end of the little volume *The Interaction between the Soul and Body* (§19) that Swedenborg appears to have changed his mind in this regard. To the exposition of their doctrine offered by the Aristotelians, the Cartesians reply:

> You reason according to appearances. Do you not know that the eye does not love a virgin or a bride from itself, but from the soul? Likewise the bodily senses do not covet the bag of silver from itself but only by the soul? And it is in the same way that the ears do not avidly receive the praises of flatterers in any other manner? Is it not perception that provokes sensation? And perception is of the soul, not of the physical organ. . . . For these and many other analogous reasons everyone concludes, if his wisdom is above the sensual things of the body, that there exists no influx from the body to the soul, but truly an influx from the soul to the body, which we call *influxus occasionalis* and also *influxus spiritualis.*

And in drawing on the various theories that follow, it is the Cartesians who win. Moreover, an angel proclaims that this outcome was not due to chance, but to the cooperation of providence.

However it may be, Swedenborg does not regard his theory as entirely identical to that of the occasionalists. In several pages of his works, he declares that so far one has been constrained to deduce the *"influxus spiritualis"* of the soul to the body and not, as he intended, from God to the soul and from thence to the body. In reality, the similarity between Swedenborg's doctrine and that of the occasionalists seems to me rather slight. As far as I can see, it is limited to this common point: like Swedenborg, the occasionalists classify the action of the body on the soul as pure appearance. At the same time, they categorically deny what Swedenborg terms *influxus spiritualis*, that is, direct action by the soul on the body. For Swedenborg, on the contrary, this deep abyss between the soul and body does not exist. The body is but the envelope of the soul: the two only make one (*Divine Love and Wisdom* §386).[245] To his mind, the difficulty consists much more in explaining how a human being can live a life of his or her own, since everything created is inanimate and is only an instrument of the Divinity, the sole living being. It is the spiritual sun that irradiates the human soul in which God has created a receptacle (*receptaculum*) for divine heat and love in the will, and a receptacle for divine light and wisdom in the mind. So, it is God himself who thinks and wills in us.

Obviously, if Swedenborg had stopped there, he would have met with the same difficulties as Malebranche, who also professes a metaphysical occasionalism of this nature. God would then become responsible for all human errors. Swedenborg finds the solution in the theory of John Locke, according to which the human soul is, at birth, a *tabula rasa*. Were human knowledge innate, like the knowledge and the instincts of animals, the human being would never attain to a degree of perfection superior to what he or she has at birth, because "the innate knowledges and sentiments of love limit this progress, while the simple innate faculties or tendencies set no bounds of this character." Consequently, humans are born without any knowledge at all, but with the faculty of learning and with an inclination toward love. The fact that we are barren of knowledge at birth and that we progressively acquire it gives us the illusion that what we receive from God comes from our own resources:

> This conception has also been given to man by God in order that he may be a man and not an animal; for from the fact that he desires, thinks, knows, understands, and possesses wisdom as of himself, accumulates knowledges, raises them to the rank of insight (*intelligentia*) and by the use he makes of these, to that of wisdom. It is thus that God conjoins himself with man; and the man to God. This unity would have been impossible if God had not ordained that man should be born completely destitute of knowledges. (*True Christian Religion* §48[14])

If human beings could not appear to act from themselves, neither will nor reason would exist, nor would love or thought, and it follows that we could receive nothing of good or truth from God: "Without this appearance there would be no rational conception of God, no charity and no faith, consequently no reformation and regeneration, and therefore no salvation"(*Divine Providence* §174).

This reasoning is already found in *Economy of the Animal Kingdom* (§299), where it is said that no human progress would be possible if we were born with entirely developed faculties. Locke's theory of knowledge, nevertheless, finds a still more important place in Swedenborg's theological system. It is only because we have no innate ideas that we are human, that we are susceptible to more and more marked progress, and that we finally may come to realize the ultimate end of creation, which is union with God.

It follows that Swedenborg passes up no opportunity to combat the doctrine of innate ideas. In *True Christian Religion* §335[7], he relates that it has been granted him to visit the spiritual world during a great discussion on innate concepts. This discussion was interrupted by an angel, who, in a loud voice, proclaimed to the assembly that no innate ideas existed. Animals are endowed with instincts, but not ideas, and with humans these only develop after birth.

> The fact that man does not possess innate ideas is clearly seen from the fact that the faculty of thought is not congenital. Now, where there is no thought, there could be no ideas, the two phenomena being interdependent—a conclusion easy to pronounce if one visualizes the newly born as only capable of suckling and breathing. . . . His physical senses themselves are in the greatest confusion and it is from this confusion that he elevates himself little by little by means of objects. Also his movements become coordinated thanks to habit, and it is only progressively and in the measure that he learns to stammer words and use them without connection with any idea of which he forms a confused image. This is clarified in turn and gives birth to a confused representation which finally engenders a confused thought. In the course of this evolution, ideas are born which, as we have said above, only become one with the thought, so that this state, implying no thought, is developed by instruction. And this is why man also has ideas which, in fact, are not connate but formed and it is from these ideas that they derive their discourse and actions.

This speech produces a great impression on the hearers. "Leibniz approached us and uttered words of consent, but Wolff departed giving expressions of approval and disapproval, for he did not possess the faculty of discernment of Leibniz."

It is nevertheless evident that only the knowledge that is born in the *mens* "apparently" undergoes this genesis. No one knows how the Divinity acts in the depth of the soul, in the *anima*, just as no one knows by what process the *anima* gives vision to the eye, hearing to the ear, and articulation to the tongue and the mouth. These are among the things that escape the perception and the sensation of human being (*Divine Providence* §174).

The genesis of our knowledge is, then, a real mystery to us. Our conceptual knowledge is only an appearance created by ourselves, and that of the *anima* escapes our consciousness. We know only one thing: it is the Divinity who operates within us without our knowing how. And it is a law of divine providence that we humans should not be capable of perceiving or sensing the providential action in ourselves; for, if we had the faculty of perceiving or feeling it, we would lose all independent life and could no longer act in full freedom (*Divine Providence* §176). But we can, through our reason, convince ourselves that we are led by God. To the degree that we acquire this conviction, we are elevated by God toward the light of truth. Those who only confirm the appearance in themselves without confirming the truth at the same time cannot remove evils from themselves. But those who confirm the appearance and at the same time the truth in themselves are freed from all evil and all sin, apparently by their own strength, but really by God (*Divine Providence* §154). Only the angels—particularly those of the third heaven, the highest of all—are susceptible of perceiving the influx of divine wisdom and love. They proclaim that they live from God and not from themselves, and they rejoice in life from God. Nevertheless, the appearance of living of themselves persists in them. It is even more marked than in other angels. And Swedenborg affirms that he has found himself in that state for several years past (*Divine Providence* §158).

Divine light and heat penetrate the soul of the human being simultaneously, but each of these is received in a different fashion. Divine light can penetrate us in our three degrees, and we are susceptible of benefitting from a wisdom close to that of the angels. But divine heat—that is, love—can only suffuse us to the degree that we abstain from evil and sin and turn toward God. An evil man can enjoy the same faculties of reason as a good man. Although he denies divine verities in his heart, he is nevertheless capable of understanding them, talking of them and preaching them or even of writing scholarly confessions. Left to his own thoughts, however, the evil man thinks counter to these verities and denies them. For then infernal love suffuses his soul and he only gives the name of verity to what accords with this love. Only by abstaining from sin with God's help and thus banishing the love of evil from his heart can the human being really succeed in acquiring divine light. For the divine light remains powerless if not united with divine heat. The light of winter is as bright as that of summer, but is incapable of opening a seed or bud. It acquires this faculty when joined with the warmth of spring. It is only from the moment when divine love in a person unites with divine wisdom that it flowers like a tree in spring (*Divine Love and Wisdom* §§244–246). As one sees, this account is identical to that of *The Worship and Love of God*. Reason teaches us how we ought to live; it leads the will and shows it the way to go, but does not direct it. The will directs the understanding and obliges it to act in absolute conjunction with it (*Divine Love and Wisdom* §244).

From the foregoing, we may conclude that our free will is in reality an illusion. It is God who desires and acts in us. But God allows us to conceive the life he puts in us as our own in order that we may live as of ourselves according to the divine laws of order and that thus we may become capable of receiving the love of God. Every created thing, animate and inanimate, possesses a certain free will, but this free will is distinguished from ours in that we "feel" our life as if it were our own. Lacking this feeling, we could not effect our union with God; our aspirations could not rise to his; we would not even be men and would not possess an eternal life (*True Christian Religion* §504). Our freedom resides in the feeling we have of forcing ourselves to do good and to tell the truth. We act in this manner to obey the orders of God and to save our souls after death. But behind these motives, an interior one is hidden, of which we are absolutely unaware: we do good for the kingdom of God and for God himself. Thus, as one sees, we have there a reasoning identical to that described in *Economy of the Animal Kingdom,* where Swedenborg declares that, when it is a matter of more elevated things and of divine things, the *mens* can desire the means, but is incapable of desiring the end, thus finding itself outside the sphere of the *anima* and, consequently, above human consciousness. Those who have recourse to the knowledge that all good comes from God and that humans of themselves are incapable of doing good as a pretext for not imposing any compulsion upon themselves and for waiting in quiescent passivity for the influx from on high are destined to abandon themselves to evil without resistance. In the world of spirits, they will be counted as among the worthless (*Arcana Coelestia* §1937).

This doctrine of human free will agrees, at least in its overall aspects, with the doctrine inspired by Malebranche, which Swedenborg had already supported in *Economy of the Animal Kingdom*. He repeats it several times in his theological works, accompanied by an ardent polemic against the orthodox Lutheran doctrine, according to which humanity, after the Fall, is entirely void of all moral fiber and retains the capacity to act in ordinary and natural things, but remains like an inert log in all spiritual and divine matters that are concerned with the salvation of the soul (see the extract from the *Formula Concordiae* in *True Christian Religion* §464).

Swedenborg declares that we would not enjoy any free will in natural things if we did not possess a certain freedom in spiritual things, since the lower faculties of the soul have their origin in the higher faculties. He adds that, with the cessation of our free will, all will and all life would come to a close. "If man were deprived of spiritual freedom, it would be as if the wheels were taken from machinery, the fans from a windmill, or the sails from a vessel. It would even be as with one who in dying sends forth his last breath; for the life of man's spirit consists in his freedom of choice in spiritual things" (*True Christian Religion* §482).

Freedom is the lot of all humans, for the divine life also suffuses the good as well as the evil. The difference is that the good "smooth the way and open the door," thus permitting the divine life to penetrate to the inferior faculties, while the evil close the door. This is why, among the evil, divine life cannot reach into the *mens* and triumph over carnal desires that block the way; but it always exists in the *anima*. Thus, they have received from God the gift of wishing well and understanding the truth (*True Christian Religion* §366). There is no original sin in the orthodox Lutheran sense of this word. We humans have never lost our free will; but after the creation, the human race has sinned in freedom. So hell was created, and thereby every person comes into the world with a tendency toward evil, a heredity transmitted in the sperm (*True Christian Religion* §469, §520ff.).

As a consequence, along with this hereditary tendency toward evil and with the evil he has acquired by himself, each person has within him such evil aspirations that, were he not sustained by God, he would precipitate himself headlong into the depth of the hells. But God constantly wars with humanity, and, through us, with hell (*Arcana Coelestia* §2046). He sends us beneficent spirits who counterbalance the evil spirits. Thus, we find ourselves in a state of permanent equilibrium that enables us to maintain a free will (*Heaven and Hell* §293) God constantly keeps his finger on the index of the scale and moderates its oscillations without violation of free will, in exercising restraint upon it (*True Christian Religion* §504).

As we see, this theory of free will is only an elaboration of the ideas of Swedenborg's *Economy of the Animal Kingdom.* Likewise, the entire thesis of the regeneration of humanity rests upon the notion of a struggle between the exterior and the inner person that we first saw posed in *Economy of the Animal Kingdom* and which has later played a leading role during the period of crisis of the *Journal of Dreams*.

The evil tendency, which is transmitted from parents to children, can only be neutralized by a new birth by the Lord (*True Christian Religion* §521). Each person must effect this rebirth "as of himself" of his own free will, in constant combat with his own evil bents. The first step on this path consists of repentance (*poenitentia*). This repentance has nothing in common with the Lutheran contrition, which only pays lip-service confession of sin, draws upon a person's head the wrath of God, and merits damnation (*True Christian Religion* §§513–516). Repentance consists of the awareness of sin and the rigorous scrutiny not only of our deeds but also of the intention of the will, searching seriously to abolish all internal evil. For evil dwells in us insofar as we fail to discard it absolutely, and God does not remove the evil without our cooperation (*True Christian Religion,*

§522,§532). The individual resembles a community in miniature; if, from the spiritual point of view, he does not act for himself, as a community does in the natural realm against criminals, he will be punished after death (*True Christian Religion* §531). Just as this repentance is a slow process, so is regeneration, for which it is the preparation, not instantaneous, but pursued during the whole life of man in order to continue and be completed after death (*True Christian Religion* §610).

Regeneration has to start within the inner person. We should first free ourselves from our individual "proprium" as well as the evil which is inherited from generation to generation and which we have aggravated by receiving into our hearts the love of self and the world that emanates from hell. If we persevere in this liberation, God creates for us a new "heavenly" proprium *(Apocalypse Explained* §585). This second birth consists of the fact that we first accept new truths through the intermediation of reason. We then learn to desire and act in accordance with them and put them into practice (*True Christian Religion* §589).

Once this new creation of the reason and will has been realized in the inner person, and once he or she has acquired knowledge of the truth and comes to know it and love it for itself, a struggle arises between the inner and outer person, between the new and the former will. This struggle bears the name of spiritual temptation, and the person is only conscious of it as remorse. It is, nevertheless, a struggle between God and the devil, that is, hell, who contend for possession of the human being. But although this fight takes place in the spiritual world, at the same time it develops in the very interior of each person, between the truths and the falsities which are found within him or her. This is because the individual is left to fight as though alone, free to act with the Lord or with the devil (*True Christian Religion* §596).

There we find the same exposition already seen in *The Worship and Love of God.* After having undergone this temptation, the internal person belongs to heaven and the external to the world. Association between humanity and heaven is reestablished and God leads us according to heavenly order. From that moment, we are endowed with a new will and a new intelligence. By regeneration, we are elevated from the lowest level of the soul, the natural region, to the spiritual region, which is the higher; in the end, we will attain the supreme, celestial region (*True Christian Religion* §603). Here we recognize Swedenborg's old dream of a state in which the divine light can freely suffuse our soul and we are directly led by the *anima*. That is the level which he says he has attained himself as a result of the crisis which he has passed through. Moreover, Swedenborg believes himself to be the only one of his contemporaries to have reached so high. He even says that, after the Council of Nicea, where "the dogma of the three Gods was established," nobody had reached a state of inner regeneration to the level where he found himself in a state of "spiritual temptation" (*True Christian Religion* §597).

Swedenborg, then, reaches a state of union of the soul with the Divinity that appears as the ultimate objective of all mysticism. But the path that leads to this differs notably from the one on which mystics generally travel; it also differs from the path to which we saw him bound in the course of his great crisis. The focal point no longer resides in the unlimited renunciation of selfhood; it is no longer by prayer, ecstasy, and contemplation that one comes nearest to God. It is in submitting oneself to an active education that one is regenerated. It lies in sharpening the thought, in disciplining the will, in waging merciless war against all evil tendencies, and in transforming all this internal life into external action. And during this whole process of moral renewal, the person must more and more convince himself it is not he himself who acts, but God who acts within him. It is an error to believe that Adam, in a state of innocence, was equal to attaining wisdom and to loving God of himself and that he had lost this free will as a consequence of the Fall. It is precisely because Adam had *wanted* to have wisdom and love by his own power that he separated himself from wisdom and love and was cast out of the earthly paradise (*Divine Love and Wisdom* §117).

But the reconciliation of man with the Divinity cannot be effected exclusively by the feeling of our own powerlessness. Every union assumes reciprocity (*reciprocitas*), and this is why the human being has received the gift of thinking as of himself. He only achieves union with God from the moment when he makes full use of this gift, believing that he thinks and acts from God. That is the reasoning which Swedenborg believes he finds in John 15:4: "As the branch cannot bear fruit by itself, unless it abides in the vine, neither can you, unless you abide in me" (*Divine Love and Wisdom* §116).

In my account, I have tried to throw light on some of the fundamental thoughts that dominate Swedenborg's theological system as well as their relation to preceding speculations. It is not appropriate to the limits of the present study to list here all of Swedenborg's heterodoxies with regard to Lutheran dogma. Nor would such an enumeration appear to offer much interest, Swedenborg himself having presented this systematically in his *True Christian Religion*. However, for the purpose of defining Swedenborg's doctrine historically, it does not appear to me useless to indicate his point of view regarding several fundamental Protestant dogmas. On that subject, the most rational procedure seems to be to compare Swedenborg's conception with that of Dippel. As we have already seen, Swedenborg had early been influenced by Dippel's views, and the resemblance between the two doctrines became, during the theological period, so accentuated that it attracted the attention of a number of contemporaries.

The analogies are particularly striking in that the critiques of Lutheranism by Swedenborg and Dippel have the same point of departure. Both consider that Lutheranism gives too much importance to the orthodox dogma and excessively neglects the importance of the religious life. "*Ortopraxis gegen Ortodoxie*" (orthopraxy versus orthodoxy) is the battle cry of Dippel, and it is basically that of Swedenborg. But in this respect, both sustain only the aspirations of Pietism toward an ardent and more vital Christianity.

What is more serious is that, in their eyes, the deficiency of Protestantism lies in the dogma of justification by faith alone. The reforms of Luther and Calvin had the purpose of depriving the pope and his subordinates of the traffic in indulgences. This only succeeded by effectively making Christ himself a trafficker in indulgences, remitting in advance the sins of humanity still captive of flesh and the devil. Such is the harsh criticism by Dippel of the Protestant doctrine of justification.[246] Although he stresses it less aggressively, Swedenborg basically shares Dippel's view. He maintains that, according to the doctrine of sudden justification, many spirits carry from this world the conviction that they will obtain instant remission of their sins and that none of their former faults would remain. Some push their folly to the point of believing that it is allowable for them to sin because, at a given moment, they will receive immediate pardon of their sins (*Spiritual Diary* §4542).

If Dippel and Swedenborg react so strongly against the doctrine of justification by faith, it is because they accord humanity a broader scope for free will than orthodox Lutheranism does. It naturally follows that they are obliged to deny the Lutheran doctrine of original sin. The sin of Adam has not at all taken away from us our free will in spiritual matters; we can cooperate in our regeneration. Swedenborg and Dippel both seem to admit that the evil created by the Fall does not consist of the fact that God has charged us with the sin of Adam. Rather it consists of the fact that, from the moment when humanity turned from God, we transmitted to our descendants the tendency to evil. *"Keine imputation, sondern eine reelle fortgepflantzte corruption,"* (No imputation, but a real, transmitted corruption) declares Dippel;[247] such also is Swedenborg's viewpoint, as was explained earlier in this chapter.

With Dippel, as with Swedenborg, the doctrine of divine wrath's weighing on humanity disappears with the orthodox doctrine of justification by faith. Dippel does not find expressions harsh enough to stigmatize this "pagan," "barbarous" conception, which portrays God, who is love, as full of anger against every mortal—a God, who, under the stress of this anger, abandons his creative plan in order to pronounce the reprobation of humankind. The difference between God's love and his wrath exists only in the sentiment of the human being. For the "fury" of God is only a form of his love, an expression of his ardor against sin, from which, quite like a physician, he intends to deliver us by bitter medicine.[248]

Swedenborg protests with just as much energy against attributing to God qualities and behavior that would appear, even among men, to be the height of cruelty. In one of his memorabilia (*True Christian Religion* §134), a pastor in the spiritual world makes an exposition of the orthodox doctrine according to which God has, in his rage, cursed the human race and has been appeased only by the suffering of his Son on the cross. The angel who hears this exposition at first stands agape with astonishment and then cries out:

> Can the Christian world be so insane, and wander away from sound reason into such mad ideas, and from such paradoxes draw conclusions about the fundamental dogma of salvation? Who does not see that these things are diametrically opposed to the very Divine essence, that is, to God's Divine love and Divine wisdom, and at the same time to his omnipotence and omnipresence? No good master could so deal with his manservants and maidservants, nor even a wild beast or a bird of prey with its young. It is horrible.

By "the wrath of God" in the Scriptures, is meant the sin of man, which is the antithesis of God. God is never angered against man.

As is well known, Dippel's negation of divine wrath leads him to the "realist" doctrine of redemption, which he structures progressively and which he considered to be his essential contribution to theology. According to the orthodox view, we are saved, not from sin, but from punishment of this sin, from the divine reprobation that threatened us. The role of Jesus Christ is not to regenerate the moral and religious life of humanity, but to give satisfaction, instead of and in the place of humankind, to God for the offense done to his glory. This doctrine is "illusory," to Dippel's mind. To it, he opposes his own theory, according to which Jesus Christ, by his incarnation in the body of a sinner like Adam, by the suffering of the cross and by his resurrection, has broken forever the chains of sin, death, and the devil. The "real" redemption consists of the fact that Jesus, serving us as a model, has shown us the way and given us the means of truly triumphing over sin.[249]

To adopt the Ritschl's formula for the views of Dippel—Christ, then, is the type of our own self-denial and sanctification.[250] Nevertheless, the significance of this doctrine of redemption is attenuated by Dippel's strongly established conception of the inner Christ, of the interior Word, a mystic conception he shares with several of his Pietist contemporaries. Basically, it is this interior Christ and not the historical Christ who is the true redeemer. It is no doubt an inestimable grace of God that Christians are not exclusively reduced to the inner Word, but that they may also have recourse to the incarnate Word, that is to say, Jesus Christ, to guide them in the right path. But the inner Word can render superfluous the outer Word, and non-Christians, be they Jews or Turks, can achieve regeneration without having knowledge of the historical Christ.[251]

Swedenborg's critique of the orthodox doctrine of redemption accords very well with that of Dippel. And to a certain extent, a concordance between both can be found in the fact that Swedenborg too sees in Christ the image of humankind's own redemption. The states through which "the Lord" passed during his incarnation accord with the immutable divine order, the order that likewise governs humanity. "Every person progresses and must progress in accordance with this order, if from being natural he is to become spiritual. In like manner it was necessary for the Lord to progress, in order to make divine his natural human" (*True Christian Religion* §105). Evidently, this theme does not play a particularly important role in Swedenborg's theology and in reality only serves to show how fully God clothes himself in the human form and submits himself to the order which he himself provided for human development.

Swedenborg energetically underscores the other side of Dippel's doctrine of redemption, that of Christ bursting the chains of sin and the devil. He delivers an ardent polemic against the orthodox doctrine according to which Jesus' suffering on the cross was in itself the redemption proper (*True Christian Religion* §132). According to him, the redemption resides in the crushing of the hells and the ordering of the heavens. At the time of the first advent of the Lord, the hells had attained such a height that they occupied the totality of the world of spirits, the intermediate realm between heaven and hell, and infested the two lower heavens as well. This reflected the fact that the whole earth had turned from God and that the Jewish church had become corrupt through the falsification and profanation of the Word. After their deaths, the people of this church overran the world of spirits, and, to oust them, it became necessary for the Lord to descend to earth. He then redeemed not only humanity but angels also (*True Christian Religion* §121).

As well as I can judge, there is no great analogy between Dippel's doctrine of redemption and that of Swedenborg. They agree in that both categorically reject the orthodox doctrine of redemption and in that they notably restrict the role of the historic Christ. If it can be reasonably sustained that, with Dippel, the interior Christ makes the historical Jesus almost superfluous, one is quite as justified in saying that, for Swedenborg, the advent of Christ on earth was in vain. When, in 1757, the Lord subjugates the hells again and reestablishes order in the heavens, he does not take on the human form again; he effects the work of redemption by commissioning Swedenborg to proclaim the spiritual sense of the divine Word. In sum, neither Dippel nor Swedenborg accords the doctrine of redemption a fundamental significance, Swedenborg even less than Dippel, for he sees in the advent of Christ only a manifestation of God (although the most important one); for him, every universal church ends in a last judgment, followed by a subsequent redemption.

It is evident that, with this conception of Christ, Dippel, like Swedenborg, cannot content himself with the orthodox doctrine of the Trinity. This appears to both as tainted by the same original error, the "tritheism," as Dippel expresses it. And both seek to escape this difficulty in the same way, by considering the Trinity from a modalist point of view. In his defense of the *Vera Demonstratio evangelica*, Dippel declares that he wanted to point out the well-informed view of ancient Greek Fathers of the Church, who considered the three persons of the Divinity as his three *modi subsistendi, "die allein in der Gottheit, und nicht in sich selbst, sowohl ihre subsistantz als Wesen haben."*[252]

There is, nevertheless, room to note that this conception of the Trinity, which is rather close to that of Swedenborg, does not play a very considerable role with Dippel. He is basically the enemy of all subtle speculation on the Deity and feels that the decadence of Christianity dates from the day when the conception of the Trinity became mingled with "philosophic chimeras." Being finite beings, we will never succeed in explaining the essence of the divine Being in terms of our own ideas, and God does not expect us to attain an adequate knowledge of his Being.[253] What is above all important, now as always, is that we become suffused by the interior Christ, who can save us, whatever be our concept of the Trinity. *"Der wahre Christ, der in Cristo seyn Heyl kennet und suchet und nur einiger Massen erfahren hat, was das Leben in Gott und ausser Gott sey, wird dergleichen*

Meinungsbilder so hoch nicht setzen können, dass die einige nöthige Influenz zum Heyl der Seelen in seynen Augen sollten haben." [254]

Here we have a flagrant contradiction with the doctrine of Swedenborg. For him, only by a correct conception of the Trinity can one gain a right idea of God. Since each one of us will have our place in heaven according to the idea we have of God, the correct conception of the Trinity has a fundamental importance for our salvation (*True Christian Religion* §163). To Swedenborg's mind, the dogma of the Trinity, as it was fixed by the Council of Nicea, has led to the belief in three gods and determined the decadence of the church. "It has extinguished the light of the Word and excluded the Lord from the church." It has brought about the abomination of desolation predicted by Daniel and in the Apocalypse. And no flesh could have been had not God created new heavens and instituted a new church (*True Christian Religion* §§177–183). Whoever has received the divine light perceives that "within the faith of the present Church, which in its internal form is a faith in three gods and in its external form a faith in one, there are swarms of falsities. . . . But how can any mind see it so long as the door to that faith and its offshoots is shut and bolted by the decree that it is unlawful for reason to look into mysteries?" (*True Christian Religion* §178). As we see, this is the reverse of Dippel's doctrine. And this difference between the two conceptions is fundamental.

It would appear that Swedenborg, who considered himself as in contact with the supersensory world, should have been particularly prepared to accept Dippel's doctrine on the interior Word, a continuous revelation that speaks in the heart of everyone who is capable of attaining regeneration, even without the help of the external word. Swedenborg, however, considers that such a direct revelation is impossible in the present state of humanity. It exists on other planets than ours, and humanity possessed it in the time of the first church but lost it through the Fall. What remains for us is an indirect revelation through correspondences. And when, in turn, this modality of knowledge was lost, the Scripture was given to humankind, after which the ties that united us to God were broken, as a means of reestablishing union with the Creator. Humanity, then, is no longer capable of receiving direct revelation of divine verities; and if we did not possess the Scripture, we would be entirely separated from heaven and deprived of all light (*Heaven and Hell* §306, §310).

It is easy to conceive that Dippel and Swedenborg thus arrive at very different conceptions of the Bible. Dippel protests against the bibliolatry that dominates theology. He criticizes the doctrine of inspiration and thinks that this can only be applied to the practical dogmas of salvation. In effect, Scripture cannot be considered as the Word of God; it is only a witness of the inner and living Word of God, incarnated in Jesus Christ. God is as close to all Christians as he was to the prophets and the apostles. A true Christian has only to create Scripture in his intercourse with God; he can write sacred texts himself.[255] The Bible does not pretend to be a theological norm but is a practical rule of life.[256]

By contrast, Swedenborg's theology rests completely on the strictest dogma of inspiration. Divine wisdom conceals itself not merely in each phrase but in each word of Sacred Scripture. The inner sense of the Bible has been hidden from humankind since its origin, and only the special mission confided to Swedenborg has permitted him to probe and proclaim it.

As should be evident from the comparison I have just made between the two theologians, Dippel has exercised an incontestable influence on Swedenborg's theology, but he does not appear to me as in any way decisive for the elaboration of the latter's theological system. Nor do I believe it likely that Dippel played a preponderant role in Swedenborg's religious conversion. As a consequence of his aspirations toward a more ethical Christianity, Swedenborg has been quite naturally led to attack the same orthodox Lutheran dogmas as Dippel has, and it is manifest that Dippel's audacious critique had a stimulating and fecund effect on the mind of Swedenborg. Yet the actual similarities between the two doctrines are really very minor.

This approach appears to me to find powerful confirmation in the Swedenborg's own estimations of Dippel in the *Spiritual Diary.* In sundry paragraphs, Swedenborg gives an account of his meetings with Dippel in the spiritual world and renders a certain homage to him for the acuity of his polemic, but Dippel's positive conceptions appear to Swedenborg to be absurd. Dippel's critiques of other authors seem full of learning and intelligence; but when he undertakes to expound his own ideas in philosophy, religion, and in all other matters, he gives the impression of a somewhat trifling simplicity. In the spiritual world, Dippel is tied so that he cannot use his powers of persuasion to corrupt his social circle, as he did by his mischievous writing while alive in the world: "*Jucundum vitae ejus fuit omnes refutare et turbas excitare*" (His joy in life was to refute everybody and to excite the crowds; *Spiritual Diary* §5995).

Here, indeed, we see the haughty superiority of the aristocratic thinker toward the democratic proselytizer. We find again, moreover, this aversion against any form of religious agitation in the judgment that Swedenborg harbors on reformers. What seems to be the characteristic of Luther is that he was a quibbler, talking unceasingly and allowing no one else to have the floor; his greatest quality was his gift of persuasion (*persuasio)*, the force of which was such that no one could resist him and which became a kind of magical witchcraft by which he blinded the multitude (*Spiritual Diary* §5105; *True Christian Religion* §796).

Concerning Dippel, Swedenborg's estimation appears basically to the point. By nature and by temperament, Dippel is a practical preacher of repentance, a violently aggressive and utterly fanatical polemicist. He detests metaphysics and syllogisms and is little concerned with ordering his ideas into a theological system. Most often he expounds his own dogmas as hypotheses and at times limits himself to defending them by purely practical arguments.

Swedenborg, on the contrary, is essentially a theoretician, a constructor of systems. We have seen that, ever since his youth, he has sought to establish the great causal connections and that the mystical elements have penetrated little by little into his mind like so many new links of his system. His whole theology is basically a transposition of his natural philosophy in *Economy of the Animal Kingdom.* His method of presentation is still soberly scholastic, whether he deals with the theory of knowledge, the nature of God, or the spiritual world.

A study of Swedenborg beginning, as is customary, with Lutheran dogmas and attempting to expose the divergences of the two doctrines in detail risks giving only a confused portrayal of Swedenborg's personality and views. The Swedenborgian doctrine is not at all a matter of critiquing Lutheran dogmatics, nor is it a collection of disparate morsels taken from the innumerable and diverse sects of the day for the purpose of creating a new religion. The preceding pages will have established, I believe, that Swedenborg's doctrinal system constitutes an attempt to coordinate logically a certain number of fundamental ideas, most of which go back to Swedenborg's scientific period and which were further developed during the course of his religious crisis. He consequently eliminates the orthodox dogmas that are incompatible with his own ideas.

It can hardly have escaped the attentive reader that Swedenborg's fundamental ideas, carried to their extreme consequences, lead to irreducible antinomies in his philosophical system. His conception of the divine Being, his doctrine of a universe created out of the very substance of God but essentially distinct from him, his theory of the birth of sin or of humankind's free will are striking examples. But Swedenborg never attempts to conceal these antinomies from the reader. On the contrary, he himself often acknowledges his inability to resolve them; he declares that the most difficult enigmas are and remain indecipherable to every created intelligence and that the angels themselves do not succeed in resolving them fully.

On the other hand, when it is a matter of dogma concerning our salvation, he is extremely zealous in conceding nothing that appears to him as contradictory or psychologically unacceptable. Thus, he rejects the orthodox doctrine of the Trinity because it requires of its adherents the visualization of something that cannot be clearly represented. We cannot and should not picture God otherwise than as the perfect man, such as he has appeared to us. The indefinable divine Being of God is beyond our human intelligence. Swedenborg equally condemns the theory of creation from nothing because it appears to him to be manifestly inadmissible that anything could be created from nothing. God is the only Being; consequently, creation can only issue from his substance.

Swedenborg therefore does not pretend to present any article of faith that implies a contradiction in itself; his philosophy aspires to satisfy the demands of reason. "The dogma established by the papists, and later picked up by the Protestants, according to which reason must be subordinated to faith in theological questions, has closed the church anew," he wrote in 1766 to the German theologian Oetinger.[257] "What could open it again if not a mind enlightened by God?" In the bosom of the New Church, he declares in *True Christian Religion* §508), it is permitted to enter intellectually all the mysteries of faith.

If one sets aside the purely dogmatic points of the *True Christian Religion,* what results is a sort of sober moral catechism, which explains the insistence on Swedenborg's rationalism and even the doubts regarding his characterization as a mystic. I have already responded to these exaggerations by pointing out the striking parallels between the religious evolution of Swedenborg and that of the great mystics. I have likewise shown that many concepts that are customarily considered as rationalistic are, in reality, derived from the mystic needs of his mind. Such a purely rationalistic and practical view of Swedenborg would be justified if one contented oneself with observing that neither *True Christian Religion* nor the other dogmatic works dating from his theological period serve as or are intended to serve as manuals of mystic religiosity of the type of certain works of German mysticism or of Spanish Quietism. Even a superficial comparison with, for example, the works of Mme. Guyon, then much read and admired in Sweden, suffices to illustrate the difference. Dippel himself, in this respect, is a much more characteristic mystic than Swedenborg.

It is evident that Swedenborg's teachings cannot be ranked among the Pietist mysticism of his century, nor can they be considered purely and simply a result of a philosophical opposition to Cartesianism and the rationalism of Leibniz and Wolff, who played such a great role in the genesis of *Economy of the Animal Kingdom*. During his theological period, moreover, Swedenborg was exposed to the clear influence of Dippel and Malebranche. But the essential part of his system is not at all covered by their doctrines, and we search in vain in the rich gallery offered by that era of sect-founding dreamers, of mystics on the prowl for philosophical speculations, for any figure presenting some similarity with that of Swedenborg. In reality, it is necessary to go back to the Renaissance to find a comparable measure of his personality.

In the first chapters of the present study, I have already indicated that Swedenborg, disciple of the great scholars who marked the end of the political grandeur of Sweden, aligns himself historically with the Renaissance. He calls attention to the fact that the qualities he has inherited from its leaders—universal interest and constructive imagination—have stamped their imprint on his theosophical doctrine as well. With the help of our preceding observations, we can now complete the parallel and identify the close bonds between Swedenborg and the Kabbalistic nature philosophy of the Renaissance.

We have already seen that the parts of his system that are manifestly based on foreign models can be related to the Platonism of the Renaissance. Several of his doctrines present in detail striking analogies with the works of Pico della Mirandola, although we cannot prove materially that Swedenborg was aware of them. We are unfortunately faced with the more or less impossibility of establishing by which route the doctrines of the Kabbalistic philosophy have reached him. I have nevertheless pointed out the existence of these doctrines in certain medical works consulted by Swedenborg. It does not appear rash to suppose the importance of a Swedish tradition, associating it with Stiernhielm, the most illustrious adept of these doctrines in Sweden. The fact that an edition of Plotinus annotated by Stiernhielm was found in Swedenborg's library already makes this hypothesis plausible. On the other hand, it is also possible that Swedenborg could have known of the speculations of Stiernhielm through Benzelius who, at the time of their closest intimacy, happened to be about to write a study of the Swedish poet. However that may have been, we are here reduced to hypotheses impossible to verify.

Nonetheless, the analogies between Swedenborg and Pico della Mirandola are striking.[258] They were raised in somewhat similar intellectual environments, and there was an undeniable intellectual kinship between them. Both were born in eras when the researches based on experimentation and exact methods were beginning to undermine the authority of faith, on which the preceding generations had uniformly built their philosophy. Both considered themselves as heralds of the new ideas. Pico della Mirandola combats astrology and divination with the same energy that Swedenborg, in his works on natural science, displays to undermine alchemy, magic, and those "*qualitates occultae*," which he believes he finds in the doctrines of the predominating philosophic schools. But the two are nonetheless born visionaries and never succeed in breaking the bonds attaching them to the past. This past binds them, on the contrary, in a fashion so much the more closely that they seek to free themselves from it and that they throw themselves all the more obstinately into meditation on the last problems that remain unresolved. When one reviews the biography of Pico della Mirandola, one gets the clear impression that—even had he not met with Savonarola—his path would have brought him irresistibly back to the medieval church, to the cloister, just as one is convinced that the conversion of Swedenborg would have been ineluctably produced one day or another, even if he had not received the external impulsion of the Pietism that prevailed in Sweden around 1730. Neither one nor the other definitively escaped what Swedenborg calls in *True Christian Religion* §653 "the current in the ocean which unobservedly draws the vessel."

Their philosophies are only attempts to cover this dualism, and this is the reason they do not at any moment become either an intimate mysticism or a rational and transparent logic. Rationalism and mysticism, antiquity and Christianity pursue a relentless struggle within the vast construction of their doctrines. They hope to resolve all the antinomies by the Neoplatonic doctrine of a transcendent unity above the sphere of thought, by the divine light that penetrates everything. In reality, everything is one; the dispersion of multiplicity exists only in the human mind. All is spiritual, endowed with a soul, divine in the measure that all is alive by the grace of God; the entire universe is only a symbol of a higher world, where every terrestrial thing has its celestial equivalent. This reasoning is confirmed for them by the Kabbalah and assures them in their conception that all human knowledge has a unique source, the Holy Scripture, through which Pythagoras, Plato, and Aristotle, by unknown ways, were disciples of Moses. And it is thus that they find their fundamental theses in their allegorical exegesis of the Bible, notably those according to which all things find their norm in humankind, from the fact that the Eternal has the human form and that the universe in its entirety constitutes the *homo maximus*.

It is in this conception of humanity as the hub of the universe that Pico della Mirandola and Swedenborg meet. I could not better illustrate this concordance than by citing Pico della Mirandola's famous passage in his *Oratio de hominis dignitate*, which is always invoked as an example of the high idea the Renaissance had of humankind:

> All other beings in nature are subject to our laws," said the Creator to Adam. "Only thou knowest no limit and by the operation of thy free will to which I, myself, have entrusted thee, thou thyself shalt write thine own laws. . . . We have created thee either mortal or immortal, in order that thou thyself canst, by thine own wish and for thine own glory, be thine own creator and sculptor and give thee the form which thou desirest. Thou canst, according to the good pleasure of thy soul, either abase thyself to bestiality, or regenerate thyself for the highest good, for divinity. . . . Animals possess from birth and carry with them in the womb of their mother all that which they later enjoy. Superior minds are, from the beginning, or at least immediately after the creation, what they are to be to eternity. It is with man, and only with man, that the Creator has deposited the seed of all things, the possibility of all forms of life."[259]

It is hardly necessary to point out how completely this conception accords with that of Swedenborg. In *Economy of the Animal Kingdom* and *The Worship and Love of God*, he has already shown that the faculty for self-development is the distinctive sign of humankind. It is the reason he maintains with so much obstinacy his theory of human free will and refuses to admit the existence of innate ideas. Heavenly beings are born with all their intelligence; animals are led by their instincts and attain from birth their full development. Only the human being is born without any knowledge and without well-marked instincts, but is endowed with a faculty of self-development towards good and evil which no other creature possesses. So it is for humanity that creation took place. During his theological period, Swedenborg develops this reasoning in a still more rigorous fashion, in which he supposes that all angels and spirits have begun their existence in the form of a human being. It follows that the human situation becomes still more unique in his theological system. We are the sole species through whom the Creator might reunite with the universe that emanates from him.

With this conception, of the dignity of humankind and of our unlimited possibility of progress, inherited from antiquity and from the Renaissance, Swedenborg must react strongly against contemporary doctrines derived from Locke's doctrine of the state of the newly born human soul as a *tabula rasa.* By this view, there is only a difference of degree between the intellectual and spiritual faculties of the human and those of the animal, and that, as in animals, it is ultimately the instinct of self-interest and survival that is the propelling force in humankind.

It is beyond doubt that Swedenborg was not ignorant of the doctrines of the Encyclopedists, whether he had come to know their English precursors during his youth or whether he was able to gather an idea of their teachings from the numerous extracts in the periodicals. However that may be, we find allusions to their principal theses in diverse passages of his later work. Thus, in *Heaven and Hell* §555, we read a violent polemic against Helvetius' doctrine that selfishness is the source of all human action. In the world, says Swedenborg, we imagine that egoism *(amor sui)* is the flame of life and that man enfeebles himself if he does not allow himself to be led by it. "It is said: 'Who, then, has accomplished whatever may be praiseworthy, useful, or memorable for any other purpose than to gain honor and glory in the eyes of others, and whence comes this desire if not from the ardor of our love of the glory and honors, that is to say, from our selfhood?'" This is evidently the reasoning of Helvetius himself. Contrary to this thesis, Swedenborg argues that egoism, the love of self, is the love that rules in hell and makes hell in the heart of man. It was therefore entirely in the spirit of their teacher when, in the *Pro Sensu Communi* polemic in the late 1780s, the Swedish Swedenborgians above all turned against Johan Henric Kellgren's proclamation of conceit as the vehicle of all human progress.

In another passage (*True Christian Religion* §692), Swedenborg underscores the contrast between the high idea formed of human beings in antiquity and the brutal doctrine of the Encyclopedists, according to which human and animal are completely equal.

It is in an "Olympian" school of the Athenaeum that the ancient sages, Pythagoras, Socrates, Aristippus, and Xenophon gather with their disciples to learn the modifications and progress of wisdom from spirits newly arriving from this world. The day Swedenborg is present he is asked the customary question: "What is the latest news from earth?" And the newcomers announce, "that a man who resembled an animal and animals who resemble man had been found in the forests." It is finally agreed that these are human creatures who have been lost in the second or third year of their lives and who have lived in the forests without having been taught to speak by anyone. Unlike animals, they are not even capable of distinguishing useful nourishment but have been nourished by all that they had found in the woods, pure or impure.

From this, it is deduced that on earth humans are by nature less intelligent and more despicable than animals and that only the faculty of emitting articulate sounds has allowed the human species to develop. If the animals had the gift of speech, they would reason with as much rigor as humans on no matter what topic. Thus, it is considered vain to believe that a human being should have more reason to live after death than an animal; religion that preaches immortality is only an artifice for governing the interior lives of the simple, as the laws of the government rules their external lives. Obviously, this episode is a reproduction, only slightly exaggerated, of the favorite doctrines of the Encyclopedists.

On hearing these words, the sages of antiquity exclaim: "Oh, what times now prevail on earth! Alas! What changes wisdom has undergone! Has it then changed into insensate rhetoric? The sun has gone down and is found on the other side of the earth at the antipode of its zenith." And they maintain later on that the discovery of the man in the forests justly proves that humankind, born in a state of innocence more complete than that of an animal, and only develops through education. The human being is only a form receiving life from God and is able to become regenerate by an eternal union with God. On earth, wisdom is actually obscured to the point that a person no longer knows anything of life or of death:

> Those who are able to know about this [the truths of life and the afterlife], but do not wish to, and consequently deny it, as many of your Christians do, we may liken to those found in the forest; not that they have become thus stupid from lack of instruction, but they have made themselves thus stupid by the fallacies of the senses, which are the obscuration of truths.

It is interesting to note that, even in this circumstance, Swedenborg remains faithful to the conception he has learned from Locke: that only instruction elevates humans above the animals. He in no way opposes the thesis according to which a human being, having grown up entirely isolated in the forests, would be condemned to remain on a level inferior to that of an animal. But to Swedenborg's mind, this only offers further proof that the human being has been created to attain perfection and to reunite with the Creator. Humans are the only creatures capable of self-development.

We shall again find this same thesis as the governing thought in the view Swedenborg will form regarding eternal life.

e l e v e n

The Spiritual World

Ever since Swedenborg's lifetime, it has been common to maintain a rigorous distinction between his theological doctrine, in a restricted sense of the word, and his conception of the spiritual world and life after death. While the former has often been considered as reasonable, sometimes even too rational and dispassionate, his speculations on the spiritual world have more often been regarded as fantastic and incoherent fancies, the products of an unhealthy mind.

I believe I have already made it clear that I do not share this opinion at all. Just as the mystical element in the theological doctrine of Swedenborg has generally been overlooked, sufficient attention has not been paid to the rationalistic elements of his eschatology or to the logical relationship between these and the rest of his theology. There has been an attraction, in a far too one-sided fashion, toward certain grotesque or picturesque details of his descriptions of the future life as well as to some of his spectacular visions and conversations with spirits; but in general, no clear idea of the structure of his eschatological system has been formed. Naturally, I cannot give a complete exposition of this system here. My task will be to show that the fundamental ideas that dominate Swedenborg's views are found again in this system and how his dreams of the spiritual world are the expression of his ideals.

The distinctive characteristic of Swedenborg's spiritual world is, as we know, that it is peopled exclusively by human beings. There are no angels directly created by God; still less is there a fallen angel, a devil, the creator of hell. Humanity is the supreme end of creation;

heaven and hell have their origin in us. God has created us to make real his eternal celestial realm, for which terrestrial life is a preparation. We have already seen these ideas pointed out in *Economy of the Animal Kingdom,* but for a long time Swedenborg hesitated to draw the final consequences. In *The Worship and Love of God,* we find angels created along with human beings; the fall of the devil has preceded and contributed to that of Adam and Eve. It is only in Swedenborg's theological system that the human being becomes the focus of the entire creation.

This initial principle explains the systematic analogy that exists between the spiritual and terrestrial worlds. In his earthly life, the human being is, in effect, internally either an angel or a devil, and the vicissitudes of natural life only serve to prepare him for the future spiritual life. The theory of correspondences teaches us, moreover, that every earthly thing possesses a higher correspondence, and the doctrine of humanity as the norm of creation allows us to find the human form again in the greater as well as in the lesser things of the spiritual world.

The three realms of the spiritual world—heaven, the world of spirits, and hell—consequently correspond to the three "parts" of the human being; and each of these, in turn, is divided into three kingdoms. It does not appear to me of great interest here to dwell any longer on these subdivisions, which are based on the three divisions of the human into *anima, mens,* and *corpus* and their subdivisions. We recall that each of these parts is subdivided, in turn, into halves: the *anima* offers a compartment for heavenly warmth—good—and another for the celestial light—truth. These two correspond, in the *mens*, to the will and the understanding, and in the body, to the heart and lungs.

This compartmentalization produces a new horizontal division of the spiritual world. The three heavens are divided into a celestial and a spiritual realm, populated respectively by celestial and spiritual angels. And we can follow similar subdivisions into hell, where they correspond to genii and spirits. As we shall see, the doctrine of marriage in the spiritual world rests on this difference between the will and the understanding. We cannot here risk being carried too far afield by following Swedenborg into all his classifications. Indeed, there is nothing in humanity which does not correspond to some "society" in the kingdoms of the spiritual world. This complicated system is really not difficult to understand if one bears in mind Swedenborg's anthropological schema.

Alongside this view, based on the doctrine of correspondences of the spiritual realms in human form, Swedenborg still makes a notably more concrete representation of the spiritual world—a conception that, in broad outline, agrees with the traditional view of most visionaries. The world of spirits, the intermediate realm between heaven and hell, appears to its inhabitants like a valley surrounded by crags and mountains. A narrow way leads to the celestial kingdoms situated above the valley; seen from the world of spirits, these kingdoms looks like clouds or brilliant white mists (*Heaven and Hell* §583). Crevices among the crags and hills lead to the hells, which are situated in the depths of the earth below the world of spirits. They have the form of black gulfs and grottos, at times resembling bogs and sheets of water. When one of them is opened, which only occurs when an inhabitant of the world of spirits is cast down there, flames and sooty smoke are emitted as from a flaming furnace (*Heaven and Hell* §585). Nauseating odors and pestilential vapors issue from these fissures, and one hears horrible cries rise from the abyss at the same time (*Heaven and Hell* §429).[260]

From this we may conclude that, to a certain extent, space and time exist in the spiritual world. Only the Divinity is free from space and time. No doubt our fixed spatial and temporal conditions are not found again in the spiritual world; but given the fact that angels and spirits see through their eyes exactly as humans do and that objects can only be seen in space, spaces apparently exist in the spiritual world. Likewise, all the events in the spiritual world, as well as in our own world, take place in apparent time. However, angels and spirits have no idea of time or space, for the changes in time or space for them are only modification of states. Everything the angels think is immediately present to them as real. When a spirit seeks the presence of another spirit, he immediately sees him or her appear before his eyes. Everything the angels see around them are correspondences of their own interior. This is how gardens and paradises, blooming with all kinds of flowers, appear to angels in a state of wisdom, among trees bearing fruit "according to the perfection of love in which the angels in a state of wisdom find themselves" (*Heaven and Hell* §176).

As a kind of analogy to the conditions of time and space prevailing in the spiritual world, Swedenborg points out that, for human thought, space does not exist, "for the things which it intensively evokes appear to him to be present." When anyone goes from one place to another, the distance seems different according to whether he or she is in a hurry to arrive or not. "The road itself is lengthened or shortened according to the desire of the traveler, although in reality it remains the same. That is an observation I have often made, to my great astonishment" (*Heaven and Hell* §§195–196).

From this, Swedenborg evidently understands that the conditions of space and time prevailing in the spiritual world are subjective and are modified according to the internal state of the observer; for celestial things do not at all exist in the same way as terrestrial things. In heaven, they exist from the Lord according to their correspondences with the inner life of the angels. They are, therefore, representations of the feelings and thoughts of the angels. From the fact that they constantly change with their feelings and thoughts, these receive the name of appearances (*apparentiae; Heaven and Hell* §§173–175). This does not prevent these appearances from having a real though still immaterial existence. All things existing in the natural world exist in the spiritual world in a more perfect form. They are substantial, although not material.

In various passages throughout his works, Swedenborg seeks to define more precisely what he means by "substantial." It is the origin of matter; it is simple, while matter is the composite. To a spirit who asks him if, in these conditions, the difference between the spiritual and the natural is not a simple question of degree, Swedenborg replies:

> Such is not the distinction. By no sort of refinement can the natural so approximate the spiritual as to become the spiritual; for the distinction is like that between the prior and the posterior, between which there is no finite ratio. For the prior is in the posterior as a cause in its effect; and the posterior is from the prior

as an effect is from its cause. Therefore the one is not visible to the other. (*True Christian Religion* §280[2])

Here we again find the old conceptions of the scientific period regarding the existence of a kind of intelligible matter which is the origin of "natural" matter. Our material body is only the envelope of the substantial body, which also has a human form and persists after death. "The *anima* of everyone resides in a spiritual body after having rejected the material envelope which it had borne in the world" (*Divine Love and Wisdom* §14). His reasoning rests, as we see, on the spatiality of the soul, a concept we can follow back to the time of the *Principia.* It follows that, by their form, the angels have all the characteristics of humans; they have a face, ears, hands, feet, etc.; they see each other and converse together, "in a word, nothing of the attributes of man is lacking, except that they are not clothed in a material body" (*Heaven and Hell* §75). They also wear clothes, except for the angels of the inmost heaven, who are nude. The splendor of their clothing corresponds to the degree of their understanding. And they find themselves in conditions of time and space similar to ours, with the difference that these conditions vary according to their inner state.

Thanks to this theory, the heaven of Swedenborg can borrow its colors from earthly dreams of happiness. The only difference lies in the fact that all objects are only appearances; they constitute a projection of the thoughts and feelings of the angels.

Swedenborg likewise describes the life of the world of spirits and of hell. Here also the inhabitants wander about in an environment that reproduces their own imaginary world in perceivable form.

The doctrine of correspondences thus permits Swedenborg to endow his spiritual world with an infinity of external details. His exposition becomes a vast universal panorama. Their proportions and reciprocal relationships are often the object of a fantastic inversion, and the doctrine of correspondences frequently removes every impression of reality from these portrayals. It is easy, however, to discover the originals.

Such is particularly the case with the world of spirits, which is often a servile copy of our own world. The majority of humans come into the world of spirits directly from earthly life and consequently retain all their individual characteristics. They have the same face, the same voice, the same habits they had during their terrestrial life, even the same desires, thoughts, and interests, although of a more exquisite essence. "It follows that once having become a spirit, the man only knows what he knew when he was in the body he occupied in the world, and does not know that he is dead" (*Heaven and Hell* §461).

Spirits continue to be near their relatives and friends. They engage in the same professions as on earth; they even continue to be distributed according to religions and nationalities. They inhabit countries and cities corresponding exactly with those they inhabited when living on earth. Consequently, there exist in the world of spirits two cities analogous to London, where the majority of Englishmen gather after death. Swedenborg gives us precise details of their topography. The Royal Exchange is located at the center of one of them, and the moderator and his staff reside there. The principal street is Holborn. To the west, as far as Wapping, live those who feel a confused love of good. The best spirits reside in the eastern quarters, which extend well beyond the city. The intelligent spirits live to the south, as far as Islington. On the other hand, in Moorfields and its surroundings, the population is mixed. In effect, here is where all those who incline toward evil are relegated, and the city is thereby purged of its bad elements. The houses, dress, and nourishment of the Londoners are exactly like what they were during their earthly life. "I asked about wine, strong drink, beer, chocolate, tea and the like, and was told that they had similar things. I also asked about the liquor called punch; they said that they also have the liquor, but it is given only to those who are sincere and at the same time industrious" (*Last Judgment [Posthumous]* §269).[261]

In the world of spirits, the Jews inhabit a city called "The Sordid Jerusalem," where they circulate in streets filled with filth to the ankles and where one is afflicted by nauseating smells. As they did during their earthly lives, the inhabitants engage in commerce and deal in diverse merchandise, particularly in precious stones, which they procure from heaven by unknown ways. The reason for this specialization is that precious stones correspond to the literal sense of the Word, which they are capable of understanding from the fact that they can read the Word in its original language. The situation provided for them in the world of spirits is so similar to that of their terrestrial life, that, less than any other people, they perceive that they have left this life (*Last Judgment [Posthumous]* §§251–261).

The Swedes are the worst European inhabitants of the world of spirits, after the Italians and the Russians. The best among them inhabit a city that resembles Gothenburg (it is well-known that Swedenborg had his first disciples in this city) and live in houses resembling those they occupied during their lifetime. The wicked are grouped in a large agglomeration of towns which, besides Stockholm, include Falun to the east, Boras to the north, etc. From the time of the absolute monarchy, fear of the king maintained a certain order among the Swedes and their gravest faults, their spirit of domination and their ambition, could not be given free rein. At the present time, they give free play to their dominating spirit and—due to the fact that they do not possess riches like other peoples—to their greed for gain. The majority among them seek public employment and titles; and, in the world of spirits, they give themselves to pernicious artifices (*Spiritual Diary* §5034ff., §5462). Members of the Swedish nobility are particularly haughty, egotistical, and ambitious. When they hold their assemblies of the nobility in the world of spirits, the angels observe that they are incapable of speaking from their inner being or distinguishing good from evil and judge everything according to their personal convenience. They are, consequently, progressively removed from their offices and finally reduced to beggary (*Spiritual Diary* §5461).

For Swedenborg, the world of spirits is the rallying area for most of the dead. Few indeed are those who are sufficiently regenerated to be accepted directly into heaven immediately after death or sufficiently degenerate to be precipitated directly into hell. During the earthly life of most people, there has been a discordance between the inner and the outer self, between the will and the understanding, which has to be overcome before they find their true place in the spiritual world. This is exactly what takes place in the world of spirits.

We have seen that, on his entry into the world of spirits, the human being retains the same face and voice as during his earthly life. Both are progressively modified, and the person has in the end a face and voice that correspond to his inner being, that is to say, his ruling love (*amor regnans*). Thus, the person becomes incapable of simulating sentiments other than those he truly feels. He finds himself constrained to speak as he thinks, and thenceforth his appearance reflects the real states of his soul (*Heaven and Hell* §457). Thanks to this transformation, the person reveals his true character, not only to other spirits, but also to his own mind. All the sins he has committed on earth, even those he has forgotten, reappear in his memory and are revealed to the angels assigned to scrutinize him. For each person possesses an interior memory on which are inscribed all he has thought, desired, said, done, understood, and seen; this memory survives his demise (*Heaven and Hell* §463). I have already mentioned Swedenborg's theory of an interior memory, in which the person preserves recollections never gathered by his external memory. During terrestrial life, no one is aware of possessing this memory.

It is exclusively the ruling love, then, that determines a person's lot in the other world. "It is man's ruling love that continues after death and this is in no way changed to eternity" (*Heaven and Hell* §477). For it is the person's will that, properly speaking, constitutes his being. "Man as a whole is such as he is in his will and consequently in his thought, so that an evil man is his own evil and a good man his own good" (*Heaven and Hell* §463). This conviction of the supremacy of the will dominates Swedenborg's whole eschatology.

It follows that no definitive reform is possible after death. In the world of spirits, the just receive instruction that prepares them for the life of heaven. And those who "are hardened in deceit" even while leading a good life, are submitted to a kind of purgatory in a place called "the lower earth" (*Heaven and Hell* §513).[262] But those whose ruling love is turned to evil are susceptible to neither instruction nor reform. When they have found their true identity, they pass directly into infernal communes that are founded in the same love (*Heaven and Hell* §512).

In this conception, we find again two of the fundamental theses of Swedenborg's theology: there is no justification by faith alone and that God is order itself. Each person creates himself through the play of his free will and through the love by which he chooses to rule his life. It is the doctrine of *Economy of the Animal Kingdom* and *The Worship and Love of God* that reappears here in full. If an individual has chosen love of the world, he can only be reformed by a radical transformation and a regeneration. And regeneration cannot operate immediately any more than a tree can grow in one day (*True Christian Religion* §586). God himself can do no more by mercy; nor can he grant the grace of salvation in violation of the laws of divine order. "The angels say that it would be easier to change a night-owl into a dove or a screech-owl into a bird of paradise than an infernal spirit into a heavenly spirit" (*Heaven and Hell* §527)

Consequently, in agreement with the Gospel of John, which he frequently quotes in this context, Swedenborg maintains that the evil pronounce their own damnation. They could not be happy among the just, whose joys they do not understand, and they are incapable of comprehending heavenly truths. The Lord excludes no one from the kingdom of heaven. Those who, at the moment of death, invoke the Lord in the belief that he can save them by immediate grace are admitted after death to the lower threshold of heaven. But when they enter there and the light of heaven flows over them, they are seized by vertigo. Their sight becomes dim, their thought is suspended, their heart throbs with unspeakable anguish, and they writhe like serpents near a flame; they throw themselves into the abyss yawning at their feet, and it is only from the moment they rejoin their like in hell that they recover their breath (*Heaven and Hell* §525; *True Christian Religion* §622).[263] God, then, does not cast down any human being into hell. The person who lives in evil has no other desire than to enter the place where his evil is at home (*Heaven and Hell* §547).

It follows that evil spirits are in their own environment in hell. They enjoy the fire of hell, its stench and its filth, and when a ray of divine light penetrates to them they seek to flee from it, preferring the infernal light, which is similar to that of smoldering coals and burning sulfur. Their faces are black and hairy and covered with pustules, ulcers, and scars; but they believe among themselves to have human form (*Heaven and Hell* §553). They give themselves to the pleasures corresponding to their desires. In the less rigorous hells, there exist rudimentary huts, agglomerated into towns with alleys and streets. From their dwellings, a noise of quarrels issues continuously, and the streets are arenas of brawls and brigandage. Other infernal spirits live in sordid houses of debauchery, while yet others wander like ferocious beasts in the obscurity of the forests (*Heaven and Hell* §586). They find their greatest pleasure in tormenting and torturing one another. They experience anguish only when angels from heaven intervene to restrain their violence, for they then feel deprived of their customary entertainment. The purpose of this chastening is not at all to reform them—that would be a vain endeavor—but to restrain them through fear. This is the only means of influencing them, for without fear of punishment hell would collapse like an earthly society deprived of laws (*Heaven and Hell* §581). Under these conditions, infernal spirits only punish themselves through the insatiability of their desires.

The same personal note is found in Swedenborg's conception of heavenly beatitude; it does not consist in perpetual enjoyment, for all pleasure, even of superior quality, induces dissatisfaction after a while. In the beautiful introductory chapter of *Conjugial Love,* Swedenborg relates that, in the world of spirits, an angel had gathered together the wise men of all Christian nations to learn what idea they had formed of heavenly bliss. He found that, despite individual divergences, they all agreed that it consisted in uninterrupted enjoyment. But the angel introduced them into spiritual "societies" where their notion of beatitude had been put into practice in order to convince them that, after a short stay, the inhabitants of these societies became weary of entertainments and sought to move out of them.

And this does not only apply to those who imagine heavenly bliss as a series of uninterrupted joys of paradise by way of strolls among rose gardens to the music of harps, but also to those who imagine this beatitude as a perpetual Sabbath, an incessant glorification of God and the permanent elevation of hearts toward the Lord. They find the spirits sitting in their temples, no longer listening to the preaching, which has dulled their hearing and wearied their minds, overcome by the interminable ecstasy and finally hurried to the doors to escape this chamber of torture. The angel finally informs them that heavenly happiness consisted in accomplishing tasks useful to oneself and to others (*Conjugial Love* §5).

In another of Swedenborg's memorabilia, three newly arrived spirits express surprise that there exists in the heavens employments, professions, commercial operations, and marvelous crafts. They had believed that, being transported from the natural world into heaven, they would rest from labor forever. But one of the ancients asks them, "Have you understood rest from all labor as perpetual idleness, where you would pass your time seated on couches inhaling pleasures into your lungs and drinking joys through your mouth?" As the newcomers respond affirmatively, the ancient one assures them that idleness engenders weariness and lethargy and so is incompatible with all true enjoyment. It is the vigor of the mind (*intensio animi)* that maintains the elasticity of the body, and this vigor can be had from activity and labor. Thus, appointments and offices exist in heaven and tribunals of greater or lesser importance, as well as arts and crafts.

The newcomers are then introduced into a library that is subdivided into sections according to the different fields of knowledge, and they are stupefied by the number of volumes, parchments, papers, quills, and ink heaven contains. From there, they are escorted to museums, schools, and colleges, where intellectual activities and competitions take place. They are eventually brought into the presence of administrators and functionaries of the city who show them the marvelous works executed in spiritual form by artists. And when they are at last convinced that eternal repose is not idleness, maidens appear, who make them gifts of articles that they have embroidered and woven with their own hands and sing a song whose heavenly melody expresses the inclination to useful labors and pleasure in accomplishment (*Conjugial Love* §207).

It follows that each angel of heaven has his task to accomplish, and his devotion is expressed by the good he does (*Heaven and Hell* §387). There exist in heaven all kinds of tasks: religious, administrative, domestic. Certain angels have the mission of educating the children who enter into heaven; others are assigned to the world of spirits to protect newcomers from attacks by malevolent spirits; others to ensure order in hell (*Heaven and Hell* §391–393). All these tasks are carried out from love of the work and the desire for useful accomplishment, for the angels do not at all work with profit in view. All the necessities of life are furnished for free: lodging, clothing, nourishment (*Heaven and Hell* §393).

Thus, each has his task to perform, but he does not dedicate himself to it without recreation, since this, too, would weary him. In the heavens, there are also days of repose; feast days, when worship takes place; and special solemnities dedicated to concerts in public squares and, on the outskirts of cities, to games and spectacles. Musicians are seated on three levels garlanded with vines, with their wind and string instruments, flanked by male and female singers, who entertain the audience with the most beautiful chants (*Conjugial Love* §17).

Even during work days, employment is intermixed with distractions, physical exercises, and artistic occupations. Every morning the soft chants of virgins and young women are heard floating on the air throughout the town from houses surrounding the public squares. When these songs come to an end, all doors and windows are closed, and the town becomes silent. No idlers are found; each one is busy at his or her tasks. Towards midday, doors open everywhere, windows also at times, and one sees girls and boys at play in the streets under the supervision of their teachers who are seated in colonnades of their dwellings. On the outskirts of the towns, girls and boys engage in varied activities, running, javelin-throwing, ball games. There are also organized competitions among boys to show who is the most alert in understanding, acting, or speaking. The winners are awarded laurel leaves. In the suburbs, theatrical pieces are also presented, where most of the actors represent the virtue of moral life. Jesters also figure among them on occasion (*Conjugial Love* §17).

The most uncommon part of Swedenborg's eschatology, as we know, is his conception of marriage in the spiritual world. It is comparatively late that his view takes the clearly dogmatic form in which we find it in his *Conjugial Love* (published in Amsterdam in 1768). Even during his lifetime, this book became the most popular and widely distributed of his writings. However, here as elsewhere, there is no difficulty in identifying the directive thought of his doctrine in the earlier scientific works.

As I have previously pointed out, Swedenborg had already propounded the thesis of a conjugal union in the future life in his *De Anima* §102, which dates from 1741, although this detail appears to have escaped the commentators. In this work, he first deals with *"amor venereus"* or sexual love (§93ff.), which he analyzes with the same physiological minuteness that we later find in *Conjugial Love.* When this carnal love emanates exclusively from the *animus*, it constitutes a drive that has only physical pleasure in mind. When, on the contrary, it originates in the *anima,* it acquires a noble and elevated purpose. In the following passage, he discusses the *"odium et adversatio veneris"* (hatred and opposition to love). He rises with alacrity against the disfavor shown to carnal love as a result of egoism, antipathy toward humanity, or senile insensibility to beauty. On the other hand, he says, we cannot censure those who condemn carnal love on principle as impure and forbidden. They possess the highest virtue, which is chastity. These distinctions conform perfectly with the Lutheran views of the day.

More peculiar are the two subsequent chapters on *amor conjugialis* (conjugial love) and *odium conjugiale* (conjugial hate). Here Swedenborg declares that love truly conjugial is not only a bodily union but also one of minds (*conjunctio mentium).* And when the two partners aspire towards a spiritual end, they likewise bring about the union of their *anima*. The result is a heavenly life on earth; and, since this conjunction of souls persists after carnal pleasure has ceased, one is warranted in believing that the two souls (*animae)* remain united in heaven. "But a marriage and a love of this nature does not develop as an effect of pure chance. They are the work of a particular intervention of divine providence" (*De Anima* §96).

In this declaration, we may look for an echo of this hope, manifested by Christian partners in all ages, that they be granted the enjoyment of the heavenly blessing together. With his characteristic taste for symmetry, Swedenborg has nevertheless, in the following chapter, sought to invent an analogous retribution for spouses who have lived in discord during their sojourn on earth. When physical pleasure ceases for them, there only remains a murderous and implacable hate that ends by overcoming their *animas*. "That is hell on earth, and we have every right to presume that their souls torture each other mutually like two harpies or two furies of Erebus. These dissensions *(disjugia)* and infernal conflicts of souls also seem to arise, not by pure chance but by a duly motivated decision of divine providence." In closing, Swedenborg declares that of the two extremes which constitute conjugal love and conjugal hate, one can deduce the nature of the innumerable intermediary forms of unions that fill the universe (*De Anima* §97).

It was certainly Swedenborg's intention to develop this theme in *The Worship and Love of God.* In the parts of this work that were written, he only speaks of the marriage of the first human couple in passing, but he does so in terms that clearly indicate that, here too, he considers marriage as of divine foundation and as constituting a union of souls. It is also observed that Swedenborg systematically recurs to marriage as symbolic of cosmic unions: union of earth and sky, of life and nature brought about in the nuptial chamber of heaven, to witness there the consecration of this union in the light of the nuptial torch, which is love. In the first part of the *Adversaria,* marriage equally has its heavenly correspondence and its exalted spiritual origin in the form of the divine union of truth and good, of the Messiah and the Church.

When Swedenborg, in his theological system, transforms the human into angel after death, he quite naturally picks up his notion of celestial marriage again. This idea is also found frequently among the Church Fathers, scholars, and Protestant theologians, who recognized angels as physical beings and even went so far as to consider them as possessing gender. We have likewise seen that it was perfectly possible, while Swedenborg was writing *The Worship and Love of God,* that he should have found this idea in Milton. This Miltonic influence seems also to emphasize the fact that, when he addresses the question of the origin and celestial correspondence of married union (*Arcana Coelestia* §§2727–2759), Swedenborg attributes to heavenly marriage the same ethereal character as Milton does. It is not at all a matter of true conjugial relations in heaven. Those who during their terrestrial life have lived in conjugial love are allowed to live together once they have become angels; sometimes they even surround themselves with their children. There exists a union among them, not of bodies, but of souls (*unio mentium*; *Arcana Coelestia* §2732). Swedenborg does not push the audacity of his thought to the point of affirming, as he had done in *De Anima,* that spouses who have lived in discord will continue to cohabit in mutual torment in hell. Here he limits himself to declaring that spouses who have not lived in a true conjugial union will be separated after death. No lewdness exists in hell. The tendency toward lewdness gives way to a depraved pleasure in filth and excrements.

Here Swedenborg develops more broadly the doctrine according to which earthly marriage issues from heavenly marriage, the union of good and truth in God. With this good and this truth, conjugial love is radiant in the world, but it changes character according to the nature of the subjects, as solar light is modified by the object it shines upon. This is of the sort that celestial beatitude can change into infernal voluptuousness (*Arcana Coelestia* §2741). It is clear that Swedenborg has already incorporated conjugial love into his emanationistic system.

In *Heaven and Hell,* which dates from around 1757, Swedenborg still considers heavenly marriage as a purely spiritual union:

> Marriages in heaven are not like marriages on earth. In heaven marryings are spiritual, and cannot properly be called marryings (*nuptiae*), but conjunction of minds from the conjunction of good and truth. But on earth there are marryings, because these are not of the spirit alone but also of the flesh. (*Heaven and Hell* §382[b])

It follows that two spouses do not carry the titles of husband and wife into the heavens. It is easy to understand why Swedenborg does not admit any marriage in the heavens. In the same passage, he recalls the words of Luke 20:35: "But those who are accounted worthy to attain to that age and the resurrection from the dead neither marry nor are given in marriage."

Over the course of time, Swedenborg cannot, however, free himself from the demands of logic. As soon as he acknowledges that angels have bodies endowed with all the physiological functions, he must admit that conjugial love among the angels will have an equivalent sexual character. That is the conclusion to which he has already been led in *Apocalypse Explained* §992, and in *Conjugial Love,* it finds its complete development. After death a man remains a man and woman a woman as before. The partners continue to have the same married relation as on earth, but they are more delightful and more blessed (*Conjugial Love* §51). Swedenborg succeeds in eluding the declarations of the Gospel that humans never contract marriages after the resurrection by a rather hasty explanation that the biblical verse applies to spiritual marriage, that is to say, to the union of man with God, which is to be realized during earthly life (*Conjugial Love* §41).

In one of his memorabilia, Swedenborg tells of three spirits newly come from earth who are greatly astonished to learn that the heavens contain the most beautiful girls and the handsomest young men. And they are still more surprised by the existence of marriages in the celestial realm and that conjugial love displays the same forms as on earth. They ask of the angels: "Is it not said in Scripture that marriage does not exist in the heavens, since we are all angels?" To which the angelic spirits respond, "Raise your eyes toward the heavens and you will find the answer to your questions there." They then see the heavens open. Two angels approach, who say that marriage exists in heaven as on earth and that the words of the Gospel apply to spiritual marriage (*Conjugial Love* §44).

This celestial love is chaste and pure because it constitutes a union, not of bodies alone, but also of souls. No infants are born of these unions, but they engender love and wisdom. By their union, the consorts impregnate each other with the human, which means the search for wisdom and attachment to what relates to this wisdom (*Conjugial Love* §§51–52).

Only this union permits "man to attain full perfection" *(homo in sua plenitudine)*. In heaven, the two consorts form only a single angel, for the man and the woman are so created that, together, they can constitute a single human being, a single flesh, each one separately being only half a man (*Conjugial Love* §37). In effect, the male has been created to comprehend the truth and the female to love the good. In the former, then, it is the reason and in the latter the will that constitutes the dominant quality. And from the fact that in God there exists a union between the good and the truth, a universal conjugial sphere (*universalis sphera conjugialis*) emanates from him which spreads throughout the entire universe, from the angels down to the worms. In conjugial love, then, there exists a descending scale across the entire creation; in its lower form, it is sexual love.

Having thus incorporated the marriage union as an indispensable element of his eschatology, Swedenborg is naturally obliged to acknowledge that new conjugial unions can be made in the future life. Most often two spouses do not meet again after death except during the first external state in the world of spirits. When they ultimately take the form according to the love that dominates them, they can no longer cohabit if their earthly marriage has been only an external union and not a true union of souls. They then separate, and each of them chooses another consort with whom they sense an internal communion (*Conjugial Love* §§47–50). Those who, in the course of their terrestrial life, have lived chastely in celibacy are authorized to marry if they have previously had the desire. If, on the other hand, they have remained reluctant to marry, they are allowed to continue their celibacy, but at the side of heaven itself. The existence of a perpetual celibate sphere in effect disturbs the sphere of conjugial love, which is the true sphere of heaven (*Conjugial Love* §54).

Conjugial love naturally has its antithesis in *amor scortatorius* (debased love), which has its origin in the Fall and consists in the conjunction of evil and falsity. It is from this love that all the impurities of hell arise (*Conjugial Love* §§425–430) and is the final destiny of all those who lack conjugial love. Here Swedenborg restates his thesis that "everyone, be he good or evil, is in his pleasure." Those who have abandoned themselves to adulterous love in their terrestrial lives are relegated to the dens of debauchery in hell, where they copulate like animals, mutually revile each other, and, despite their voluptuousness, feel only disgust and revulsion for their companions.

It is in the description of the lives of the various categories of adulterous consorts that Swedenborg gives perhaps the widest scope to his poetic genius. The scene he paints of hell truly has something demonical and frightening that cannot fail to impress even a modern reader. The reprobates are led into hell by sirens who seduce them by their radiant beauty, but who, at the moment when one wants to embrace them, become horrible monsters. If, in spite of everything, they do not renounce their unrestrained lust, they are cast down into still deeper hells. Their faces are pale and appear to be composed exclusively of skin. Their voices are excessively dry, hoarse, their clothing is in rags, their gait is stooped. They eventually lose all sexual potency, possessed by sex to the point of satiety (*Conjugial Love* §505, §510).

Conjugial Love is not, however, exclusively concerned with carnal love in the future life; it gives also a detailed psychological analysis of marriage and erotic love on earth. We cannot give here a detailed exposition of this analysis, which, moreover, would be superfluous because we find the psychological schema of Swedenborg again here. Like the sphere of conjugial love that descends from heaven, the sphere of adulterous love rises from hell. Their meeting ground, which, in the spiritual world, is the world of spirits, is in the *mens* of the human being (*Conjugial Love* §437). It does not appear to me to be necessary to pursue a description of Swedenborg's exposition of the state of equilibrium and of the intervention of free will.

In the human being, the state of marriage exalts the faculties of the soul: with men, the *mens* rises toward a purer light; with women, toward a more ardent warmth. The inner levels of the soul open wider and wider so that the male sees and knows God intuitively, while from the *anima* light and love flow down into the lower parts, which are thus ennobled (*Conjugial Love* §191). This exaltation of the faculties is transmitted to the offspring in the form of receptivity to love and wisdom (*Conjugial Love* §204). It is evidently the contrary that occurs in adulterous love.

Truly conjugial love is chaste in all its manifestations. But it is absolutely pure neither with humans nor angels. Beneath the spiritual in humankind, there exists a natural level that is not chaste, and between the two there is a door on hinges. When this door is open, the chaste is mixed with what the unchaste (*Conjugial Love* §146).

What I have just expounded appears to me to be sufficient to excuse me from further insistence on Swedenborg's conjugial doctrine. As we have seen, it is no more than a repetition of the psychology of his *Economy of the Animal Kingdom,* applied in a truly ingenious fashion to sexual conditions.

Although Swedenborg's doctrine of conjugial love can, in its minute details, be included in his system, we may nonetheless wonder what motivated him to give marriage and carnal love such an important place in his doctrine. Already in connection with the dreams of his religious crisis, I have pointed out the strangely marked erotic character of Swedenborg's dispositions. Unfortunately, we do not know much about his amorous encounters. The anecdote found in most of his biographies of his unhappy love for Emerentia, the youngest of Polhem's daughters, seems to have been somewhat romanticized. It owes its origin to a rather doubtful source—an anonymous document that was read in 1789 at the Exegetic-Philanthropic Society in Stockholm.

According to this document, Polhem gave Swedenborg a written commitment to give him his daughter Emerentia in marriage, and would have obliged the young girl, who at the time was not more than fifteen, to sign this promise.[264] The girl was so chagrined by this that, moved by pity, her brother Gabriel stole the contract from Swedenborg, whose sole joy it was to reread it daily. He was so moved by this loss that Polhem insisted on learning the cause of his sorrow, and then he declared himself ready to return the document to him. But in view of the young lady's despair, Swedenborg himself renounced his rights and left the Polhem home. He solemnly declared that he would never again become attached to any woman and that he would never again entertain the idea of becoming engaged. Following this, he undertook his voyages abroad. Finally, this document tells us that Swedenborg had later, in his old age, assured Emerentia's daughters and their husbands, when they visited him in his garden, that he talked to their late mother as often as he wished.

The only document that permits us to verify the above account is a letter from Swedenborg to Benzelius dated September 14, 1718 (*Opera* I, 286). From this letter, it appears that Polhem had first promised him his elder daughter Maria: "The older daughter of Polhem is affianced to a gentleman of the King named Manderström; I ask myself what people say, for she was my promised; the other daughter is in my opinion much prettier."[265] As we see, Swedenborg seems to have easily recovered from his repulse, consoling himself with the hope of marrying the second Polhem daughter. In any case, as Tafel remarks on the basis of a letter from Polhem to Benzelius, Swedenborg had broken all relations with Polhem, by whom, according to the latter, he had been pampered like a child.[266]

It is possible that, during the following six months, Swedenborg may have demanded the hand of the younger sister, Emerentia, and that his repulse in this new project may have provoked the break. Nevertheless, it appears more likely that his animosity toward Polhem may have been due to the deception he experienced in not becoming his son-in-law at all, rather than his rather sudden love for Emerentia. This supposition is furthermore confirmed by the fact that, in a conversation with the Danish General Tuxen,[267] Swedenborg certainly alludes to the blow to his project of marriage with Maria Polhem when he tells his interlocutor about his sole incursion on the way to marriage.[268] But he does not speak of any vow never to marry, and there are several reasons to believe that later he was not absolutely opposed to the idea of making a good marriage.

On the rest of his loves, we are, if possible, even less informed. Robsahm relates in his memoirs: "It is known further that Swedenborg has possessed a mistress whom he abandoned after she had deceived him, but otherwise one finds no trace of illicit *amours*."[269] Tafel has vainly taken infinite pains to prove that this piece of information was due to a false interpretation of Swedenborg's demand for the hand of Emerentia Polhem. Using strange reasons, he has also tried to show what was implausible in Tuxen's anecdote, in which he asked Swedenborg whether he had succeeded in remaining free from all carnal temptation. Swedenborg replied, "Not completely; in my youth I had a mistress in Italy."[270]

Given the complete absence of any contradictory declaration by Swedenborg himself and of any contrary affirmation by contemporaries, it is clearly impossible to rebut these assertions categorically as false. On the contrary, they appear to be corroborated by the *Journal of Dreams,* where Swedenborg declares that "the taste for women" was "his dominant passion." This, moreover, confirms the terribly sensual character of his dreams. Like his extremely detailed descriptions of married love in *Conjugial Love,* these seem to completely exclude the possibility that Swedenborg may have lived in chastity all his life; moreover, he never claimed to. He also declares in *Conjugial Love* that, in certain individuals of violent passions, carnal love cannot be repressed without danger, if they do not have occasion to marry when reaching adolescence. Without any doubt, he put himself in this category. Also extramarital relations *(fornicatio)* seem to him a minor sin in the degree they relate to conjugial love. That is to say, one is internally in marital love to the degree that one prefers this love to the impure state of fornication. And if we then continue to have extramarital sexual relations, it is by necessity (*Conjugial Love* §§450–452). For in *fornicatio*, conjugial love can be concealed like the spiritual within the natural (*Conjugial Love* §449). *Fornicatio* constitutes an intermediate stage between conjugial love and debauchery and can be a preparation for either. Thus, he counsels young men who cannot marry and do not feel capable of mastering their desires to take a mistress in order not to be perverted by promiscuity.

Thanks to the crisis of the *Journal of Dreams*, Swedenborg considered himself to have been cured from his "dominant passion"; and during the final thirty years of his life, he probably lived in absolute celibacy. He seems to have been rather intimidated by women, and this timidity seems to have increased during his solitary bachelorhood. Robsahm relates that Swedenborg never allowed a woman to enter his chamber without the presence of a third party, "for he knew that woman is artful and that he could be accused by one of them of having sought to know her too intimately."

The facts that I have attempted to assemble above as impartially as possible appear to me to lead to this conclusion: that Swedenborg was never permitted to taste the pure joy of love, although the intensity of his erotic instincts made it appear to him as the highest of all earthly joys. This is why he transposes these joys to the future life. It is for him not only a logical necessity, but even a true psychic need, to include in celestial marriage all the physical pleasures of terrestrial union. His indiscreet and uselessly detailed descriptions of conjugial joys in heaven—the constant amorous ardor of male angels, the "sixth sense" of female angels, "this sense of the joys of conjugial love in the male"—are explained by this need. And it is also why *Conjugial Love,* along with many passages in poor taste, includes passages of sublime lyric beauty and elevation that are not found elsewhere in Swedenborg's works.

That Swedenborg himself may have hoped to enjoy in another world all the conjugial joys that had been denied him in this one is indicated by a testimony that has been transmitted by a tradition among Swedenborgians and was published for the first time by J. J. G. Wilkinson. It offers a clue that bears all the signs of authenticity. According to this tradition, Swedenborg was accustomed to say that it had been given to him to see his future spouse in the spiritual world, who was waiting for him there; on earth, she had borne the name of Countess Gyllenborg. This countess was the wife of Fredrik Gyllenborg, born Elisabeth Stierncrona, a lady of Pietistic tendencies and authoress of a book of piety in two volumes, *The Best Part of Mary.* Since 1733 at least, Swedenborg was intimately associated with her husband and with her father, Fredrik Gyllenborg, who died in 1759 and was relegated by Swedenborg to hell because of his dominating spirit. It is known that Gyllenborg was a politician given to intrigue, one of the most rabid of the "era of liberty." His widow, who survived him by ten years, could then look forward to a divorce and a new marriage in the future life.

It would be not at all just to build a romance on these simple facts. It may well be that the lady remained ignorant of the position that Swedenborg reserved for her in the future life. It may even be conceded that the idea of making her his celestial bride only came to Swedenborg after the countess's death. Even with this reservation, the anecdote is no less interesting in that it supports the close connections between Swedenborg's doctrine of heavenly marriage and his own amorous hopes. Swedenborg evidently considered himself as one of those who lived in celibacy but had longed for a companion and may be admitted into heaven to contract marriage there. Finally, it appears from this anecdote that, during several years at least, and perhaps since the death of Fredrik Gyllenborg and his relegation to hell, the dreams of Swedenborg of the holy "joys of marriage" had a precise objective.

If one wishes to judge the sexual ethic of Swedenborg equitably, such as he professes it in *Conjugial Love,* it is evidently necessary to consider it against the background of the epoch when he lived, one of the most profligate known in history. It would have been rather futile for Swedenborg to preach moral austerity. Although he lived apart from mundane life during his whole theosophical period, he could not avoid seeing to what degree the obligations of marriage were neglected, and he complained of it repeatedly in his works. He harbored no illusions about the purity of human behavior. When he describes the proposal of marriage, he maintains that the choice belongs to the man, not to the woman, because the love of the man is addressed to the sex in general, while that of the woman has the object of a single representative of the opposite sex. "If you wish to be convinced," he adds, "ask the men you meet if they prefer monogamy or polygamy, and you will find hardly a single one who does not pronounce for polygamy" (*Conjugial Love* §296).

It is this pessimistic view of the male incapacity to observe sexual continence that explains the tolerance that serves so often to prove his moral norm. We recall here his opinion of *"fornicatio"* and the counsel he gives to young people who are not capable of controlling their desires. In certain cases, he would even allow a husband to take a concubine. Clearly, one cannot judge his morality by the measure of our own, no more than one can with the sexual morality of Luther. It is beyond doubt that *Conjugial Love,* which one sees frequently classified as an immoral work, even in the most modern expositions, was written with the object of reestablishing the sanctity of marriage. This book, then, earns a rank among the tenacious attempts made in this regard in all countries during this period. It is not by pure chance that Swedenborg is a contemporary of Richardson and Rousseau. *Conjugial Love* is, more than any other work of the century, an apotheosis of marriage and family life.

For Luther, the human sexual instinct is a necessity of nature. Human beings have been created by God to live in a state of marriage, not of celibacy. Also it is the married, and not the cloistered, life that can bear the name "*Order der reinen Keuschheit*" (the order of chastity). To shackle this natural instinct by vows of chastity is the equivalent of placing an obstacle to the work of the Divine, and thus monastic vows cannot be binding. "In the absence of any divine miracle, true chastity hovers protectively in the highest degree over marriage, and in the weakest degree over the state of virginity."[271]

Swedenborg pushes this concept to purely paradoxical consequences. For him, not only is marriage itself chaste, but sexual intercourse is as well.[272] All the enjoyments of a true marriage, even the most exalted, are chaste (*Conjugial Love* §144). The expressions "chaste and unchaste" are only specifically applicable to marriage and to all that depends on it (*Conjugial Love* §139). We may not, then, qualify as chaste those who have made the vow of celibacy, unless the love of a truly conjugial life persists within them. Swedenborg says he asked angels whether those who have sought piety, consecrated themselves to the adoration of God, have turned away from the vanities of the world and desires of the flesh, and who have made a vow of chastity, will be accepted in heaven. The angels answered him that such people could not stand the sphere of conjugial love and that a place is reserved for them outside of heaven. After their death, monks and nuns are therefore released from their vows so that they may choose between the conjugial life in heaven and the celibate life outside of heaven (*Conjugial Love* §155).

Just as Swedenborg, in condemning the traditional doctrine of the redemption and in proclaiming the activity of love, believed he was pursuing the route Luther was engaged in without having been able to travel it to the end and thought he had destroyed the last vestiges of the spiritual traffic in indulgences, so he also believed that his doctrine of spiritual marriage effaced the last traces of monastic mysticism that persisted in Lutheranism. We have already seen that, in the course of his crisis, he gives free course to an ecstatic love of the Christ that is certainly related to the Moravian doctrine. During his theological period, he busies himself in a diametrically opposite way. His exposition of the "marriage of the Lord with the Church" is particularly sober and abstract, and he denies explicitly that this union has an equivalent in celestial or terrestrial marriages.

It is thus incorrect to relate, as is so often done, Swedenborg's doctrine of spiritual marriage to this aspiration towards the divine Bridegroom that is found again and again in Christian mysticism, particularly in Catholic mysticism. His doctrine, on the contrary, has the purpose of combatting this confusion between the love of God and erotic longing. By giving eros a purpose in eternal life, he raises it to the yearning towards the heavenly spouse. Conjugial love remains, therefore such as it is, in the future life.

Even though Swedenborg's affirmation of the sexual and marital character of love in its most noble form contradicts the eros of Plato, his system presents, as Lagerborg has proposed, a marked Platonic imprint in the universal role that he attributes to love.[273] It is the fundamental love (*amor fundamentalis)* for all that is heavenly and spiritual and, consequently, natural love (*Conjugial Love* §65). Born of the union between the good and the true, between wisdom and love, it conducts those who possess it not only to a greater love but also to a higher wisdom (*Conjugial Love* §188). It follows that it is the treasure of human life and of the Christian religion (*Conjugial Love* §457). It is also the source of beauty. For it is neither wisdom alone nor love alone that creates beauty, but the conjunction of the two. Beauty is an enjoyment of sight, born of the union of love with wisdom. It is the reason virgins in heaven sparkle with light like diamonds, while wives reflect the fire of rubies (*Conjugial Love* §384). It is plain that this erotic metaphysics and this esthetic eroticism ultimately go back to Platonic impulses, even though Swedenborg may have modified these doctrines according to his own ends.

On the other hand, it seems to me difficult to follow Lagerborg when he claims that Swedenborg is full of "mythological phantasmagoria." One might perhaps discover a remote affinity with Plato's idea of the primordial androgyne, or the perfect hermaphrodite, in Swedenborg's idea that the consorts united in heaven are fused into one angel. No doubt the earthly man is, for Swedenborg, but a half that will only become complete in the future life, by the union with his better half. But since Swedenborg never acknowledges the doctrine of preexistence here, any more than elsewhere, this analogy does not reach very far. It is by moral conduct during his life on earth that a man determines the person with whom he will conjoin himself in the future life.

For Swedenborg, spiritual marriage gives to heavenly happiness its idyllic—one is tempted to say pastoral—character. For these are, in reality, the contemporary dreams of an Arcadia of eternal spring, an eternal youth, eternal innocence, and eternal fidelity in the love that Swedenborg reproduces in his descriptions of marriage in heaven. Heavenly couples of the Golden Age live under their tents, raised on a plateau, amid forests of cedar and olive trees and surrounded by vines laden with dark-blue grapes. Men are clothed in hyacinth-hued mantles and white tunics, the women in purple togas. One even sees rams and ewes that are "representatives of the innocence and peace among the mountaineers." And when these couples converse regarding marital love, their tents take on hues of gold (*Conjugial Love* §75).

In most of his memorabilia, Swedenborg introduces us into a fairyland; rose gardens, groves with limpid springs, lawns surrounded by trees cheerfully interlaced by winding grapevines. He likewise discovers that everywhere in heaven there exist sites where weddings are conducted, little gardens surrounded by intertwining branches of trees, flowering shrubbery exhaling a soft fragrance. These are "nuptial gardens" (*Conjugial Love* §316). It appears that the southern nature Swedenborg had occasion to admire during his voyages and of which no trace is found in his travel notes, has reappeared in a form embellished by time, along with the dreams of celestial unions in his old age.

Here I would like to relate several of the more beautiful of Swedenborg's memorabilia, which rank among the most poetic passages of his writings and of all the literature of eighteenth-century Sweden. The unequaled richness of their fablelike morality does not permit me to realize this desire, however. Moreover, their complicated symbolism makes them entirely accessible only to a reader who is familiar with Swedenborg's system. Nevertheless, I believe I should briefly summarize at least one of these visions, which, if not one of the most beautiful, has the advantage of being one of the more intelligible.

Meditating one day on conjugial love, Swedenborg sees two naked infants approaching him from a distance, bearing baskets and accompanied by a flight of turtledoves. As they come nearer, he perceives that they are crowned by roses and that garlands of lilies and bluish-purple roses hang on them obliquely from shoulder to waist, held together by a chain of foliage mixed with olive twigs:

> But as they came yet nearer they did not appear as infants, nor naked, but as two persons in the first bloom of life, clad in robes

> and tunics of shining silk, into which were woven flowers most beautiful to the sight. And as they came close to me there breathed upon me from heaven through them a vernal warmth, with fragrant odor as of the earliest blossomings in gardens and fields. They were two married partners from heaven.

Swedenborg then learns from them that they have been united in heaven for centuries and that there reign in heaven a sun and a perpetual spring. This is what the vision symbolizes. And they conduct Swedenborg into other interiors of heaven, where everything, even housekeeping utensils, have celestial forms and sparkle with gold and rubies. He then learns that the wives who now look like maidens were old women and that the husbands who appear to be young men were, at the time of their death, tottering old men. They loved each other reciprocally, and their religion caused them to avoid adultery as the worst of sins. This is the reason God has led them back to the most beautiful age of their life for eternity (*Conjugial Love* §137).

To Swedenborg's mind, then, it is conjugial love that gives all its poesy to the blessings of heaven. And it is thanks to this love that angels live perpetually in sunny Elysian fields, that they appear to each other as young people in the flower of youth, and that they are surrounded by delicious gardens and perfumes of springtime verdure and flowers of spring. For youth, light, fragrances, and the warmth of spring are only representatives of the warmth of their own love and the light of their own wisdom. The more closely they are united in love, the more the golden air that bathes them shines, the softer the odors of flowers become, and the younger they appear in their own eyes and in those of their companions. For as Swedenborg writes elsewhere (*Arcana Coelestia* §553), "they who are united in heaven in mutual love perpetually advance to the springtime of their youth, a springtime becoming ever more enchanting and ever more holy; in the measure that their common life accumulates thousands of years."

In my exposition of Swedenborg's ideas of the spiritual world, I have deliberately avoided drawing detailed parallels with earlier eschatological systems. Comparisons I myself have made have no doubt revealed certain analogies with prior conceptions of the nature of angels, heavenly life, purgatory, hell, etc.; but it has been in general a matter of details without great importance for Swedenborgian doctrine as a whole. The relationship between this doctrine and diverse biblical representations of a future life derive from biblical quotations Swedenborg almost never fails to invoke in support of his theses.

Nevertheless, here is reason to bear in mind the freedom of interpretation that validates his exegetical method. The deep imprint of antiquity on his descriptions of celestial beatitude is also so manifest that it hardly needs mentioning. It is notably to this source that there is reason to attribute the role he gives to physical exercises and the fine arts in the life of angels. All his descriptions of heavenly joys quite naturally recall the picture of the Elysian fields given in the *Aeneid*. And again in the philosophical discussions under the porticos of the schools of wisdom, which recur so frequently in his work, we find the environment of Plato's Dialogues. The links that some have occasionally wished to establish with Dante tend to conflate the biblical and classical representations of the future life. Nothing allows me to assume that Swedenborg had known Dante or felt his influence.

On the other hand, Swedenborg's representations of the future life, in their totality, clearly bear the imprint of his time and his own personality. In the world of spirits, where the dead have lost only their external physical envelope, we find a faithful reflection of terrestrial conditions as they appear to him. He has given us his judgment of the characteristics of the different nations and the effects of different religions on their adherents. That he had early felt a lively interest in ethnology is a fact that is attested by his traveler's notebooks, in which he provided ample space for comments on the characteristics of diverse peoples and churches. No doubt one finds numerous eccentricities in his descriptions of corresponding conditions in the world of spirits. But it would be vain to deny that he gives frequent proof of a psychological perspicacity and a familiarity with the habits of life of different peoples that one would hardly expect of a traveler who had led such a retiring life abroad.

It has been objected, not without reason, to the portrayals of the celebrated dead he meets in the world of spirits, that they lack distinctive traits and that all of them express themselves in nearly the same fashion. But to a certain extent, this is the natural consequence of his belief that each one, in his future life, is recreated in the image of his own interior, of his dominant drives. If, in this spirit, we read the characteristics Swedenborg gives them, in most cases we come to form a fairly clear idea of the manner in which he conceives them. When, later, he is to have the vision of the Last Judgment, he will find added occasion to pass in review over all his contemporaries, individuals, sects, societies, and peoples. With Swedenborg, no ardent hate of parties is found, such as that which gives such color to Dante's *Inferno*. But thanks precisely to their sober and measured tone, the judgments of Swedenborg give an impression of inexorable severity. It is thus that, in the sepulchral description he gives, for example, of a promenade in the streets of Stockholm in the world of spirits, there unfolds an impression of funereal terror. The majority of the houses are closed and silent, for their owners are spiritually dead.

Heaven and hell are objects of a more fantastic description, but here too we again find without difficulty the characteristic traits of the epoch. To Swedenborg's mind, hell is not at all a place of punishment. Unlike in the classical and many of the Christian accounts, the reprobates are not condemned to be deprived of what was their pleasure on earth or forced to occupying themselves with what they detested here. On the contrary, even in hell, they harden themselves in their crimes and sins. For the Lord punishes no one; evil is so intimately attached to its own punishment that it cannot be separated (*Heaven and Hell* §550). Also hell becomes the type of criminal, lawless society, which so many of the satirists of the eighteenth century described in a more or less veiled form. Its inhabitants, possessed by egoism, experience neither remorse nor repentance, which would be the first indication of reform in them. Every trace of conscience among them has been forever extinguished, and they have no other ambition than to do evil. They want to dominate everything, they seek to injure each other and to enjoy themselves at each other's expense. It is precisely the impossibility of satisfying all their desires that constitutes their torture.

Likewise, Swedenborg's heaven is the realm of Utopia. It is the land of promise for marriage and family life, where the pure joy of love, so rare on earth, becomes the lot of the pious. It is the land of innocence, of the beauty of youth of the Golden Age of which the poets sing—or rather nature in its state of integrity to which Rousseau dreamed of returning humanity.

The habitual representations of beatitude are basically rather alien to Swedenborgianism. For Swedenborg, celestial joys are not at all passive ones: they consist of action, of doing something useful for oneself or others. Thus, the celestial realm includes workshops, trades and tradesmen, handicraft, courts of justice, and libraries where each of the angels can find occupations that best respond to his or her tastes. Do we not find in these dreams of the blessings "of usefulness" a true son of the century of power and rural economy, with all its zealous utility? Do we not see, outlined behind the religious dreamer, the image of an indefatigable traveler of the spirit, for whom undisturbed work at his desk was in reality the only true happiness?

But this spiritual world, where we all laugh and cry, love and hate, work and play, quite like in our own, could never become a gross copy of reality. For there all things are only representations, equivalents of states of soul of the inhabitants. All these marvelous sceneries, all their handsome adolescents, all their beautiful maidens appear to the eyes of the angels according to the state of their love and wisdom. They change, disappear, and reappear like mirages according to the degree of modification of the thoughts and feeling of the angels. "Whoever becomes an angel carries within himself his own heaven" (*Conjugial Love* §10). Likewise, the inhabitants of the world of spirits and hell live in an environment that perfectly harmonizes with their interior, and which itself is irradiation.

It is in this thought that we find perhaps the most genial trait of Swedenborg's eschatology, and in the fashion he develops it, we find perhaps his grandest artistic contribution. Thanks to his gift for surrounding his spiritual world with a net of symbolism, structured in earthly representations, he has succeeded in giving it something of the fantastic character, dreamlike and ethereal, that it probably had in his own visions.

t w e l v e

THE LAST JUDGMENT AND THE NEW JERUSALEM

The ten last years of Swedenborg's life were for the most part devoted to apocalyptic speculations. His thoughts revolved constantly around the Last Judgment that it had been given him to witness in the spiritual world, and the consequent institution of the new Jerusalem.

Swedenborg's earlier conceptions of the Last Judgment do not seem to be far removed from the orthodox views. The mention of these which he made in the *De Anima* (*Animal Kingdom* VII, 249) carries no individual imprint and even when, in the first part of the *Adversaria* (222) he interprets the biblical account of the destruction of Sodom and Gomorrah allegorically as a prophecy of the Last Judgment, he remains faithful, point by point, to the letter of the Apocalypse. The Messiah himself will come, surrounded by his angels, to judge the living and the dead in heaven and on earth.

Little by little, Swedenborg begins to find that this interpretation contradicted his eschatology. We recall that, to his mind, the judgment will strike every human being after death; and, after an often very long sojourn in the world of spirits, the individual will go to heaven or to hell and remain there for eternity. Furthermore, Swedenborg does not acknowledge the orthodox doctrine according to which the human being is, at the end of the world, reintegrated into the body he or she occupied on this earth. Above all, he cannot accept the customary interpretation of the apocalyptic prophesies, for he considers the created world as everlasting. The world is a nursery conceived with heaven in view; therefore, it is to stand forever.

Thus, at a rather early date, he comes to think that the Last Judgment was not destined to strike our earth literally, but only the world of spirits, into which, with the passage of time, a certain disorder had slipped in. As early as 1747, he has visions that are portents of a last judgment in this sense (*Spiritual Diary* §220).[274] And in the *Arcana Coelestia* §931[2], he declares that those who await a universal catastrophe on the occurrence of a last judgment are in error. This final reckoning refers to the last days of the church. Every church undergoes its last judgment when it is corrupted and when it no longer possesses a living faith. The first church, which disappeared in the Deluge, has already been struck by its last judgment; the same applies to the Jewish church, which perished with the descent of Jesus Christ upon the earth. The judgment is now imminent for the current Christian church, which will be replaced by a new one.

It is clear that, from the beginning, Swedenborg is thinking of his own doctrine. It is he who, like a new messiah, will announce his doctrine to the world and who will create, in the form of a new church, the new heaven and the new earth of which the Apocalypse speaks. The primitive Christian religion was made up of love and faith, but it has degenerated and is no more than a religion of external adoration. The Christianity that now rules is ripe for replacement by a New Church, by a New Jerusalem (see, for example, *Arcana Coelestia* §1850). And by all signs, he observes that the time is near. The world of spirits is so full of genii and evil spirits that humanity is perpetually exposed to deadly influences from them and that even the angels are barely able to resist them (*Arcana Coelestia* §2121 passim).

In the *Spiritual Diary* §765, Swedenborg relates that one day—February 13, 1748—he had a vision of the number 57. He appears to have at first interpreted it as 1657, the significance of which he did not understand. He did not delay, nevertheless, in connecting this number with his expectations of a last judgment, following which degenerate Christianity would give place to a new church, of which he himself would be the revelator, at a time he fixes in 1757.

Over the greater part of that year, it is given to him to see this Last Judgment, which he has prophesied, become a reality. His experiences in this regard we find mentioned for the first time in the *Spiritual Diary*, where they often take the form of grandiose visions, at times illustrated by drawings, later revised and published in his work entitled *The Last Judgment and Babylon Destroyed* (1757); in a later work, the *Continuation of the Last Judgment;* and in a posthumous work on the same subject, which was mentioned in the previous chapter (see note 261). In addition, we find descriptions of and commentaries on the Last Judgment in his later works, above all in the two commentaries the *Apocalypse Explained* and the *Apocalypse Revealed.* Although the initial descriptions of the *Spiritual Diary* may be more colorful and interesting, I must base my argument on the works published by Swedenborg himself, where the rather diffuse exposition of the *Spiritual Diary* has been systematized.

When the Book of Revelation announces that the first heaven and the first earth shall pass away and be replaced by a new earth and a new heaven, this does not at all mean, Swedenborg explains, that our earth and the heaven of angels are to be destroyed and make place for a new earth and a new heaven. God does not judge humanity during earthly life, nor does he deprive those who are in heaven of the celestial bliss. Consequently, the Last Judgment cannot affect the humanity presently alive or the angels.

By the first heaven is to be understood the dwelling places which, after the first coming of Christ upon earth, were assigned to those who have been externally good, but not internally just. They may have been just and honest according to civil and moral law, but not regarding divine laws. Since divine order requires that all those who could be saved should be saved, they had been allowed to stay in these dwelling places as long as they could endure to live among the good. They had created for themselves spiritual societies on the highest levels in the world of spirits, most often on mountains and rocks, and had even created the appearance of a heaven.

This collection of pretended pious beings, who aspired to become angels but were powerless to attain this state, had become so numerous that it absorbed the rays of divine light and heat. These societies extended like a dense fog across the sky, obscuring the rays of the divine sun. The living races on earth thereby risked becoming unable to maintain the equilibrium between heaven and hell that is necessary to safeguard their free will. The danger continued to intensify; in the course of the degeneracy of the church, the number of beings going to hell became greater and greater while that of the beings admitted into heaven diminished in an equal proportion, so that the divine influx continuously weakened in relation to that from hell (*Last Judgment* passim; *Apocalypse Revealed* §865).

The great Babylon of which the Book of Revelation speaks is found among the Catholics.[275] Swedenborg gives a particularly severe exposition of the Catholic Church, which he abhors primarily because it has falsified the word of the Bible and kept it hidden from the people, thereby closing the door to heaven. In the world of the spirits, the Catholics have set up a complete replica of their organization on earth, with papal consistory, cloisters, saint worship, and so forth (*Last Judgment* §§55–56).

It would lead us far afield here to recapitulate the destruction of that Babylonian structure during the Last Judgment, how it was devastated by earthquakes and storms from the east and its inhabitants thrown into a dark sea. These reports are written with a certain dramatic energy that is exceptional in Swedenborg's writings. This time his visionary fantasy has surely been tinged by the profuse color of the Apocalypse of St. John. The Muslims and the Gentiles are found outside the sphere of the Catholics in "the first heaven." Inside, in the center of heaven, Protestants of various confessions have their abode. Among the former, the Africans are particularly accomplished. When they are instructed by the angels, they grasp and receive the truths better than others because their way of thinking is more internal and spiritual (*Continuation of the Last Judgment* §75)

Swedenborg's preference for Africans goes back very far. In the *Spiritual Diary* §453, he relates that, in 1748, he had met African spirits who, in the other life, wished to be chastised and tortured. They told him that they detested their black bodies, for they knew that their souls are white. He also learns that more souls from Africa came into heaven than from any other continent. I do not know the cause of Swedenborg's love for the blacks of Central Africa, which fits the age of Rousseau so well. In any case, he kept it all his life; and in the *Last Judgment* §76, he affirms that Africans likewise have the same pious character in our terrestrial world. In the interior of their continent, there exists a revelation that has spread widely but has not yet reached the coasts. The angels orally teach the natives the same doctrines that Swedenborg himself has professed in *The New Jerusalem*.

The Reformed are admitted at the very center of heaven because they have read the Bible and worshiped the Lord, and therefore they have enjoyed a more brilliant light. They have, however, the common fault: their religion is purely external. They have attended worship, been present at all the rituals, and confessed their faith in God; but they have neglected the moral prescriptions of the Gospel and have not amended their lives. It is they who are symbolized by the dragon of the Apocalypse (*Continuation of the Last Judgment* §§14–16). At the center of all the Christians dwell the best of the English. These in effect have a double theology, one of which has its source in the doctrine of faith and the other in that of life. This latter theology is found among those who do not belong to the clergy (*Continuation of the Last Judgment* §§40–45).

The description of the Last Judgment itself is an allegorical paraphrase of the Apocalypse. It is presaged by a storm cloud, after which the upper heavens come down. In the clarity of the light of heaven, the internal world of the spirits opens, and the impious appear no more like Christians but like devils, and a feverish struggle begins among them regarding God, Scripture, faith, and the Church. All the glory by which they have been surrounded in their imaginary heaven vanishes. Their palaces become miserable huts, their gardens seas of mud, and their churches a heap of filth (*Continuation of the Last Judgment* §23). They then receive the visit of angels who try to the end to persuade them to renounce their evil ways. These angels succeed in separating some just spirits who are among the evil. But the others persevere in their sins and consequently are unable to escape the judgment.

The Lord then appears in a luminous cloud, and the fanfares of trumpets are heard, which invites the angels to assemble the just from all directions. For the Lord does not desire the perdition of the sinner and limits himself to freeing them from all contact with the evil; these are then left entirely to their own devices. They reassemble in the form of an enormous dragon, which rears as though he sought to destroy heaven. But the attempts fail, and he sinks down into hell (*Continuation of the Last Judgment* §§23–28).

I have cited these descriptions because they confirm how much Swedenborg seeks to show that God does not condemn anyone, not even in the Last Judgment. He is the Redeemer who saves his faithful; he and is not the judge, properly speaking. The malevolent judge themselves when their inner being is stripped naked and they lose the veneer of respectability and piety that had covered them in the world of spirits. They hurl themselves into hell because only there do they feel among their peers. Like the newcomers, the dragon tries to rise toward the divine light; but it is too strong for him, and he falls blindly into the abyss.

The state of the world after the Last Judgment will be what it was before. The great change of the spiritual world will entail no perceptible modification of our world. There will be, as previously, nations, wars, and periods of peace. From the superficial point of view, there will also be, as in the past, different churches, each with its different dogmas. But church members will now enjoy a greater independence in questions of faith because they will have recovered their spiritual freedom. Order has now been reestablished in the heavens and in hell, and the normal equilibrium reigns anew between them. Thus, the spiritual sense of the Scriptures can be unveiled without room for doubt that it may be misunderstood or profaned (*Last Judgment* §73).

The most important consequence of the Last Judgment is, nevertheless, the creation of the New Jerusalem, the New Church that Swedenborg, as we have seen, had long before announced. The new heaven created by God after the Last Judgment is destined to yield place to this church, which is to include the best among Christians and also among pagans who have lived since the epoch of Christ (*New Jerusalem and Its Heavenly Doctrine* §§2–3). From heaven, the New Jerusalem will later descend upon the earth.

During the Last Judgment, Swedenborg had already had visions that seemed to presage a descent of this New Church upon the earth (*Spiritual Diary* §5543), but he delays in declaring its full accomplishment. In a letter of 1767 addressed to a favorite disciple, Gabriel Beyer, who had asked when one might expect the constitution of a new communion, he declares that it is given him to see daily how God prepares and orders the new heaven and that the New Church will be formed gradually in proportion to the completion of this heaven. Two years later he writes from Amsterdam to Beyer that the Church will only come about to the extent that the doctrines of salvation and of imputation will have been exterminated. Moreover, the Christian Church was not born immediately after the ascension of Jesus Christ, but developed gradually.[276] In *True Christian Religion* §791, he declares that the very day he finished this work, June 19, 1770, the Lord has gathered his twelve disciples and sent them out through the spiritual world, there to "preach the gospel that the Lord Jesus Christ reigns and that his reign will endure from eternity to eternity."

Swedenborg is convinced that this concerted work will assure the triumph of his doctrine. "I am persuaded," he writes to Beyer in the course of its publication, "that our Redeemer Lord will act both directly and indirectly, when the book will have appeared, in order that the *New Church* which is founded on this theology, will be instituted throughout all Christianity." And in the last chapter of the book, he develops the mission that has been entrusted to him to create new universal churches destined to supplant the present age. The predictions of the prophets, the evangelists, and the Apocalypse, in effect, have in view his own exegesis. When it is said that the Lord shall come in the clouds of heaven in His glory and power, this does not mean that Christ will descend again in person upon the earth. According to the Gospel of John, God is the Word, and it is in this quality that he is to come on the earth. "It is idle, therefore, to believe that the Lord will appear in the clouds of heaven in person; but he is to appear in the Word, which is from him and therefore is himself" (*True Christian Religion* §777.)

The Second Coming of the Lord will then take place

> by means of a man, who is able not only to receive these doctrines in his understanding but also to publish them by the press. That the Lord manifested himself before me, his servant, and sent me to this office, that he afterward opened the eyes of my spirit and thus introduced me into the spiritual world and

> granted me to see the heavens and the hells, and to talk with angels and spirits, and this now continuously for several years, I affirm in truth; as also that from the first day of that call I have not received anything whatever pertaining to the doctrines of that church from any angel, but from the Lord alone while I have read the Word. (*True Christian Religion* §779)

The proud awareness of his own mission, explicit in this passage, is not a new thing for Swedenborg. But this is the first time that he proclaims it publicly and signs his name on the title page under "*Domini Jesu Christi Servus*" (servant of the Lord Jesus Christ). And in one of his memorabilia in *True Christian Religion* §508, he says he has had the vision of a temple with a door of mother-of-pearl and wells of crystal. It signified the New Church, and "when I drew nearer, I saw this inscription above the door, *Nunc Licet*, which signified that now it is permitted to enter intellectually into the mysteries of faith."

It is no coincidence that this vision recalls Swedenborg's first visionary revelation, the luminous redemptive vision that revealed to him the existence of a "holy temple" in the brain and brought him back to the state of innocence of the first man. The association with the Divinity, broken by the Fall, and which was at that moment regained thanks to his biblical exegesis, was conquered once again for the totality of all humanity. "Enter henceforth into the mysteries of the Word hitherto closed," an angel from the third heaven instructs him, "for these particular truths are so many mirrors of the Lord." By the revelation of the Word, the world has become a resplendent temple where the glory of the Lord is reflected in the eyes of whoever wishes to see.

In my investigation, I have sought to elucidate the diverse stages of this evolution. We have seen that Swedenborg had early undergone great discouragement on the scientific front, which he then considered as the only one accessible to humanity, and that he had longed for a knowledge that was not reduced to traveling the long, unsure, and roundabout route of sensory testimony. In this state of mind, he received the first divine sign, the interior light that gave a higher confirmation to this hypotheses. Shortly afterwards, his explanation was completed: it is the *anima* that is irradiated by the very light of the Divinity. All knowledge and all life are emanations of the spiritual sun.

This doctrine of a higher intuitive quality of the soul beyond reason, of a spiritual sun above our own sun, gives new life to half-effaced recollection of his childhood. He believes again that he is connected with a supersensory world. How denuded of value the uncertainties of science then appear compared to the doctrine that sees in external phenomena only symbols of a higher life, and in natural things only reflections of things spiritual! In the doctrine of correspondences, he rediscovers the wisdom humanity enjoyed at the beginning of time, but which it lost when it turned away from the Divine. His entire energy now focuses on a single goal: to become worthy of this higher wisdom. The *Journal of Dreams* and the account he gives in *The Worship and Love of God* of the state of innocence of Adam inform us how he came to the purpose he proposed for himself through unreserved renunciation and annihilation of his own selfhood.

Once he himself had been admitted into the spiritual world and had been allowed to contemplate its glory, the aim of his life became to reveal to humanity the spiritual sense of the Word. All the inexpressible wisdom of the angels, in which the awakening of his inner sight permitted him to share, is found concealed in the Word that has been given to humanity as a link between us and the Creator, but which we have forgotten and whose true sense we have not been able to preserve since our love has been diverted from heavenly things toward worldly things. And when Swedenborg has finished his mission and has revealed the spiritual sense of the Scriptures and related to humanity what he has seen in the spiritual world, a new era will be born in the history of our species. The Last Judgment has cleansed space in the spiritual world for the New Church that will again conjoin the human race to God and lead creation to its final end.

Thus, in the light of Swedenborg's inner evolution, we come to understand that his mind was prepared for the idea that his own biblical exegesis constitutes the return of the Messiah, which the prophets had announced.

Chapter 1, "Early Years," pages 3–23

1. Quoted according to Henry William Tottie, *Jesper Swedbergs lif och verksamhet* (Uppsala, 1885–1886), vol. 1, 271.
2. *Festum Magnum* (Skara, 1724), 22, 26.
3. Gustaf Lizell, *Svedberg och Nohrborg* (Uppsala, 1910), 250.
4. Tottie, vol. 2, 34.
5. Gilbert Ballet, *Swedenborg* (Paris, 1899), 30.
6. Ill. *Sv. Litt. Hist.,* 2nd ed., vol. 1, 530.
7. *Festum Magnum,* 206.
8. *Guds Barns Heliga Sabbats-Ro* (Skara 1710–1712), 76–82. A *fontang* is a congenital cranial deformity named for the extravagant hairstyle of Louis XIV's mistress, Marie Angélique de Scorailles, countess of Fontange.
9. See the study on this theme by Bööks in *Edda,* 1914.
10. *Sanctificatio Sabbati* (Norrköping, 1934), 494ff.
11. Ibid., 692.
12. Quoted in Tottie, vol. 1, 42.
13. *Sanctificatio Sabbati,* 24.
14. *Festum Magnum,* 163ff.
15. *Sabbats-Ro,* vol. 1, 1285.
16. *Festum Magnum,* 180, 186ff.
17. See Tottie, vol. 1, 27.
18. Ibid., vol. 1, 9, 23; vol. 2, 19ff.; *Sabbats-Ro,* vol. 2, preface.
19. Tottie., vol. 1, 25ff.
20. This comparison is maintained by Hjalmar Holmquist in an article that appeared in the journal *Bibelforskaren* (1909), 41.
21. Tottie, vol. 2, 29.
22. Ibid., vol. 1, 37.
23. Ibid., vol. 2, 9.
24. Ibid., vol. 2, 30.
25. Ibid., vol. 2, 11.
26. Ibid., vol. 2, 270.
27. Published in *Samlingar för Philantroper* (Stockholm, 1788). [The letter can also be found in R. L. Tafel, *Documents concerning the Life and Character of*

Emanuel Swedenborg (London: Swedenborg Society, 1877), vol. 2, part 1, document 243, pp. 279–280.]

28. Tafel, vol. 1, 145.
29. Hjalmar Holmquist, in his essay "Swedenborg's Period of Natural History and Natural Philosophy" (*The Finnish Society of Church History Annual,* 1914, p. 7), quoted a medical opinion, which gives a physiological explanation of this phenomenon. The main point is that the blood that flows to the brain due to the inhibited respiration is not purified by oxygen and therefore induces a state of trance. I am not in a position to judge if this explanation is correct.
30. *Tessin och Tessiniana*, 355ff.
31. See Hans Ludwig Forssell's study of Benzelius, *Erik Benezelius den yngre: minnesteckning för Svenska Akademiens Handlingar* (Stockholm, 1883), 58.
32. Letter to Benzelius, Oct. 1710, in *Opera* (Academy of Sciences edition) I, 207.
33. Ibid., vol. 1, 26.
34. *Enny Mening om Planeternas gangochstand; Opera,* vol. 3, 294.
35. See Henrik Schück, article on Rudbeck in *Ill. Sv. Litt. Hist.*, 2nd ed., vol. 1, 377ff.
36. *Opera* (Academy of Sciences edition), III, 286.

Chapter 2, "The Mechanistic View of the World," pages 24–49

37. Cf. Holmquist, *Bibelforskaren* (1909), 47.
38. Ibid., 55.
39. *Sabbata-Ro,* vol. 2, 952. On the other hand, in his *Animal Kingdom* (III, §447), dating from the period of his evolution toward mysticism, Swedenborg refers to this statement of his father's among other scientific materials.
40. Wilhelm Windelband, *Geschichte der neuer Philosophie*, 4th ed., vol. 1, 304.
41. G. F. Hertling, *John Locke und die Schule von Cambridge* (Freiburg, 1892).
42. Ibid., 263.
43. Ibid., 91.
44. Ibid., 83.
45. Ibid., 70.
46. Ibid., 245.
47. Ibid., 197–199, 202.
48. John Locke, *Essay Concerning Human Understanding*, II, i, 2; IV, ii, 1.
49. Samuel Ebbe Bring, *Christopher Polhem, Minnesskrift utgifven af Svenska Teknologforenengen* (1911), 64ff.
50. A. H. Stroh, in the introduction to Swedenborg's *Opera* (Academy of Sciences edition).

51. *Spiritual Diary* §4722 and elsewhere. Cf. Tafel, vol. 1, 615.
52. Bring, 68ff.
53. Ibid., 60.
54. *Tankar om Andarnass warelse*. Manuscript in the Stockholm Royal Library.
55. Bring, 64.
56. Andreas Rüdiger, *Physics Divina* (Frankfurt, 1716), 347ff.
57. Bring, 68.
58. Both have been translated into English and published under the title *On Tremulation* (Boston, 1899).
59. Bring, 91.
60. Cf. Holmquist, 226.
61. In his *Miscellanea Observata* of 1722 (Academy of Sciences edition, I, 130), we also find the same reasoning. The hypothesis of H. Schlieper *(Emanuel Swedenborgs System der Naturphilosophie*, Berlin, 1901, 10), according to which it is under the influence of Leibniz that Swedenborg would have granted substantial value to the point, appears to me correct. The reasonings that follow on the origin of motion also seem to argue in favor of the influence of Leibniz.
62. Notably the works of Schlieper and of Stroh. In his introduction to the Academy of Sciences' edition of Swedenborg's works (vol. 2), Svant Arrhenius gave a very clear account of Swedenborg's cosmological theories, a subject upon which we have no cause to enter here.
63. *De Mechanismo Animae et Corporis.* So far only published in an English translation by A.H. Stroh (*Scientific and Philosophical Treatises,* 1905, 21).
64. Henry More, *Philosophical Writings* (London, 1662). R. Zimmermann, *Henry More und die vierte Dimension des Raumes* (Academie der Wissenschaft). Vienna, Sitz. Ber. B. XCVIII. Cassirer, *Das Erkenntnisproblem* (Berlin, 1906), vol. 2, 362. Swedenborg cites More in *Economy of the Animal Kingdom* I, 630.
65. *Opera* (Frankfurt, 1707), 664ff.
66. *Acta Eruditorum*, 1735, 559.
67. Wolff, *Theologia Naturalis* (1736), vol. 2, 610ff.
68. *Resebeskrifningar* (Uppsala, 1911).

Chapter 3, "A Mystical Philosophy of Nature," pages 50–68

69. Kurd Lasswitz, *Geschichte der Atomistik vom Mittelalter bis Newton* (Hamburg, 1890), vol. 2, 580.
70. Ibid., 484–485.
71. See Heinrich Haeser, *Lehrbuch der Geschichte der Medicin und der epidemischen Krankheiten* (1865–1868), third ed., vol. 2, 519ff.

72. V. Hirsch, *Geschichte der medicinischen Wissenschaften in Deutschland,* (*Geschichte der Wissenschaften in Deutschland,* vol. 21), 166.
73. These parallels have been noted by Rufus M. Jones, *Studies in Mystical Religion* (London, 1909), 67–68.
74. Tafel, vol. 2, 1236.
75. The volume bearing the signature of Swedenborg and Stjernhjelm's marginalia, the Latin translation of Ficino, is in the Linköping library. See also the manuscript of Lidén of "Historiola" and the article on Swedenborg in *Svenskt biografiskt Lexicon.*
76. Photolithograph, ms. vol. 3, 121.
77. The proof of this lies in his occasional use of their occult terminology. So we find in his *Economy of the Animal Kingdom* the name "Alkahesi." According to Paracelsus and van Helmont, this would be a universal elixir that would reduce every natural body into its initial components.
78. Tafel, vol. 2, 1237ff. In another passage (p. 1088) Tafel—apparently with reason—comes close to this affirmation of the mandate Swedenborg claims to have received from God, on April 25–26, 1744, not to read any work on theology or similar subjects. It would seem to follow that, prior to this date, Swedenborg considered himself to be entirely free in this respect.
79. *Swedenborgs Resebeskrifningar,* 65.
80. *Bibelforskaren,* (1909), 226; *Finska Kyrkohistorika Samfundets Arisbok*, vol. 3, 39.
81. Van Helmont, 255ff.
82. *Swedenborgs Drömmar,* 1744 (Stockholm: G.E. Klemming, 1859).
83. *Economy of the Animal Kingdom* II, 10, 42. Cf. Tafel, vol. 2, 1116.
84. Cf. Tafel, vol. 2, 143.
85. *Arcana Coelestia* §9281, §805. Cf. Tafel, ibid.
86. *Adversaria* III, §7012. Cf. Tafel, vol. 2, 145, note.
87. Tafel, vol. 2, 145, note.
88. William James, *Den religioesa erfarenheten* (The Varieties of Religious Experience), Swedish translation (Stockholm, 1906), 231ff.
89. *Resebeskrifningar,* 74, Sept. 6, 1736: "*Conciperade min ingressum ad transactiones, quod anima sapientiae sit agnitio et cognitio numinis.*" See also note of Sept. 7.
90. James, 233.
91. Locke, IV, ii, 1.
92. E. Cassirer, *Das Erkenntnisproblem in der Philosophie und Wissenschaft der neueren Zeit* (1906–1907), vol. 1, 190.
93. *Economy of the Animal Kingdom* II, 276; also cf. Locke, IV, xvii, 14.

Chapter 4, "The Philosophy of Economy of the Animal Kingdom,*" pages 69–94*

94. "Nothing in the created universe is *anything* except by its form; or what amounts to the same thing, there is nothing in the world but is a series and in a series" (*Economy of the Animal Kingdom* II, §286).
95. We note incidentally the manifest influence of monadology that can be seen here, as is frequently the case when Swedenborg deals with the relationships between microcosm and macrocosm.
96. Photolithograph ms., VI, 58.
97. See the passages cited in Stöckl, *Geschichte der Christlichen Philosophie zur Zeit der Kirchenväter*, (Mainz, 1981), 307.
98. We find confirmation in the fact that, in one of his last theological works, *De Commercio Animae et Corporis* (The Interaction of the Soul and the Body [1769]), where he explains that the spiritual sun, emanating from God, appears to the angels in the form of a globe, just like our sun. He points out that everyone knows from experience that spiritual light assures certitude, "for man perceives the light of his reason to the extent that he achieves certitude. . . . I have often seen that spiritual light. It immensely exceeds natural light in whiteness and also in splendor, for it is as whiteness and splendor themselves and appears like bright and dazzling snow, as the garments of the Lord appeared when he was transfigured" (Ibid., §6).
99. See quote by Spiess, *J.B. van Helmonts System der Medicin,* (Frankfurt, 1840) 5, note 3.
100. See "Hieroglyphic Key" (§48) included in *Psychological Transactions.*
101. Published under the name of *Oeconomia Regni Animalis III* (London, 1847).
102. In reality, then, the *fluidum spirituosum* is the organ of the soul, as the eye is the organ of vision. At any rate, it makes no difference whether we give the *fluidum spirituosum* itself the name of *anima* or of spirit, or whether we restrict that nomenclature to the faculty it possesses of representing the universe and having the intuition of ends. For among the highest unities of the series, we cannot distinguish the substance from its functions (*Economy of the Animal Kingdom* II, §303). Swedenborg also uses throughout the term *fluidum spirituosum* as a synonym for *anima*.
103. It is not within the scope of this study to deal here with the epoch-making localizations of cerebral phenomena established by Swedenborg. Those interested in the matter will find a general exposition by M. Ramström in the commemorative publication of the Society of Sciences entitled "Emanuel Swedenborg's Investigations in Natural Science," (Uppsala, 1910). In the *Upsala Läkareföreings Förhandlingar* (vol. 16, fasc. 1), under the title "Upon What

Is Swedenborg's Conception of the Cerebral Functions Based?", Ramström gave a very interesting exposition of the hypothesis at the root of the results Swedenborg achieved in his research into cerebral psychology. This is, as far as we know, the only historico-critical study of Swedenborg's scientific theories undertaken to date [1917].

104. Under the rubric of "ideas," Swedenborg manifestly includes (like Descartes) the whole content of our understanding. Under "material ideas" (also a Cartesian term), it seems necessary to include sensory perceptions. They appear to be identical with "images," which, according to the theory expounded above, are the impressions evoked in the *anima*.

105. This Aristotelian concept, which also betrays the influence of the traducianism of Tertullian and the later Church Fathers (cf. *Economy of the Animal Kingdom* II, §310), is maintained in Swedenborg's theological works.

106. Regarding the following, cf. Spiess, 58ff.

107. In his theological period, Swedenborg likewise joins the *animus* and the *mens*. For example, we find in Cornelius Agrippa an exact equivalent of the clarification given in the *Economy of the Animal Kingdom.* For him, the soul consists of the *mens*, the *ratio,* and the *idolum.* The *mens* is the receiving organ of divine light that thereby penetrates the *ratio.* The *idolum* is in communication with the body and its organs. With Agrippa, however, this system is rather rudimentary. Cf. his *De occulta philosophia,* III, xliii, and Auguste Prost, *Corneille Agrippa* (Paris, 1881), vol. 1, 85.

108. Drawn from *De Anima,* written about 1741 and printed by Tafel under the title *Regnum Animale* VII (London, 1849). The modern English translation is entitled *Rational Psychology* (Philadelphia: Swedenborg Scientific Association, 1950), has numbered paragraphs; but the *Regnum Animale* does not. The corresponding reference in *Rational Psychology* is found in paragraph 350.

109. Eduard Zeller, *Die Philosophie der Griechen in ihrer geschichtlichen Entwicklung Hildesheim,* second ed., vol. 2, 457ff.

110. Ibid., vol. 3, 616.

111. See *Essais de Théodicée,* I, 22ff. The agreement with Leibniz likewise extends to other parts of the Swedenborgian exposition of life and volition. We do not insist, however, on these concordances, which in no way deal with the essential conception of the will and which is basically different from that of Leibniz.

112. Cf. Ollé-Laprune, *La Philosophie de Malebranche* (Paris, 1870), vol. 2, 287ff. See also Jodl, *Geschichte der Ethik,* vol. 1, 268ff.

113. Malebranche, *Traité de morale* (Lyon, 1697), 114.

114. Malebranche, *Traité de l'amour de Dieu* (Lyon, 1697), 30.

115. See Tottie, 115–117.

116. Isaak Dorner, *Geschichte der protestantenischen Theologie* (1867), 637.
117. W. Bender, *J.K. Dippel* (Bonn, 1882), 204.
118. *Rational Psychology,* 535. It is almost superfluous to point out that this reasoning, which plays such a major role in the development of Swedenborg's eschatological system, is supported by the Leibnizian principle of *"identitatis indiscernibilium."* The whole Swedenborgian conception of this *"varietas harmonica"* that must govern our world as well as the world of spirit is manifestly inspired by Leibniz.

Chapter 5, "The Doctrine of Correspondence," pages 95–122

119. Photolithograph mss., vol. 3, 183ff.
120. Cf. Zeller, vol. 2, 1, 631.
121. Here I closely follow Ad. Franck, *La Kabbale* (Paris, 1843), 218–219.
122. Pico della Mirandola, *Opera omnia* (Basel, 1672), 7. Cf. Stöcke, *Philosophie des Mittelalters,* vol. 2, 176.
123. Pico della Mirandola, 7.
124. See, for example, Cornelius Agrippa, *De occulta philosophia,* I, xiff.
125. Pico della Mirandola, 166ff.
126. Ludwig Diestel, *Geschichte des Alten Testaments in der christlichen Kirche* (Jena, 1869), 376ff.
127. Glassius, *Philologia Sacra* (Frankfurt, 1633), 284.
128. Ibid., 312.
129. Ibid., 322ff.
130. Hans Schlieper, *Emanuel Swedenborgs System der Naturphilosophie, besonders in seiner Beziehung zu Goethe-Herderschen Anschauungen* (Berlin: Gustave Schade, 1901).
131. *Rational Psychology,* §§526–528. This reasoning appears in flagrant opposition to Swedenborg's statement in the *Economy of the Animal Kingdom* that the soul cannot degenerate. But he specifies that this applies only to the intelligence of the *anima*, which remains constant from infancy to old age, and is the same with all human creatures. On the other hand, the knowledge of the *anima*, that is, the nature of its love, is continually modified during its whole life.
132. Plotinus supposes (*Enneads,* IV, 3, 18) that, in the intellectual world, souls communicate through intuition, not words.
133. *Economy of the Animal Kingdom* III, §523. I have consulted Professor Ramström, the greatest expert on Swedenborg's psychological works. He was also of the opinion that Swedenborg speaks of hallucinations.

134. Tafel, vol. 2, 1092.
135. *De sec. art.* part L. I, Chap. 4; cf., Fr. Dieterici's edition, *Die sogenannte Theologie des Aristoteles*, 8 and footnote 182.

Chapter 6, "The Religious Crisis," pages 123–159

136. With regard to this and the following, see H. Delacroix, *Études d'histoire et de psychologie du mysticisme* (Paris, 1908), particularly the chapter headed "*Les peines mystiques*."
137. Delacroix, 342.
138. Stockholm, 1859. New ed. by K. Barr (Stockholm, 1924). [See also *Journal of Dreams,* trans. J. J. G. Wilkinson, commentary by Wilson Van Dusen (New York: Swedenborg Foundation, 1986. See also Lars Bergquist, editor, *Swedenborg's Dream Diary,* trans. Anders Hallengren (West Chester, Penna.: Swedenborg Foundation, 2000).]
139. Tafel, vol. 2, 1125.
140. See Tafel, vol. 2, 1072.
141. James, 249.
142. Tafel, vol. 2, Doc. 208, no. 10, p. 148.
143. *Sydsvenska Dagbladet,* 1903, no. 220; Kandinsky, *Kritische und Klinische Betrachtungen im Gebiete der Sinnestäuschungen* (Berlin, 1885), 58.
144. Cf. Kandinsky, 56.
145. See the quotation above as well as his explanation a few days later: "I experienced an intense joy, but at the same time also a bodily pain, unable to bear the delights of the heavenly soul" (*Journal of Dreams* 79).
146. Today we find the mystical ecstasy described and analyzed in numerous works on religious psychology. Let us simply refer to Murisier, *Le sentiment religieux* (*Revue Philosophique*, 1898) and J. H. Leuba, *Tendances religieuses ches les mystiques chrétiens* (*Revue Philosophique,* 1902). See especially the chapter on the "*Tendance à la jouissance organique*," 459ff.
147. For Tafel, in fact (II, 158, note**), Swedenborg's words that at the moment when "I was thrown down, I became wide awake" signified that his spiritual life had been activated so that he could penetrate the world of spirits, where the rest of his vision took place. That is certainly an inexact interpretation of Swedenborg's actual words. Swedenborg indeed believes that Christ had come down to him.
148. Delacroix, 435–450.
149. Ibid., 441.
150. My interpretation of the course of this vision appears to be supported by the

fact that it has repeated tendencies to reproduce itself several times under analogous conditions, but without going on to the clear objectification of the person of the Christ. Indeed, two weeks later we read: "I held my hands together. In the act of waking, it seemed to me that they were pressed together by a hand or finger; which, with God's help, signifies that our Lord heard my prayers" (*Journal of Dreams* §155).

During the night of July 1 or 2, he is overcome by intense tremors "as when Christ showed me divine grace"; he awaits "being thrown upon my face as the previous time." At the moment of the final tremor he feels a "back. I laid hold of the whole back, as well as put my hands under to the breast in front. Straightaway it laid itself down, and I saw in front the countenance also, but this very obscurely." This vision is also produced, in his opinion, in a state between dream and wakefulness: "This was a vision when I was neither waking nor sleeping, for I had all my thoughts together. It was the inward man separated from the outward that knew this." He concludes that this time it was the case of an angel because he was not constrained to prostrate himself (*Journal of Dreams* §209–210).

Yet another vision of the same kind, of July 30 or August 1, is weaker. He feels the tremors, has the sensation of being "thrown on his face," but he is not certain of it. A moment later he is "snatched" from his vision "and found under my back one who it seemed was an acquaintance." He becomes irritated because this person had "taken me from it [the vision]."

151. Cited in Albrecht Ritschl, *Geschichte des Pietismus,* vol. 3, 410.
152. *Memoirs of Robsalm* (Skandinavisk Nykyrk-tidning, 1876), 154.
153. Cf. Tafel, vol. 2, 389ff.
154. Herrlin has pointed (*Sydsvenska Dagbladet,* 1903, n. 220) to Swedenborg's entry of August 26–27: "In the night the soles of my feet appeared altogether white, which signifies that my sins have been forgiven." He indicates that this relates to the washing of feet of which Brockmer speaks. It is likewise in the entry dated July 22–23 (*Journal of Dreams* §22): "I saw a boy running away with my shirt, and set out in pursuit. May mean that I had not washed my feet" (cf. also *Journal of Dreams* §91). As to the declaration that Swedenborg would have offered to be the Christ, I have found in the *Journal* no confirmation other than the enigmatic passage where it is said (*Journal of Dreams* §276): "He appeared to me to be Jesus Christ himself, with whom I had a relationship as with anyone else." In any case, it was only a matter of a dream here. It seems hardly likely that in this case Swedenborg imagined himself to be the Messiah: his intimate journal would certainly not have failed to make some allusion to this belief.
155. In a lecture entitled "On Swedenborg's Psychosis," before the Swedish Medical Society (printed in *Svenska Läkaresällskapets förhandlingar,* 1914, fasc. 9),

E. Kleen concluded that Swedenborg suffered from a paraphrenetic condition. For a more complete discussion of Swedenborg's mental state, see Lagerborg, *The Case of Swedenborg*, (Helsinki, 1924); and T. Andrae, *Mystikens psykologi*, (Stockholm, 1926), 307–38.

156. See Martin Dibelius, *Die Geisterwelt im Glauben des Paulus* (Göttingen, 1909). 75.
157. At times, he doubts that God demands absolute chastity of him. See the journal entries for May 19–20 (*Journal of Dreams* §200).
158. A. Lehmann, *Overtro og Troldom* (Copenhagen, 1896), vol. 3, 13.
159. Tafel, vol. 2, 1074–1082.
160. Printed in an English translation in Tafel, vol. 1, doc. 5, 30–51. The Swedish text appeared in *Skandinavisk Nykyrk-tidning* (1876), 60ff.
161. This letter is reproduced from the facsimile of Tafel in *Sammlung v. Urkunden* (Tübingen, 1845), vol. 4, 79. [See also Tafel, doc. 254, vol. 2, 426 (3).]
162. Tafel, vol. 1, 623. [Tafel indicates *Adversaria* II.]
163. Cf. Tafel's discussion, vol. 2, 1118ff.
164. In a series of articles appearing in *Sydsvenska Dagbladet*, Aug.–Sept. 1908, no. 220.
165. Leuba, 29.
166. Tafel, vol. 1, doc. 5, 34–35.

Chapter 7, "The Worship and Love of God," pages 160–194

167. Published with Swedenborg's notes in the photolithograph edition by Tafel (Stockholm, 1870). The entire work, as Swedenborg left it, was published in an excellent English translation by A.H. Stroh and F. Sewall, *Worship and Love of God* (Boston, 1914; rpt. West Chester, Penna.: The Swedenborg Foundation, 1996). An extensive article by Stroh, which highlights the relation of the work in question with Swedenborg's scientific works, can be found in *The New Philosophy* (April 1902).
168. *Opera* (edition of the Academy of Sciences) XII, §324.
169. Tafel, vol. 2, 257.
170. Zeller, vol. 3, 2, 513.
171. Published by Tafel in *Adversaria* I, §§1–25 (London, 1847).
172. Stroh, 45ff. Cf. *De Divino Amore* §§83–89.
173. Stroh, 62ff.
174. The Neoplatonic origin of these concepts appears more clearly, perhaps, in *The Worship and Love of God* than in previous works. Thus, in §67, note k, which discusses the love of every person, at its beginning, be it a heavenly love

(the love of the greatest good) or its antitheses (the love of evil suggested by the Prince of the World), we read *"Typus omne suum trahit ab idea, secundum quam effigiatur; ubi nulla idea, etiam nulla effigies ideae possibilis"* (The type derives all that is has from the idea, according to which is is effigied; where there is no idea, no effigy also of an idea is possible).This is one of the rare passages where Swedenborg applies the word *idea* to the denomination of the celestial prototype.

175. Plotinus, *Enneads*, vol. III, book 5, chapter 6. Cf. Zeller, vol. 3, 2, p. 343, 471ff., 510ff.
176. *De Divina Sapientia Secundum Aegyptios,* book 4, chapter 6, note 3: *"Spiritus vocare videtur caelestes intelligentias, de quibus Arist. inulta colligit lib. 12. Metaph. Neque hoc omnino alienum est ab eo quod spirituum nomine Angelos at Daemones significare solemus. Sic enim nos cum vix quicquam cogitatione possimus concipere nisi corporeum, rebus omnino incorporeis spirituum naturam cum populo tribuimus."*
177. *Opera* (Ed. Acad. Sci.) I, 215.
178. Swedenborg himself declares in *The Worship and Love of God* §73, note g, that the fables of antiquity were only representations of heavenly things. He explains two of them according to the doctrine of correspondences, which, he claims, the ancients knew, their souls being closer to heaven than ours.
179. A reminiscence of Milton might also be assumed in a passage where Swedenborg narrates (*The Worship and Love of God* §73) how knowledges transform evil spirits into rampant and hissing serpents in Adam's presence. In *Paradise Lost*, book 10, l.508, there is an account in which the demons, similarly transformed into serpents, hiss around their prince. In both passages, again, we find the same allusion to Gorgons. In any case, the theme appears to me to be ordinary and natural enough to warrant a conclusion of Miltonic influence.
180. See D. Masson, *The Life of John Milton* (London, 1880), vol. 6, especially the last chapter, "Milton's Treatise of Christian Doctrine," 814–840.
181. Quoted according to Masson, vol. 6, 826.
182. Tafel, vol. 2, 710.

Chapter 8, "The Spirit Seer," pages 195–223

183. Robsahm, op.cit., 15. See also Tafel, document 5, vol. 1, p. 33.
184. Lidén, *Resedagbok*, ms., Uppsala Library, X, 398, 484.
185. A. Scheler, *Aufzeichnungen eines Amsterdamer Bürgers über Swedenborg* (Hanover, 1852). Referred to hereafter as "Cuno."
186. Robsahm, 74; Tafel, 32

187. Cuno, 40.
188. Robsahm, 74–75; Tafel, 32.
189. Cuno, 38.
190. Robsahm, 75; Tafel, 32–33.
191. Robsahm, 74; Tafel, 32.
192. Cuno, 44.
193. Ibid., 155.
194. Ibid., 36–37.
195. Ibid., 163.
196. Robsahm, 122; Tafel, 43.
197. Ulrika Arfvidsson (c. 1734–1804), constantly consulted by the Swedish court; she was known for her powers of soothsaying by coffee grounds.
198. Cuno, 154.
199. Tessin and Tessiniana, 357–358; 368.
200. *Svenska Siare och Skalder,* second ed., vol. 1, 52ff.
201. Tafel, vol. 2, document 290, 721.
202. Tafel, vol. 2, document 255, 434.
203. Robsahm, 105; Tafel, 40.
204. Ibid.; Tafel, 39.
205. Tafel, vol. 2, document 267, 558.
206. *Economy of the Animal Kingdom* II, §285. Cf. Ramström, *Uppsala Läkareförenings Förhandlingar,* N.F., vol. 16, f. 1, 14.
207. Séglas, *"Hallucinations psychiques et Pseudo-Hallucination verbale," Journal de Psychologie* (1914): 294–295.
208. Kandinsky, 84.
209. Séglas, 307. Cf. Baillarger, cited in Delacroix, 430. My conception of the interchanges between Swedenborg and spirits by way of verbal pseudohallucinations differs from those of Ballet (121–123), who considers them psychosensory. He bases his view on a quotation from *Heaven and Hell* that describes the intercommunication between man and spirits as follows (248): "The language of the angel or spirit is heard in a manner as sonorous as the speech of man to man; but it is heard by him alone and not by others who are present. That is because the language of the angel or spirit flows first into the thought of the man and by an inner way, into his ears and thus activates that organ *interiorly,* while the speech of man to man first flows over the air and by an external way into his ears, and activates the ear externally. From this it is evident that the speech of the angel and of the spirit with man is heard inside man, and that, because it likewise activates his organ of hearing, it is also heard in a sonorous manner." From this Ballet concludes (p. 121) that we are dealing with an auditory psychosensory hallucination. "These hallucinations,

as one knows, present all the characteristics of auditory perceptions as genuine; the same sonority, same externalization." It seems to me, on the contrary, that the above quotation indicates that this language of the spirit was *not* externalized. Had Swedenborg wished to indicate that it had the character of a true auditory perception, he would naturally turn his ear interiorly and not vice versa. Swedenborg does not believe he perceives this language through the ears, since he ultimately makes it "inflow" into the auditory organ. This is clear from the passage following the quotation cited by Ballet: "The fact that the speech of an angel or of a spirit flows from the interior into the ear appeared to me clearly from the fact that this language flows equally into the tongue where it causes a slight vibration, but no movements of the kinds which are produced when the man himself articulates sounds of the speech." This phenomenon is mentioned by Ballet several pages further on when citing the conversation of Swedenborg with a spirit from Mars. Ballet considers this to be a mental hallucination (that is to say, according to the theory, a mental representation with a delirious interpretation), accompanied by a motor phenomenon. As it appears to me, the sole difference between the two resides in the fact that, in his conversation with the inhabitant of Mars, Swedenborg does not perceive the tone of voice. It is clearly this "internal resonance" of which Séglas speaks that Swedenborg has in view when he declares that the speech of the spirit is just as "sonorous" as though it had issued from his tongue and his lips, even though it is not translated by a sound. The "cognitive language" which Ballet also considers as a psychic hallucination, differs from the two preceding in that there is no verbal form. Our preceding quotation no doubt accurately refers to this direct transmission of the thought emanating from the spirits.

In *Arcana Coelestia* §1763, Swedenborg speaks of spirits talking out loud, whose speech resembles the murmur of water or the rolling of thunder. He seemed to perceive, not distinct voices, but the murmur of a whole crowd. Here it seems to be a matter of sonorous hallucinations, even thought of elementary nature. Swedenborg moreover declares that this type of speech is very rare.

210. Séglas, 308.

211. Case reported by Karl Jaspers, *Allgemeine Psychopathologie* (Berlin, 1913), 40.

212. Kandinsky, 97.

Chapter 9, "The Exegete," pages 224–237

213. *Adversaria* I, 47. Cf. Tafel, vol. 2, document 313, 951.

214. Siegfried, *Philo von Alexandria* (Jena, 1875), 163.

215. A. Franck, 164; cf. his citation from Origen, 167.
216. Siegfried, 162, 351.
217. Ibid., 161, 322.
218. Zeller, vol. 3, 202.
219. According to Swedenborg, this idolatry involved the personification of God into so many divinities over whom the idolaters imagined Jupiter as sovereign master, and whose name Swedenborg believed was derived from "Jehovah."
220. Zeller, vol. 3, 2, page 304.
221. Quoted according to Franck, 313.
222. Zeller, vol. 3, 2, page 360, note 2.
223. Ibid., vol. 3, 2, page 357.
224. Siegfried, 360, 380.
225. Sundelin, *Swedenborgianismens historia i Sverige* (Uppsala, 1886), 9.
226. Cf. Diestel, 233, 321.

Chapter 10, "God and the World," pages 238–289

227. My analysis follows Franck, 168–173, very closely, as well as that of Stöckl, vol. 3, 235.
228. *Prot. Realencyklopedie,* "Swedenborg," vol. 19, 190.
229. Ibid.
230. I should take this opportunity to underscore in passing the absurdity of the claim, first expressed by Cornelius and afterward repeated by a number of authors, that the Swedenborgian doctrine of the Trinity recalls that of Zinzendorf. The analogy lies in the importance accorded to Jesus Christ. Based upon my exposition, one might conclude that, quite to the contrary of Zinzendorf's view, Swedenborg has set the historic personality of the Christ in the background. He particularly opposed the doctrine of vicarious atonement that, for Zinzendorf, is essential for Christianity.
231. That Swedenborg may have been even tempted to reach pantheistic conclusions is clear from his account in *Conjugial Love* §328 of a conversation with several spirits: "And I told them that I once considered the omnipotence and ubiquity of God, that is, before the creation, and I conceived, from the anxiety in not being able to discard from my mind ideas of space and time, for nature was substituted for God. But I was told: 'Discard the representations of space and time and you will see.' And it was given to me to eliminate these notions, and I saw. And from that time I could visualize God from all eternity . . ."
232. Stöckl, *Geschichte der Christlichen Philosophie,* vol. 2: *Zeit der Kirchenväter*, 320 and quotations.

233. Zeller, vol. 3, 2, 444–453 and the passages of the *Enneads* cited by him.

234. *Enneads*, V, 6, 4.

235. I cannot refrain from pointing out in passing the manifest external analogy between the triadic system of Proclus and the "discrete degrees" of Swedenborg such as they are expounded during his theological period. Proclus, who, like Swedenborg, combined a clearly systematic and visionary temperament with a marked tendency toward scholastic formalism, sought to systematize the emanationist process, by which multiplicity arises from unity, through a triadic scheme. Just as unity creates the multiplicity from its own emanation without undergoing any modification itself, and just as each lower rung of the evolution finds itself, at the same time, separated from the higher rung as well as united with it by a causal relationship, the effect, which finds itself in the cause, separates itself from the cause to reunite itself with it. These three stages reproduce themselves at each stage of the evolutionary chain, which passes from perfection to imperfection, the lower rung being unable to receive in itself all the power of the higher one. With Proclus as with Swedenborg, this triadic schema is universal and is applied equally to the two which, with Proclus, forms a kind of triadic hierarchy. Clearly nothing keeps us from assuming that Swedenborg may have had direct knowledge of the system of Proclus, whose works, like those of other Neoplatonists, were published in Latin during the Renaissance. I have equally attempted to make a comparison with the edition of Patrizzi of the *Elementa theologica* (Ferrara, 1583), in which Proclus expounds his doctrines in the form of mathematical demonstrations, as Spinoza did later. However, I have not discovered any decisive proof of a direct influence. Since the doctrine of series and degrees is not associated with the triadic schema at the time of its appearance, it appears probable that Swedenborg has reasoned out his system independently of Proclus. The observed analogy can for the most part be explained by the fact that the two authors separate themselves from the emanationist doctrine of Plotinus, where the three stages on which Proclus structures his schema are already found, although they may not be applied to the various phases of the evolutionary chain. Cf. Zeller, vol. 3, 2, 713.

236. L. Stein, *Die Psychologie der Stoa* (Berlin, 1886), vol. 1, 207.

237. J. Kroll, *Die Lehren des Hermes Trismegistos,* (Münster, 1914), 159. See also Lobeck's account in *Aglaophamus,* 908–925.

238. Franck, 179. Lorenzo Hammarsköld seems to have perceived similarities with Kabbalistic notions when juxtaposing the "*maximus homo*" concept with "the Adam Kadmon of the Kabbalists, and the Neoplatonic Macrocosm" (*Historiska Anteckningar till det Philosophiska Studium,* 232).

239. Cornelius Agrippa, I, iii, 13, entitled "*De membris Dei et eorum in nostra membra influxu*"("On the Members of God and Their Influx into Our

Members"); chapter 36 is entitled *"De homine quomodo creatus ad imaginem Dei"* ("On How Man Is Created after the Image of God").

240. Pico della Mirandola, 61: *"Primum igitur illud aduertendum, uocari a Mose Mundum, hominem magnum. Nam si homo est paruus mundus, utique mundus est magnus homo, hinc sumpta occasione, tres mundos, intellectualem, coelestem, et corruptibilem, per tres hominis partes aptissime figurat, simul indicans, hac figura, non solum contineri in homine mundos omnes, sed & quae hominis pars cui mundo respondeat, breuiter declarans. Cogitemus igitur in homine tres partes, supremam caput, tum quae a collo ad umbilicum protenditur, tertiam, quae ab umbilico extenditur ad pedes, sunt enim & hae in hominis figura, uarietate quadam disclusae et separatae. Sed mirum quam pulchre, quam examussim, per exactissimam rationem, tribus mundi partibus, proportione respondeant . . ."*

241. Paracelsus, *Paramirum alterum,* book 2, ch. 11.

242. Cf. Zeller, vol. 3, 2, 490.

243. *Enneads,* Vol. 1, 1.

244. Ollé-Laprune, vol. 1, 378ff.

245. It cannot be admitted, as Schlieper does (p. 35) after having reviewed the above "memorable relation," that Swedenborg had returned to the dualism of Descartes. In his last work, *De Consummatione Saeculi* (published in *Spiritual Diary* vol. 7), he still asserts that what prevents knowledge of the relationship between soul and body resides in the hypotheses "of Descartes and several others that the soul is a substance distinct from the body." Swedenborg himself ties his conception of the links between soul and body to the doctrines of classical antiquity (Ibid., 145.)

246. Bender, 53.

247. Dippel, *Vertheidung seines Tractats Vera Demonstratio Evangelica* (1731), 19.

248. Dippel, *Auffrichtiges Glaubensbekänntniss* (1732), 75; Bender, 219.

249. According to Bender, 183–185.

250. Ritschl, *Geschichte des Pietismus,* vol. 2, 334.

251. Bender, 137; Ritschl, vol. 2, 335.

252. Dippel, *Vertheidung seines Tractats Vera Demonstratio Evangelica*, 264.

253. Bender, 198.

254. Ibid., 220.

255. Ibid., 177–180.

256. Ibid., 74–75.

257. Tafel, *Sammlung v. Urkunden* (Tübingen, 1839), vol. 2, 356.

258. Cf. the introduction by A. Liebert to *Giovanni Pico della Mirandolas Schriften* (Jena, 1915), who unfortunately gives only a summary description of the philosophy of Pico della Mirandola.

259. Pico della Mirandola, 314ff.

Chapter 11, "The Spiritual World," pages 290–319

260. Ritschl, op. cit., I, 248ff.) seems to relate Swedenborg's theory on the world of spirits to the interest shown by many Pietists in the intermediate state. He is still forced to recognize that these are determined by quite another motive than that of Swedenborg—the belief in the apocatastasis. It seems to me superfluous to research Swedenborg's sources for the topography of the spiritual world. In its broad lines, it reproduces the notions of Christianity, which may be attached to the Bible, and can be found, in one form or another, in various writers. Plato's exposition of the other world (*Republic* 10, 614) is itself based on the same topography.
261. This short work is found in Swedenborg's *Posthumous Theological Works,* 2nd ed. (West Chester, Penna.: Swedenborg Foundation, 1996. See also Tafel, *Spiritual Diary* (London, 1846), vol. 7, §88.
262. Swedenborg declares that he found this place indicated in Ezekiel 32:18.
263. This description probably has nothing to do with the famous description given by Plato (*Republic* vol. 7, 515) of the subterranean cave: it is more likely a development of the fundamental idea found in the Gospel of John, which says, "And this is the judgment, that the light has come into the world, and men have loved darkness rather than light, because their deeds were evil" (John 3:19). Swedenborg constantly quotes this passage with regard to the men who pronounce their own condemnation.
264. Tafel, vol. 1, document 5 (Robsahm's memoirs), 50.
265. In the *Spiritual Diary* §4729, Maria Polhem is described as vain and worldly. "Her principal preoccupation in social circles is her appearance and cooking."
266. Tafel, vol. 1, note 33, pp. 635–636.
267. Ibid., vol. 2, doc. 255, §18, p. 437.
268. Ibid., vol. 1, note 31, p. 635.
269. Robsahm, 122; Tafel, doc. 5, §36, p. 43.
270. Tafel, vol. 2, p. 437. Tafel's only argument that could be discussed seriously is that Swedenborg visited Italy for the first time at the age of fifty. But the expression "in my youth" could be a mistranslation of "when I was younger" (in effect we only have the account of Tuxen in the English translation made by Nordenskõld) or a misstatement by Swedenborg, who at the time of the interview, was eighty-two years old. He could thus well have erred regarding the time of his voyage to Italy.
271. Sundelin, *Luthers Etik* (Ups. Univ. Årsskrift, 1880), 43–46.
272. This concept goes back to his scientific period and is a consequence of his theory of series and degrees. In the *Journal of Dreams* he maintains in effect that

every drive has its source in the love of God and forms a series. Physical love is a subclassification of this love and is consequently pure in itself.

273. Lagerborg, *Die platonische Liebe* (Stockholm 1915), 109.

Chapter 12, "The Last Judgment and the New Jerusalem," pages 320–328

274. Cf. B. Worcester, *Life and Mission of Emanuel Swedenborg* (1883), 282.

275. A parallel to this view can be found in the identification established between the papacy and the Antichrist. Just as Luther sees in the decadence of Catholicism a presage of the Last Judgment, so also Swedenborg sees a sign of the same tenor in the decadence of Christianity in its entirety. Both, then, link their apocalyptic expectations to those of the definitive triumph of their doctrine.

276. *Samlingar för Philantroper,* fasc. 1. See also Tafel, vol. 2, doc. 234, p. 260–262, for Swedenborg's letter to Beyer, dated February 1767; and Tafel, vol. 2, doc. 240, p. 273–274, for his letter to Beyer, dated March 15, 1769.

Index